D1593406

*The Saintly Politics of Catherine of Siena*

# The Saintly Politics
# of Catherine of Siena

*F. Thomas Luongo*

CORNELL UNIVERSITY PRESS

*Ithaca and London*

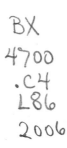
First published 2006 by Cornell University Press

Printed in the United States of America

Library of Congress Cataloging-in-Publication Data

Luongo, F. Thomas (Francis Thomas)
    The saintly politics of Catherine of Siena / F. Thomas Luongo.
        p. cm.
    Includes bibliographical references and index.
    ISBN-13: 978-0-8014-4395-4 (cloth : alk. paper).
    ISBN-10: 0-8014-4395-4 (cloth : alk. paper).
    1. Catherine, of Siena, Saint, 1347–1380—Political and social views.
2. Church and state—Italy—Tuscany—History.  3. Christianity and politics—
Italy—Tuscany—History.  4. Women in politics—Italy—Tuscany—History.
5. Tuscany (Italy)—Church history.  I. Title.
BX4700.C4L86 2005
282'.092—dc22                                                2005018410

Cornell University Press strives to use environmentally responsible suppliers and
materials to the fullest extent possible in the publishing of its books. Such materials include vegetable-based, low-VOC inks and acid-free papers that are recy-
cled, totally chlorine-free, or partly composed of nonwood fibers. For further
information, visit our website at www.cornellpress.cornell.edu.

Cloth printing      10 9 8 7 6 5 4 3 2 1

*To Lisa*

# Contents

# Maps and Illustrations

## Maps

## Illustrations

# Acknowledgments

Earlier versions of chapter 4 appeared as "Catherine of Siena: Rewriting Female Holy Authority," in *Women, the Book, and the Godly: Selected Proceedings of the St. Hilda's Conference,* 1993, vol. 1, edited by Lesley Smith and Jane H. M. Taylor (Oxford: D. S. Brewer, 1995), 89–104; and as "The Evidence of Catherine's Experience: Niccolò di Toldo and the Erotics of Political Engagement," in *Siena e il suo territorio nel Rinascimento,* edited by Mario Ascheri (Siena: Il Leccio, 2001), 53–90. And expanded treatment of one theme dealt with in chapter 1 appears as "Cloistering Catherine: Religious Identity in Raymond of Capua's Legenda maior of Catherine of Siena," *Studies in Medieval and Renaissance History* n.s 3 (2005).

In the earliest stages of this book I received the support of a Fellowship from the National Endowment for the Humanities; the Perrota Scholarship from the National Italian-American Foundation; Notre Dame's Zahm Travel Grant; and fellowships from the University of Notre Dame, the University of Toronto, and the Pontifical Institute of Mediaeval Studies. The completion of this book was made possible by the support of Newcomb College's Eva-Lou Joffrion Edwards Fellowship; research fellowships from the Georges Lurcy Charitable and Educational Trust; and a Tulane University Committee on Research Summer Grant.

I am grateful for the patient guidance of John Van Engen, and for the distinct and valuable contributions of Kathleen Biddick, Theodore Cachey, Jr., and Edward English. I was fortunate in my teachers at the Medieval Institute of Notre Dame, the Centre for Medieval Studies at the University of Toronto, and Columbia University. Thanks, in particular, to J. N. Hillgarth and Giulio Silano at Toronto, and to my undergraduate adviser at Columbia, the late John H. Mundy, who first awakened in me a fascination with medieval Italian cities. I am grateful too for the insight and high standards of the lively and generous communities of graduate students at Toronto and Notre Dame. Thanks in particular to Lezlie Knox, Rachel Koopmans, and Lisa Wolverton for insights on the early versions of this project.

I have benefited crucially throughout the writing of this book from the encouragement and advice of Carol Lansing. And I am especially grateful to Suzanne Noffke, OP, who has always been a model of generosity in sharing the fruits of her research on Catherine. Many others have offered encouragement, criticism, and suggestions on specific points in this book, including Mario Ascheri, Daniel Bornstein, William Bowsky, Isabelle Chabot, Laura de Angelis, Maiju Lehmijoki-Gardner, Maureen Miller, and Jane Tylus. Edward English generously read a draft of the book and offered many corrections and suggestions. Elena Brizio shared her research when I made my first forays into the Sienese archives, has since offered much practical assistance, and caught many mistakes in a careful reading of an earlier draft of this book. I have benefited from the hospitality of the staffs of the Archivio di Stato di Siena and the Biblioteca Comunale degli Intronati in Siena. I am grateful for the encouragement of John Ackerman, director of Cornell University Press, and his care in shepherding this book through the review process, and for the keen insights of Cornell's two anonymous reviewers, whose suggestions for revision improved the work immensely. At Tulane I have enjoyed the support and encouragement of my colleagues in the History Department and Medieval Studies program. Thanks to Donna Denneen for many patient administrative interventions. And a special thanks to Scott, Brendan, Ross, Brandon, and the rest of Catch-22 Track Club in New Orleans, for many miles of good company and help keeping *mens sana in corpore sano.*

My final debts are my deepest, and most beyond my ability to repay. My parents, Francis and Mary Anne Luongo, have offered unstinting support. I finish this book in thanksgiving for the good health of my children, Benedict, Tobias, and David, who have been sources of cheerful mayhem and deep joy. And I thank Lisa Boyett Luongo, my wife, to whom I owe more than I can express. This book is dedicated to her.

F. T. L.

# Brief Chronology

c. 1347    Catherine born.

1348       Black Death strikes Italy.

1355       Fall of the Nove, beginning of the regime of the Dodici.

1362       Death of Catherine's sister, Buonaventura.

c. 1363–   Catherine's period of spiritual education under the direction of
1368       Sienese Dominicans. First contacts with the mantellate.

1368       Fall of the Dodici, replaced by a coalition of nobles, Nove, Dodici, and members of the popolo minuto.

           22 August. Death of Iacopo di Benincasa.

           (After 1368) Catherine enrolled in the community of the mantellate.

1370       Death of Pope Urban V, election of Pierre Roger II as Pope Gregory XI.

1371       Revolt of the Bruco and Salimbeni/Dodici coup attempt. Catherine saves her brothers from enemies during the unrest. Banishment of the Salimbeni and disenfranchisement of the Dodici. Beginning of the regime of the Riformatori.

1374       Catherine travels to Florence to attend the General Chapter of the Dominicans. Meets elite members of the Florentine Parte Guelfa. Probable occasion for the writing of the Miracoli. Receives Raymond of Capua as her confessor.

           The Salimbeni and allies revolt in the Sienese contado.

           Plague and famine in Tuscany. Death of Catherine's brother, Bartolomeo di Iacopo.

| | |
|---|---|
| 1374 (cont) | Papal governors refuse to supply Florence with grain. Rumors of church-sponsored plots against Florence and intensification of tensions between Florence and the Papacy. |
| 1375 | Catherine travels to Pisa, returning in June to attend the execution of Niccolò di Toldo. |
| | *June.* Peace between the papacy and Barnabò Visconti, signore of Milan. Catherine writes to Barnabò. |
| | Army of John Hawkwood released from papal service. Hawkwood extracts payments from Florence, Siena, and other cities. |
| | *July.* Formation of mutual defense treaty between Florence and Milan. Florentines call on Siena, Pisa, Lucca, and others to join league against the church. |
| | Election in Florence of the "Eight Saints" to tax clerical property. |
| | *November.* Siena joins the Florentine league. |
| | *Winter.* Revolts of Perugia and other cities of the Papal States. |
| 1376 | *January.* Catherine's first letter to Gregory XI. |
| | *March.* Pisa and Lucca join the Florentine league. Bologna revolts. Florence placed under interdict by Gregory XI. |
| | *April.* Visionary letter to Raymond of Capua (in Avignon) on persecution of the church and her own mission. |
| | Catherine travels to Florence, resides with Niccolò Soderini. |
| | *May.* Catherine travels to Avignon, arriving on 18 June. |
| | *September.* Pope Gregory XI departs Avignon for Italy. After negotiations, Rome submits to the pope on 21 December. |
| | *November.* Catherine departs for Italy. |
| 1377 | *February.* Slaughter at Cesena. |
| | *April.* Founding of Catherine's convent at Belcaro, near Siena, former fortress of Nanni di ser Vanni. |
| | Raymond of Capua elected prior of the Dominican community of Santa Maria sopra Minerva, in Rome. |
| | *Late summer–winter.* Catherine travels to Salimbeni territory. Responds to Sienese suspicions that she was plotting against the regime, and writes to reassure Sienese followers. Experiences "Dialogue" vision and writing miracle. |
| | *October.* Tensions in negotiations between Florence and Gregory XI. Florentine Signoria orders violation of the interdict. |
| 1378 | *Winter.* Catherine travels to Florence, residing with Niccolò Soderini and Piero Canigiani. |
| | *27 March.* Death of Gregory XI. Election of Pope Urban VI on 8 April. |
| | *June.* In Florence, Catherine targeted, but not harmed, during initial unrest connected to the Revolt of the Ciompi. |

*28 July.* Peace between Florence and the Pope Urban VI.

*20 September.* In Avignon, Robert of Geneva elected as Pope Clement VII, in opposition to Urban VI. Beginning of schism.

*November.* Catherine travels to Rome. Raymond of Capua enlisted as papal ambassador.

1379    Catherine in Rome with a group of her followers, writing in support of church reform and unity under Urban VI. Her health deteriorates.

1380    *29 April.* Catherine dies in Rome.

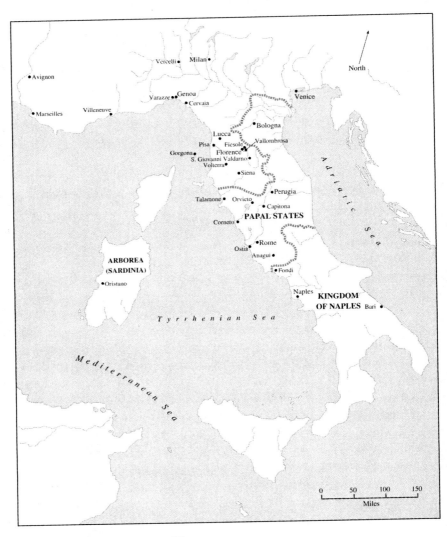

Map 1. The World of Catherine of Siena.

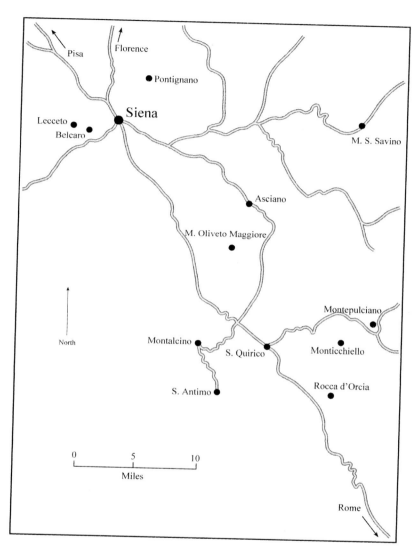

Map 2. Siena and Its Environs, ca.1370.

*The Saintly Politics of Catherine of Siena*

# Introduction

In late summer 1377, Catherine of Siena traveled with a group of her followers—her *famiglia*—into Sienese territory to the south of the city, spend-
ing several months at the stronghold of Agnolino di Giovanni Salimbeni,
head of the Salimbeni clan. The Salimbeni, the most potent of the Sienese
magnate families, had long sought to achieve signorial control of the city
and had been in almost constant rebellion against the governing regime in
the early 1370s. At this time, a period of high tension in the contest between
Florence and the papacy known as the "War of Eight Saints," the Salimbeni
were suspected of introducing troops from ecclesiastical armies into the
Sienese *contado,* the territory over which the city claimed jurisdiction. The
mission to the Salimbeni of this charismatic young holy woman, already
known as "santa Caterina," whose followers included politically active
sons of Sienese noble families as well as several men known to be opponents of the governing regime, drew the anxious attention of the Sienese
magistrates, prompting a flurry of letters between Catherine, the Sienese
*signori,* and several of her highly placed contacts in Siena. The magistrates, attentive to the political implications of her movements, apparently demanded that Catherine return to Siena to undertake a peace
mission within the city walls. This prompted an acerbic letter from
Catherine to a highly placed member of her network:

> I trust in our Lord Jesus Christ, and not in men. I will continue to do so. The
> more they slander me and persecute me, and I return tears and constant
> prayers, that much more grace God will give me! And whether the demon wants
> it or not, I will strive to carry out my life in the honor of God and the salvation of

souls for the whole world, and especially for my city. The citizens of Siena do a
very shameful thing in believing or imagining that we are here for making plots
in the lands of the Salimbeni, or in any other place in the world.[1]

Catherine here addressed with remarkable specificity the Sienese suspicions of her activity and indignantly professed her innocence. She and
her *famiglia* were not involved in any way in partisan politics. They were
saving souls, not plotting with the Salimbeni. In this and in other letters
Catherine wrote at this time, while asserting her innocence and upbraiding the Sienese for their suspicions, she also rejected the magistrates'
authority over her. She trusted in Jesus Christ, not men. Her mission was
ordained by God and her sphere of operations lay beyond the world of
civic loyalties and jurisdictions. She refused to be drawn into the city, the
realm of a worldly politics that had nothing to do with her.

Historians have taken Catherine at her word. Just as she claimed for
her domain a space beyond worldly plots, and juxtaposed "saving souls"
with "making plots in the lands of the Salimbeni," scholars have consistently abstracted Catherine from the political and social scene in which
she moved. Catherine is remembered today as a saint, a religious
reformer, a canonical figure in the library of Catholic spiritual literature,
and a minor figure in the history of early Italian prose. She is known for a
visionary book (her *Libro di divina dottrina,* known today usually as the
*Dialogo*) and more than 380 extant letters: one of the largest collections
of epistolary prose from the Middle Ages and the largest by a woman.
And Catherine figures especially prominently in the recent wave of historical scholarship on late medieval piety, sanctity, and female religiosity. But
studies of Catherine have almost never explored in any depth her relation to the public politics and cultural ferment of the late *trecento*. Nor
does she figure at all in other historical narratives of Italian politics and
culture in this period. This is despite the fact that Catherine was one of
the most notable public figures of her day, famous—and in some quarters
notorious—for moving in public and intervening boldly in worldly affairs.
She traveled throughout central Italy and to the papal court in Avignon,

---

[1]  Letter 122 September 1377, to Salvi di Ser Pietro: "Io mi confido in Domino nostro
Jesu Christo, e no negli uomini. Io farò così. E se daranno a me infamie e persecuzioni, e io
darò lagrime e continua orazione, quanto Dio mi darà la grazia. E voglia il dimonio o no, io
mi impegnerò di esercitare la vita mia nell' onore di Dio e la salute dell' anime per tutto
quanto il mondo, e singolarmente per la mia città. Gran vergogna si fanno i cittadini di
Siena, di credere o immaginare che noi stiamo per fare i trattati nelle terre de' Salimbeni, o
in veruno altro luogo del mondo." In references to Catherine's letters, I have maintained
the numbering system employed in the editions of Niccolò Tommaseo and in Piero Misciattelli's reissue of Tommaseo's edition, and repeated in Antonio Volpato's edition, which I
have used in this book. I have added in roman numerals the number assigned to letters
included in Dupré Theseider's partial edition. All translations are my own.

2

and sent letters to civic and ecclesiastical leaders on pressing matters of public concern. Catherine asserted authority at a time when public authority was contested in Italy, disrupted by recurrences of the Black Death; social revolutions; the ominous banding of mercenary troops on the outskirts of many cities; and a war between the papacy and a Florentine-led league of Italian city-states: the "War of Eight Saints." Nevertheless, despite the public character of her life, Catherine of Siena survives in history removed from the social and political dimensions of her career. In light of her historical reputation, the accusation that Catherine was plotting against the Sienese in 1377 might seem a category error, a complete misunderstanding of her career and its place in history.

But Sienese concerns were not unreasonable, nor should Catherine's denial of political involvement be accepted as simply or unproblematically true. This book seeks to return Catherine to her history, showing her emerging sanctity as bound to the social and political tensions of a particular moment, a process more complex than the terms of her historical reputation. The usual ways in which Catherine has been classified by historians cannot take account of her career, which dramatically crossed boundaries and transgressed inherited categories. For instance, her identity as a female penitent placed her somewhere between the lay and religious states, fitting clearly into neither. Through her travels Catherine violated expectations of both secular and religious women, transgressing the gendered borders of social space and mixing conspicuously in the world of men. And her letters, a completely novel combination of inspired language and mundane genre, expressed an even more ambitious mobility by creating her own network of contacts across the structures of ecclesiastical and social institutions. Through her letters she not only sent her words where she as a woman could not easily go but addressed an audience few men could achieve: popes, kings and queens, and other ecclesiastical and secular dignitaries. The boundary-defying features of Catherine's life and travels, as well as the experimentation that marked her writing, were essential to her ability to enter into public life in Italy by moving authoritatively across the borders of political, social, religious, and cultural institutions and authorities.

Catherine emerged as a figure on the Italian stage at the outset of the "War of Eight Saints," a conflict between Florence and the papacy that represented a response to an increasingly fragmented Italian political map and in a new way placed in question the relationship between political power and spiritual authority.[2] The War of Eight Saints can be seen as

---

[2]   On the War of Eight Saints and Florentine relations with the papacy in this period, see Marvin Becker, "Church and State in Florence on the Eve of the Renaissance (1343–1382)," *Speculum* 37 (1962): 509–27; Gene Brucker, *Florentine Politics and Society,*

an early conflict in late-medieval and early-modern battles over peninsular hegemony, in which Florence, Milan, and the papacy sought to achieve dominance in central and northern Italy. Several factors led Florence to break with the papacy, its political and financial ally since the creation of the Guelf confederation in 1267: the emergence within Florence of "new men," less bound financially and politically to the papacy, who sought to undermine the political hegemony of the pro-papal Parte Guelfa; a climate of anticlericalism (resulting in part from papal interventions in Florentine ecclesiastical affairs); and fears about the expansionist ambitions of the governors of the Papal States and of the pope himself, as Gregory XI contemplated returning the papal Curia to Rome from Avignon. On the Florentine side, the conflict was fought largely through propaganda, as the Florentine chancellor Coluccio Salutati sent letters to the cities of Tuscany as well as the Papal States, calling on them as Italians to embrace *libertas* and resist the predations of a foreign (i.e., French, or Limousin) Curia and ecclesiastical hierarchy. By mid-November 1376, most of the Tuscan cities had joined the Florentine league, and most of the cities of the Papal States north of Rome, including Bologna, had rebelled against their papal governors. The Florentines retaliated for church aggression by taxing the clergy of the city and sequestering some ecclesiastical estates; the committee designated to implement these measures was known as the "Eight Saints."[3] Gregory XI countered with the papacy's traditional spiritual weapons, placing Florence under interdict and declaring Florentine merchants outlaws, to be expelled from all Christian nations and their goods seized. Florentine citizens, supported by influential clerics, rejected the interdict and defended the war as a justified defense of Florentine *libertas* against corrupt prelates aggressively trespassing in temporal politics. On the ideological level, the War of Eight Saints was an occasion for Salutati and others to articulate a vision of Florentine secular republicanism as an identity for Florence and for

---

*1343–1378* (1962), 131–44, 265–355; Richard C. Trexler, *The Spiritual Power: Republican Florence under the Interdict* (1974); and David S. Peterson, "The War of Eight Saints in Florentine Memory and Oblivion," in William J. Connell, ed., *Society and Individual in Renaissance Florence* (2002), 173–214.

[3] While the term *church* (*chiesa*) as I have used it here and throughout this book is inherently ambiguous, it as an accurate reflection of the language used by Italians in the 1370s to refer to the papacy and the ecclesiastical establishment in general. The Papal States were defended by armies of the "church"; opponents of Florence in the War of Eight Saints were identified as members of the "church" party. The lack of precision in the term *church* is in fact important and meaningful. Those with political and economic ties to the papacy, like the Parte Guelfa elite in Florence, were rewarded with appointments for family members to prominent local ecclesiastical offices. And political opposition to the temporal ambitions of the pope and the governors of the Papal States often overlapped with a more general anticlericalism.

Italy, before the more famous conflicts with Gian Galeazzo Visconti two decades later.[4]

Sienese politics in this period were also significantly affected by relations with the church, and the Sienese experienced similar tensions over the political effects of spiritual authority, but colored in their case by sensitivity to the regional ambitions of Florence, their more powerful near-neighbor and potential overlord.[5] As in Florence, changes in power within Siena in the late 1360s and early 1370s brought about the replacement of a regime that had economic ties to the papacy and was strongly supportive of papal projects in Italy with one that was much more skeptical of the government of the Papal States. The regime of the Riformatori, which ruled Siena from 1371 to 1385, was a coalition government based on an uneasy balancing of the political ambitions of several distinct political groupings, including an emergent radical *popolo minuto,* embodied by the militant wool workers of the company of the Bruco. And it was unified by the threat of subversion or rebellion by two groups that had been politically outlawed in 1371, at the inception of the regime, after they had attempted a coup: the Salimbeni clan and the Dodici, a group of wealthy leaders of the major guilds who had ruled Siena from 1355 to 1368, and whose overthrow had been a prelude to the establishment of the Riformatori. The stability of the regime of the Riformatori was also in no small measure based on a close patron-client relationship with the Florentines, who had among other objectives in helping the new regime the defense of Florentine hegemony in southern Tuscany against incursions by the governors of the Papal States. Along with the Florentines, the Sienese regime and its supporters feared, apparently with good reason, that ecclesiastical authorities (Gerard du Puy in particular) were conspiring with the Salimbeni and

---

[4]  In "The War of Eight Saints in Florentine Memory and Oblivion," David S. Peterson has described the process whereby the War of Eight Saints was written out of Florentine history by fifteenth-century humanists in favor of the more thoroughly secular conflict with Milan, producing a version of Renaissance Florentine history that has continued to be influential in modern scholarship.

[5]  There exists no synthetic study of Sienese politics in this period. My treatment here depends partly on my own reading of chronicles and archival records, as well as on studies of specific aspects of Sienese politics: Elena Brizio, "Siena nel secondo Trecento: Organismi istituzionali e personale politico dalla caduta dei Dodici alla dominazione viscontea," Ph.D diss., Università degli Studi di Firenze, 1992; Andrea Giorgi, "Il carteggio del Concistoro della Repubblica di Siena (Spogli delle lettere: 1251–1374)," *Bullettino Senese di Storia Patria* 97 (1991): 193–573; A. K. Isaacs, "Magnati, Comune e Stato a Siena nel Trecento e all'inizio del Quattrocento," in *I ceti dirigenti nella Toscana tardo comunale* (1983), 81–96; D. Marrara, "I magnati e il governo del Comune di Siena dallo statuto del 1274 allo fine del XIV secolo," in *Studi per Enrico Fiumi* (1979), 239–76; Valerie Wainwright, "Conflict and Popular Government in Fourteenth-Century Siena: Il Monte dei Dodici, 1355–1368," in *I ceti dirigenti nella Toscana tardo comunale* (1983), 57–80; idem, "The Testing of a Popular Sienese Regime. The *Riformatori* and the Insurrections of 1371," in *I Tatti Studies: Essays in the Renaissance* 2 (1987), 107–70.

Dodici and other elements within Siena to destabilize the governing coalition and topple the regime, in the interests of replacing it with a regime more friendly to the governors of the Papal States. After some months of hesitation, the Sienese entered into the Florentine league against the church in November 1375.

What the Sienese magistrates saw when they observed Catherine's movements in 1377 was not only an ascetic and mystic holy woman surrounded by a group of adoring followers, but also a spiritual authority mobilized for a hostile cause, supported by a politically engaged group of clerics and laymen that included some obvious and outspoken opponents of the Sienese and their Florentine allies. As will be seen, Catherine's own family background as well as the profile of her network placed her and her spiritual *famiglia* on the political map in a way that would have been inescapably obvious to a contemporary Sienese. And once Catherine's movements and letters are examined alongside the events that dominated her career, the political trajectory of her movements and the political meanings of her letters are hard to miss. Returning Catherine to her political context reveals that her assertion of spiritual goals can also be read as political rhetoric. That the spiritual and the political spheres in the Middle Ages ought not be treated as mutually exclusive is a historiographical axiom. But the situation here is even more complicated. In a dispute like the War of Eight Saints, in which the secular authority of the spiritual power was at stake and "sanctity" was attributed to political leaders charged with taxing the clergy, the distinction between the "spiritual" and the "political" was itself particularly contested. On the one side, the pope and supporters like Catherine saw the Florentines and their allies as rebelling against the church and committing sacrilege by violating the interdict. On the other side, the Florentines and their defenders argued that they were opposing an unjust extension of the political jurisdiction of corrupt, worldly prelates, and so were not liable to the spiritual punishment of the interdict. In other words, the rhetoric of the dispute entailed a disagreement about whether what was at issue was spiritual or political. Thus Catherine's response to the Sienese that she was engaged not in plotting but in "saving souls" must have seemed to beg the question, for in this context "saving souls" might very well have meant plotting with the Salimbeni.

In addition, while in her letter Catherine claims for herself a place outside of civic jurisdiction and politics, by traveling into Salimbeni territory in the Sienese *contado* Catherine was moving deeply into politically contested space. The Salimbeni lands in the Sienese *contado* were only nominally under the governance of Siena. In fact, Salimbeni military might threatened Siena, and the Salimbeni had their own network of familial and other allies within Siena and spread throughout Tuscany and the Papal States: in other words, a power base that transcended individual cities and crossed the boundaries of civic jurisdiction, just as Catherine's network, fostered largely through her letters, moved across the Italian map. But moving outside of civic jurisdiction, in a sphere transcending civic politics, did not make Catherine and her followers apolitical. In the context of the War of Eight Saints and emerging political contests that transcended civic politics and civic particularism, Catherine's movements and letter-writing reflected the new cartography of politics in the late fourteenth century.[6]

Without intending to reduce Catherine to politics, this book argues that this crisis of political and spiritual authority set the terms for Catherine's career and licensed the anomalies of her category-defying life and writings. These anomalies were later written out of her life in the creation of her saintly identity, and they have not been recovered in the terms by which Catherine figures in modern scholarship. By reading Catherine's letters within their original political settings, I situate Catherine's spiritual authority and emerging sanctity within contemporary political and cultural developments, to show how Catherine's emergence into a public role was due to the political situation of the church in Italy as well as to a culture that privileged female spirituality and prophetic speech, and not merely to her own remarkable personality and abilities. I conclude that, despite a hagiographical tradition and recent historiography that has placed Catherine at a mystic remove from the politics of her day, Catherine acquired her public authority within late-medieval debates over Italian political and cultural identity. These debates are more usually associated with the battles between Florence and Milan in the early fifteenth century, conflicts at the ideological level over the relative virtues of republican and absolutist systems of government, but these wars were in fact engaged already in the 1370s during the contest between Florence and the papacy. At this moment Catherine emerged as a propagandist for a third model of political and cultural identity, a prophetic polity based on Christian unity, ecclesiastical reform, and the pastoral leadership of the pope as head of Christendom—a perspective that nevertheless led her to frequent criticism of the actual leadership of the pope and prelacy even as she rejected Florentine opposition to the church.

This book confronts the central irony in Catherine of Siena's historical reputation as a woman famous for her public life but who has almost always been examined as if the Italian political and social scene were irrelevant, or at best a mere backdrop, to her saintly career. Scholarly disinterest in

[6] On the spatial dimension of Italian politics, I am especially indebted to Randolph Starn, *Contrary Commonwealth: The Theme of Exile in Medieval and Renaissance Italy* (1982).

Catherine's relationship with her world is due in large part to the categories through which Catherine has been studied, all of which in a variety of ways place her apart from politics and the larger culture of the period in which she lived. In this, historians have, perhaps unconsciously, inherited the terms of Catherine's saintly persona established by her followers and promoters in the years between her death in 1380 and her canonization in 1461.

Hagiographic accounts and the promulgation of manuscripts of her writings set the terms for an enduring understanding of Catherine as a public figure who nevertheless transcended the particulars of her own public career. A tension between Catherine's sanctity and her own history is evident in the most authoritative and influential account of her life, the *Legenda maior*, composed by her confessor, Raymond of Capua, in the decade after her death, and promulgated when Raymond had succeeded to the generalship of the Dominican order.[7] Raymond's challenge in this long and highly sophisticated work of hagiography was to reconcile Catherine's exceptionally active and public career with the standard expectations of female sanctity. Raymond's Catherine was a would-be contemplative forced into the world in obedience to divine commands, and protected by her engagement with God in a mystic cell that she inhabited perpetually despite mixing in the world. While Raymond emphasized Catherine's public life in her acts of charity toward and conversions of both lay and clerical men and women, he pointedly avoided depicting her in public settings and generally steered clear of her higher-profile activities.[8] For Raymond, Catherine moved in the world but was not part of it, and the authority of her life and writings depended on her essential distance from the world, gendered as male. Employing a familiar paradox in the discourse of female sanctity in the Middle Ages, Raymond appealed to Catherine's deficiencies as a mere woman, unlearned and frail by nature, to explain the authority of her words and deeds. God sent Catherine and other saintly women in order to shame learned and powerful men who had become puffed up with pride.[9]

A series of source-critical studies in the first half of the twentieth century verified many details of Catherine's life and career, and clarified the manuscript tradition of her writings.[10] But with very few exceptions,

[7] Raymond of Capua, *Legenda Sancti Catherine Senensis*, in *Acta Sanctorum*, vol. 3, (1866), 862–967; hereafter referred to as *LM*.

[8] Sofia Boesch Gajano and Odile Redon, "La *Legenda Maior* di Raimonda da Capua, costruzione di una santa," in Domenico Maffei and Paolo Nardi, eds., *Atti del simposio internazionale Cateriniano-Bernardiniano, Siena, 17–20 aprile 1980* (1982), 15–36.

[9] *LM*, especially chaps. 4 and 122.

[10] This scholarship is summed up comprehensively in Eugenio Dupré Theseider, "Caterina da Siena, santa," in *Dizionario biografico degli Italiani*, vol. 22 (1979), 361–79. See also F. Thomas

Catherinian scholarship has not addressed with any specificity or depth Catherine's relationship to the public, political culture of her day.[11] Neither does Catherine figure at all in histories of *trecento* Italian politics, even Sienese politics, despite recent interest in the role of religious authority and ecclesiastical jurisdiction in Italian civic politics and emerging states.[12] Similarly, Catherine has almost never been treated as part of the same world as contemporaries such as Petrarch, Boccaccio, and Coluccio Salutati—men associated with the late-medieval cultural movement retrospectively known as the Italian Renaissance—despite the fact that her network included men who were also part of Petrarch's Florentine circle. With the exception of Jane Tylus's recent provocative argument for Catherine's link to the ethical concerns of early humanism, narrow and gendered definitions of "Renaissance" and "humanism" have excluded Catherine from the narrative of the cultural movements of her time.[13] Assumptions about the secular nature of fourteenth- and fifteenth-century Italian culture have been corrected in the last thirty years by studies of the role of piety in humanism by Paul Oskar Kristeller, Salvatore Camporeale, Nancy Struever, Charles Trinkaus, and others; and by studies of the role of religion and ritual in Italian civic culture by such scholars as Richard Trexler,

Luongo, "Catherine of Siena," in T. J. Cachey Jr. and Z. B. Baranski, eds., *Dictionary of Literary Biography. Italian Literature of the Fourteenth Century* (forthcoming). Some of the most important of these publications are Eugenio Dupré Theseider, "La duplice esperienza di Santa Caterina da Siena," *Rivista storica italiana* (1950): 533–74; idem, "Il problema critico delle lettere di Santa Caterina da Siena," *Giornale storico della letteratura italiana* 69 (1933): 117–278; idem, "Il supplizio di Niccolò di Toldo," *Bullettino senese di storia patria* 12 (1935): 162–64. Robert Fawtier, *Sainte Catherine de Sienne: Essai de critique des sources,* 2 vols. (1921–1930); Édouard Jourdan, "La date de naissance de santa Caterina," *Analecta Bollandiana* 40 (1922): 365–411; Pierre Mandonnet, "Santa Caterina da Siena et la critique historique," *Année dominicaine* 52 (1923): 6–17, 43–52.

[11] Exceptions include the still-useful biography by Edmund Gardner, *Saint Catherine of Siena: A Study in the Religion, Literature, and History of the Fourteenth Century in Italy* (1907), as well as two essays by Franco Cardini: "Caterina da Siena, la repubblica di Firenze e la lega antipontificia. Schede per una riconsiderazione," *Bullettino Senese di Storia Patria* 89 (1982): 300–325; and "L'idea di crociata in S. Caterina da Siena," in Maffei and Nardi, eds., *Atti del simposio internazionale Cateriniano-Bernardiniano* (1982), 57–87.

[12] Especially influential in revising the secular vision of Renaissance Italian politics have been Donald Weinstein, *Savanarola and Florence: Prophecy and Patriotism in the Renaissance* (1970); Giovanni Miccoli, "La storia religiosa," in *Storia d'Italia,* vol. 2 of *Dalla caduta dell'impero romano al secolo xviii* (1974); Denys Hay, *The Church in Italy in the Fifteenth Century* (1977); Richard C. Trexler, *Public Life in Renaissance Florence* (1980). More recently, see David S. Peterson, "State-Building, Church Reform, and the Politics of Legitimacy in Florence, 1375–1460," in William J. Connell and Andrea Zorzi, eds., *Florentine Tuscany: Structures and Practices of Power* (2000), 122–43; and idem, "Out of the Margins: Religion and the Church in Renaissance Italy," *Renaissance Quarterly* 53 (2000): 835–79.

[13] Jane Tylus, "Caterina da Siena and the Legacy of Humanism," in Joseph Marino and Melinda W. Schlitt, eds., *Perspectives on Early Modern and Modern Intellectual History: Essays in Honor of Nancy S. Struever* (2001), 116–41.

John Henderson, and Edward Muir.[14] But interest in the Renaissance and humanist religion has included only certain kinds of religious expression, and those mostly the preserve of men, a gendering of the Renaissance as male that is supported by the pervasive association of Renaissance culture with Latin humanism and the *studia humanitatis*. The exclusion of the vernacular not only rules out the language in which Catherine and most literate women of the period functioned but also sets up an artificial barrier in a Tuscan book culture in which the texts favored by the humanists were read also in Italian vernacular translation by cultivated merchants.

Where Catherine has received scholarly attention, readers have tended to impose ahistorical categories that have forestalled rather than explored the more interesting and novel features of her career as an author. Among saintly women in later medieval culture, Catherine's career involved an almost unique engagement in the practice of writing, and her use of the personal letter as a favored genre of writing had no precedent among female religious figures in Italian history. Rather than explore the relationship between Catherine's reputation as an inspired prophetess or mystic and her intense and continuous engagement with literature, studies of Catherine's writings have tended simply to set her texts apart from literature ordinarily understood, and forestalled inquiry into the relationship of her writings to the larger culture of her time. Recent exceptions include Jane Tylus's article cited already, as well as Marina Zancan's definitive introduction to Catherine's letters, in which she argues for Catherine's relationship to writing as a fundamental feature of her career.[15] There has also been some fruitful, if doctrinaire, inquiry into the sources that influenced Catherine's writing, studies that begin to lay the groundwork for a real appreciation of the complexity of her relationship to a variety of sources and models.[16] But Catherine and her writings have almost always been treated as

[14] For example, Charles Trinkaus, *In Our Image and Likeness: Humanity and Divinity in Italian Humanist Thought* (1970); Salvatore Camporeale, *Lorenzo Valla: Umanesimo e teologia* (1972); Paul Oskar Kristeller, *Medieval Aspects of Renaissance Learning* (1974); Trexler, *Public Life in Renaissance Florence;* Edward Muir, *Civic Ritual in Renaissance Venice* (1981); idem, "The Virgin on the Street Corner: The Place of the Sacred in Italian Cities," in Steven Ozment, ed., *Religion and Culture in the Renaissance and Reformation* (1989); Ronald F. E. Weissman, *Ritual Brotherhood in Renaissance Florence* (1982); Nancy Struever, *Theory as Practice: Ethical Inquiry in the Renaissance* (1990); *Christianity and the Renaissance: Image and Religious Imagination in the Quattrocento,* edited by Tomothy Verdon and John Henderson (1990); Daniel Bornstein, *The Bianchi of 1399: Popular Devotion in Late Medieval Italy* (1994); John Henderson, *Piety and Charity in Late Medieval Florence* (1994).

[15] Marina Zancan, "Lettere di Caterina da Siena," in Alberto Asor Rosa, ed., *Letteratura italiana. Le opera,* vol. 1 of *Dalle origini al cinquacento* (1992), 593–633; also "Lettere di Caterina da Siena. Il testo, la tradizione, l'interpretazione," *Annali d'Italianistica: Women Mystic Writers* 13 (1995): 151–61.

[16] Giacinto D'Urso, *Il genio di S. Caterina: Studi sulla sua dottrina e personalità* (1971); Alvaro Grion, *Santa Caterina da Siena, dottrina e fonti* (1953); Benedict Hackett, *William Flete,*

essentially estranged from the world of literature and "ordinary" texts. The features of Catherine's reputation that allowed Raymond of Capua to place Catherine beyond or above ordinary knowledge and writing—her femininity and the inspired nature of her texts—have usually caused modern critics to see Catherine as other than an author. This includes the dismissive assessment of her poetic skills by Risorgimento and post-Risorgimento critics such as De Sanctis, Croce, and Sapegno.[17] But it also includes the judgments of more friendly critics such as Giovanni Getto, Vittore Branca, and Giorgio Petrocchi, who have in different ways set Catherine apart from ordinary literature and historical situations by labeling her writings essentially "female" (Getto and Branca), "oratorical" (Petrocchi), and "mystical" (Getto).[18] Getto's interpretation of Catherine's letters is rich with fundamental insights into the character of her writings, and his abundantly enthusiastic interpretation of Catherine's writings has decisively influenced subsequent readings. Getto urged that Catherine's letters be read exclusively for their mystic content and evidence of her spiritual experience, explicitly setting aside historical and other mundane elements.[19] For Getto, the historical situations that prompted Catherine's letters were merely incidental, and the epistolary form a mere container of mystic, spiritual insights, and so Getto's interpretation has helped forestall inquiry into Catherine's letters as a cultural project. In this context, Michel de Certeau's injunction against imposing "ready-made" definitions on texts labeled "mystic" is especially apropos.[20] More

---

O.S.A., and Catherine of Siena: Masters of Fourteenth-Century Spirituality, The Augustinian Series, 15 (1992). D'Urso argues for a Dominican, and more specifically, a Thomistic Catherine; Grion emphasizes the influence of Franciscans, and particularly Ubertino da Casale; and Hackett links Catherine to the Augustinian tradition. On the other hand, I would agree with Getto (cited below) in emphasizing the heterogeneous character of Catherine's influences.

[17] Francesco De Sanctis, Storia della letteratura italiana, ed. Niccolò Gallo (1958); Benedetto Croce, "Letteratura del Trecento. Letteratura di devozione," La Critica, 3rd ser. 29 (1931): 321–22; Natalino Sapegno, Scrittori d'Italia: antologia per lo studio della letteratura italiana nelle scuole medie superiori (1963).

[18] Vittore Branca, I mistici: Fioretti di San Francesco, Lettere di Santa Caterina (1964); Giovanni Getto, "L'intuizione mistica e l'espressione letteraria di Caterina da Siena," in Letteratura religiosa del trecento (1967), 107–267; Giorgio Petrocchi, "La letteratura religiosa del trecento," in Storia della letteratura italiana, Emilio Cecchi and Natalino Sapegno, eds., vol. 2 of Il Trecento (1965), 637–82.

[19] Giovanni Getto, "L'intuizione mistica."

[20] Michel de Certeau, "Mystic Speech," in Heterologies: Discourse on the Other, trans. Brian Massumi (1986), 82: "In the beginning, it is best to limit oneself to consideration of what goes on in texts whose status is labeled 'mystic,' instead of wielding a ready-made definition (whether ideological or imaginary) of what it is that was inscribed in these texts by the operation of writing." Following De Certeau, Sarah Beckwith argues for historicizing "mystic" texts in Christ's Body: Identity, Culture and Society in Late Medieval Writings (1993), esp. chapter 1, "The Transcendent and the Historical: Inventing the Discourse of Mysticism," 7–21: "If we are to consider mysticism as a practice, and as a specifically late medieval practice, then we will have to pay heed to manifestations which are not merely the husk, the externalities

recently, Karen Scott's insightful studies of Catherine's letters have emphasized Catherine's activity in the world and read Catherine's letters more as
ordinary rather than mystic communication. But Scott in turn has argued
that Catherine's culture was essentially oral (her "basic mentality remained
that of an illiterate person") and her writing a form of speech only inciden-
tally or secondarily textual—effectively steering away from a more complicated understanding of the cultural meaning of Catherine's letters.[21]

One symptom of Catherine's alienation from Italian literature is that
there still exists no complete, modern critical edition of her letters. Eugenio Dupré Theseider published a single volume of a proposed four-volume critical edition of the letters in 1940. This volume, with some
revisions, was translated into English by Suzanne Noffke in 1988, again as
part of a planned four-volume series.[22] The Italian scholar Antonio Volpato has attempted to take up and continue Dupré Theseider's work in
order to produce a complete critical edition of the letters. While no critical edition has yet appeared in print, Volpato has issued, as part of a CD-
Rom collection of Catherine's writings, a newly edited text of the letters.[23]
All references in this book are to Volpato's edition. In the meantime,
Suzanne Noffke has continued her own work on the letters, employing lin-
guistic analysis to stabilize their chronology and translating the remaining
letters into English from working editions based on especially authoritative manuscripts. In 2000, Noffke issued a new first volume of the letters,
including seventy letters, with original commentary and a chronological
order slightly different from that in Dupré Theseider's edition, and subsequently has published a second volume, including an additional seventy-
three letters; further volumes are anticipated.[24] Thus we have the ironic
situation of a translation into English of something close to a critical edition of Catherine's letters, including attention to textual variations, before

---

of a phenomenon that is already described without them, but exist as particular and specific
utterances, oriented towards the world of their embodiment" (18).

[21] Karen Scott, "*Io Caterina*: Ecclesiastical Politics and Oral Culture in the Letters of
Catherine of Siena," in Karen Cherewatuk and Ulrike Wiethau, eds., *Dear Sister: Medieval
Women and the Epistolary Genre* (1993), 87–121 (quotation is on p. 113). Also by Scott: "'This
is Why I Have Put You among Your Neighbors': St. Bernard's and St. Catherine's Understanding of the Love of God and Neighbor," in Maffei and Nardi, eds., *Atti del simposio internazionale Cateriniano-Bernardiniano* (1982), 279–94; "St. Catherine of Siena, 'Apostola,'"
*Church History* 61, no. 1 (March 1992): 34–46; "Urban Spaces, Women's Networks, and the
Lay Apostolate in the Siena of Catherine Benincasa," in E. Ann Matter and John Coakley,
eds., *Creative Women in Medieval and Early Modern Italy*, (1994), 105–19.

[22] *The Letters of Catherine of Siena*, vol. 1 (1988).

[23] "Le lettere di Santa Caterina da Siena," edited by Antonio Volpato, in *Santa Caterina
da Siena: Opera Omnia*, edited by Fausto Sbaffoni (2002).

[24] *The Letters of Catherine of Siena*, translated and edited by Suzanne Noffke
(2000–2001). All references to Noffke's edition and translation of Catherine's letters are to
the second edition, begun in 2000.

a critical edition is available in Italian. Throughout this book I have generally accepted Dupré Theseider's and Noffke's datings of the letters; where
I have departed from or added precision to their datings, I have presented
my reasoning. Translations are my own throughout. I have opted for a
more literal and less colloquial translation of Catherine's letters than Noffke's. At the same time, I have depended on Noffke's translations, where
available, to help in deciphering rough patches in Catherine's sometimes
very confusing syntax, and I gratefully acknowledge this debt.

The fact that Catherine continues to be studied apart from what are
considered the main political and cultural developments of her day is
also linked to the considerable recent work on late-medieval and early-
modern religious women and feminine religiosity, scholarship that has
succeeded in creating for itself an autonomous place within the historical
discipline. Catherine is a prominent point of reference in the last two
decades' wave of scholarship on religious women in medieval and early-
modern Italy, including the work of such scholars as Anna Benvenuti,
Gabriella Zarri, Roberto Rusconi, and Daniel Bornstein.[25] A large number of individual studies and conference proceedings have addressed
individual saints; local and regional cults; and the legal/institutional situation of religious and quasi-religious associations of pious women in Italian cities.[26] Catherine also surfaces frequently in broader studies as an
important exemplar of female Eucharistic piety, asceticism, and visionary
religiosity, as in André Vauchez's landmark studies of medieval canonization and lay piety.[27] At the same time, the very success of this scholarship

[25] Anna Benvenuti-Papi, *"In Castro Poenitentiae": Santità e società femminile nell'Italia
medievale,* Italia Sacra, 45 (1990); Daniel Bornstein and Roberto Rusconi, eds., *Mistiche e
devote nell'Italia tardomedievale* (1992); available in revised form in English as *Women and Religion in Medieval and Renaissance Italy* (1996); Gabriella Zarri, *Le sante vive: profezie di corte e
devozione femminile tra '400 e '500* (1990), esp. chapter 2: "Pietà e profezia alle corti padane:
le pie consigliere dei principi," and chapter 3: "Le sante vive."

[26] See the excellent introduction to this scholarship in Daniel Bornstein, "Women and
Religion in Late Medieval Italy: History and Historiography," in Bornstein and Roberto Rusconi, eds., *Women and Religion* (1996), 1–27. Among the most notable Italian conferences
focused on women's religiosity, see Roberto Rusconi, ed., *Il movimento religioso femminile in
Umbria nei secoli XIII–XIV: Atti del convegno internazionale di studio nell'ambito delle celebrazioni per
l'VIII centenario della nascita di S. Francesco d'Assisi, Città di Castello, 27–29 ottobre 1982* (1984);
*Temi e problemi della mistica femminile trecentesca, Centro di studi sulla spiritualità, Todi 14–17 otto-
bre 1979* (1983); Claudio Leonardi and Enrico Manesti, eds., *S. Chiara da Montefalco e il suo
tempo: Atti del quarto convegno di studi storici ecclesiastici organizzato dall'Arcidiocesi di Spoleto, Spoleto 28–30 dicembre 1981* (1985). Among important collections in English are Craig Monson,
ed., *The Crannied Wall: Women, Religion, and the Arts in Early Modern Europe* (1992); E. Ann
Matter and John Coakley, eds., *Creative Women in Medieval and Early Modern Italy: A Religious
and Artistic Renaissance* (1994); Lucetta Scaraffia and Gabriella Zarri, eds., *Women and Faith:
Catholic Religious Life in Italy from Late Antiquity to the Present* (1999).

[27] André Vauchez, *Les laïcs au moyen âge: Pratiques et expériences religieuses* (1987) (English
translation, *The Laity in the Middle Ages: Religious Beliefs and Devotional Practices,* trans. Margery J.

has tended to throw together women of very different backgrounds and social experiences, approached always through the a priori category "religious women," in isolation from the cultural, economic, and political aspects of their particular social locations. The inadvertent effect has been to reinforce the image of Catherine existing at a distance (prophetic or otherwise) from male politics and culture. It has become all too easy to know where to place Catherine in a historical narrative in which politics and literary culture are gendered male, and religious women and feminine religiosity occupy a space apart.[28]

Above all, Catherine's emergence as a saint exemplifies what a variety of scholars have presented as a "feminized" religious culture in the later Middle Ages, a characterization that has received its most brilliant and persuasive treatment in the influential works of Caroline Walker Bynum.[29] This cultural movement reversed the values in a series of gendered tropes traditionally derogatory toward women. Bynum has summed up these tropes as a series of binaries: "Male and female were contrasted and asymmetrically valued as intellect/body, active/passive, rational/irrational, reason/emotion, self control/lust, judgment/mercy, and order/disorder."[30] But with the more intense focus on Christ's humanity in the religious culture of the later Middle Ages, a constellation of images associated Christ and the salvific suffering of the crucifixion with women's powerless social position as well as women's ordinary experience of the suffering and nurturing roles of mothers. Thus the dominant image of Christ became "feminine" and often female. And new value was placed on "feminine" experience of religious matters, for instance emotional engagement in the suffering of Christ on the cross and in the sorrow of the Virgin Mary, as opposed to the theological abstraction associated with "masculine" intellectuality.

Thus, as Bynum has argued, the very marginalization of women from the main centers of male authority and culture created a positive image of women alongside traditional misogyny, and by extension privileged women's religious experience, allowing some women to assert power by

---

Schneider [1993]); *La sainteté en occident aux derniers siècles du moyen âge: D'après les procès de canonisation et les documents hagiographiques* (1981 (English translation, *Sainthood in the Later Middle Ages*, trans. Jean Birrell [1997]); *La spiritualité du moyen âge occidental* (1975).

[28] Tylus, "Caterina da Siena and the Legacy of Humanism," 119: "The otherwise welcome spate of studies on medieval women and religion in Italy has tended to generate a picture in scholarship in which humanism is gendered as generally male and late medieval religion as feminine if not female."

[29] *Fragmentation and Redemption: Essays on Gender and the Human Body in Medieval Religion* (1991); *Holy Feast and Holy Fast: The Religious Significance of Food to Medieval Women* (1987); *Jesus as Mother: Studies in the Spirituality of the High Middle Ages* (1982).

[30] Caroline Walker Bynum, "'And Women His Humanity': Female Imagery in the Religious Writings of the Later Middle Ages," in *Fragmentation and Redemption* (1991), 151.

embracing the spiritual equivalents of women's social roles.[31] Whereas the power of men was asserted through institutions that excluded women, mystics and holy women could articulate through spiritualized feminine personae a kind of authority and independence from which women were otherwise excluded. In a culture that increasingly valued a more emotive, immediate, and ascetic piety, women—considered both more fleshly and more emotional than men—offered proud intellectuals a site of redemptive transformation. In short, men sought feminine images of Christ and female holy authorities because of their distance from ordinary male experience. At the same time, since the feminine already signified religious engagement, the roles embraced by women reflected a transformed version of women's ordinary experience: "Medieval women, like men, chose to speak of themselves as brides, mothers and sisters of Christ. But to women this was an accepting and continuing of what they were; to men it was a reversal."[32] The authority of holy women derived from their distance from male society and power—from being the opposite of men.

There is indeed abundant reason to identify Catherine with this model of female-holy authority. Catherine identified herself as Bride of Christ and spiritual mother to her followers, who in turn called her "Mamma." Catherine used motherhood as her preferred metaphor for spiritual affiliation; "I am giving birth to you in my soul" was her most characteristic description of her spiritual interventions. Her letters, in which she exhorted her correspondents mentally to embrace the crucified Christ on the cross and nurse from his wounds, are emotionally charged and full of ecstatic images of Christ's fleshliness. Catherine's incessant rhetoric of hunger and feeding in reference to the Eucharist, *imitatio Christi,* and evangelization—conversion, for Catherine, was "eating souls"—as well as her preoccupation with the salvific and nurturing blood of Christ crucified, all accord well with Bynum's observations concerning female saints and food. Her hagiographers told how the uneducated Catherine confounded proud intellectual clerics, converting them by miraculously reducing them (or raising them) to tears and a more emotional, experiential piety. Raymond of Capua argued for the authority of Catherine's life and writings by appealing to a model of sanctity that associated femininity with affective spirituality and special access to divine gifts, characteristics

---

[31] This argument is made in Bynum's enormously influential *Holy Feast and Holy Fast* (1986), and more concisely in "'. . . And Women His Humanity.'" For a similar formulation, see Karma Lochrie, "The Language of Transgression: Body, Flesh, and Word in Mystical Discourse," in Allen J. Frantzen, ed., *Speaking in Two Languages: Traditional Disciplines and Contemporary Theory in Medieval Studies* (1991), 115–40.

[32] "Women's Stories, Women's Symbols: A Critique of Victor Turner's Theory of Liminality," in *Fragmentation and Redemption* (1991), 48.

that made Catherine simultaneously less than and greater than contemporary male society. And Catherine's other male followers similarly valued her for a gendered alterity, describing her as the Bride from the Song of Songs, an exotic and prophetic woman. Catherine's authority depended precisely on her embodiment of a series of specifically female spiritual roles and, by the contradictory logic of late-medieval religious culture, on her difference from men and exclusion from institutions of male power—whether ecclesiastical, academic, or political. Thus, as Daniel Bornstein has argued, Catherine "from a position of structural weakness and ideological subordination was able to exercise a profound influence on her world."[33]

But while the dominant discourse of female sanctity elevated Catherine by setting her apart, Catherine was not in fact separated from worldly affairs. This book argues against understanding Catherine simply according to categories—religious woman, female saint, mystic—that treat her a priori as someone separate from worldly affairs and worldly power, approaching the world always from a position apart, whether that position is understood as prophetic distance or "structural weakness." Gender categories are not fixed, but change according to time, place, and circumstance; what it meant to be a "woman," even a "religious woman," in the Middle Ages was different for Catherine of Siena than it was for Hildegard of Bingen.[34] The category "religious women" is itself a cultural construct, the product of hagiography and other normative literature. But discussion of women in medieval religion has tended to take gendered religious identities as representations of the experience of late-medieval women, and so has naturalized and reified the discourse of late-medieval female religiosity. Studying women's religious experience in isolation from the social, economic, and political aspects of medieval culture, and assuming some experience common to "religious women," almost inevitably ends up eliding the particularities of individuals.[35]

[33] Daniel Bornstein, "Women and Religion in Late Medieval Italy," 5–6.

[34] This is not a novel or highly theorized argument, but I should acknowledge the basic influence of Denise Riley, *"Am I That Name?" Feminism and the Category of "Women" in History* (1988). Also relevant here is Judith Butler's idea of gender as "performative," as a way to understand how a person's actions create that person's gender identity, not in isolation from culture, but in a kind of dialogue with cultural norms. See *Gender Trouble: Feminism and the Subversion of Identity* (1990); and *Bodies That Matter: On the Discursive Limits of 'Sex'* (1993).

[35] Sharon Farmer, in an essay that addresses particular attention to Bynum's formulation of the medieval male/female binary, has recently raised precisely this point in critiquing the idea that in medieval male writings women were simply more closely associated with the body than men: "Gendered categories are always constructed within, and in relationship to, other categories of difference—such as social status or ethnic or religious difference" ("The Beggar's Body: Intersections of Gender and Social Status in High Medieval Paris," in Sharon Farmer and Barbara H. Rosenwein, eds., *Monks and Nuns, Saints and Outcasts: Religion in Medieval Society*

The irony of this situation is especially clear in the work of Bynum. While her most influential studies are premised on an argument for understanding gender and the body as culturally constructed—indeed, it is this point that has proved most influential, even to the extent of transforming the historiography of medieval religion—her method undercuts this basic premise by throwing together women of very different backgrounds and social experience. This approach inevitably reproduces certain dominant categories of medieval discourse—regarding female sanctity, for instance—as representative of women's experience, just as it excludes the experience of women who did not fit into those categories. In the case of Catherine, this approach elides tensions in her career by allowing the hagiography of Raymond of Capua and others to dominate interpretation and prejudge reading of her writings. More fundamentally, such a move from discourse to representation in the work of Bynum, among others, inevitably misses the ways in which cultural terms are constituted in specific social, political, and economic situations—turning, as David Aers puts it, "processes and complex (sometimes contradictory) effects into essence, verbs into nouns."[36]

In other words, what both Catherine and her followers said about her were claims, not simple facts or reflections of some essential identity.[37] Catherine was not simply the person Raymond of Capua and others said she was. And Catherine's own statements were not simply expressions of self-identity; as will be seen, Catherine's writings at times functioned as a kind of autohagiography appealing to, and sometimes challenging, the

---

[2000], 153–71]). It is worth observing that a more socially complex approach to gender has become relatively common within medieval history as whole, outside of the literature devoted especially to religious women and feminine religiosity, even in work less overtly grounded in feminist and postcolonial theory than Farmer's. For example, within Italian history, one might mention the work of Christiane Klapisch-Zuber and Diane Owens Hughes; essays by Robert C. Davis, Sharon Strocchia, and Stanley Chojnacki, in Judith C. Brown and Robert C. Davis, eds., *Gender and Society in Renaissance Italy* (1998); and, more recently, Carol Lansing, *The Lament for the Dead* (forthcoming). Outside of medieval Italian history, exemplary studies include Judith M. Bennett, *Ale, Beer, and Brewsters in England: Women's Work in a Changing World, 1300–1600* (1996); Martha C. Howell, *The Marriage Exchange: Property, Social Place, and Gender in Cities of the Low Countries, 1300–1550* (1998); Ruth Mazo Karras, *Common Women: Prostitution and Sexuality in Medieval England* (1996). This is not even to account for the many studies of medieval gender in the last decade devoted to masculinities.

[36] David Aers, "The Humanity of Christ: Reflections on Orthodox Late Medieval Representations," in David Aers and Lynn Staley, *The Powers of the Holy: Religion, Politics, and Gender in Late Medieval English Culture* (1996), 15–42; see also Kathleen Biddick, "Genders, Bodies, Borders: Technologies of the Visible," *Speculum* 68 (1993): 389–418, reprinted in Biddick, *The Shock of Medievalism* (1998). I am indebted to both of these more thoroughgoing critiques of Bynum and the historiography of late-medieval female religiosity, though my own approach to this material offers a corrective in a different direction than the points emphasized by Aers and Biddick.

[37] Joan Scott, "The Evidence of Experience," *Critical Inquiry* 17 (1991): 773–97.

terms in which Raymond and others were prepared to accept her. Catherine's saintly identity was a verb, not a noun, just as sanctity itself, as Aviad Kleinberg has argued, should be viewed as "not an attribute or a quality, but a process of negotiation."[38] This is a distinction that is difficult to see through the lens provided by the standard narrative of medieval female sanctity. But it is an important distinction; for to miss it is also to miss some of the most dramatic and interesting features of Catherine's career. Raymond's portrayal of Catherine does largely confirm Bynum's model, but identifying Catherine too closely with what was said about her after her death makes it impossible to appreciate the ways in which in her life and writings Catherine transgressed the boundaries of female sanctity—as indeed she crosses the categories of medieval and Renaissance historiography.[39] When Catherine as an historical agent is occluded within an identity like "female saint" or "mystic," it is difficult to see the ways in which she and her followers deployed the discourse of female sanctity and feminine religiosity to further specific political and social programs. An understanding of the discourses of female sanctity and feminine religiosity so dramatically revealed by Bynum and subsequently studied by others is basic to my argument. But this book is not about these discourses; rather, it is about what Catherine and others did with them. Cultural terms like sanctity and gender gain meaning only as they are constituted in specific situations and engaged by specific actors. Rather than view Catherine through the retrospective categories of hagiography or historiography, this book seeks to understand the process of negotiation by which Catherine asserted her authority, and the specific situation that shaped the articulation of her saintly identity, the cultural moment of the War of Eight Saints.

࿔

There is a clear connection between the categories into which scholars fix Catherine—the generic space in which they place her—and their disinterest in exploring the more profligate geography of her movements in

---

[38] Aviad M. Kleinberg, *Prophets in Their Own Country: Living Saints and the Making of Sainthood in the Later Middle Ages* (1992).

[39] Jane Tylus has commented that the "deeply transgressive nature of Catherine's letters" has rarely been appreciated (Tylus, 139n). As Tylus notes, exceptions include Roberto Antonelli, for whom Catherine was "autrice in proprio di alcuni fra i più inquietanti testi mistici della cultura europea, oltre che protagonista rilevante nelle storia politica e religiosa del Trecento" ("L'Ordine domenicano e la letteratura nell'Italia pretridentina," in *Letteratura italiana*, vol. 1, Albert Asor Rosa, ed., *Il letterato e le istituzioni* [1982], 701). On the tensions between Raymond's portrayal of Catherine and Catherine's self-presentation, particularly involving her physicality and her writing, see Claudia Rattazzi Papka, "The Written Woman Writes: Caterina da Siena between History and Hagiography, Body and Text," in *Annali d'Italianistica* 13 (1995): 131–47.

the 1370s. Instead of reiterating the categories of Catherine's posthumous reputation, I argue for a vision of Catherine in which the defining feature of her career is the violation of inherited categories, a transgressivity that also carries her across the boundaries of conventional historiographical classification.

Catherine's travels in public and her interventions by letter into politically sensitive matters challenged accepted norms for ordinary female behavior, let alone for female sanctity. While these trangressive features of her life were sanctioned because of particular circumstances and needs, after her death Catherine's life and writings needed to be abstracted from the particularities of the 1370s and broadcast in new terms. Raymond of Capua's portrait of Catherine in his authoritative *Legenda maior* continues to set the terms for discussion of Catherine's role in the world, particularly as it confirms neatly the terms in which recent historiography has discussed the valorization of "saintly" women and female religiosity in the later Middle Ages. Chapter 1 offers a new look at Catherine's early career before she became a public figure, examining the drama of her emerging religious vocation, which was far from conventional, or even formally religious. It also explores the political situation of her family during the Sienese revolutionary period 1368–71, exactly the moment when Catherine established a novel identity as an independent religious woman with a public persona and sphere of action. Catherine's public position in the 1370s owed more to the social and political circumstances of her family than has previously been recognized, and especially to the example and protection of her mother, a powerful and independent woman. By interrupting Raymond's account with other narratives and sources, this chapter exposes tensions in his narrative and reveals a complex story hidden not only by the authoritative hagiography but also by the standard historiography of gender in late-medieval spirituality. Raymond's construction of Catherine's saintly identity is not a description of female religiosity in the late fourteenth century, but an argument for a particular kind of sanctity. It confirms nicely the model of female sanctity described by Caroline Bynum, among others, but it does so by excluding alternative experiences of real women in the late fourteenth century.

The remaining chapters track Catherine's movements on the Italian political map and her involvement in the politics of the War of Eight Saints, returning her letters to their historical settings. Chapter 2 examines the network of clerics and elites that set the stage for Catherine's emergence as a public figure in 1374, when church leaders recruited her to replace the recently dead Birgitta of Sweden, whose prophetic authority had bolstered papal policy. But Catherine broke with mystic precedents by communicating with the world through letters. While Catherine's letter-writing innovated by embodying inspired speech in a mundane, domestic genre, her epistolary project was nevertheless part of a larger culture of letter-writing in late-medieval Italy, placing her in the company of Petrarch and Coluccio Salutati. Catherine engaged the innate ability of the epistolary genre to cross class and other barriers in order to seek authority and relocate discussion outside the bounds of particular institutions—ecclesiastical, civic, or academic. And along with her humanist contemporaries she took advantage of the relative fluidity of the epistolary form—its lack of formal constraints, unbounded by institutionalized modes of discourse—to approach from new perspectives issues of public importance. Looking at Catherine's letters as letters, with the full implications of letter-writing as a cultural practice, reveals Catherine as something other than the "mystic" author she has become in the literary canon. Far from being disinterested in worldly affairs in her writings, Catherine employed the generic and institutional mobility of the letter to carry prophetic speech into worldly affairs, and thereby challenge the terms of worldly politics.

Chapter 3 illustrates dramatically the potential of letter writing in Catherine's hands as a means to foster her network and communicate her authority in politics. Here I offer a new reading of Catherine's most famous letter, in which she describes for Raymond of Capua her conversion of a young man who had been arrested and condemned to death by the Sienese government. The letter is a tour de force of mystic eroticism, in which Catherine plots her encounter with the young man as a marriage culminating in consummation on the scaffold in the moment of his death, employing a constantly shifting series of gendered images that play on her own reputation as a saintly woman, as well as on the imagery of the dominant discourse of feminine religiosity. Less obviously, the letter also traces Catherine's engagement in a highly charged political episode: the condemned young man had been arrested in Siena as agent of the papacy. Catherine appeals in the letter to assumptions concerning female religiosity and to her own reputation, in terms that anticipate to some extent the construction of her saintly authority. But she violates the accepted discourse of female sanctity by politicizing it, carrying her authority provocatively into the public and political domain at the beginning of her public career and the outset of open hostilities between the Tuscan city-states and the papacy.

Chapters 4 and 5 address directly Catherine's movements on the Italian political map between 1375 and 1378 and her involvement in the politics of the War of Eight Saints. Chapter 4 places Catherine directly within Sienese and Tuscan politics by examining the political connections and activities of her spiritual "family" in Siena. While the young men who formed her *famiglia* later recalled their association with her as involving a complete and categorical conversion from the world, most of them entered religious life, if at all, only after Catherine's death. Her noble followers in particular continued to hold political offices in Siena during the time when they were attached to her. Indeed, the Caterinati might very well have functioned at times as a party within Sienese politics, united in opposition to the Sienese regime and in loyalty to the cause of the church in Italy—just as the Sienese regime apparently feared in 1377, during the episode with which I began this introduction. More basically, this chapter continues the process of moving Catherine from an unworldly and ahistorical cloister into the complications and tensions of social and political life in the 1370s. Being part of Catherine's *famiglia* did not remove her spiritual children from the world, any more than Catherine's own saintly authority developed apart from the exigencies of social and political affairs. Just as Catherine occupied a space between religious and secular status, and wrote letters that mixed the prophetic and political, association with Catherine involved for her followers a sometimes tense mixing of spiritual ambitions with mundane social and political concerns.

Chapter 5 concludes this study of Catherine's politicized sanctity by presenting Catherine as a woman mixing unapologetically in the world and moving in Italian political space. Here I trace Catherine's movements and the circulation of her letters alongside a narrative of Sienese and Tuscan politics drawn from a mixture of published and unpublished evidence. This narrative dramatizes the relationship between Catherine's emergence as a saintly figure and her participation in papally sponsored diplomatic missions as the conflict between the church and Florence intensified. This chapter brings together several main themes of Catherine's letters—reform of individuals and the church, peace in Italy, the return of papacy to Rome, and the launching of a general Crusade to Jerusalem—to show how her rhetoric on these themes was shaped by and responded to the political exigencies of the War of Eight Saints. Catherine's epistolary efforts on behalf of the church in the war culminated in late 1377 with an astounding epistolary description to Raymond of Capua of Catherine's mystic dialogue with God, and an even more shocking announcement that, while her letters had previously been dictated to scribes, she has now learned miraculously to write. I argue that this controversial letter, one that has caused discomfort within the Catherinian tradition from Raymond of Capua to recent scholarship, demonstrates how the content of Catherine's most profound and long-lasting spiritual text, the *Libro di divina dottrina* or *Dialogo*, which she began composing at this time, was occasioned by and grounded in the exigencies of the War of Eight Saints.

This book reveals a Catherine not contained within the bounds of conventional historical categories and argues for an understanding of Catherine as a historical figure one of whose defining characteristics was the violation of categories—an extraordinary mobility across boundaries, both cultural and geographical. Her violation of categories should be viewed in light of other moments of late-medieval cultural experimentation; Catherine through her travels and letters was herself a kind of experiment with genres, the mobilization of female holy authority within a religious and political contest. That is what her travels and writing were for, and that is presumably why they were sanctioned and encouraged by clerical authorities in spite of their transgressing gender norms and models of religious life. After her death and the passing of the moment that had called her extraordinary gifts into public life, these exceptional features of Catherine's life were softened or written out of her life as a more acceptable saintly persona was constructed. The potential for female religious figures to step into the fissures created in political disorder has been recognized for the early-modern period by, among others, Gabriella Zarri and Michel de Certeau[40] The War of Eight Saints was such a crisis, an early episode in the Renaissance contests over political order and the form and meaning of the Italian map. To return to the scene with which the introduction began, Catherine's response to the Sienese regarding her relationship with the Salimbeni ostensibly put her beyond civic politics, but the Sienese would have understood, as most historians have not, that her response gestured to a prophetic distance that in fact authorized her entry into politics, and was the mark of her authority. Catherine was not really apolitical, but was carrying out a new and different kind of politics in response to the ideological demands of the battles between the church and Florence. Reading Catherine's letters and actions in this way moves her from the particular critical and historiographical space of female religiosity and mysticism into the assumed male and secular cultural ground of late-medieval and Renaissance politics, challenging not only the conventional image of Catherine but also conventional accounts of fourteenth- and fifteenth-century cultural developments. Catherine, in her brief career, thus provides a link between gender, religion, and politics, and a window onto the cultural and political contests of late-medieval Italy.

[40] Zarri, *Le Sante vive;* and Michel de Certeau "Mystic Speech," 87: "To gain a perspective on the process which slowly replaced a divided Christianity with national *political* units, breaking down the social organization of universal belief into sects, 'retreats,' and '*spiritual*' communities, it is necessary to take a more general view that includes a recognition of the sociopolitical instability of the age and the fragmentation of its frames of reference. As a matter of fact, the 'Machiavellian Moment' and the 'mystic invasion' coincide. The project of constructing an order amid the contingencies of history (the problem of the reason of State) and the quest to discern in our earthly, fallen language the now inaudible Word of God (the problem of the spiritual subject) arose simultaneously from the dissociation of cosmic language and the Divine Speaker. In addition, these two complementary restoration projects have recourse to the same 'ecclesial' heritage of a unifying whole, although they express it in henceforth specialized modes: for one, the reason of State, for the other, the 'community of saints.'"

CHAPTER 1

# Catherine's Vocational Years: Worldliness and Female Sanctity

In the *Legenda maior* of Raymond of Capua, Catherine on her deathbed addresses criticism of her unorthodox life as a woman who carried out her vocation outside the cloister, violating the gendered boundaries of social space. To critics who asked, "Why does she not stay in her cell, if she wishes to serve God?" Catherine, in nearly her final words, asserts that she mixed in society only for "the praise of God and his true glory!"—not for fame or praise.[1] That Raymond has Catherine address this issue at this climactic moment of his narrative signals how much of a challenge it was to portray Catherine in terms acceptable for a female saint in light of the anomaly of her mixing in the world and intervening in public affairs. Enough evidence of criticism has filtered through the hagiographic net to know that Catherine was indeed attacked on occasion for the public nature of her life. For example, in a *lauda* written to Catherine during her lifetime, the Gesuate poet Bianco da Siena warned Catherine against presumption in exercising a prophetic authority in public and urged her to "escape to the cell" in order to avoid the spiritual dangers of publicity and the world.[2] The Florentine

---

[1]   Raymond of Capua, *LM*, par. 365, 953: "Unde plures quandoque de ipsa loquentes, etiam mihi dixerunt: Ut quid ista gyrovagando discurrit? Mulier est. Quon manet in cella, si vult Deo servire? Quibus, si quis diligenter advertat, sufficienter responsum est. Vanam gloriam (inquit) numquam, sed laudem et veram gloriam Dei utique. Ac si aperte diceret: Non propter vanam gloriam discurrebam, aut alia quaecumque opera faciebam: sed propter laudem et gloriam nominis Salvatoris omnia operabar."

[2]   Verse 8: "Molti santi sono stati / Che so' stati frequentati:/ Per non esser vulnerati / Son fuggiti alla celata." Verse 14: "Guarda che la tentazione / Del profetico sermone / Non ti metta in suo prigione: / Tardi t'averà lasata." The complete thirty-two stanza poem is

Figure 1. The Church of San Domenico, standing over Fontebranda and the neighborhood of Catherine's family. Source: Alinari/ Art Resource.

Vallombrosian abbot Giovanni dalle Celle was an outspoken supporter of Catherine and wrote several letters in the mid-1370s defending Catherine against clerics attacking her for her conspicuously public wielding of spiritual authority.[3] But when Giovanni in 1376 learned that a nun named Domitilla, who was under his supervision, had been invited by Catherine to join her on what Catherine assumed was an imminent Crusade to the Holy Land, Giovanni strongly rejected this plan as "the enemy of all chastity, the gate of perdition and dispersion of all virtue, the loss of all innocence and purity," and ordered his young charge to remain in her cloister.[4]

This tension over Catherine's social and religious status has largely been lost in both the hagiographical and historical memories of Catherine, in which her public persona is assumed, sometimes even exaggerated—as in the tradition by which she is credited with convincing Pope Gregory XI to return to Rome—but not considered a problem worth deeper analysis. In medieval religious history, Catherine is identified with unambiguous institutional status, as a member of the Dominican Third Order or Order of Penance. More generally, she is cited as a representative of late-medieval piety: as a bride of Christ and a mother to a spiritual *famiglia,* Catherine adopted spiritualized equivalents to ordinary female roles in almost perfect accordance with Caroline Walker Bynum's model of late-medieval female sanctity. These historical and hagiographical identities treat Catherine's status as fixed and already set apart from the world in which she moved, and so have forestalled certain kinds of questions about the development of her career. The designation "saint" itself, whether in hagiography or in historical scholarship, presumes exceptionality, and so tends to place beyond or beneath analysis social particularities involved in the saint's career. So the question remains, what was so unusual or problematic about Catherine's position in the world, that Raymond of Capua would have been prompted to raise the issue prominently in his case for Catherine's sanctity?

This chapter seeks to recover some of the tension and novelty to which Raymond was responding by taking a fresh look at Catherine's youth and early career, the period before she attained renown beyond Siena, to

---

printed in *I Fioretti di santa Caterina da Siena,* ed. Innocenzo M. Taurisano (1950), 131–36.

[3] Giovanni dalle Celle and Luigi Marsili, *Lettere,* ed. Francesco Giambonini, Vol. 2 (1991). The specific charges Giovanni answers concern the alleged "novelty" of Catherine's declaring a desire for martyrdom, taking upon herself punishment for the sins of others, and allowing her hands and feet to be kissed in adoration.

[4] Giovanni argued that while Catherine's uncloistered life was licit, she was an exception—not a model to be imitated. And in any case, Catherine gained the perfection necessary to lead such a life through a long seclusion. Giovanni responded to this young nun's desire to follow Catherine by arguing, paradoxically, that Domitilla should imitate Catherine by staying in the cloister, not by leaving it (Giovanni dalle Celle, *Lettere* 2: 305–10).

describe the social and political circumstances in which she emerged as a public figure. It focuses on the drama of Catherine's emerging religious vocation amid competing models of female propriety and religious life, a drama with social resonance that has been lost, in part, through hagiographic rewriting of Catherine's story. In particular, Catherine's ordinary family life has largely vanished from her story in accordance with the demands of hagiography—what Anna Benvenuti has referred to as the *territorio negato* of the domestic life of the saint.[5] This chapter examines the social and political situation of Catherine's family, especially during the revolutionary period in Siena of 1368–71, exactly the moment when Catherine began to establish her novel identity as an independent religious woman with a public persona and sphere of action. Catherine's subsequent career as a public figure was bound in basic ways to the experience of her family during those years.

Any attempt to describe Catherine's life before her letters and other evidence of her movements and actions must depend on the methodologically risky approach of sifting through hagiographical constructions for positive evidence. Indeed, the evidence of Catherine's early life is so bound up in hagiographical tropes that a critical and thorough biography of Catherine during these years is impossible. For biographical details, Catherinian scholars have depended almost exclusively on Raymond of Capua's *Legenda maior*. In this highly sophisticated argument for Catherine's sanctity, Raymond sought to explain, justify, and sometimes erase problematic features of Catherine's career, especially her public life, even as he emphasized her identity as an ascetic visionary and Bride of Christ. Indeed, in creating Catherine's saintly identity Raymond wrote certain disturbing aspects of her career out of her life, even to the extent of revising the chronology of her early years. This chapter uses archival sources and an earlier account—the *Miracoli di Caterina di Jacopo*, written by an anonymous Florentine shortly after Catherine's visit there in 1374—to restore some social tensions and ambiguities that Raymond's narrative hides.[6] There is no way of knowing whether Raymond ever read the *Miracoli*, but his lengthier and much more sophisticated treatment of Catherine's life is at least indirectly related to the vernacular collection of anecdotes by the anonymous Florentine. For their information on Catherine's early life both authors relied on the accounts of Catherine's

---

5  Anna Benvenuti-Papi, "La famiglia, territorio negato," in *"In Castro Poenitentiae,"* 171–203. See also Alessandro Barbero, *Un santo in famiglia: Vocazione religiosa e resistenze sociali nell'agiografia latina medievale* (1991), esp. chap. 7.

6  On the *Miracoli* and the circumstances of its composition, see the introduction to *I miracoli di Caterina da Iacopo da Siena di Anonimo Fiorentino*, edited by M.-H. Laurent and Francesco Valli (1936). An English translation of the *Miracoli* is now available in *Dominican Penitent Women*, edited and translated by Maiju Lehmijoki-Gardner (2005).

early confessors and other Dominican advisors. For instance, Raymond cites a now-lost written account by Catherine's first confessor, Tommaso dalla Fonte; the *Miracoli* author seems to have learned stories of Catherine's early life directly from Tommaso dalla Fonte and other Sienese Dominicans who traveled to Florence with Catherine in 1374, and possibly even possessed a copy of Fra Tommaso's text. The *Legenda maior* and *Miracoli* are not, therefore, completely independent versions of Catherine's life, and it is reasonable to read Raymond's account as a reworking of the earlier tradition on which the *Miracoli* is based, if not a reworking of the *Miracoli* itself.

As for the relative reliability of the two accounts, both are works of hagiography, and must therefore be read with sensitivity to hagiographic tropes. But the *Miracoli* has the advantage over the *Legenda maior* of being closer to the scene and, unlike Raymond's account, not driven by a programmatic concern to promote Catherine's canonization and enlist her in support of reform of the Dominican Order. The *Miracoli* is an account of a saint in mid-career, and so is by its very nature unfinished, provisional, and relatively inconclusive—even to the extent of including a dramatic story of Catherine's failing as an intercessor. The author tells how a young religious, drawn to Catherine by her holy life, develops for Catherine a "wicked love" (*cattivo amore*). The young man leaves his order, attempts to kill Catherine, and finally hangs himself in despair—in spite of Catherine's prayerful battle with the demons attempting to seize his soul.[7] This shocking story was intended, perhaps, as a cautionary tale for the young clerics in Catherine's circle. Whatever its purpose, it is an item that would be wildly out of place in Raymond's carefully structured and finished presentation of Catherine's sanctity. It would be a mistake to read the *Miracoli* account as a simple representation of Catherine's early life, but there is ample reason to prefer its version of events to Raymond's when the two accounts differ. Something of the circumstances of Catherine's early career can be reconstructed by reading between the two versions, informed by archival and other evidence regarding Catherine's family and Sienese society during the formative period of Catherine's life.

## Family Conflict and Catherine's Vocation

The public nature of Catherine's vocation lurks as an issue in the Catherinian hagiography, sometimes in unexpected ways. For example, the *Miracoli* tells how a seven-year-old Catherine, already spiritually sensitive and inclined to hide from her family in order to recite her *Pater nosters*

[7] *Miracoli,* chaps. 16, 14.

and *Ave Marias,* decided to seek solitude in the "desert" outside the city walls, and so hid herself in a grotto outside the Porta di Sant' Ansano, where she prayed to the Virgin Mary to be espoused to Jesus; Catherine found herself levitating, and the Virgin Mary appeared carrying the Christ-child, and with a ring espoused Catherine to Him.[8] (This is the first of two espousals in the *Miracoli* account: here a child Catherine marries the Christ child under the aegis of the Virgin Mary, while later Jesus himself espouses an adult Catherine.) Raymond's version adds that after Catherine came back down to earth God informed her that it was not "in this way that He intended her to leave her father's house." He then transported her miraculously back within the city walls, underscoring the message that it was God's choice, not Catherine's, that she fulfill a public vocation, in the city, rather than a reclusive life in the "desert" or in cloistered seclusion from the world—a preemptive defense of Catherine's public persona. But there is another way to read this story. The area in which Catherine sought her grotto, outside the Porta Sant' Ansano (what would today be the Vallepiatta neighborhood, down the hill from the Duomo and near the church of San Sebastiano), was in the fourteenth century a region of the city in which there were a number of communities of female hermits, living religious lives unattached to any particular religious order or rules. And many references in Sienese statutes, testaments, and other documents make it clear that these women, though hermits, were also very public figures, identified and acknowledged throughout the city as recipients of individual and civic alms.[9] Though not the point of this episode in the hagiography (and the Florentine author of the *Miracoli* might very well not have understood the significance of the location), the story reveals Catherine at a young age possessing some sensitivity to the pious topography of Siena, and emulating women who had chosen a public and independent form of religious life.

The *Miracoli* author, like Raymond, tells how Catherine's spiritual ambitions became a point of tension as she neared or reached adolescence and eligibility for marriage, precipitating a series of battles with her family over her resolve not to marry at the time when a respectable family probably would have begun planning seriously her marriage prospects. A clash with her family over marriage was practically a hagiographical requirement for a saintly virgin, among other things to confirm the saint's resolve to embrace

---

[8]  Ibid., chaps. 3, 4.

[9]  There were large numbers of such hermits in Siena in the early fourteenth century, clustered around the Porta Romana and the Porta Camollia (the points at which the ancient pilgrim's route, the Via Francigena, intersected the city) as well as in Vallepiatta. They are referred to in religious testaments from this period, especially testaments of women. See, for example, Siena, Archivio di Stato (hereafter referred to as ASS), Diplomatico, Archivio Generale, 11 settembre 1335.

virginity and reject the world. Hagiographic tropes probably influenced Catherine's behavior; Catherine herself must have known that for a young woman religious aspirations required a contest with her family over the question of marriage. But it is also reasonable to expect that her family would have balked at her resistance to conventions and to family needs, especially considering that Catherine's was an upwardly mobile and increasingly prominent *popolo grasso* family that had secured highly advantageous matches for Catherine's older siblings.

Modern commentators have consistently understated the status of Catherine's family in Siena, partly a generalized effect of hagiography (it makes a better story to describe Catherine emerging from modest beginnings) and partly because the social and political situation in Siena in the second half of the fourteenth century has often been misunderstood. Raymond of Capua states at the outset of the *Legenda maior* that Catherine's parents, "although common [*plebeii*], . . . possessed an abundance of worldly things in accordance with their state of life, and they were by birth highly respectable members of the *popolo*."[10] Perhaps their status was humble from the perspective of Raymond, whose family, the delle Vigne, was deeply entrenched within the ruling class of the kingdom of the Two Sicilies (and could boast of an illustrious ancestor mentioned by Dante, albeit in *Inferno*). But Catherinian scholars have interpreted Raymond's statement freely, made anachronistic assumptions about what it meant to be a dyer and member of the *popolo* in fourteenth-century Siena, and gone further than Raymond to lower Catherine's social standing.[11] In fact, Raymond's description is technically correct; the real issue is what it meant in their case to be "highly respectable members of the *popolo*." The designation *popolo* is inherently misleading, including on the one hand *popolo grasso* elites, who participated in the oligarchies that governed republics like Siena and Florence in the fourteenth century, and who were often socially indistinguishable from urban nobles, and on the other hand the much larger group of artisans as well as poor and disenfranchised workers,

---

[10] *LM*, 23 (p. 868), regarding Jacopo and Lapa: "Hi sic matrimonialiter conjuncti, et in simplicitate uniti, quamvis plebeii, rebus tamen temporalibus juxta conditionem propriam abundabant, et de satis laudabili popularium genere orti erant."

[11] For example, in his translation of the *Legenda maior*, Conleath Kearns translates Raymond's *popularium genere* as "working class" (*The Life of Saint Catherine of Siena by Raymond of Capua*, trans. by Conleth Kearns [1980], 23); Gardner refers to the political group of Catherine's family, the Dodici, as "the class of the petty tradesmen and small notaries" (*Saint Catherine of Siena*, 39); Dupré Theseider labeled them as *popolo minuto* ("Caterina da Siena, santa," 261); and Karen Scott has recently called Catherine "an uneducated *populana* of the artisan class" ("*Io Caterina*," 87). These judgments are all ill-informed. Catherine's family would not have been considered "popolo minuto," and contemporaries in the 1370s and 1380s identified the "artisan class" with the supporters of the Riformatori, the political coalition that displaced the Dodici.

the *popolo minuto*.[12] But there is no question about where to place Catherine's family in the wide range of status denoted by the term *popolo*.

Catherine was born into a family that, while not one of the most wealthy or influential in Sienese society, was nevertheless close to the highest levels of social and political power. Her father, Iacopo di Benincasa, came from a family that, in the thirteenth century, had produced notaries and several well-to-do merchants.[13] The family background of Catherine's mother, Lapa, was far from inconsequential: Lapa's father was Nuccio (or Puccio) di Piacente, a Sienese poet of the *dolce stil novo* who participated in the literary world of the Tuscan poetic elite in the late thirteenth century, writing at least one lyric to the Florentine associate of Dante, Guido Cavalcanti.[14] Iacopo and his sons Benincasa, Bartolomeo, and Stefano, were dyers by profession, but they were *lanaiuoli* and not *lavoranti*—that is, they were wool masters and shop owners rather than wool workers. They were affiliated with the sociopolitical grouping of the *monte dei Dodici*, which controlled the Sienese government from 1355 to 1368; during Catherine's childhood her father would have been numbered among the dominant political class of the city.[15] The Dodici were so-named after the twelve-man signorial board they instituted when they

---

[12] On class distinctions in Florence and elsewhere in this period, see Alessandro Stella, *La révolte des Ciompi: Les hommes, les lieux, le travail* (1993).

[13] Giovanni Cecchini, "I Benincasa di Cellole," *Bullettino Senese di Storia Patria* 56 (1949): 114–20.

[14] M.-H. Laurent, "Alcune notizie sulla famiglia di S. Caterina," *Bullettino Senese di Storia Patria* 44 (1937): 365–66. Lapa is identified as "filia quondam Puccio Piagentis" in a contract of 1346 in which Benincasa, the eldest son of Iacopo and Lapa, rents a workshop (M.-H. Laurent, ed., *Documenti [1936]*, 19). As Laurent points out (p. 366n.), the profession of Nuccio (or Puccio) is given in a rubric introducing some of his verses in Siena, Biblioteca Comunale H.X.47; Nuccio was a *coltraio*, evidently one of the *arti* linked to the *arte della lana*. On Nuccio see also Giovanni Crescimbeni, *L'istoria della volgar poesia* (1698), 26; and *Canzoni d'amore e madrigali di Dante Alighieri, di M. Cino da Pistoia, di M. Girardo Novello, di M. Girardo da Castel Fiorentino, di M. Betrico da Reggio, di M. Ruccio Piacente da Siena, riproduzione della rarissima edizione del 1518*, ed. Giulio Piccini (1899).

[15] Technically, the *monti* were not political parties in the modern sense; nor did they correspond precisely to socioeconomic classes. But while affiliation with a *monte* in this period meant nothing more than a recognition of eligibility for election to the governing magistracy under a particular regime, the regimes themselves represented particular socioeconomic groupings. On the patterns of social and political status in Siena in the second half of the fourteenth century, see Elena Brizio, "Siena nel secondo Trecento"; idem, "L'elezione degli uffici politici nella Siena del Trecento," *Bullettino Senese di Storia Patria* 98 (1991): 16–62; A. K. Isaacs, "Magnati, Comune e Stato a Siena," 81–96; *La rivolta dei Ciompi di Siena: 1371*, ed. G. Cherubini (1970–71); D. Marrara, "I magnati e il governo del Comune di Siena," 239–76; C. Rosa, "Il personale politico-amministrativo dello Stato senese (1385–1399)," Tesi di laurea, Università di Siena, 1985; Victor Rutenburg, "La vie et la lutte des Ciompi de Sienne," *Annales E. S. C.* 20 (1965): 95–109; Valerie Wainwright, "Conflict and Popular Government in Fourteenth-Century Siena," 57–80; idem, "The Testing of a Popular Sienese Regime," 107–70.

toppled the regime of the Nove, which had ruled since 1287. While the Nove constituted a patrician merchant oligarchy (the magistracy was confined to members of the *mercanzia,* the merchant's guild), the regime of the Dodici was a broader oligarchy, representing the increasingly prosperous and socially mobile leaders of the Sienese guilds, as well as notaries, wealthy shop owners, and other prominent men who had been excluded from the regime of the Nove.[16] This shift in power in no way meant the enfranchisement of the lower classes: the *popolo minuto* (also known as the *popolo maggiore,* "the people of the greater number") were still largely excluded. Valerie Wainwright has demonstrated that by the end of their regime the members of the Dodici had begun to establish themselves as among the most wealthy and socially prestigious members of Sienese society, as reflected in their tax assessments and their ability to intermarry with Nove, and even noble, families.[17]

Iacopo and Bartolomeo appear on the rolls of the Capitudini delle Arti around 1350, in the *capitudine* of the *lanaiuoli,* showing that they had attained recognition among the guild elite before the fall of the Nove and establishment of the Dodici in 1355.[18] Bartolomeo was elected to the Signoria in February 1368, just before the end of Dodici rule.[19] During the period of transition between the fall of the Dodici and the establishment of the regime of the Riformatori in 1371, he was a representative of the Dodici in the coalition magistracy in September 1368 and was once again elected to the Signoria in May of 1370.[20] Benincasa, the eldest son, and Stefano achieved political office in September 1368, with the radical expansion of eligibility in the immediate post-Dodici governments. They did not enter political life as representatives of the Dodici (one could not have become Dodici after the fall of that regime), but would nevertheless have shared with their father and brother the prestige—and later the stigma—of being Dodici. Moreover, the family was far from poor. The evidence suggests that Bartolomeo and his brothers by 1370 had achieved substantial business success, including expansion of the family business to Florence, probably well before October 1370, when Catherine's three brothers obtained citizenship there, and where Catherine wrote her brothers on three occasions. Scholars have assumed that the brothers' migrated to Florence after the failure of the family business in Siena.[21] But this is a clear misunderstanding of the nature of citizenship in Italian

[16] Wainwright, "The Testing of a Popular Sienese Regime," 120.
[17] Wainwright, "Conflict and Popular Government," 77ff.
[18] ASS, *Arti* 165, f. 38r.
[19] ASS, *Concistoro* 45, f. 1.
[20] ASS, *Concistoro* 1859, f. 43 and *Concistoro* 55, f. 1.
[21] For example, Suzanne Noffke (*Letters of Catherine of Siena,* 1: 62) repeats this assumption in dating Catherine's letters to Benincasa and to her three brothers.

cities as well as an incorrect chronology of the business misfortunes of Catherine's brothers. It was a common practice for merchants to seek dual citizenship in foreign cities in order to avoid paying import taxes, to receive the protection of the local merchant's guild and its courts, and to avoid punitive economic measures directed against their home cities during wars or diplomatic disputes.[22] And in any case the Florentine government was not in the business of offering citizenship to failed merchants.[23] (The brothers did go bankrupt, but later.) And the clearest indication that Catherine's family had attained social prominence is the marriage of Catherine's older sister, Buonaventura, to Niccolò Tegliacci, a member of one of the leading Dodici families, and the marriage of Bartolomeo to Lisa, daughter of the Nove Castaldino Colombini; the family of Iacopo di Benincasa was evidently considered sufficiently respectable for intermarriage into the highest levels of the *popolo grasso*.[24]

Thus one can imagine that weighty family expectations were among the pressures Catherine had to negotiate in order to avoid marriage. But Catherine's vocational choice seems also to have been influenced by observing at close-hand the dire effects of marriage when her sister Buonaventura died in childbirth in 1362, when Catherine was around fifteen. According to the *Miracoli*, the Dominican friar Tommaso dalla Fonte, who was related to Catherine's family by marriage, and thus in effect a family member as well as Catherine's first confessor, encouraged Catherine to take her sister's death as a warning: for "she had been vain and lascivious like other young women."[25] Catherine then vowed to promise her virginity to Christ, a resolve which brought her into conflict with her family. Raymond, on the other hand, has Catherine's vow and even the family conflict predate Buonaventura's death (perhaps to disassociate Catherine's

---

[22] On merchants holding multiple citizenships, see Trexler, *Public Life in Renaissance Florence*, 42–43.

[23] I am grateful for the insights of Laura de Angelis on this issue, and in particular for her comments on the brothers' petition for citizenship. The petition is in Florence, Archivio di Stato, *Provvisioni* 58, f. 102r–v; and published in Laurent, ed., *Documenti*, n.7, 26–8. The petition is absolutely standard for its period in, among other stipulations, requiring of the new citizens substantial investment in Florence: "Hoc in predictis acto, dicto et declerato quod predicti Benincasa et fratres infra unum annum proxime venturum, postquam presens provisio obtenta fuerit in consilio domini potestatis et comminis Florentie, teneantur et debeant in ipsa civitate vel eius comitatu emere vel acquirere possessiones et bona immobilia, in ipsa civitate in ipsa civitate [*sic*] vel comitatu positas, pretio adminus librarum mille florenorum parvorum" (Laurent, ed., *Documenti*, 27).

[24] "Lisa filia quondam Castaldini et relicta Bartali quod Jacobi Benincase tintoris olim de popolo sancti antonii de senis" names a procurator in a document dated 7 November 1384 (ASS, *Diplomatico, Spedale della Scala*). The 18th-century Sienese archivist Celso Cittadini identified Lisa as daughter of Golio di Picco Colombini, known as "Castaldino." (Cittadini's genealogical tree of Catherine's family is published as an appendix to the Tommasèo edition of Catherine's letters.)

[25] *Miracoli*, 5.

pious resolve from an aversion to marriage and motherhood). But both authors agree that Catherine's austerities and determination intensified after the death of Buonaventura, as did the battles with her family.

According to Raymond, family resistance ended when Catherine's father, Iacopo, having more spiritual insight than the rest of the family, perceived a dove hovering over Catherine as she prayed and subsequently insisted that the family accept Catherine's resolve, arguing that her "marriage" to Christ more than compensated for the loss of a temporal marriage. Catherine's story at this point departs from the usual hagiographical line, and breaks dramatically with social expectation. One would expect Catherine's spiritual aspirations to be resolved by entrance into a monastery. Instead, the question of her precise vocation was apparently left open: she remained in her own home, though still under the influence of the local Dominicans. Both Raymond and the *Miracoli* author note that Catherine spent a number of years in secluded prayer in her own home, a point stressed by Raymond and other of Catherine's clerical supporters in justifying her later public profile.[26] Between around 1362 and 1368 or 1369, Catherine apparently lived at home as a kind of holy recluse, receiving instruction from Fra Tommaso and perhaps from other Dominicans, and (according to Raymond) also engaging in some charitable activities. This was clearly a crucial period in the development of Catherine's spiritual gifts, and the highly personal, immediate, and energetic point of view on spiritual and theological issues that later emerged in her writings. While Raymond and other hagiographers would later stress the supernatural origins of Catherine's knowledge, much of the theological content that undergirds her later writings was probably gained during this period through instruction by Tommaso dalla Fonte and perhaps other Sienese Dominicans. Through her own reading Catherine at this time probably developed the close familiarity with the texts that influenced her thought and writing: scripture, especially the Gospels, Pauline epistles, and Book of Revelation;[27] the major texts of Tuscan vernacular religious culture, for instance the writings of Domenico Cavalca, Iacopone da Todi, Iacopo Passavanti, Iacopo da Voragine, and her Sienese near-contemporary Giovanni Columbini; and

[26] The *Miracoli* author states that Catherine spent seven years in seclusion, but places that period after the death of her father—which is not possible. The author, apparently not knowing that Iacopo di Benincasa died in 1368, apparently reversed the chronology. It is likely that this order made more narrative sense, for reasons that will be made clear later in the chapter in explaining Raymond's narrative strategies in his account.

[27] It is likely that Catherine had at least sufficient familiarity with Latin (the kind of rudimentary Latinity common in Italian vernacular culture) to absorb liturgical texts read during Mass and from her own reading of the divine office; as Suzanne Noffke demonstrates in her translation and edition of the letters, Catherine occasionally dwelled on passages or images from readings in the lectionary for the season or feast on which she was writing.

vernacular translations of saints' lives and the affective spiritual literature that circulated especially within the Franciscan world, for example the pseudo-Bonaventuran *Stimulus amoris*.[28] And from Fra Tommaso and perhaps other Dominicans she also began learning about the religious life, and probably began her contacts with the female penitents or *pinzochere* living in their own homes and associated with the Sienese Dominicans, women known in Siena as *mantellate* on account of their distinctive habit.

In the *Legenda maior*, Catherine has to overcome continued interference by Lapa and initial resistance by the *mantellate* themselves before she is admitted to what Raymond calls the "Order of Penance of St. Dominic," an event that his narrative implies (though never actually states) took place before her period of seclusion and shortly after her father's approval. Catherinian scholars have uniformly followed Raymond's lead in placing Catherine's entry into the *mantellate* in or near 1363, when Catherine was around fifteen. On the other hand, it is hard to see how Catherine could have lived in domestic seclusion and been one of the community of *mantellate*, at least in the full sense, since membership entailed meetings of the community in San Domenico as well as acts of public charity. Indeed, a series of rubrics appended to an early-fourteenth-century set of guidelines for the Sienese *mantellate* requires invested members who become recluses to give up the habit of the order and forbids recluses from receiving the habit of the order.[29] In addition, the location of Catherine's name on the membership list of the *mantellate* suggests that her name was added closer to 1370 than to 1362.[30] But the strongest evidence that Catherine's religious vocation was still in some sense a live issue in the late 1360s is a dramatic anecdote in the *Miracoli*, which the author states, without apparent hagiographic purpose, took

[28] On Catherine's sources, see Noffke's notes in her translation and edition of the letters, and Giacinto D'Urso, *Il genio di S. Caterina*; Alvaro Grion, *Santa Caterina da Siena*; Benedict Hackett, *William Flete*.

[29] Siena, Biblioteca Comunale, MS T.II.8b, 2ᵛ: "Quod nulla vestita possit effici reclusa nisi deponat habitum numquam reassumptura. Quod nulli recluse concedi possit habitus vestitarum nostrarum. Quod nulla vestite nostre possit dari licentia intrandi aliquam reclusarum. Idem dicitur quod ad omnia de monasteriis et monialibus et heremitis."

[30] Siena, Biblioteca Comunale, MS T.II.8. Laurent's transcription of the list (in *Documenti*, 22–24) is not accurate; Robert Fawtier (*Sainte Catherine de Sienne*, 1: 234–36) provides photographs of the list and a more accurate (although not perfect) transcription. See also Timoteo Centi, "Il memoriale delle mantellate Senesi contemporanee di S. Caterina," *Rivista di storia della chiesa in Italia* 1 (1947): 409–18. Catherine's name is inscribed as the first in a list in the same hand, followed immediately by "Katerina Enghecti," also known as "Caterina Ghetti." Against Fawtier's badly reasoned assertion that Catherine was entered on the list in 1352, Centi argues from evidence in Caterina Ghetti's entry in the S. Domenico necrology (n. 1415, p. 173) that Caterina Ghetti was about fifteen in 1370. If this is true, she probably was inscribed on the list no earlier than 1370, and probably at least a little later. Catherine of Siena's name appears to have been added not long before Caterina Ghetti's.

place after the death of Catherine's father. We know that Iacopo died in 1368, when Catherine was around twenty-one and past her prime as a candidate for marriage.

In the *Miracoli*, Fra Tommaso, knowing that Catherine's mother and brothers are determined to thwart her pious aspirations, advises Catherine to cut her hair in order to preserve her virginity. Catherine hesitates—oddly she wonders whether her mother will be pleased or displeased by this action—but eventually heeds the advice of Fra Tommaso and cuts her hair. This precipitates a final battle with her mother, a colorfully domestic scene that begins with Lapa complaining to Catherine and a visiting relative about how quickly Buonaventura's husband remarried:

> In speaking about this, she mentioned wanting to see this maiden [Catherine] married. And the woman who was there said to the mother, "What are you saying? Catherine would not wish for a husband." When the maiden affirmed that this was true, her mother quarreled with her about it, and in anger cried out: "If I lay my hand in your hair, I will tear out more than seven of them!" To this the maiden responded immediately, retorting: "Go ahead and take my hair, if you can!" Then she uncovered her head.[31]

After Lapa's expected uproar Catherine goes to her brothers and assures them that, if they leave her alone, she will not cost them anything more than the bread and water she needs to live (though it is not immediately obvious why her upkeep is an issue) and her brothers and mother accede to her wishes. The *Miracoli* author then adds, incongruously, that Catherine spent the next eight years in solitude in her own home—an obvious mistake if indeed her definitive break with her family came after her father's death in 1368.

Both the *Miracoli* and *Legenda maior* report that Catherine joined the *mantellate* after being inspired by a vision, but the *Miracoli* differs from the *Legenda maior* version by emphasizing the dangers of Catherine's position as a woman moving independently in public.[32] In the *Miracoli*, some time after the confrontation with her mother and brothers, Catherine finds herself in a place "out of this world, in which she saw a multitude of people engaged

[31] *Miracoli*, chap. 6, 6–7: "Venne di parlare a dire di volere maritare questa fanciulla. E la donna che v'era dicendo verso la madre: 'Che dite voi? La Caterina non vorrà marito,' e questo affermando la fanciulla, e la madre quistionandone collei, turbata disse: 'Se io ti metto mano ne' capegli, io te ne caverò più di sete.' A questo detto la fanciulla, rispondendo presto, desse alla madre: 'Ora gli pigliate pure, se voi potete, I miei capelli,' e palesossi il capo."

[32] In the *Legenda maior* (chap. 53), the founders of various religious orders appear and attempt to recruit Catherine, but among them St. Dominic assures her that she will one day wear the habit of the Sisters of Penance, the *mantellate,* and encourages her not to lose heart. Raymond's account of the vision is highly visual, evoking tropes of sacred painting, and has none of the public drama and sexual tension of the *Miracoli* vision.

in many occupations, and wrapped up in a variety of businesses." Catherine is too confused and frightened to dare to move through the crowd, but suddenly St. Dominic appears to her and tells her that in order to pass through the crowd she must hide herself under something white; he then calls on her to "come and receive my habit." But as she moves toward St. Dominic to take the habit, Catherine is accosted by two prostitutes:

> And as she began to go she saw coming behind her two dishonest women, adorned and beautiful, who were sisters. They caught her at the back by her clothes, holding her and pulling her with all their might. Catherine turned on them and struck out at them and struggled to make them let go, so much so that she escaped from their hands. And going on alone, she saw that some people had seized the two sisters, while she went on safe and sound.[33]

This vision raises dramatically the sexual tension implicit in Catherine's status: an unmarried woman, unprotected and in the world, might be drawn to prostitution, and she might even be equated with a prostitute. The *Miracoli* thus underscore the social novelty of Catherine's status as a virgin *pinzochera,* someone effectively outside the domain of male protection in a society preoccupied with the necessity of maintaining women either within the father's or husband's house, or within the walls of a monastery. But the veil will guarantee Catherine's integrity even in the world. As a result of the vision, Catherine "decided to become a *pinzochera di santo Domenico,*" and induced Lapa to join as well: "not only [Catherine], but even her mother was convinced to take the habit with her."[34] The *Miracoli* reports that when this took place Catherine was around twenty-three years old, that is, "at the end of 1370 or thereabouts."[35] And indeed,

---

[33]  *Miracoli,* chap. 7, 7–8: "Poi così perseverando, le venne una visione in questo modo. Parevale vedere uno certo luogo fuori di questo mondo, nel quale ella vedea moltitudine di gente fare diverse operazioni e viluppi di svariati traffichi, non sappiendo discernere ella il che nè 'l come, e concenivale passare per lo mezo di tutta quella gente, e non ardiva. E ella stando così tutta spaventata e paurosa, si udì una voce che le disse: 'Se tu vuogli passare tutta questa gente, e' ti conviene nascondere sotto una cosa bianca.' E levando ella gli occhi verso quella voce, vidde santo Domenico in quella forma che veduto l'avea dipinto nella chiesa, il quale le disse: 'Vieni e ricevi l'abito mio.' E essendo mossa per andare, vide venire dopo sè due disoneste femine, molto adornate e belle, le quali erano sirocchie, e pigliarono lei di dietro per gli panni, tenendola e tirandola alloro potere, e quella rivolgendosi loro adosso, e percotendole, e sforzandosi di farsi lasciare, tanto fece che ella uscì loro delle mani. E andando oltre sola vidde che quella gente aveano prese quelle due sirocchie. E ella passava oltre sana e salva."

[34]  *Miracoli,* chap. 8, 8: "Questa visione revelando ella al confessore suo, prese partito di presente di farsi pinzochera di santo Domenico, e così fece, e non solamente ella, ma eziandio la madre indusse a pigliare l'abito con esso lei."

[35]  *Miracoli,* ibid.: "E continuando in casa sua l'usata vita della aspra penitenzia, sempre crescendo el desiderio suo di servire a Dio, e cominciò a volersi comunicare ogni mattina quasi a ora di terza del corpo di Cristo. E essendo già d'etade di ventitrè anni o in quel torno, e cominciato che elle ebbe a fare così, e valorosamente in ciò perseverando, vennele

Catherine's mother, Lapa, as well as her sister-in-law Lisa, appear on the list of *mantellate* in a grouping of names briefly removed from Catherine's, suggesting that they were enrolled shortly after Catherine.

In effect, the *Legenda maior* and *Miracoli* contradict each other about when Catherine became a *mantellata*, and each contains internal ambiguities as well: in the *Legenda maior*, Catherine's reclusive life after joining this very public group; and in the *Miracoli*, Catherine's seven years of solitude after her father's death. But more important than dating Catherine's entrance into the *mantellate* is the question of what it meant for her to become a *mantellata*, a question that bears directly on the character of her social and religious status in the early years of her saintly reputation. In fact, it is a mistake to treat Catherine's becoming a *mantellata* as if she had experienced a complete and unequivocal change in status, comparable to entering the cloister. While scholars (following Raymond) have represented Catherine as a member of the Dominican Order of Penance or Third Order, during Catherine's lifetime there was in fact no "Order of Penance," and the group Catherine joined had none of the formality or clear relationship to the Dominican Order that this term implies. Rather than being members of a religious order, female penitents like Catherine, whether they were known as *mantellate, pinzochere,* or *vestitae,* were ambiguously placed in a margin between the secular and religious worlds. There were many attempts to limit and regularize the religious lives of women in the later Middle Ages, for instance by prohibiting "domestic" monasticism, attaching *pinzochere* to the protection and authority of male mendicant houses, and imposing strict claustration on all members of women's religious communities.[36] But in practice, strict categorical distinctions between cloistered and uncloistered, regular and irregular religious women broke down, and women—especially widows with income from dowries or other property—had a wide variety of options available to them and seem to have adopted modes of religious life and even moved between forms of religious life independent of rules and canonical norms.[37] *Mantellate* and others like them were not, for

---

voglia di lasciare affatto quello poco del cibo corporale che ella solea pigliare, e così fece, cominciando nelle fine dell'anno del MCCCLXX, o in quel torno."

[36] The movement to prohibit the ancient practice of "domestic" monasticism among women (a prominent feature of the Christian communities of Ambrose and Jerome, for example) began with canon 26 of Lateran II, *Ut sanctimonialies in privatis domibus non habitent,* which imposed a common life on such women. Claustration was imposed on all female members of the existing religious orders in 1298 with the decretal *Periculoso* and again in 1309 with the decretal *Apostolicae sedis.* On the canonical norms relating to the *pinzochere,* see R. Guarnieri, "Pinzochere," in *Dizionario degli istituti di perfezione,* vol. 7 (1983), 1721–49. On the legal issues surrounding claustration, see Elizabeth Makowski, *Canon Law and Cloistered Women: Periculoso and its Commentators, 1298–1545* (1997).

[37] Katherine Gill, "*Scandala*: Controversies Concerning *clausura* and Women's Religious

example, bound canonically by the standard religious vows of poverty, chastity, and obedience. As Maiju Lehmijoki-Gardner has recently pointed out, what was represented by Tommaso Caffarini in the early fifteenth century as the rule of the Order of Penance by the thirteenth-century Dominican Master General Munio of Zamora was in fact a reworking of a simpler set of *ordinationes* issued by Munio not as a rule for an order but as a set of guidelines originally for a group of Orvietan *pinzochere* (he calls them *vestitae*); these *ordinationes,* not Caffarini's more elaborate rule, were employed by the Sienese *mantellate* in the fourteenth century. Raymond's reference in the *Legenda maior* to an "Order of Penance" was in fact the first use of the term, a retrospective invention of a regularity of status the *mantellate* did not possess during Catherine's lifetime.[38]

The improvisational nature of the *mantellate* as a religious community is illustrated in a document connected to the Sienese *mantellate* in the generation preceding Catherine. The 1352 preamble to what became the group's membership list down to the 1370s (the first of two lists on which Catherine's name is found) announces that the "sisters wearing the habit of the Friars Preachers in the city of Siena . . . in order to refute the scandalous words of certain evil-speakers and to retain the aforesaid habit more firmly and devoutly, by their own free will, have promised by vow and by oath, each one touching the missal, to persevere until death in the aforesaid habit in the manner which they had begun."[39] That the Sienese *mantellate* were objects of scandal was not a unique situation: the independence, public lives, and lack of clear rules or fixed religious status opened the *pinzochere* to a wide range of suspicions, however common they were on the Italian urban scene.[40] The accusations against the

---

Communities in Late Medieval Italy," in Scott L. Waugh and Peter D. Diehl, ed., *Christendom and Its Discontents: Exclusion, Persecution, and Rebellion, 1000–1500* (1996), 177–206. As Gill points out, historians have often erred in imposing an anachronistic categorical clarity on women's religious communities in the Late Middle Ages.

[38] Maiju Lehmijoki-Gardner, "Writing Religious Rules as an Interactive Process—Dominican Penitent Women and the Making of Their *Regula,*" *Speculum* 79 (2004): 660–87.

[39] Siena, Biblioteca Comunale, MS T.II.8: "Pateat omnibus evidenter quod sorores portantes habitum fratrum Predicatorum in civitate Senensi, simul congregate in ecclesia predictorum fratrum, anno Domini M. CCC. LII, die XVIIa augusti, ad refellendum verba quorundam male loquentium scandalosa et predictum habitum firmius et devotius retinendum, mote propria voluntate, voto et iuramento promiserunt, quelibet siggilatim tacto missali supradictum habitum, modo, que inceperunt, se usque ad diem sui obitus esse servaturas."

[40] Katherine Gill, "Open Monasteries for Women in Late Medieval and Early Modern Italy: Two Roman Examples," in Craig A. Monson, ed., *The Crannied Wall,* 15–48. Gill (21) notes the 16th-century dance called "The Pinzochera," which had women dance to traditionally male parts, and vice versa, as evidence that the *pinzochere* defied gender roles. She also notes that *pinzochere* were frequent subjects of bawdy songs; the lyrics of one such, "The

Sienese *mantellate* in 1352 are not made explicit in the document, but the sisters' response to the "scandal" is strongly suggestive: they reaffirmed their way of life and their commitment to the wearing of the habit, implying strongly that complaints against them concerned the lack of stability or permanence of their way of life, unregulated as it was by solemn religious vows. All they had was their habit as an outward sign of a way of life; they in fact remained in the world. Nothing prevented these women from acting as relatively independent laywomen, using dotal income to buy and sell property, for example. Indeed, such economic activity might have been a sine qua non of the *pinzochera*'s life, predicated as it was on female economic independence. The promise to persevere "by vow and by oath" by the Sienese *mantellate* addressed precisely their public status: it clearly aimed to strengthen their identity as a religious group in the eyes of the civic community. Of course, the adding of an action like this to the customary practice of the Sienese *mantellate* was an improvisation, revealing precisely the kind of irregularity that might have called their status into question in the first place. This action in itself confirms that the Sienese *mantellate* did not abide by a fixed or formal rule governing their entry into the community and their way of life as penitents, for otherwise they would not have needed the additional "vow and oath."

The lack of a fixed status explains the ambiguities in both the *Legenda maior* and *Miracoli* on the question of when Catherine became a *mantellata*. Perhaps she came into contact with the *mantellate* during the period of seclusion, and perhaps even entered on some sort of provisional membership, but was only formally admitted and enrolled on the membership lists after 1368, when she was around twenty-one and past her prime as a candidate for marriage. If later practice is any guide, the *mantellate* in Catherine's time probably had a period of initiation (though none is prescribed in Munio's *ordinationes*).[41] Catherine's novel situation as a virgin entering a group normally consisting of widows might very well have caused the leaders of the Sienese *mantellate* to extend her period of initiation. In any case, the oath taken by the *mantellate* in 1352 confirms that there were more

---

Pinzochere Who Have Been to Rome," suggest that *pinzochere* possess secret magical knowledge which enables them to assert influence over people.

[41] Caffarini's vernacular version of the Rule of the Order of Penance includes a ceremony of profession after the investment, in which the invested candidate promises "to strive to live according to the rule of the sisters and brothers of this Order of Penance of St. Dominic, from now until death," and which takes place whenever the master, prioress, and the community of sisters judge the individual fit—normally a year after the investment, although it can occur sooner (*Tractatus de Ordine FF. de Paenitentia S. Dominici di F. Tommaso da Siena* [1938], 172). A one-year period of probation may indeed have been the norm in late-medieval rules for *pinzochere* affiliated with the mendicants, as can be inferred from the existence of such a provision in a 15th-century rule of Franciscan penitents cited by Anna Benvenuti-Papi (*"In Castro Poenitentiae,"* 589).

steps to entry into the *mantellate* than is represented in the *ordinationes* of Munio, or than is represented in Raymond's account of Catherine's taking the habit of the Order of Penance.[42] And that it was possible for a woman to be enrolled in the order in some sense without being a full-fledged member is confirmed by a 1378 membership list of the Sienese *mantellate*. After a list of the members of the order compiled by the friar responsible for their supervision, there is added in a later hand a list of "secular ladies" who have been received into the order, but who will receive the habit during their lives only if they become widows, and in any case will be buried in the habit after their deaths.[43] The existence of a marginal or provisional membership, left unmentioned in Munio's *ordinationes* or in Caffarini's rule, suggests that there might have been other gradations of membership not reflected in the written canons.

To return to the question of when Catherine joined the *mantellate*, she might very well have been a member in some sense before her father's death, and still have had her vocation unresolved when her father died. Joining the *mantellate* did not provide the categorical resolution of Catherine's status that entering the cloister would have done. Catherine's condition as she entered upon her public life was ambiguous, an ambiguity that Raymond sought to elide by showing Catherine entering the *mantellate* in one decisive moment, regularizing a conversion that was, in canonical terms, never so clear. He was also thereby able to show Catherine entering the *mantellate* at a younger age and under the authority of her parents, in the manner of a postulant entering into a monastery, rather than as a fully grown woman embarking on a self-determined vocation. Tommaso Caffarini, in his translation of the *vita* of another *pinzochera* saint, Giovanna of Orvieto, similarly (and probably for the same reasons) rewrote the earlier account of Giovanna's life, changing the age at which she became a *pinzochera* from twenty to fourteen.[44] Both Raymond and Caffarini undoubtedly sought to avoid for their subjects any hint of the scandal that might have been attached to an unmarried adult woman living in the world, and represented these saints' vocations as similar to

---

[42] A *ceremoniale* of the Order of Penance produced by Caffarini includes the detail that the sisters are to make their profession with a hand on the "book of the sisters"—exactly the practice adopted by the Sienese mantellate in 1352, as described above (*Tractatus de Ordine FF. de Paenitentia*, 182). As is confirmed by Maiju Lehmijoki-Gardner's study of the penitent rule ("Writing Religious Rules as an Interactive Process"), Caffarini seems to have constructed his rule and other norms by taking older texts like the *ordinationes* of Munio and adding, under the guise of Munio's authority, practices adopted over time by the Sienese and other communities of *mantellate*.

[43] Siena, Biblioteca Comunale, MS T.II.8; transcribed in *Laurent, ed., Documenti*, 49: "Ista sunt nomina dominarum secularium que recepta [*sic*] sunt in capitulo Mantellatarum, que debent recipere abitum in articulo mortis vel in istatu viduali."

[44] I am indebted to Maiju Lehmijoki-Gardner for this observation.

monastic conversions. Raymond seems to have rewritten Catherine's story to make her entry into the *mantellate* as early as possible in order to have her vocation resemble as much as possible a conventional religious vocation.

Indeed, Catherine's vocation was not conventional. Catherine's early public life was transgressive; she was a quasi-religious woman conspicuously independent of the cloister as well as the usual structures of male protection. But some sense of the tensions engendered by her status can be teased out of the *Miracoli* account of her life as well as from archival sources. For example, the *Miracoli* episode in which Catherine cuts her hair highlights social and economic tensions implicit in Catherine's peculiar status, as any contemporary reader almost certainly would have recognized, tensions signaled in the episode by the apparently unimportant detail that her father was dead, and by her final promise not to cost her brothers anything beyond her creature needs. As a young woman neither married and given a dowry nor cloistered, Catherine was a potential drain on family resources in addition to being a social embarrassment. Contemporaries in Siena and elsewhere were very sensitive to the problem of daughters diverting resources from patrimonies, and sought to restrict their ability to inherit. Roman law norms guaranteed a female child an equal part in inheritance, but Siena like other Italian civic governments in the late Middle Ages took pains to limit daughters' rights to inherit, in the interests of preserving patrimonies within the agnatic line.[45] Toward this end the Sienese applied the principle of "exclusio propter dotem," denying daughters any rights beyond their dowries where there were male children to inherit; the dowry was the totality of their inheritance.[46] The Sienese statutes in force during Catherine's life reaffirmed thirteenth-century statutes, providing that, if one or more male heirs existed, a daughter who was dowered was not entitled to a portion of the inheritance of either her mother or her father.[47] It is not clear that these restrictions were effective in practice, but in any case they would not have applied to Catherine.[48] In assuring

[45] On civic practices that nullified women's theoretical rights of inheritance, see Isabelle Chabot, "La loi du lignage. Notes sur le système successoral florentin (XIVᵉ–XVᵉ siècles)," *Clio. Histoire, femmes et sociétés* 7 (1998): 51–72, esp. 57–58; and Idem, "Diritti e risorse patrimoniali," in *Storia delle donne italiane*, vol. 2 of *Il lavoro delle donne, Parte I: L'età medievale*, edited by A. Groppi (1996), 47–70.

[46] Gianna Lumia, "Morire a Siena. Divoluzione testamentaria, legami parentali e vincoli afettivi in età moderna," *Bullettino Senese di Storia Patria* 103 (1996): 103–285, esp. 117–18. Lumia gives the relevant rubrics from the Sienese Constitution of 1262.

[47] Siena, ASS, *Statuti di Siena* 26 (Statutes of Siena begun in 1337), see for instance Rubric 214 (f. 123ʳ⁻ᵛ): "Quod mulier dotata non succedat extantibus masculis;" and Rubric 216 (123ᵛ): "Quod mulier dotata ad successionem uel divisionem non veniat cum fratribus."

[48] On the difference between the theory and the practice of dowries in Siena, see Elena Brizio, "La dote nella normativa statutaria e nella pratica testamentaria senese (fine sec.

her brothers that she would not cost them anything beyond her food and drink, Catherine was in effect renouncing her dowry rights and any inheritance from her father's estate.[49] In addition, she was reassuring her brothers that she would not interfere with their use of Monna Lapa's dowry—though this was a promise it seems that Catherine could not keep.[50] Catherine's final plea for her brothers' permission to maintain her peculiar status thus speaks precisely to the issue of Catherine's economic rights and the anomalous position she was in as an adult woman living unmarried and uncloistered. The *Miracoli* shows Catherine reassuring her brothers by stepping outside the bounds of patrilineal authority; Catherine's solution to the complications of her position was to emancipate herself and declare her independence.

## The Political Trials of the Family of Iacopo di Benincasa

The drama of Catherine's emerging vocation and autonomy played itself out against a backdrop of civic unrest and political change that affected profoundly the fortunes of her brothers and contributed in several ways to the shape of her career. The same year that Iacopo di Benincasa died saw the fall of the regime with which Catherine's family was associated; the Dodici were ousted in early September 1368, leading to a three-year period of political struggle in Siena, resolved only in 1371 and

---

XII—metà sec. XIV)," <http://www.storia.unisi.it/pagine/strumenti/Le%20doti/Home%20page.htm>, Università degli Studi di Siena, Dipartimento di Storia, "Fonti e materiali per la storia di Siena e del territorio," February 2004 (accessed 24 July 2004).

[49] On a woman's right to a dowry see the standard account by Manlio Bellomo, *Ricerche sui rapporti patrimoniali tra coniugi* (1961), 61–130. On Italian dowry laws and practice in general, and their implications for women's property ownership, see Diane Owen Hughes, "From Bridepiece to Dowry in Mediterranean Europe," *Journal of Family History* 3 (1978): 262–96; David Herlihy and Christiane Klapisch-Zuber, *Tuscans and Their Families* (1985), 202–28; Christiane Klapisch-Zuber, "The 'Cruel Mother': Maternity, Widowhood, and Dowry in Florence in the Fourteenth and Fifteenth Centuries," in *Women, Family, and Ritual in Renaissance Italy* (1985), 117–31; Thomas Kuehn, "Some Ambiguities of Female Inheritance Ideology in the Renaissance," in *Law, Family, and Women: Toward a Legal Anthropology of Renaissance Italy* (1991), 239–57.

[50] On a woman's right to a share of her mother's dowry, and the competing family interests that would have favored her renunciation of that right, see Thomas Kuehn, "Women, Marriage, and the *Patria potestas* in Late Medieval Florence," in *Law, Family, and Women*, 197–211, esp. 207: "A daughter had a right to a share of her mother's dowry equivalent to each of her siblings. This right could become very important, especially to a father who found himself in dire financial straits. A father, then, might emancipate his daughter so that she could renounce her right to the maternal dowry or give it to her brothers and sisters. . . . Furthermore, if a woman did not renounce her mother's dowry, it was important that she at least declare that her claims to it had been satisfied."

the formation of the coalition regime of the Riformatori.[51] The Dodici fell to a coalition of magnate families supported by the as yet unenfranchised *popolo minuto*—a broad range of men who had not been eligible for office under the Nove and Dodici, and whose numbers included artisans in the wool trade and other industries as well as more substantial and socially elevated men whose particular occupation had not been recognized in the system of guild representation established by the Dodici. This revolution led to a short-lived regime of noble *Consoli*, which was toppled on September 23, when the Salimbeni—the most powerful magnate family—made common cause with elements of the Dodici and *popolo minuto* to create a broad-based popular regime. In this new arrangement, the Salimbeni were recognized as members of the *popolo* and guaranteed a special unelected status within the government, clearly a move toward dominance of the republic from within the government—in other words, a constitutional coup, and a de facto signory. Both executive and legislative power briefly rested in a popular coalition, the Council of the Riformatori, on which a new political grouping—the *monte del popolo minuto* or *popolo parvo*, eventually to be called the *monte de' riformatori*—was given almost as many representatives as the Dodici and Nove combined. As events quickly proved, the apparent unity of this coalition disguised real tensions. Radical members of the Riformatori sought sole rule for their *monte*, fearing the influence of the more politically experienced Dodici. The Dodici, only recently deprived of political hegemony, resented the presence in government of their traditional *noveschi* rivals as well as the upstart *popolo minuto*. And the Salimbeni were determined to manipulate the *popolo minuto* and to play groups off against each other in order to maintain influence over the government and achieve personal rule for their clan. The *popolo minuto* recognized that their only strength lay in numbers, and by December 1368 began to attempt to counter the influence of the Salimbeni and Dodici by reorganizing government in favor of greater representation for the *popolo minuto*. In 1369 they introduced the noble families into the governmental coalition in order to counterbalance Salimbeni pretensions. The reentry of the nobles, as well as the disproportionate representation of the Riformatori, allowed the new political men to consolidate their hold on power. But the governing coalition was constantly pulled in two directions, threatened on the one hand by *minuto* radicals who sought to exclude other nonnobles (the Nove and Dodici) in favor of exclusive government by the *popolo minuto*, and on the other hand by continuous plotting by the Salimbeni/Dodici alliance to attain absolute governmental control.

[51] On political developments at this time see Valerie Wainwright, "Conflict and Popular Government," and "The Testing of a Popular Sienese Regime."

A story in the *Miracoli*, intended clearly to emphasize Catherine's growing reputation as well as the protection in public afforded her by the habit of the *mantellate*, brings home the extent to which Catherine's family was implicated in this political turmoil. During a period of revolution in Siena, "in one of those years in which the government changed," Catherine's brothers find themselves in defeat, targeted by their enemies in the victorious party. A friend comes to warn them that a mob is on its way seeking to harm or even kill them, and recommends that they take refuge in the local parish church of Sant' Antonio, where others of their allies were hiding. But Catherine insists that they not go to the church, but rather follow her:

> Catherine took her mantle and put it around her and said to her brothers: "Come with me and do not fear." She went among them and turned towards the quarter [*contrada*] of their enemies. They met them, and passed through their midst, with all of them bowing before her in reverence, so that Catherine and her brothers passed on safe and sound. She led her brothers into the hospital of Santa Maria in Siena, and there she recommended them to the governor of the hospital and left them with him, saying to them: "Remain hidden here for three days, and at the end of these days return home in safety." And so they did.[52]

The detail that matters to the author is apparently that, before entering into the strife-torn streets, Catherine dons her mantle—the habit of the *mantellate*—and this sign of her status enables her to protect her brothers and move freely with them in the midst of a threatening mob. But if the story is accurate even in its bare details, it also places Catherine's family politically. Catherinian historians have always assumed that the events described in the story must have taken place before October 1370, when the brothers petitioned for Florentine citizenship. But this petition has been misunderstood, and at least two of Catherine's brothers, Bartolomeo and Stefano, still resided in Siena even as they obtained Florentine citizenship and the favorable trading status that came with it. In fact, the *Miracoli* story can be placed with confidence in the summer of 1371 during the "Revolt of the Bruco," a wool-workers revolt that anticipated the more famous Florentine Ciompi revolt by seven years, and which proved a watershed event in the formation of the new Sienese regime.

---

[52] *Miracoli*, chap. 16, 12–13: "La Caterina pigliò il suo mantello, e ponselo adosso, e dice a' frategli: 'Venite meco e non temete.' E ella entrò in mezo di loro. E dirittamente gli mena per la contrada de' nemici loro; e trovandogli, e passando per lo mezo di loro, con reverenzia inchinando allei, passarano sani e salvi. E menogli nello spedale di Santa Maria a Siena, e quivi gli raccomandò e lasciò al signore dello spedale, e disse loro: 'Istatevi celati qui tre dì, e in capo di tre dì sicuramente venitene accasa.' E così feciono."

In July 1371 a dispute between wool workers and their masters, the *lanaiuoli*, grew into a political insurrection as economic hardship fueled dissatisfaction among the less wealthy *popolo minuto* (sometimes therefore referred to as the *minutissimi*) with their representation in the new regime.[53] The affair began on 16 July when a group of wool workers, mostly from the company and ward of Il Bruco del Pian d'Ovile (one of the poorest areas of Siena, on the side of the hill leading down to the church of San Francesco), sought redress from the government in a dispute with their masters, the *lanaiuoli*, over terms of employment. Denied entrance to the Palazzo Pubblico, the crowd stormed through the streets of the city, threatening to kill their masters. When three wool carders (possibly instigators of the riots, which appear to have been orchestrated to some extent by *minuti* radicals) were arrested by the senator and sentenced to death, the crowd attempted to set fire to the senatorial palace.[54] The wool workers apparently blamed the Salimbeni and Dodici for the arrests and the governmental repression of their protests, and the uprising turned quickly into a political demonstration. After the wool carders were released through the armed intervention of the *capitano del popolo*, who with his troops attacked the senatorial palace, the men of the Bruco moved on to the Palazzo Pubblico, and demanded the expulsion of the Nove and Dodici members of the Signoria. The government capitulated immediately, replacing the Nove and Dodici representatives with members of the *popolo minuto*. The men of the Bruco proceeded through the city, attacking eminent Dodici and others suspected of ties with the Dodici and Salimbeni, and removing from the Palazzo Salimbeni the banner of the *popolo* (placed there when the Salimbeni were given the right to be considered *popolari*, and thus eligible for all governmental offices, after the revolution of September 1368).[55] Attempting to return to the Palazzo Pubblico, the protestors were confronted by a group of nobles from the Malavolti, Tolomei, and Montanini, who were able to repulse the men of the Bruco, and protect for the moment the suspected Dodici and Nove.[56]

The revolt was a victory, at least initially, for the Bruco and the more radical *minuti*. The regime sought to settle the unrest by capitulating to the demands of the protestors, expelling from governmental offices all the Dodici and Nove considered opponents of the *popolo*.[57] None of the

---

[53] An account of the affair is in the chronicle of Neri di Donato (*Cronaca Senese di Donato di Neri e di suo figlio Neri*, in *Cronache Senesi*, Alessandro Lisini and Fabio Iacometti, ed., *Rerum Italicarum Scriptores* vol. 15, pt. 6 [1936]), 639–42. See Valerie Wainwright, "The Testing of a Popular Sienese Regime."

[54] Neri di Donato, 639.

[55] Neri di Donato, 639–40.

[56] Ibid., 640.

[57] Ibid., 640. The decision is recorded in ASS, *Consiglio Generale* 181, 52v (27 July 1371).

*popolo minuto* protestors were punished, despite having killed several prominent Dodici. In reaction, the Salimbeni and Dodici attempted a coup on 29 July.[58] The plot was detected when the *capitano del popolo,* who had been paid off by the conspirators, was discovered in the middle of the night, along with his troops, fully armed and prepared to open the doors of the Palazzo Pubblico to the Salimbeni/Dodici armies, which were poised at the city gates.[59] On 30 July the Salimbeni/Dodici armies entered the city anyway, taking out their anger by indiscriminately slaughtering residents of the quarter of the Bruco. Many of the nobles and Nove, with good reason to fear the political ascendancy of the Salimbeni and Dodici, came to the aid of the *minuti* and helped to defeat the conspirators. The fighting extended from the Pian d'Ovile to Camporegio, Catherine's family's neighborhood. At least two days of violent reprisals followed. A number of Dodici and other conspirators were immediately arrested and executed, including the *capitano del popolo,* who was beheaded in the Campo on 1 August. More than two hundred other Dodici and suspected "friends of the Dodici and Salimbeni" were fined amounts from six hundred florins to twenty-five lire. In the end, the oligarchy restored their control, allowing the "new men" some additional representation, but also returning the Nove to the governing coalition. The Salimbeni and Dodici, on the other hand, were proscribed, and new measures effectively barred from political office all Dodici and their descendants.[60]

The *Miracoli* episode places Catherine and her brothers in the middle either of the initial assault of the Bruco against the wool masters, or of the violent reprisals against the conspirators and their supporters in the days immediately following the Salimbeni/Dodici coup attempt on 29–30 July. As Dodicini and masters in the wool guild, Catherine's brothers and their friends were indeed of the party attacked by the Bruco and also targeted after the coup attempt. This is strongly implied by the description of Catherine leading her brothers toward the *contrada,* or quarter, of their

---

[58]  Unnamed chronicle, cited by Brizio ("Siena nel secondo Trecento," 49): Siena, Biblioteca Comunale, MS A.IV.1, 306v.

[59]  Neri di Donato, 640–41.

[60]  This action established the Riformatori, a coalition of *popolo minuto* and Nove representatives with the significant backing of the Tolomei family, the traditional enemies of the Salimbeni, a regime that lasted until 1385, when the Dodici and other noble families reentered the government and banished the *minuti* who had ruled under the Riformatori. The decision to exclude the Dodici from the Signoria was taken on 2 August (ASS, *Consiglio Generale* 181, 34r [2 August 1371]. Later in August, the Riformatori decided that all Dodici and their sons and grandsons, would be ineligible for all offices within the commune, and could no longer bear arms. Moreover, Dodici notaries were prohibited from working in the most lucrative governmental offices, those of the Defensori, Biccherna, and senator. See Wainwright, "The Testing of a Popular Regime," 163; Brizio, "Siena nel secondo Trecento," 54.

enemies: the only political group that had a distinct geographical identity in Siena in this period was the Bruco, associated with the Pian d'Ovile.[61] In addition, the reprisals taken by the Bruco and the other *minuti* did in fact extend into the neighborhood in which Catherine's brothers lived and worked, and included their close associates. Catherine's family lived in the southwestern wing of the Terzo of Camollia, near the Dominican church of San Domenico in Camporegio and the fountain of Fontebranda, a section of town dominated by the masters of the wool guild, and which included the *contrade* of Sant' Antonio and of San Pellegrino.[62] Neri di Donato lists among those beheaded immediately following the coup, "Antonio di Bindotto Placidi de' Nove" and "Nicolò d'Ambruogio di Nese tentore de' Dodici," both residents of San Pellegrino.[63] Niccolò d'Ambrogio di Nese, a dyer like Catherine's father and brothers, was the nephew of Catherine's first confessor, Tommaso dalla Fonte, as well as related by marriage to Catherine's family.[64] The *Miracoli* story, then, is a dramatic demonstration of the political situation of Catherine's family, associated with the guild oligarchy, enemies of the *popolo minuto,* and (at least indirectly) partisans of the Dodici/Salimbeni alliance. If the *Miracoli* account is completely accurate, they were probably among the twenty-six Sienese who, according to Neri di Donato, were fined one hundred florins as part of the reprisals taken by the government after the coup attempt.[65] Perhaps as a result of this political setback, by the end of 1372

[61]  The political geography of Siena was on a smaller scale similar in this respect to that of Florence, in which the wool-workers who took part in the Ciompi uprising in 1378 resided in the city's outlying suburbs. See Stella, *La révolte des Ciompi: Les hommes, les lieux, le travail,* 125–33.

[62]  The two *contrade* were in different *terzi,* but really part of one larger neighborhood, including most of the masters of the wool guild (Duccio Balestracci and Gabriella Piccinni, *Siena nel Trecento. Assetto urbano e strutture edilizie* [1977], 127).

[63]  Neri di Donato, 641. Niccolò d'Ambrogio was beheaded immediately, on 30 July, the day of the coup attempt (as is evident in his entry in the necrology of San Domenico; see *I Necrologi di San Domenico in Camporeggio* (1937), n.1519.

[64]  One of Catherine's older sisters, Niccoluccia, had married Palmiero di Nese della Fonte, who after her death apparently became a lay brother in the hospital of Santa Maria della Scala. According to Caffarini (Thomas Antonii de Senis "Caffarini," *Libellus de Supplemento,* edited by Giuliana Cavallini and Imelda Foralosso [1974], 370), Tommaso was practically raised in the household of Catherine's family. Fra Tommaso is usually referred to in hagiographical accounts and other documents merely by a geographical designation—Tommaso of the Fountain—without a patronymic. In fact, Tommaso, like Palmiero, was the son of one "Nese della Fonte." He is referred to as "Tommasus Nesis de Fonte" in two testaments he witnessed in 1373 (ASS, *Diplomatico, Patrimonio dei Resti, S. Domenico,* both dated 29 July 1373). Niccolò's father Ambrogio was probably Fra Tommaso's brother. Both Niccolò and Ambrogio were entombed in San Domenico, a connection to the Dominicans consistent with their common relation to Fra Tommaso and with their social status as Dodici wool masters (*Necrologi di S. Domenico,* n.355, "Ambrosius Nese tinctor," buried 22 May 1340; n.1519, "Nicholaus Ambrosii tinctoris," died 30 July 1371).

[65]  Neri di Donato, 642.

the family business evidently failed, and the sons of Iacopo di Benincasa were declared bankrupt.[66]

## Caterina di Monna Lapa

Another episode in the history of Catherine's family in the early 1370s brings together the economic situation of the sons of Iacopo di Benincasa and Catherine's vocation, and shows how her religious status itself was shaped by declarations of women's autonomy and a break with the family's patrimonial interests. Alongside the entry for "Bartolo di iachomo benenchasa," Catherine's older brother, who died in the plague of late 1374, in a volume of Sienese tax records for 1375, there is a later note recording a decision rendered by the prior of the Biccherna with reference to Bartolomeo's tax liabilities. Bartolomeo was bound to pay 3 *denarii* on the behalf of Monna Lapa his mother, and 7 *denarii* on the behalf of Monna Lisa his wife, for a house in Fontebranda and a vineyard in Santa Maria a Pilli, properties that were owed to them by virtue of debts incurred to their dowries by the father, Iacopo di Benincasa. The two women were not obliged to pay any additional tax on these properties or on their goods, except some material for dying obtained from Bartolomeo's workshop.[67] The vineyard mentioned was purchased by Bartolomeo in 1372; the house in Fontebranda was probably the family home of Iacopo and Lapa.[68] It is clear that Lapa and Lisa were declared owners of the two properties mentioned, and Bartolomeo was to pay the assessed tax in repayment for debts to their dowries inherited from his father.[69] The dowries of the two women must have been invested by their

[66] Records show Bartolomeo, in particular, acquiring properties in the city and in the Sienese *contado* from 1367 through July 1372 (see ASS, *Spedale della Scala* 516, f. 132; *Gabella* 77, f. 13v; *Gabella* 81, f. 61v; *Gabella* 82, f. 90r). But in December 1372 Bartolomeo and Stefano together sold two properties, a residential house and a dyer's shop along with all the dying tools therein—apparently an entire dying operation (ASS, *Gabella* 83, f. 21v). This was followed by further liquidation of family property in May 1373 (*Gabella* 84, f. 72r and September 1373; *Gabella* 85, f. 37r), and on 7 October 1373 the Florentine government wrote to the Sienese government seeking redress for debts incurred in Florence by the three sons of Iacopo di Benincasa (ASS, *Concistoro* 1783, 69).

[67] ASS, *Lira* 14, 100v.

[68] While Bartolomeo himself bought property in the area of Fontebranda and owned a house there, he divested himself of this property in 1372 and 1373. Thus the house mentioned in the tax record must be another house—most likely the family home of Iacopo di Benincasa and Lapa.

[69] The judgment as recorded is ambiguous. It is possible that Bartolomeo maintained possession or use of the two properties, and the note is added to his entry to make explicit that the ownership had passed to Lapa and Lisa. It is also possible that the tax money is part of what Bartolomeo owed the two women, in addition to the properties.

husbands in property and the family's business enterprises.[70] While husbands controlled the dowries of their wives, those dowries in theory and in practice always remained the property of the wives, and could be reclaimed under certain circumstances. In particular, a woman had the right to sue her husband for her dowry, and would be recognized as his first creditor, if her husband was tending to insolvency.[71] When the family went bankrupt, Lapa and Lisa evidently asserted their rights under law to be considered their husbands' prior creditors, and sued for restitution of their dowries. At this point, these properties and some movable goods left unsold from Bartolomeo's workshop passed into the possession of the two women as repayment for their dowries.[72] As a result of the judgment, Lapa and Lisa maintained possession of the family house, which was recognized as Catherine's residence as well: a tax assessment of 1385 lists "Monna lapa dona fu di Jacomo tintor e caterina mantellata e monna lisa" (outdated information, since Catherine had died in 1380) as property-holders resident in the *contrada* of Sant' Antonio, which is the location of the "house in Fontebranda" they received in 1375.[73] Other records show Lisa, after Lapa's death, residing alone there some years later.[74] Lapa sold the vineyard in Santa Maria a Pilli in 1382.[75]

[70] The reason why Iacopo, and not Bartolomeo, is named as debtor for Lisa's dowry is probably that, except in cases where a son had been legally emancipated, the father normally took control of his daughter-in-law's dowry; accordingly, the father could also be sued by his daughter-in-law for return of the dowry if he should become insolvent (Julius Kirshner, "Wives' Claims against Insolvent Husbands in Late Medieval Italy," in Kirshner and Suzanne F. Wemple, eds., *Women of the Medieval World. Essays in Honor of John H. Mundy* [1985], 280.)

[71] Julius Kirshner, "Wives' Claims against Insolvent Husbands," esp. 257–59. In Roman law, although the dowry was considered among the husband's goods, it was also considered to belong to the wife. Accordingly, the husband could not alienate dotal land without the permission of the wife, although he could alienate movable goods for which a value had been fixed by explicit agreement. The wife had an implied *hypothec*, or security, over all her husband's goods for restitution of the dowry; this took precedence over all other *hypothecs* or securities. The Roman law title *Ubi adhuc* (*Codex* 15.12.29) was appealed to in order to support the right of a wife who was *sui juris* to take physical control of her husband's goods, as well as any *donatio ante nuptias* and *res extra dotales*, by an *actio hypothecaria*, if her husband became insolvent during marriage; the wife was the preferred creditor. Kirshner shows how jurists in the thirteenth and fourteenth centuries tended to uphold and even strengthen the rights of women to file suits to reclaim their dowries.

[72] This assertion of dowry rights was not simply a legal ploy on the part of the husbands to protect wealth from creditors outside the family, since the property declared to be theirs in 1375 was not redistributed to other family members—for instance, the eldest son, Benincasa, who was still alive and running the Florentine branch of the family business—but remained in the possession of Lapa and Lisa. Lapa sold the vineyard in 1382 (ASS, *Gabella* 103, 50v [30 October 1382]).

[73] ASS, *Lira* 21, 146.

[74] ASS, *Lira* 28 (1394) fol. 94: "Monna Lisa dona fu di Bartolo di Jacomo tintor," in Sant' Antonio, assessed 1d.

[75] ASS, *Gabella* 103, 50v (30 October 1382): Sano di Maco, acting as procurator and

Lapa and Lisa joined the *mantellate*, apparently at around the same time since they are listed together in the membership list. This was not long after Catherine, who probably was enrolled as a member in around 1370.[76] Their action to recover their dowry rights can be seen as assuring them the necessary autonomy to embark upon life as *pinzochere* and independent widows, and it is likely that these women provided Catherine with her means of support as well as her home. Indeed, Lapa and Lisa accompanied Catherine in some of her travels in subsequent years. Their autonomy might have been gained, however, at the expense of the men of the family; the action of Lapa and Lisa to regain their dowries likely interfered with the efforts of the sons of Iacopo to salvage their business by liquidating properties and repaying their creditors. And indeed tension over debts lay behind an evident rift between Lapa and her sons at around this time. In one of her earliest extant letters, probably in 1374, Catherine wrote to her brother Benincasa in Florence counseling him to endure his trials with patience, and upbraiding him for complaining that Lapa has not done what she could to help her sons:

> I beg you, dear brother, that you bear [your troubles] with every patience. And I would not like you to overlook the correction of your ingratitude and thoughtlessness (*ignorantia*), that is concerning the debt that you bear towards your mother, to whom you are bound by God's commandment. And I have seen that you have so much compounded your thoughtlessness that, not just have you not rendered your debt to help her—let us say for the moment that I excuse you for this, since you have not been able—but I do not know whether you would have done so, since you only care for words. Oh ingratitude! You have given no thought to the pains of childbirth nor to the milk that she gave from her breast, nor for the many pains she bore for you and all the others. And if you say to me, "she has shown no concern for us," I reply that this is not true, that she has had such great concern, for you and the other [brother], that it has cost her dearly. But let us say that it was true. You are obligated to her, not her to you. She did not take flesh from you, but gave you hers.[77]

---

creditor for the dowry of "domine lise [*sic*] uxoris Iacobi benecase" sells for her dowry, for 100 florins and 40d., certain possessions and goods with a vineyard and a house in Santa Maria a Pilli, which had been possessions of the aforesaid Iacobus and Bartolus his son. The document has confused Lisa for Lapa.

[76] It is not certain when they became *mantellate*. They are listed together in the extension of the membership list begun in 1352, and the *Miracoli* author in late 1374 describes Lapa as already a *mantellata*. Bartolomeo seems to have died in the plague of 1374–75, and it is likely that Lisa only joined after this time. On the other hand, as has already been noted, it is a mistake to try to establish precision with respect to entry into the *mantellata*.

[77] Letter 18/XIII; *Epistolario*, 57–58: "E però vi prego, carissimo fratello, che voi portiate con ogni pazienzia. E non vorrei che vi uscisse di mente el correggiarvi della vostra

Suzanne Noffke takes Catherine to be faulting her brothers for not being sufficiently attentive to their mother, whom Noffke suggests was at this point left in Catherine's care.[78] But Lapa's assertion of her dowry rights suggests that what is at issue here is more than filial neglect. The debt Catherine mentioned was likely a real debt to Lapa's dowry, a debt the brothers had not been able to pay because of the failure of their business. And the brothers' complaint about their mother's care concerned her assertion of her rights in spite of their business interests. Rather than Lapa being in Catherine's care, it is more likely that Catherine as a *pinzochera* was dependant on her mother for support.

Catherine entered into the public view in Siena in the early 1370s, and began to form the network of layman and clerics who would constitute her *famiglia*, with the support of her mother and her sister-in-law and as one of a community of *mantellate*—in other words, as an independent woman among independent women. For Raymond, Catherine's status as a *pinzochera* must have seemed a very unpromising position from which to launch a new saint, further complicating his already difficult task of justifying the public nature of her life. Raymond in fact takes great pains with this issue in the *Legenda maior*, emphasizing how Catherine entered on her unusual career in response to Christ's mandate and against her own desire to retreat from the world. In Raymond's account, Catherine's ability to move unscathed in the world is provided by her development, during her period of domestic seclusion, of an internal cell within herself, to which she could retreat and remain continually in mystic communion with Christ even as she mixed in public life. And Raymond compensates for Catherine's public profile by avoiding representing her in public places. As Sofia Boesch Gajano and Odile Redon have observed, houses, rooms within houses, and otherwise carefully delimited enclosures compensate in Raymond's account for Catherine's lack of the stability and protection of a monastic life.[79] As in her status as a *mantellata*, Raymond's

---

ingratitudine e ignoranza, cioè del debito che avete con la madre vostra, al quale voi sete tenuto per comandamento di Dio. E io ò veduto moltiplicare tanto la ignoranzia vostra che, non tanto che voi l'abbiate renduto el debito d'aiutarla, poniamo che di questo io v'ò per scusato, però che non avete potuto; e se aveste potuto, non so che voi aveste fatto, però che solo delle parole l'avete fatto caro. O ingratitudine! non avete considerato la fatica del parto né 'l latte ch'ella trasse del petto suo, né le molte fatiche ch'ella a avute di voi e di tutti gli altri. E se mi diceste ch' ella non abia avuto pietà di noi, dico che non è vero; ch' ella n' à avuto tanta, di voi e dell'altro, che caro le costa. Ma poniamo caso che fusse vero: voi sete ubrigato a lei, e non lei a voi. Ella non trasse la carne di voi, ma ella dié la sua a voi."

[78] Noffke, *Letters of Catherine of Siena*, 1: 31. Out of context, of course, Noffke's reading of the letter makes sense. However, I do not see what justifies her translation of the phrase, "però che solo delle parole l'avete fatto caro," as "because you've scarcely kept in touch with her" (*Letters of Catherine of Siena*, 1: 33).

[79] Sofia Boesch Gajano and Odile Redon, "La *Legenda maior* di Raimondo da Capua,"

careful description of the origins and status of the "Order of Penance" suggests stability and regularity where none in fact existed. And in order to distance Catherine even further from the more scandalous implications of her status as a *mantellata,* Raymond draws a clear distinction between the lukewarm and conventional spirituality of the widows who dominated the *mantellate* when Catherine joined and the more ambitious and lively spirituality of Catherine and a group of younger women, including several virgins, who joined the group in imitation of Catherine. In Raymond's account, the older, widowed *mantellate* resist Catherine's pious desire to join the group, harbor suspicions of her, and even accuse her of violating her virginity. Such attention to Catherine's status, and the distinction between Catherine and the typical *pinzochere,* reflects Raymond's awareness of the anomaly Catherine represented as a woman, let alone a saint, moving independently in the city and mixing in public affairs.

Less obviously, Raymond's most ambitious way of distancing Catherine is in his subtle rewriting of the chronology of Catherine's vocational years, a revision that appears especially ironic in light of the economic tensions in Catherine's family when she was beginning her public life. Raymond's reworking of Catherine's early years is a complicated issue, and there is room here for only a summary of the main features of his revision.[80] In the *Legenda maior,* Catherine's struggle with her family is resolved by Catherine obtaining Iacopo's explicit and solemn approval of her prospective "husband." As already noted, Raymond implies at least that Catherine entered the Order of Penance shortly after receiving her father's approval. Later, after she has been tested and proven as a visionary and ascetic during her years of seclusion, Catherine receives the command from Christ Himself to emerge into the world. Catherine's vocation is authorized when Christ accedes to Catherine's longstanding desire to become his bride; in Raymond's account, Catherine's espousal to Christ finalizes her conversion to the religious life, seals her against the dangers of her public life, and validates her status as a religious woman mixing in

---

15–36. The miracles Catherine performs during her life take place mostly in private rather than public settings, and occasions when she must venture into public are carefully circumscribed and limited in duration. Where she asserts saintly authority in public, she is shown doing so against her will. For example, Raymond tells how, in Pisa, Catherine miraculously causes an abundance of delicious wine to flow from a dry and long unused cask. But when this marvel begins to attract a crowd, Catherine not only retreats from the public eye, but undoes the miracle, turning the wine into dregs and sediment (*LM,* pars. 307–9). Similarly, Catherine's *stigmata* inflicts internal pain on her, but unlike that of Francis, leaves no outward trace (*LM,* par. 195).

[80] This argument is made at length in F. Thomas Luongo, "Cloistering Catherine: Religious Identity in Raymond of Capua's *Legenda maior* of Catherine of Siena," *Studies in Medieval and Renaissance History* n.s. 3 (2005).

the world of men. The espousal serves as conclusive authority for Catherine's position in the world and a preemptive response to any social scandal caused by a young unmarried woman acting independently in public. The narrative structure of Raymond's account of Catherine's early years thus depends not only on her eventual espousal to Christ, but on the authorization that she receives from her earthly father. Lapa is damned with faint praise: she is a formidable woman ("of the old sort"), but an inadvertent agent of the devil in her attempts to sway Catherine from her vocation. In Raymond's story, Lapa is ultimately made irrelevant in Catherine's progress. Real authority over Catherine passes from her earthly father to her heavenly father and spouse, and Lapa is merely a foil in Catherine's surmounting of feminine weakness and sensuality. Indeed, the juxtaposition of the spiritual acumen and rationality of Catherine and Iacopo with the volatility, emotionality, and purely motherly affection displayed by Lapa—who loves *carnaliter,* not *spiritualiter*—allows Raymond to present Catherine with apparently contradictory characteristics. Catherine graduates from her family home and her father's protection as a "wife," fulfilling a female role in all propriety. But in his description of Catherine's espousal of Christ, which occurs at the crucial moment when Catherine moves out into the world, Raymond tells how Christ commanded Catherine "carry out manfully, without any hesitation, whatever by order of my providence may be laid in your hands."[81] While Catherine enters the world as a wife, and will eventually become mother to her disciples, Raymond takes pains to show that Catherine acts in the world as if she were a man. Unlike Lapa, Catherine is not feminine in the ordinary (and dangerous) sense.

While the Catherinian tradition, beginning with Raymond, has tended to disparage Lapa, her independent status and authority over her daughter was recognized during Catherine's lifetime. In Sienese public documents, the records of the *mantellate,* and even papal bulls in the second half of the 1370s, Catherine is identified by her mother's name and not—as one would usually expect—by her father's. During her short adult life and public career, Catherine was known not as "Caterina di Iacopo" but as "Caterina di Monna Lapa."[82]

---

[81] *LM* par. 115, p. 891: "Age igitur, filia, viriliter amodo, absque cunctatione quacumque, illa, quae ordininante mea providentia, tuas deducentur ad manus."

[82] Some change in the manner of designating Catherine seems to have occurred between 1374, at which time the *Miracoli* author identifies her as "Caterina di Iacopo"—and August 1376, when a bull of Gregory XI calls her "Caterina Lape de Senis" (Archivio Vaticano, *Reg. Vat.* 288, fol. 159r–v; transcribed in Laurent, ed., *Documenti,* 14). She is "Katerina domine Lape de contrata Fontis Brandi" in the minutes of the Sienese Consiglio Generale for 25 January 1377, which records Catherine's petition for the conversion of the fortress of Belcaro into a monastery (ASS, *Consiglio Generale* 187, fol. 9r–v), and "Caterina domine Lape" in the 1378 list of *mantellate* (cited above).

By casting Catherine in the role of a saint and religious woman, set apart from ordinary society and from ordinary women like her mother, a *legenda* like Raymond's has fed into the establishment of "female saints" and "religious women" as historical categories that can easily miss the more complicated stories involved in the lives of the women who are their subjects. It is worth considering how Raymond's construction of Catherine's identity as bride of Christ involved not simply the authorization of an autonomous woman, but the rejection of a model of female independence: the model of the *mantellate,* represented by Monna Lapa. Historians have in this case absorbed the hagiographical construction uncritically: Catherine has become emblematic of the authority of saintly women in late-medieval religious culture, but one hears little or nothing about the more common and conventional model of female piety of Monna Lapa and widowed *mantellate.*

This reconsideration of Lapa's role begins to restore some of the real life that the hagiography obscures—not a real life completely removed from hagiographical discourse, but rather the complex process of negotiation in real life of gender, sanctity, and other constructions of identity. There is undoubtedly more drama in this story than will ever be disclosed by the hagiographical and archival sources. Monna Lapa may indeed have been emotionally overbearing, perhaps the stereotypical nagging mother she has become in the Catherinian tradition. One suspects, however, that in many ways Catherine was indeed her mother's daughter. Lapa seems to have facilitated Catherine's vocation through her economic support; she must also have been responsible for her daughter's first Christian instruction, and also provided Catherine with a model of initiative and independence. Monna Lapa must have faced no small challenge in living with a daughter determined to become a saint, and for this, if nothing else, Monna Lapa deserves better than to be shunted off into the negative role she has come to play in Catherine's story.

Catherine by the end of 1374 was acting under the authority or protection of the Dominican Order and the papacy. But the issue of Catherine's religious vocation is fraught with ambiguities, despite the apparent clarity imposed on Catherine's status by Raymond of Capua and Tommaso Caffarini, and repeated by Catherinian scholars. While it is easy in retrospect to see that Catherine's extraordinary talents would have been stifled by the cloistered life, it is still surprising that Catherine's clerical advisors (apparently) supported and encouraged her entry into the *mantellate,* a group comprised of widows with independent means. Catherine's status as a *mantellata* was a problematic novelty, so as her fame grew why was this saintly virgin not encouraged, or even compelled, to enter the cloister and embrace a more conventional manner of life, one much less open to censure?[83] One answer is that her supporters, Dominicans and otherwise, already in the early 1370s saw her as helping to lead a reform movement, a movement for which she would become a saintly authority by the late 1390s. One might even speculate that Catherine's becoming a *pinzochera* instead of a Dominican nun was part of a strategy on the part of Catherine's early advisors to employ the informal structure of the *mantellate* to introduce reform into female Dominican monasticism, rather than fight the resistance of established women's monasteries attached to the Dominican order—as in effect was done later by Giovanni Dominici in foundations like Corpus Domini. Another answer, however, is that the relative flexibility and mobility of Catherine's status as a *mantellata* was sanctioned precisely so that she could play a political role. Indeed, one can certainly say that Catherine's status as a *mantellata*, free of strict rules governing the form of her life, made possible the social and political mobility that defined her career.

Finally, the direction of Catherine's career as she entered into the larger theater of Tuscan and ecclesiastical politics was not a break with her background, but was in fact consistent with the social and political character of her family and her earliest network of supporters and acquaintances. Catherine's family were not the humble artisans of pious convention, but members of the guild elite and *Dodicini*—and so presumed allies both of the Salimbeni and the papacy. While Catherine's supporters and Catherine herself articulated her authority by claiming for her a place apart from ordinary economics and politics, Catherine's experience and authority were in fact grounded in specific and real connections to family and a web of social and political interests in Siena and Tuscany. And this web of interests was responsible, in large part, for Catherine's entry into ecclesiastical and Tuscan politics in 1374.

[83] Indeed, as has not previously been recognized, during Catherine's lifetime the Sienese Dominicans had under their supervision a female monastery, the monastery of Santa Caterina (of Alexandria), located just inside the city walls at the Porta Laterina. Several of Catherine's early Dominican directors were associated at various times with the monastery, and several of her fellow *mantellate* made bequests to that community. Evidence of the Dominican supervision of this convent as well as the relationship between individual *mantellate* and the nuns, can be found in ASS, *Patrimonio dei resti*, 2181 (records of the monastery of Santa Caterina) and 2144 (records of the *mantellate*) as well as many testaments, for instance ASS, *Diplomatico, Patrimonio dei resti, S. Domenico*, 26 luglio 1346; 29 luglio 1373; 22 ottobre 1373; 17 aprile 1408; and 27 aprile 1408.

# CHAPTER 2

# Catherine Enters Tuscan Politics: Networks and Letter Writing

In a letter in March 1374, Catherine announced the visit to her of the Spanish monk and bishop Alfonso da Vadaterra, confessor of the visionary queen Birgitta of Sweden, who had died the previous July.

> I tell you that the supreme goodness has prepared for us the ways and times for doing great things through him. And so I have told you that you should seek to increase your holy desire, and do not be content with little things, because He wants great things. And in order that you may do this, let me tell you: the Pope sent his vicar here, the one who was spiritual father of that countess who died at Rome, and he renounced the episcopate for love of virtue. He came to me on behalf of the Holy Father, that I ought to make special prayers for him and for holy Church, and as a token he brought me the holy indulgence. Be glad and rejoice, that the Holy Father has begun to turn his eye toward the honor of God and Holy Church.[1]

This letter was sent to the Sienese Dominican friars Bartolomeo Dominici and Tommaso Caffarini, who were at the Dominican *studium* in Pisa. Birgitta in a series of prophetic writings had admonished popes (Innocent

---

[1] Letter 127/XX: "Io vi dico che quella somma bontà ci à apparecchiati e' modi e tempi da fare e' grandi fatti per lui. E però vi dissi che fuste solleciti di cresciare el santo desiderio, e none state contenti alle piccole cose, però che elli le vuole grandi. E per tanto io vi dico: el papa mandò di qua el suo vicario, e ciò fue el padre spirituale di quella contessa che morì a Roma, ed è colui che renunziò el vescovado per l'amore de la virtù: venne a me da parte del padre santo, ch'io dovesse fare speziale orazione per lui e per la santa Chiesa, e per segno mi recò la santa indulgenzia. [Gaudete ed exultate], ché 'l padre santo à cominciato ad eccitare l'occhio verso l'onore di Dio e della santa Chiesa."

VI, Urban V, and Gregory XI) and church leaders about the state of the church, and had called with urgency for a return of the papal court to Rome. In her later life, Birgitta focused on the Italian situation and the preparations for the pope's return, and maintained contact with Pierre d'Estaing and Gerard du Puy, the governors of the Papal States, through whom she issued prophetic pronouncements to the pope about the need to return to Rome and about matters such as the prosecution of the Visconti wars.

Birgitta's prophetic role apparently satisfied two requirements of Gregory XI: his desire for divine knowledge and the need for prophetic authority to buttress policies the pope favored (such as the return to Rome), but which other political forces opposed. Gregory XI does not cut a distinguished or even distinct figure in the history of medieval popes, and his personality and character are difficult to assess. He is often remembered as a timid, vacillating man, a reputation that is due in part, at least, to Catherine's characterization in some of her more outspokenly critical letters. On the other hand, he vigorously prosecuted papal interests in Italy and returned the papal court from Avignon to Rome in spite of the opposition of the king of France and his own Curia. A fairer assessment of Gregory XI is that he was an intelligent and capable administrator, but a captive of the machinery of papal government rather than an innovator or far-seeing leader. Given his background and career, this is hardly surprising. Pierre Roger II was born into a Limousin noble family whose prestige was based largely on ecclesiastical preferments. He became a canon by the age of eleven; was made a cardinal by his uncle, Pope Clement VI, when he was only eighteen; studied civil and canon law at Perugia; was elected pope when he was only forty; and died at the age of forty-seven.[2] An interest in prophecy might not seem to fit into this picture of a very conventional career prelate, but in fact prophetic literature and eschatological language about the meaning and role of the pope was a part of the culture of the Avignon court, and sometimes a preoccupation of the Avignon popes, however much they might have condemned particular prophecies as unorthodox.[3] Thus there is nothing surprising in the attention paid by the pope and his vicars to Birgitta, whether they sincerely valued her insights or found her prophetic voice politically useful, or both. In any case, after her death

---

[2]  Paul R. Thibault, *Pope Gregory XI: The Failure of Tradition* (1986); G. Mollat, *The Popes at Avignon, 1305–1378*, trans. Janet Love (1963), 59–63.

[3]  Amanda Collins has drawn particular attention to the use of apocalyptic language by Gregory XI's uncle, Clement VI, in *Greater than Emperor: Cola di Rienzo (ca. 1313–54) and the World of Fourteenth-Century Rome* (2002), 108–15. On the place of prophecy at the papal court, see also Jean de Roquetaillade, *Liber secretum eventum*, ed. Robert E. Lerner, trans. Christine Morerod-Fattebert (1994).

there was an immediate attempt to find a successor, and Catherine's name came to the attention of the pope.

Shortly after the visit from Alfonso da Vadaterra, Catherine was summoned to attend the Dominican general chapter in Florence in the summer of 1374. This was the occasion that prompted the writing of the *Miracoli*. This event has usually been described as if she had been summoned to face accusations of heresy, but it is much more likely that Catherine was brought to Florence to be vetted for a role that had already been conceived for her, as a political visionary—a second Birgitta. The period from Alfonso's visit until the Dominican chapter was the defining moment in Catherine's career, launching her almost immediately into the Italian theater of ecclesiastical politics. Whatever interest Catherine had previously had in the issues at stake in the increasingly hostile relationship between the papacy and the Tuscan city-states, her interventions in worldly affairs outside Siena commenced only after the Dominican general chapter. Probably it was at the general chapter that Raymond of Capua was assigned to her, an affiliation that in itself brought Catherine unambiguously into the ambit of papal diplomacy in Tuscany and engaged her directly in the pursuit of Gregory XI's main political goals: the pacification of Italy to make possible the return of the papal court to Rome and the unification of Christendom through (or in preparation for) a full-scale Crusade. And while we possess several letters Catherine had written between about 1372 and 1374, her letter-writing campaign seems to have begun in earnest only after her trip to Florence.

Catherine's fame and scope of activities had spread quickly following her movement into a public role after 1368. Papal interest was a result of Catherine's enormous talents, including an unusual intelligence, an engaging personality, and a gift for vivid and stirring expression. But the development of Catherine's career and saintly reputation was also shaped decisively by the political scene in Siena and Tuscany at the time, particularly by the growing tension between Florence and the papacy leading to the War of Eight Saints. A brief look at some of these political tensions will describe the stage on which Catherine emerged as a public figure and as an author of letters.

The Papacy and Political Tensions in Florence and Siena

The most important feature of Florentine politics in the early 1370s was increased opposition to the government of the wealthy merchants and bankers of the Parte Guelfa (which had dominated Florentine politics throughout the century), pressure that was exacerbated by an economic depression that affected all of Tuscany.[4] While the Parte held sway, Florence was the papacy's staunchest ally, particularly in the papal wars against the Visconti of Milan in the early 1370s. And Parte leaders enjoyed privileged economic ties with the Curia and the fruits of papal patronage in appointments to high ecclesiastical offices. But political resistance to the Parte by *gente nuova* who resented the *popolo grasso* monopoly of power within Florence combined with anticlericalism to make the Florentines ambivalent about the papacy and its political goals. Florentine religious culture had long been colored by the kinds of critiques of clerical wealth and worldliness found, most famously, in the writings of Dante, Petrarch, and Boccaccio, as well as in the preaching of the Fraticelli against the institutional church.[5] At the same time, governors of the Papal States under Innocent VI and Urban V sought to strengthen control of their territories as part of the anti-Viscontean struggle. Throughout the early 1370s, suspicions grew in Florence that the papacy, whose political bases were in Perugia to the southeast and Bologna to the northeast, was plotting to expand its area of control westward into the territory of the independent Tuscan city-states. As a result of these fears, what might previously have seemed an unalloyed good for all Italians—the return of the pope to Rome—now appeared to pose a threat to Florence. As the political climate within Florence became increasingly unsympathetic to the papacy, the Florentines ceased to provide the kinds of economic and direct military support needed by the governors of the Papal States to successfully defeat the Visconti and prepare the way for a triumphant return of the papal court to Rome.

Gregory XI consistently denied that the church had any expansionist ambitions in Tuscany: his avowed goal of returning the papal court to Rome required a resolution of the Visconti wars and the pacification and consolidation of the church's temporal possessions in Italy. But expansion of the church's influence into Tuscany clearly was a goal of the ambitious and energetic French prelates who governed the Papal States: the papal vicar-generals in Bologna, Pierre d'Estaing and Guillaume Noellet, and the vicar-general in Perugia, the pope's nephew and abbot of Montmajeur, Gerard du Puy. Whether or not these men ever contemplated actually subjugating the Tuscan city-states and absorbing them into the Papal States, the replacement of unsympathetic regimes in Florence and Siena with more supportive ones would have given them economic and other assistance in defeating the Visconti and consolidating control of the Papal States. Thus the papal governors had good reason to support the Albizzi faction, who sought a return to Guelph hegemony

---

[4]    For a more detailed description of Florentine politics in the years leading up to the War of Eight Saints, see Brucker, *Florentine Politics and Society*, 244–96.

[5]    Brucker, *Florentine Politics and Society*, 301–3.

in Florence. In this context it is worth recalling that both Machiavelli and Guicciardini thought that the traditional aim of papal policy, or at least its effect, was to destabilize Italy.[6] The papacy through its territorial power in Italy provided an alternative authority to whom subversive elements within the city-states could apply for assistance in their plots to overthrow local governments.

Whatever the actual designs of the pope and the governors of the Papal States, a series of events in the first half of the 1370s rapidly intensified anxieties within Florence. Gregory XI's responses to complaints from Florence and elsewhere showed insensitivity to these fears and demonstrated that the governors of the church's temporal possessions were outside his control. In this respect, Gregory's pontificate commenced badly when Pierre d'Estaing subjugated Perugia in May 1371. With papal armies established at Bologna and Perugia to the northeast and southeast, Florence and the Tuscans feared a pincerlike westward expansion.[7] In 1372, troops battling the Visconti conquered some land on the Florentine borders. At the same time, there were rumors that the Ubaldini, a rebellious noble clan based in the Appennines, might subject themselves to the church. And then the Sienese discovered a plot to overthrow their regime, in which church officials were allegedly implicated. The appointment of Gerard du Puy to the vicar-generalship in Perugia in September 1372 was another cause for concern, since Gerard was suspected of conspiring with leaders of the Albizzi faction to take over Florence, and with Sienese rebels to topple that commune's regime. When Gerard organized a military campaign to aid papal armies on Lombardy in October 1374 and requested a safe-passage from the Sienese, both Florence and Siena suspected an invasion. Not only did the Sienese not grant a formal safe-passage, but Florence sent an army to defend the city against attack by the papal armies.[8] A

---

6  Starn, *Contrary Commonwealth*, 34–35.

7  The atmosphere of accusations and suspicions of the church's political ambitions, and the extent to which those suspicions had been assimilated into a general critique of clerical worldliness, are illustrated in Gregory's self-justificatory response to Florentine complaints after the fall of Perugia: "The clergy are falsely accused of not being satisfied with their possessions, and of seeking to aggrandize themselves at the expense of Tuscany. The Popes have always defended the peace and liberty of Italy." (Brucker, *Florentine Politics and Society*, 271). Pierre d'Estaing's letter to the Sienese government announcing his entry into Perugia might also have fed Sienese fears: "Intravimus hanc nobilem civitatem Perusii, quam cum omnibus comitatus et districtus eiusdem castris et fortaliciis ad honorem et statum S. matris Ecclesie sub tranquillo dominio gubernamus, nec sit aliquis qui possit in corde vestro ponere subgestionibus falsis quod contra status vestrum aliquid attentamus." (ASS, *Concistoro* 1794, 54 [11 June 1371]; G. Mollat, "Relations politiques de Grégoire XI avec les Siennois et les Florentins," *Mélanges d'Archéologie et d'Histoire* 68 [1956]: 360.)

8  Brucker, *Florentine Politics and Society*, 276; Mollat, "Relations politiques," 341. Gerard du Puy requested a safe-passage on 2 October 1374 (ASS, *Concistoro* 1785, 5). On the Sienese reaction, see Neri di Donato, p. 655.

number of other alleged plots were uncovered, culminating in 1375 with the most publicized provocation, which might very well have been fabricated by the Florentine regime to foster antipapal feeling: the "discovery" of a plan by a friar in Prato to deliver that Florentine possession to Berenger, abbot of Lézat and papal nuncio in Italy.[9]

The Sienese political situation during these years was even more unstable than that of Florence. The regime of the Riformatori remained vulnerable to continued plotting by the Salimbeni and Dodici, as well as the designs of discontented nobles and Noveschi. Like the Florentines, the Sienese suspected church-sponsored subversion aimed at the overthrow of the Riformatori. As in Florence, the Riformatori were much more skeptical of the government of the Papal States than the previous propapal regime of the Dodici.[10] The Sienese concerns about the establishment of church authority in Perugia in 1371 were even more immediate than the Florentine anxieties, since the church territory governed from Perugia bordered on the southeastern Sienese *contado*. In June 1371, a Sienese diplomat in Perugia reported a meeting between Pierre d'Estaing and a nobleman from Montepulciano, a Sienese subject town in the southeastern *contado*, in which the noble offered to instigate a rebellion and deliver Montepulciano to the church. The ambassador reported that the offer was rejected, but this sort of episode could only increase fears of potential papal interference.[11] Another plot to give Montepulciano to the church, this time instigated by some Dodici who had fled or been banished from Siena in 1371, was uncovered in spring 1372.[12] The Sienese in 1373 and 1374 received ambassadors from Barnabò Visconti, an excommunicate and the pope's chief enemy in Italy. The first visit prompted communications from Sienese representatives at the Curia, who reported the pope's anger and his suspicions that the Sienese and Visconti were conspiring against the church.[13] Pierre d'Estaing also communicated his displeasure

[9]   Also, in June and July 1373, two different residents of Civitella, a town in the Florentine territories, were denounced for sponsoring a plan to turn that town to the papacy. A friar was accused of inciting rebellion in Volteran territory by informing his neighbors that "a better government is that of the church of Rome" (Brucker, *Florentine Politics and Society*, 281).

[10]   The dangers of generalizing on the basis of class identity have been stressed in the recent historiography, but this common mistrust of the papacy might nonetheless be related to the increasing ascendancy of members of the *popolo minuto* in both cities, since the economic and political benefits of papal patronage tended to be enjoyed by the larger bankers and merchants, and by members of the feudal nobility.

[11]   ASS, *Concistoro* 1781, 48 (18 August 1371); Brucker, *Florentine Politics and Society*, 281.

[12]   Andrea Giorgi, "Il carteggio del Concistoro," 274.

[13]   Mollat, "Relations politiques," 339. The pope's secretary, the Sienese Francesco Bruni, wrote to Siena on 22 December 1373, recounting the pope's concern and his own efforts to excuse the commune (ASS, *Concistoro* 1783, 84; Mollat, "Relations politiques," 361–62).

to the Sienese, warning them in January 1374 to avoid being "infected by the pestilential virus of the Milanese serpent."[14]

Sienese anxieties centered on the alleged relationship between the rebellious Salimbeni and Gerard du Puy. These concerns were not unreasonable. The Salimbeni strongholds in the southern *contado* bordered on Perugian territory and Gerard had an established relationship with the Salimbeni, having rewarded members of the clan for assistance in the campaigns against the Visconti.[15] Moreover, the *capo* of the Salimbeni, Agnolino di Giovanni, was related by marriage to Trincio dei Trinci, lord of Foligno and standard bearer of the duchy of Spoleto, one of the main administrative divisions within the government of the Papal States.[16] When the Salimbeni and their allies rose up in autumn 1374, seizing a number of strategic castles in the *contado* and threatening to force themselves back into power, the Sienese regime, noting that the Salimbeni had in the past received honors from Gerard du Puy, charged the papal governor of Perugia with complicity in the rebellion. Francesco Bruni, a Sienese papal secretary, brought the commune's complaints to the pope, who denied the charge on his own behalf, responding in language that suggested that he was not entirely in control of his deputies in Italy: "We do not believe that the Vicar General has given aid to the Salimbeni. We do not wish this and we will not allow it."[17] Gregory instructed Gerard to help reconcile the Salimbeni with the Sienese, which he did—after a fashion. While he refused military aid to help defend the city from the Salimbeni forces, he sent ambassadors to the city to help arrange a peace treaty. These ambassadors, arguing that the Salimbeni were too strong to be defeated, urged the Sienese government to concede to one of the chief Salimbeni demands—the reinstatement of the Dodici in the governing coalition. This was, in effect, to suggest that the Riformatori cooperate in their own demise, and the ambassadors were mocked and sent on their way.[18]

The Salimbeni revolt was eventually settled with the help of the Florentines, who sent troops to defend Siena and ambassadors who were able to

[14] Mollat, "Relations politiques," 339–40. The letter is in ASS, *Concistoro* 1783, 91 and Mollat 362–3.

[15] The Salimbeni had aided in 1370 in the occupation of Sarteano and of Cisterna. See Neri di Donato, 635; Mollat, "Relations politiques," 343.

[16] Trincio dei Trinci was the brother of Agnolino's wife, Biancina. See Eugenio Dupré Theseider, "La rivolta di Perugia nel 1375 contra l'abate di Monmaggiore e i suoi precedenti politici," *Bullettino della R. Deputazione di storia patria per l'Umbria* 35 (1938): 105–6.

[17] Mollat, "Relations politiques," 342–43.

[18] Neri di Donato, 656: "L'abate di Perogia mandò ambasciadori a Siena a mostrare di volere far pace fra 'l comuno di Siena e' Salimbeni. Sposero a' signori e poi a vedere come le terre de' Salimbeni erano forti; in breve la pace loro si era, a pitizione de' Dodici e de' Salimbeni, di volere che li Dodici regiessono. Fu lo risposto saviamente, e in effetto fu fatto beffe di loro; montaro a cavallo e andarsene."

broker a peace treaty in July 1375. Florence acted on several other occasions in the early 1370s to assist the Sienese regime: for instance, by sending military assistance to help stabilize Siena after the Revolt of the Bruco in the summer of 1371. The Sienese were able to turn to Florence for help also in 1372 when the first of the Montepulciano plots was uncovered, and in 1374 for defense against the Salimbeni and the papal army. The Riformatori maintained frequent contact and a privileged relationship with Florence.[19] Since the Florentines feared that political turmoil in Siena would make that city more susceptible to takeover by the church, thus exposing Florence to direct attack from the south, maintaining a stable Siena was an important part of Florentine defensive strategy in these years. It also suited Florence's hegemonic ambitions in Tuscany to form a patron-client relationship with the new Sienese regime, which the ascendant Florentine *gente nuova* found much more sympathetic than the previous regime of the Dodici, which had formed a very close alliance with the papacy, particularly in the league against the Visconti. And just as the Salimbeni opposed the Riformatori throughout its rule and maintained connections to the Papal States, the traditional blood enemies of the Salimbeni, the Tolomei clan, dominated the new regime and became particularly strong allies of the Florentines during the dispute with the papacy. The political constellation shaped by these alliances and interests dominated the fifteen-year regime of the Riformatori. In general, the Tolomei and the Riformatori (particularly its more radical *popolari* wing) sided with Florence, while the Salimbeni/Dodici alliance sided with the papacy.[20]

## Catherine's Network and Church Diplomacy

It was in this climate of building tension that Catherine was drawn into Italian politics. Catherine did not emerge onto this larger stage (pace Daniel Bornstein) simply "from a position of structural weakness and ideological subordination," but as part of a web of politically and socially powerful interests.[21] Again, Catherine's brothers were among the proscribed Dodici. In the years following the death of her father and the

[19] For evidence from the diplomatic communications between the two communes, see Giorgi, "Il carteggio del Concistoro," 263.

[20] Indeed, this constellation in some ways survived the regime. When the Riformatori regime was toppled in 1385 by an alliance of the Salimbeni and other noble families with elements of the Dodici and Nove, the new regime rejected the Tolomei and the special relationship with Florence, turning instead to the Gian Galeazzo Visconti for protection against Florentine ambitions. The Tolomei in the late 1380s then played the role of the Salimbeni in the 1370s, becoming an outlaw family at war with the new Sienese government.

[21] Daniel Bornstein, "Women and Religion in Late Medieval Italy: History and Historiography," 6.

commencement of her public career as a *mantellata,* Catherine moved in circles dominated by nobles and merchant and guild elites. This is implied, at least, by the individuals named by Raymond of Capua as subjects of Catherine's interventions in the early part of her public life, men to whom she was presumably introduced by her clerical advisors. Karen Scott is correct in noting that Raymond of Capua represents many of Catherine's early activities as centered in her family's neighborhood and a community of women.[22] But a closer look at some of the names mentioned in stories of Catherine's early miracles suggests that her activities quickly transcended a neighborhood milieu and were not limited to women. For example, Raymond describes how Catherine's intercession accomplished the deathbed conversion of a wealthy man named Andrea Naddini, a notorious gambler and blasphemer, who fell gravely ill in December 1370.[23] This man is identified by both Tommaso Caffarini and Bartolomeo Dominici in their testimonies for the *Processo Castellano* as one of the Bellanti, a politically and socially prominent Nove family with connections to the Dominicans, whose residences were in the *popolo* of San Stefano—not at all in the same neighborhood as Catherine's family.[24] Raymond also describes how Catherine through prophetic insight discerned a secret sin of Messer Niccolò de' Saracini, a member of a noble family whose residences were in the very wealthy *popolo* of San Paolo, at the center of the city and adjacent to the Piazza del Campo.[25]

Even more striking is how Catherine's letters show that she forged relationships with three of the Sienese senators and their families in the early 1370s. The senator was a military and law enforcement position that in this period was always assigned to a non-Sienese member of the feudal nobility. Vico da Mogliano, Pietro Marchese del Monte Santa Maria, and Andreasso Cavalcabuoi were feudal nobles, temporary residents of the city and elites on a Tuscan and Italian rather than a merely local stage, yet Catherine wrote all of them letters implying more than a passing acquaintance. More will be said in chapter 3 about Catherine's relationship with Pietro di Monte Santa Maria. For now, one example of her contact with the senators will suffice, a letter Catherine wrote in 1374 to Madonna Mitarella, the wife of Vico da Mogliano. As Catherine notes within the letter, Madonna

---

[22]  Karen Scott, "Urban Spaces, Women's Networks," 113.

[23]  *LM,* pars. 224–27.

[24]  *Processo Castellano,* 44 and 296–97. Andrea di Naddino Bellanti served on the Sienese executive board after the Salimbeni led coup of September 1368; the election records identify his *terzo* and *popolo.*

[25]  *LM,* 278–80. This Niccolò, whom Raymond describes as "well versed in arms" was possibly Messer Niccolò di Messer Guido de' Saraceni, who held a variety of civic offices and ambassadorial posts in the 1370s. On the Saraceni possessions, see Balestracci and Piccinni, *Siena nel Trecento,* 118.

Mitarella had written to Catherine in fear, seeking the "prayers of the Servants of God" in response to a crisis in the affairs of her husband, to which Catherine responded by exhorting Mitarella to put her hope in God and accept this trial as an opportunity for redemptive suffering.[26] The crisis that prompted this exchange was probably events that took place in May 1374, after the senator had led a civic army in retaking the Sienese subject community of Perolla. This town had been seized by a group of Sienese rebels that included one of the Salimbeni and a member of the Tegliacci (a prominent Dodici family to which Catherine was related by the marriage of her sister Buonaventura).[27] After the rebels were captured, and several of them executed by order of the senator, Vico resisted executing the Salimbeni prisoner, which prompted a *minuti* uprising led by the Compagnia del Bruco. As had happened in 1371, civic officials offered no resistance to the uprising, and the men of the Bruco were able to take justice into their own hands. They began by attempting to seize the senator in his palace, but Vico had fled to refuge in the Palazzo Pubblico. The Bruco leaders satisfied themselves with judging and executing the Salimbeni prisoner.[28] This dramatic threat to the senator's life is probably the event that prompted such fear on the part of Mitarella, who may have been left in the senatorial palace to face the angry crowd of wool workers.[29]

By 1374 Catherine had become someone to whom an elite member of Sienese society would turn to for spiritual solace; her contacts in Siena far transcended the milieu of family, neighborhood, and the pious association of the *mantellate*. And while Catherine's letter is in itself not in any way political, it does show her giving spiritual comfort and support to a victim of the same kind of political terror that endangered her own brothers just a few years earlier.

Even Catherine's connection to the Dominicans gave a particular social and political color to her network of contacts and supporters. As in Florence, the Dominicans in Siena were identified with the *popolo grasso*

[26] Letter 31/XII.
[27] Neri di Donato, 653.
[28] Ibid., 654.
[29] Fawtier (*Sainte Catherine de Sienne*, 2: 301) assigned this letter to the aftermath of the invasion of Perolla, but mistakenly thought that affair occurred in 1373. Dupré Theseider (*Epistolario*, 51) and Gardner (*Saint Catherine of Siena*, 112–13) place the letter in 1373. Dupré Theseider's dating appears to derive from the rubric accompanying the letter in one of the MS groups, but the rubric merely states (some 20–30 years after the fact) that Vico da Mogliano was senator in 1373—not that the letter was sent in 1373. There was an uprising in 1373, but unlike the Perolla affair, accounts of that earlier unrest mention no threats to the senator's life. Indeed, while Gardner gets the date wrong, he clearly intends to refer to the events of the Perolla affair, "when the senator attempted to restore order by sentencing noble and plebeian criminals alike to execution. In the rioting Ludovico's life was threatened, as well as the safety of his entire household."

guild and merchant elites, whereas the Franciscans were relatively more firmly established among the *popolo minuto* working classes.[30] For example, Bernadette Paton, in her study of mendicant preaching in Siena from 1380–1480, uses the homiletic writings of Catherine's disciple, the Dominican Tommaso Caffarini, as an example of a particularly Dominican "repulsion of the rich for the physical and moral degeneracy seen to be inherent in chronic poverty."[31] The church and friary of San Francesco was situated in the heart of the wool-workers' quarter in Ovile (the geographical base for the Compagnia del Bruco); San Domenico was in close proximity to the center of the wool trade and the residence of the guild masters in the *contrade* of San Pellegrino and Sant'Antonio. Indeed, while during Catherine's lifetime the *lanaiuoli* made the church of San Pellegrino their base of operations, the 1292 statutes of the *lanaiuoli* show that the wool guild masters had previously convened in San Domenico.[32] Catherine's first confessor, the Dominican Tommaso dalla Fonte, was from her neighborhood and also from a Dodici family of *lanaiuoli* targeted in the reprisals after the Bruco unrest.

Catherine's Dominican connections were certainly responsible for the distinctly *popolo grasso* character of her following in Florence, where the prominent merchants and bankers of the Parte Guelfa made the Dominican church of Santa Maria Novella their spiritual home. As Franco Cardini has noted, Catherine's Florentine lay contacts were almost exclusively members of the upper classes, and especially of the Albizzi faction and propapal Parte Guelfa hierarchy.[33] These were men whom she probably met through her Dominican advisors during her trip to Florence in 1374, though her fame would certainly have preceded her in the ambit of the Dominican community. Among her Guelf followers were Carlo Strozzi; Niccolò Soderini; Piero Canigiani and his sons Ristoro, Barduccio, and Cristoforo; Stoldo di Bindo Altoviti; Lapo di Castiglionchio and his son, Buonaccorso di Lapo. These men were among the patricians

---

[30] While there exists no comprehensive study of the socioeconomic backgrounds and constituencies of the several mendicant orders in Siena, on the social clientele of the Florentine mendicants in the late thirteenth century, see Daniel R. Lesnick, *Preaching in Medieval Florence: The Social World of Franciscan and Dominican Spirituality* (1989).

[31] *Preaching Friars and the Civic Ethos: Siena, 1380–1480*, 203: "Caffarini's lurid descriptions of St. Catherine's ministrations to the ungrateful poor and diseased convey a strong sense of revulsion on the part of both writer and saint. Indeed, her charity is held to be the greater because of her repugnance for the work she undertakes amongst the indigent. . . . It is not, perhaps, surprising that for the Sienese Dominicans in particular, whose very convents with their artistic treasures added so much to the city's cultured wealth, poverty was a spiritual ideal which had little in common with the reality of lay mendicancy."

[32] Filippo-Luigi Polidori, ed., *Statuti Senesi scritti in volgare ne' secoli XIII e XIV e pubblicati secondo i testi del R. Archivio di Stato in Siena*, (1863), 1: 177.

[33] Franco Cardini, "Caterina da Siena, la repubblica di Firenze e la lega antipontificia," 309–12.

most closely associated with Florence's propapal foreign policy, and among those attacked and exiled when their political opponents gained the upper hand during the Ciompi uprising of 1378.[34] As will be seen more clearly in chapter 5, these connections had crucial implications for Catherine's diplomatic activity and position in Tuscan politics during the War of Eight Saints and brought her into ill-repute within Florence as a presumed agent of a hostile papacy.

One of Catherine's clerical supporters outside the Dominican order also gives a distinct political color to her network and illustrates clearly the interrelation between piety and politics during this period. The English Augustinian hermit William Flete, who resided in the hermitage at Lecceto (a short distance from Siena), was prominent in Catherine's clerical circle, and as a religious of a distinctly "spiritual" bent, no doubt contributed significantly to shaping the reformist agenda of Catherine and her followers. A meeting between Catherine and Flete in 1376 is documented, although she must have known of him from a much earlier date, and there is little doubt that Catherine's early Dominican advisors were in touch with William and the other hermits at Lecceto before 1374.[35] Flete became an important participant in Catherine's circle and an active defender of her during her lifetime, and it was to him that Catherine entrusted leadership of her *famiglia* after her death.

Flete's perspective on the War of Eight Saints and Catherine's activities during it is clear in his writings about her after Catherine's death: "She fought single-handed against the heretics of Florence and strove to extinguish their heresy as much as she could."[36] And he bewailed the lack of support she received from the Sienese during this time, despite the fact that it was only through her prayers that the city was saved from a deserved punishment for its sins—presumably a reference to the Sienese alliance with Florence against the church.[37] Moreover, William Flete was

---

[34] Ibid., 324. The one possible exception to this observation among her regular correspondents—the Florentine tailor Francesco di Pippino and his wife—actually proves the rule, since it is clear from remarks within Catherine's letters to these two that the couple were intimate with members of the Parte Guelfa elite.

[35] For general details of Flete's life and writings, see Hackett, *William Flete*. Flete by 1359 had migrated from England to the Augustinian hermitage of San Salvatore at Lecceto (about four miles from Siena), the center of the reform movement within the Augustinian order. Catherine's early Dominican advisors clearly knew Flete and held him in high regard. For an assessment (more than a little overstated) of Flete's influence on Catherine, see Grion, *Santa Caterina da Siena*, esp. 274–99. The author of the *Miracoli* states without equivocation that, at the time of his writing (October 1374), Catherine and William had not yet met, although they were known to each other: "Questi non vide mai la Caterina, nè ella lui ma ánno conoscimento l'uno dell'altro per istinto di Spirito Santo, in tanta che l'uno parla de' fatti dell'altro con solennità e con grande reverenzia, quale più puote" (*Miracoli*, p. 15).

[36] Hackett, *William Flete*, 205.

[37] Ibid., 205–6: "If the Lord had not through her guarded the city of Siena, in vain

known to the Sienese government not only as a holy man and religious reformer, but also as an advocate for the Dodici in their efforts to regain participation in the governing coalition under the Riformatori. From Lecceto he wrote at least two letters to the Sienese government when the Dodici were excluded from the governing coalition, urging that the Dodici be readmitted into power. Although one of these letters is lost, the one that survives (in an eighteenth-century copy) was written sometime after the Dodici were expelled from government, either immediately after the 1368 revolution or after the Revolt of the Bruco and the Salimbeni/Dodici coup attempt in 1371.[38] In this letter, Flete employed scriptural authority to call on the Signoria to come to peace with the Dodici despite opposition from within the ranks of the *popolo:*

> Let it be known to you that your predecessors ill-used those good men who are called the Dodici, and in consequence evils fell by chance upon your community; and unless you establish peace, charity, and concord with them and with all your neighbors and fellow citizens worse will happen, but not by chance, in accordance with divine judgment, for *every kingdom divided against itself will be laid waste.* . . . Follow Christ, who worked for peace. *Peace be with you; my peace I leave with you.* Do to all as a good conscience dictates; one who goes against conscience is building up for Gehenna. Do not follow the frenzy of the *popolo* nor their evil counsels, but rather the counsels of good men, otherwise you can easily go wrong. As far as it is possible for you, strive to save your souls, for *you will not escape the hands of God. It is a fearful thing to fall into the hands of the living God.* Seek the peace of the city, and the God of peace will be with you. Amen.[39]

---

would *its guardian have kept watch* (Ps 127:1)—indeed it may have deserved to go down to the depths of hell. . . . Ungrateful men of Siena, unmindful of her goodness! Most wretched grumblers, incredulous fools, slow of heart to believe in all that God worked through her; lukewarm sons of your mother, neglectful of her love and her teaching, you have become cold and are bound to the things of the world in your actions, thoughts and affections. As regards many she can say: *I am forgotten as one dead from the heart* (Ps 30:13). Let you all return to judgment, for *not one jot or one tittle shall pass from the law until all is fulfilled* (Mt 5:18), until all who grumble about her and disobey her receive their punishment. Remember, degenerate men of Siena, how you were saved by her merits; now and always let us cry to heaven, and by her intercession our God shall have mercy on us."

[38] The eighteenth-century copy of the letter is in Siena, Biblioteca Comunale B.IX.18, ff. 205r–v, and is transcribed by M. H. Laurent in "De litteris ineditis Fr. Willelmi de Fleete (cc. 1368–1380)," *Analecta Augustiniana* 18 (1942): 303–27. An English translation is given in Hackett, *William Flete,* 164–65. Laurent, "De litteris ineditis"(307), dated this letter to 1368–69. It seems to me more likely that the letter was addressed to the Riformatori after the Dodici were excluded in 1371, given that the Dodici did participate at various times in the governing coalition between 1368 and 1371.

[39] "Vobis innotescat quod predecessores vestri male tractabant istos bonos viros qui vocantur Duodecim, propterea evenerunt forte comunitati vestre mala; et nisi pacem, charitatem et concordiam cum eis et cum omnibus vicinis et civibus vestris habueritis, sine forte iuxta sentenciam divinam evenient peiora, quia *omne regnum in se ipsum divisum desolabitur.* . . . Sequami[ni] Christum, qui contulit ad pacem. *Pax vobis; pacem meam relinquo vobis* et faciatis

Flete thus intervened on behalf of a group whose manifest ambition was the overthrowing of the coalition government. By extolling the "counsels of good men" as opposed to the "frenzy of the *popolo*," he offered an apology for oligarchical government, and so embraced the cause of the avowed enemies of the *popolo minuto*. Indeed, by recommending the reintroduction of the Dodici, Flete endorsed as a solution to civic strife precisely the measure that would be later sought by the Salimbeni and their advocates in negotiations after the Salimbeni revolt of 1374, a solution that would in short order have toppled the regime of the Riformatori. In short, Flete's intervention in the interests of peace in Siena was no more apolitical than the "peacemaking" of Gerard du Puy and the other papal governors as the conflict between Florence and the papacy intensified. As I will describe in chapter 4, while Flete in his letters was urging the Riformatori to readmit the Dodici to power, he had clear contacts with at least one Dodici insurgent—Nanni di ser Vanni Savini—who was working with the Salimbeni to seize power by force. Indeed, given his relations with Catherine and her spiritual *famiglia* as well as his sympathies and connections to the Dodici, Flete might be the answer to one of the most important of the unanswered questions regarding the Sienese dimension of Catherine's career: how did she come into contact with the Salimbeni? Given his political sympathies and his position as spiritual advisor to Nanni di ser Vanni, a notorious Salimbeni ally or client, Flete seems to have been perfectly placed to provide this connection and is the likeliest candidate among Catherine's contacts for having introduced her to the Salimbeni.

The political complexion of her network before 1374 was confirmed when, after the Dominican chapter, Raymond of Capua was assigned as Catherine's spiritual director. When Raymond met Catherine, he was a prominent and learned friar who had already undoubtedly acquired the reputation he held later as an ecclesiastical statesman. He was born into a socially prestigious family of jurists in the kingdom of Naples (tied politically to the papacy), the "delle Vigne." His father was a trusted advisor to King Robert of Naples (predecessor to Giovanna I), his brother Antonello was *miles camerarius* to King Ladislao (1386–1414) and legate to Innocent VII (1404–05), and his brother Nicola was royal chamberlain and *capitano* of Piperno.[40] A third brother, Luigi, fought in the army of

omnibus secundum bonam conscientiam; qui facit contra conscientiam, edificat ad gehennam. Non sequamini furorem populi nec mala consilia eorum, sed potius consilia bonorum virorum, aliter faciliter potestis deviare. Quantum est vobis possibile, nitamini salvare animas vestras, quia non effugiatis manus Dei. *Orrendum est incidere in manus Dei viventis,* queriteque pacem civitatis, et Deus pacis erit vobiscum. Amen" (Laurent, "De litteris ineditis," 308–9).
[40] For Raymond's genealogy, see H. M. Cormier, ed., *B. Raymundi Capuani XXIII Mag. Gen. O.P. Opuscula et Litterae* (1899), 143.

Giovanna I in the papal assault against Viterbo in 1376, when he was captured by pro-Florentine forces.[41] Raymond himself, before entering the Dominicans, studied law at Bologna, an education that probably helped prepare him for career as an ecclesiastical diplomat. Raymond's clerical career before meeting Catherine shows offices of increasing prestige, both within his order and the church at large.[42] His appointment as spiritual director to Catherine occurred some time probably after 1 August 1374, by which time Raymond was acting as lector at San Domenico in Siena and awarded a prominence within the friary just below that of the prior.[43]

The question of why Raymond was chosen as Catherine's director—indeed, why it was necessary to look for direction for her outside the Sienese Dominican community—is too rarely raised in the Catherinian historiography. Certainly, one reason for the appointment might have been the preparation given by Raymond's earlier position as pastor to the Dominican women's convent in Montepulciano, from which he perhaps had gained experience in the spiritual direction of religious women. But it is wrong to assume that Raymond was attached to Catherine purely in order to nurture her spiritual gifts. This assignment was clearly part of a plan to employ Catherine in larger ecclesiastical programs, as can be seen from a papal letter of 17 August 1376 responding affirmatively to Raymond's petition for papal confirmation of his role as Catherine's advisor. In his petition Raymond had noted that Elias, master general of the Dominicans, had placed him in charge of Catherine "for the saving of souls, the Crusade, and other business of the Holy Roman Church."[44] The

---

[41]   Catherine intervened on Luigi's behalf by writing to Pietro Tolomei, a powerful force within the Sienese government and a notable ally of the leaders of the Italian league, as described in chapter 5.

[42]   On Raymond's career, see A. W. Van Ree, "Raymond de Capoue: Éléments biographiques," *Archivum Fratrum Praedicatorum* 33 (1963): 159–241. Raymond was ordained a priest in around 1355, becoming *lector* in friaries in Bologna and then Rome. From 1363 to 1366 he was rector of the Dominican women's convent in Montepulciano, during which time he wrote a *Vita* of the local saint, Agnese da Montepulciano (see *LM*, ns. 199, 281, 325). During the period of Urban V's abortive return of the papal court to Rome (1367–70), Raymond served as prior of the Dominican mother house in Rome, Santa Maria sopra Minerva (see *LM*, n. 422). He is known to have been in residence in Florence at Santa Maria Novella by August 1373, on which date he witnessed a document along with the other friars of the monastery. Raymond's name appears immediately after the names of the prior and subprior and before 28 others, suggesting that he was a prominent member of the community. (On the meaning of the placement of his signature, see the differing interpretations of Fawtier, *Sainte Catherine de Sienne*, 1: 162, and Van Ree, "Raymond de Capoue," 167n.

[43]   Raymond's name appears on a document of this date (ASS, *Diplomatico, Patrimonio Dei Resti, San Domenico,* 1 August 1374), on which his name is given immediately after that of the prior. (Van Ree, "Raymond de Capoue," states [p. 168n], erroneously, that Raymond is listed after the prior and subprior.)

[44]   " . . . circa animarum salutem et ultramarini passagii et alia sancte Romane ecclesie negocia occupabat" (Arch. Vat., Reg Vat. 288, f. 159r–v; in Laurent, ed., *Documenti*, n. 38).

language of this letter makes it reasonable to assume that Raymond's assignment to Catherine was made in anticipation of precisely the sorts of missions they would undertake together, particularly in Pisa and Lucca 1375–76, where they sought support for the Crusade and strove to keep those two communes out of the Florentine league. And the course of Raymond's career after his two years as Catherine's director only increases the sense that his assignment to Catherine had involved political and diplomatic goals. In October 1377, Raymond left Catherine in order to consult with leaders of the Florentine Guelfs and advise Pope Gregory XI in Rome concerning negotiations with Florence.[45] Thereafter he served once again as prior of Santa Maria sopra Minerva and as a chief ambassador for Urban VI during the schism (sent, for instance, to obtain the support of the king of France). Raymond received increasingly greater responsibility within the Urbanist party of the Dominicans, culminating in his appointment as master general of the Roman Obedience in May 1380, shortly after Catherine's death. Perhaps Raymond's assignment to Catherine interrupted his steady progress toward a position as a prominent ecclesiastical statesman and leader, a progress that resumed suddenly in October 1377. But it makes much more sense to view his time with Catherine as consistent with the kind of work for which the Dominican authorities and the popes thought Raymond suited. In light of the evidence of the papal letter cited above—not to mention the clear indications of Catherine's participation in papal diplomatic efforts during the War of Eight Saints, as below—Catherine's association with Raymond takes on a much more obviously political complexion than is possible to recognize when Catherine and her spiritual gifts are made the undisputed center of the story.

It is clear that Catherine did not emerge into the public eye in 1374 as a solitary figure. Rather, she entered public affairs at the instigation of high church leaders and with an already established network of politically aware and active clerical supporters/promoters. This social and political context set the terms for Catherine's movement from a local to an Italian, and eventually a European, stage. After the visit from Alfonso da Vadaterra, Catherine's attendance at the Dominican chapter at Florence, and her acquisition of Raymond of Capua as confessor, Catherine's celebrity moved rapidly onto a broader stage just as the conflict between Florence and the papacy was nearing the opening of outright hostilities. And while her new role involved traveling to hot spots in the conflict, Catherine's more far-flung and more characteristic interventions came through her letters, which at this point took on a defining importance in her career.

---

[45]  *LM*, par. 422.

## Epistolarity and Catherine's Public Career

Catherine's letters are marked by a strikingly regular structure, one that seems to have developed very early in her letter-writing career. She begins by identifying herself according to an almost unvarying formula, "I Catherine, servant and slave of Jesus Christ." She then announces her desire for her correspondent's spiritual welfare, according to an image or theme which introduces the initial and sometimes the main concern of the letter. For example, a letter to Raymond of Capua (102), after an invocation, begins, "I Catherine, servant and slave of the servants of Jesus Christ, write to you in his precious blood, with the desire to see you a true husband of the truth, and a follower and lover of that same truth." Catherine then amplifies the initial theme in a variety of ways, including theological excursus, mystic apostrophe, and practical advice or admonition. Typically, Catherine does not develop images in a logical or linear way, but rather invokes them in patterns or constellations around a theme as her ideas become more complex. Catherine usually ends the main body of the letter with a simple, "I won't say more." A final protocol usually ends with "remain in the holy and sweet love of God," followed by the invocation "Sweet Jesus, Jesus love." In letters to popes and other significant ecclesiastical and secular dignitaries, she usually adds before the final part of the protocol an expression of humility, for example, "pardon me for my great presumption." In some of the letters—those that survive in the original and those that have been preserved from early collections made by her followers for their personal use—there follows a short, more personal postscript with news and other practical communication.[46]

Catherine's letters are not intellectually innovative, but represent her own highly personal, immediate, and energetic point of view on traditional teachings. Her letters are full of generous affection for her correspondents and emphasize filial relationships: she is *mamma* to her spiritual children and famously addresses Gregory XI and Urban VI as *babbo* (daddy). The paramount theme of Catherine's letters (as well as her *Libro*) is love. She returns continually to the joy and consolation of perfect love of God, and the love of neighbor, which is an expression of love of God. For Catherine, the chief vice and source of all vices is self-love, which clouds the intellect and caused people to mistake truth for lies, and lies for truth. As a corrective to self-love, she repeatedly and energetically exhorts her correspondents to seek proper self-knowledge, at the basis of which is the recognition

---

[46] These postscripts seem to have been regular features of Catherine's letters, but were excised in the manuscripts intended for wider dissemination, probably because they were irrelevant to the purpose of spiritual edification for which those collections were made (Fawtier, *Sainte Catherine de Sienne*, 2: 122; Noffke, *Letters of Catherine of Siena*, 1: xxiv–xxv).

of a fundamental dependence on God, and of the need for a fundamental reorientation of one's love to God. So Catherine diagnoses all manner of social and political ills as deriving from self-love and lack of self-knowledge—for instance, leading Italian citizens to rebel against the papacy during the War of Eight Saints, and bishops to support the Avignonese "antipope" after the schism of 1380. Self-love is also to blame for the corruption of the prelacy and clergy, and is at the root of Gregory XI's ineffectuality in correcting abuses and his vacillations over returning the papal Curia from Avignon to Rome—two failings for which Catherine frequently and energetically chided the pope.

But it is a mistake to read Catherine's letters as abstract treatments of spiritual topics, as if the historical situations that prompted Catherine's letters were merely incidental, and the epistolary form as a mere container for mystic communication. Ignoring the settings of Catherine's letters, and the implications for her career of letter writing as a cultural practice, is to miss on several levels some of the most important and innovative features of her life. First of all, in a culture in which, as Dyan Elliot has concluded, a medieval "female mystic's authenticity was proportionate to her degree of aversion to publicity in general and to the writing process in particular," Catherine's career was marked by a constant and conspicuous engagement in writing—to a degree unprecedented among female religious figures in Italy and rarely matched by female religious figures in Europe.[47] For models, Catherine might have looked to Angela da Foligno, and even more to Birgitta of Sweden, as visionary or saintly women identified with their texts; as mentioned, Catherine was recruited as a second Birgitta by churchmen who must have seen her as the inheritor of a tradition of visionary women in Italy and Europe. But Catherine's letters in their form, content, and style were a very different sort of literature than Birgitta's *Revelations*. Catherine's letters show almost no interest at all in eschatological claims or predictions, and show little if any influence of Joachimite and other traditions of prophetic literature current in Italian culture.[48] Above all, Catherine defied generic expectations of female sanctity and spiritual writing by adopting the mundane and domestic genre of the personal letter for her communications. The Italian critical tradition

[47] Dyan Elliot, "*Dominae* or *Dominatae?* Female Mysticism and the Trauma of Textuality," in Constance M. Rousseau and Joel T. Rosenthal, eds., *Women, Marriage, and Family in Medieval Christendom: Essays in Memory of Michael M. Sheehan, C.S.B.* (1998), 47–77, esp. 49.

[48] Marjorie Reeves was certainly wrong to place Catherine alongside Birgitta in the tradition of Joachimite prophecy (*The Influence of Prophecy in the Later Middle Ages: A Study of Joachimism,* [1969], 422). On Catherine's lack of interest in eschatological and prophetic claims, see Eugenio Dupré Theseider, "L'attesa escatologica durante il periodo avignonese," in *L'attesa dell'età nuova nella spiritualità della fine del Medioevo, 16–19 ottobre 1960* (1962), 119; and Roberto Rusconi, *L'attesa della fine: Crisi della società, profezia ad Apocalisse in Italia al tempo del grande scisma d'Occidente (1378–1417)* (1979), 27–34.

has sought to categorize Catherine's writing in a variety of ways, but Catherine's letters are essentially heterogeneous, not easily categorized. For instance, she mixes elements of high formality (for example, the superpapal self-identification as "servant and slave of the servants of Jesus Christ") with a chatty style typical of a personal letter (for instance, the informal and simple closing, "I won't say more," a typical element of Tuscan secular and mercantile letters).[49] The tone of Catherine's letters is not popular or colloquial, but frequently strikes a lofty and prophetic register; nevertheless, consistent with the style of the personal letter, her language is her own Sienese vernacular, immediate and familiar, a "low" form of language.[50] Most religious prose in Italian consisted in translations from Latin, or imitations and popularization of Latin genres and forms. But Catherine produced a completely novel body of writings through her own *volgare* and by way of a vernacular genre, the personal letter.

However unusual Catherine's letter writing was, she chose as her principle form of public communication a genre that was particularly appropriate for experimentation. Notwithstanding scholarly emphasis on the *ars dictaminis* and its culture of imitation and formal technique, the letter in the Middle Ages was in fact a relatively open genre, without strict rules and formal requirements. The epistolary genre was defined only by the basic features of salutation and subscription, and by the fact that it represented speech to someone not present, even if the person was imaginary or dead—as in Petrarch's letters to Cicero—or if the intended audience was someone other than the addressee.[51] Catherine was unique as a virtuoso of the vernacular letter (though she did have the model of her near-contemporary, the Sienese founder of the Gesuati, Giovanni Colombini), but she wrote at a time marked by experiments with the Latin letter as a literary form, most famously by Petrarch and Coluccio Salutati but also by a host of other writers in the orbit of burgeoning humanistic culture, including authors close to Catherine such as Giovanni dalle Celle, an intimate of Luigi Marsili and the Florentine Christian humanists of Santo Spirito. Catherine took advantage of the fluidity of the epistolary form, its lack of formal constraints and institutionalized modes of discourse—a feature even more true of the vernacular letter than of the Latin letter—to confront her correspondent in her own words with her inspired take

---

49 Scott, "'*Io Caterina*,'" 96.

50 Getto, "Intuizione e espressione in Caterina da Siena," 137–38.

51 A point emphasized by Giles Constable in his definitive general treatment of medieval letter-writing, *Letters and Letter-Collections* (1976). See also Alain Boureau, "The Letter-Writing Norm, a Mediaeval Invention," in Roger Chartier, ed. *Correspondence: Models of Letter-Writing from the Middle Ages to the Nineteenth Century*, trans. Christopher Woodall (1997), 24–58: "The very hallmark of distinguished letter-writing is the open contempt that is displayed for rules that are taught but that nobody wants to or can apply" (24).

on the crisis of the church and the world, carrying revelation and prophetic speech into worldly affairs. Catherine's mixing of the eternal and the temporal, a heterogeneity that has complicated the hagiographic as well as scholarly image of Catherine as a writer, is an example of Catherine's virtuosity in manipulating the transgressive potential of the letter as a literary form, what made the letter an ideal vehicle for Catherine to carry prophecy into politics.[52]

In addition, while Catherine was famous (and notorious) for crossing boundaries—her mixing of the lay and religious lives, her travels—her letters are an expression of an even more ambitious mobility. Catherine had audiences with Gregory XI in Avignon and Urban VI in Rome, but it was only by letter that she was able to address the queen of Naples; Barnabò Visconti; the *signori* of Florence, Lucca, and Pisa; the king of France; the count of Anjou; and many others. This is not to say that Catherine's letters were merely substitutes for more potent face-to-face encounters. While Karen Scott has pointed out that Catherine sometimes in her letters declared a preference for direct speech over epistolary communication, wishing she could speak in person to her correspondent rather than write letters, this stated preference for direct speech is in fact a standard trope of letter writing. In these statements Catherine is merely invoking the letter's definition: all letters are based rhetorically on the premise that they serve as substitutes for direct speech the correspondents cannot share because they are not together in the same place.[53]

Moreover, while epistolary rhetoric might imply that the letter is a weak substitute for speech, letter writers of all eras know that epistolary discourse sometimes allows for a more intimate and direct manner of communication than is possible through a face-to-face encounter. An underlying assumption in the rhetoric of medieval letters was the friendship between the writer and the addressee (whether any friendship actually existed), a friendship that bypassed the strictures of social class and formal relations that would have dominated personal encounters between people in the Middle Ages—what Alain Boureau refers to as letter writing's "illusion of unbounded communication: the humblest citizen may dispatch a missive to the highest reaches of the political, social or cultural hierarchy."[54] The assumption of friendship is basic to all Catherine's

<hr />

[52] On the mixing of the eternal and temporal in letters, see Boureau, "The Letter-Writing Norm, a Mediaeval Invention," 28.

[53] Thus the letter was defined in the Middle Ages as "sermo absentium quasi inter presentes," words which make present to each other those who are apart (Constable, *Letters and Letter-Collections*, 13).

[54] Boureau, "The Letter-Writing Norm," 24. On *amicitia* as the basis of the epistolary contract, see Constable, *Letters and Letter-Collections*, 15–16; Struever, *Theory as Practice*, 6; and Martin Camargo, "Where's the Brief? The *Ars Dictaminis* and Reading/Writing between the

letters, even those to people with whom she was in stark disagreement, included in her standard declaration of her desire for her correspondent's spiritual good ("I Catherine . . . write to you in the precious blood of Christ, with the desire to see you . . ."). And the assumption of friendship also lies behind the way in which Catherine engaged even some of her more prominent and less actually intimate contacts through filial language, for example, by addressing John Hawkwood and his mercenary soldiers as "my brothers in Christ" (letter 140/XXX) and the queen of Naples, Giovanna d'Anjou, as "mother and sister in Christ" (letter 138/XLI). Through her own solicitude and by evoking an affectionate spiritual filiation with her correspondent, Catherine's letters addressed her correspondents in ways in which she could never have done in face-to-face speech. For all her complaints to Gregory XI about not being able to obtain personal audiences with him, it is hard to imaging that Catherine ever addressed Gregory XI and Urban VI in person as she did in her letters—as *babbo* (daddy).

The fact that Catherine wrote to popes, kings, cardinals, and civic *signori,* and the intimacy with which she addressed them, functioned as an important comment on her own authority much more than as a description of her actual relationship with such prominent figures. Catherine's letters expressed the scope and prestige of the space—indeed, constructed the space—within which Catherine's saintly authority was meant to be recognized. Catherine's correspondence expressed a network of intimate contacts among a wide variety of prominent secular and ecclesiastical leaders, an effect of the apparent ability of the letter to travel anywhere and address anyone directly and intimately, crossing not only geographical boundaries but barriers of gender and class as well as formal constraint. Catherine took advantage of the opportunity in epistolary discourse for informality and direct appeals to create a community, using the letter's assumption of a relationship of friendship to create a space for her own voice beyond the bounds of existing institutions—ecclesiastical, civic, academic—in which she had no standing.[55]

This last effect of letter writing worked for Catherine regardless of whether her correspondent in any particular case was moved by her letters or even received her letters, because of the effect Catherine's letters might have had on people other than the putative addressees of individual letters. The way in which letters functioned to create and foster Catherine's network of followers and supporters is an essentially important feature of letter writing in her saintly career. Whereas direct speech

---

Lines," *Disputatio* 1 (1996): 1–17.

[55]  I am indebted here to Nancy S. Struever's discussion of Petrarchan epistolary strategy in *Theory as Practice,* chap. 1, "Petrarchan Ethics: Inventing a Practice."

is restricted to the immediate audience and bound to a particular moment, in the Middle Ages even personal letters were understood to be public documents, let loose to a larger, more indeterminate audience.[56] In fact, Catherine's letters are often best understood as communications for an audience other than their putative addressees. We have no way of knowing whether any particular letter was even sent to its addressee, let alone whether it was received, read, and taken to heart. It is clear in a few of Catherine's letters that her correspondent initiated contact to seek Catherine's insight or intercession, but it is almost certain that some, and perhaps many, of her letters to prominent secular and ecclesiastical rulers never made it past the filter of court secretaries (assuming they were delivered at all).[57] This is perhaps especially true of the letters Catherine wrote in the last two years of her life, after the outbreak of the schism, to prominent supporters of the French observance like Giovanna of Naples and Pietro Cardinale di Luna, opponents of Catherine who would have had no interest in encouraging her interventions. But Catherine's messages to these and other correspondents were not meant to be private. In some cases this was acknowledged by Catherine, for instance, in the several cases in which she addressed her entire *famiglia* in a letter to one particular follower, and when she addressed to some high ecclesiastical official a message explicitly intended to be passed on to the pope (for instance, her letters to Nicola da Osimo in 1375 and 1377, discussed in chapter 5). But even where she does not address a larger audience directly, Catherine's letters, as letters, were simultaneously private and public documents, addressed to individuals through the rhetoric of intimacy, but intended to be read also by others. Whether the letters ever reached their putative addressees, they did circulate among Catherine's followers and their associates, and throughout a network of interested readers in Tuscany and beyond. Catherine's followers sent copies of her letters to each other, and Catherine's scribes, some of whom (like Cristofano di Gano Guidini and Barduccio Canigiani) were professional notaries, at some point evidently began keep a register of copies of her letters, from which other copies were made which circulated among her network of followers, to be copied again as desired by new readers; the first manuscript collections of her letters were generated out of the exchange of letters and copies among Catherine's followers.

Catherine's letters, addressed to particular individuals and circulating among a larger group of interested readers, functioned within a larger

[56] Constable, *Letters and Letter-Collections*, 11.
[57] It is worth recalling that in the case of Gregory XI and a number of Catherine's more prominent addressees, Catherine's letters required the additional help of a translator in order for her words to reach their intended recipients.

epistolary culture in which the exchange of letters created webs of influence and affiliation that overrode religious and civic particularism. Catherine's network intersected, for example, with a larger network of reform-minded clerics to whom Catherine would refer as "the servants of God," attributing to them an organic unity and clear identity which they did not in fact have, except through their exchange of letters. (A demonstration of the strictly "virtual" nature of this community came when Catherine, after the creation of the schism of 1378, sought unsuccessfully to gather Giovanni dalle Celle, William Flete, and other "servants of God" in Rome in support of Urban VI: William Flete, in particular, was unwilling to leave his hermitage.) While Petrarch and his network might be the most prominent model for such epistolary association, Catherine would have had the more immediate model of the letters of Giovanni Colombini and Giovanni dalle Celle. Giovanni dalle Celle's letters to both supporters and detractors of Catherine, for example, demonstrate dramatically the effect of letters in the Catherinian network, revealing his own participation in epistolary exchange with other Caterinati and the larger epistolary conversation going on around Catherine during her career.[58] For example, Giovanni wrote in 1376 to the English Augustinian reformer William Flete, who from his hermitage outside of Siena had become an intimate of Catherine some years earlier, denying that a certain letter of Giovanni's that had come to the attention of Flete was critical of Catherine.[59] Giovanni noted the evidence of his admiration for Catherine in letters he had written to her critics—letters which he assumed were already in Flete's possession—and declared himself grateful for the instruction about Catherine's virtues that he gained from reading Flete's letters about her. Other letters written by Giovanni dalle Celle acknowledged receipt of one of Catherine's letters and several of Flete's, and make it clear that Flete was keeping him abreast of Catherine's movements.[60] When Catherine's supporters communicated their views on her by letter, explaining her identity in scriptural and theological terms and glossing the meaning of their experience with her, their letters and the sentiments they contained circulated throughout the Catherinian network and beyond, building up her reputation and establishing the terms of her authority in a way that face-to-face conversation alone could not have done. Catherine's followers' letters about her, just like Catherine's own letters, were not merely supplements or stand-ins for face-to-face conversation. Catherine's network was itself a creation of the circulation

---

[58] Giovanni dalle Celle's letters survive, in turn, because they too were valued, copied, and shared among reform-minded religious.

[59] This was the letter Giovanni dalle Celle wrote to the nun Domitilla, cited in chapter 1, arguing against her following Catherine's example in planning a pilgrimage to the Holy Land.

[60] Giovanni dalle Celle, Luigi Marsile, *Lettere* 2: 361.

of letters, and this epistolary network was a key stage in the production of Catherine's sanctity, setting the terms of her authority and spreading her reputation.

While Catherine's letter writing has almost never been considered alongside the epistolary experiments of her contemporaries like Petrarch and Salutati, it is nevertheless important to note that Catherine wrote from within a culture marked by optimism about the potential of letters to imitate speech, but in a more direct and rhetorically more potent form.[61] In fact, Catherine's public letter-writing campaign began at almost precisely the time that Coluccio Salutati was breaking with Florentine chancery tradition by entrusting to letters the kinds of emotional rhetorical appeals on behalf of Florentine state policy that had previously been conveyed only in person by ambassadors.[62] The War of the Eight Saints was a conflict fought mostly through propaganda, and Salutati used the contest with the papacy as an occasion to articulate a republican (and distinctly Florentine) political identity for Italy, anticipating by a decade the development of the "civic humanism" famously credited by Hans Baron to the Florentine response to conflict with Milan in the 1390s. As tensions increased between the papacy and Florence, Salutati wrote to independent cities and cities subject to the papacy, invoking Republican Rome as a vision of Italian political independence (and republican Florence as the special heir to the Roman tradition), and calling on the cities to unite as Italians against the Limousin governors of the Papal States.[63] While Salutati and Catherine are hardly ever treated as inhabiting the same cultural or historical space, the connection between them was more substantial than a mere coincidence of timing. Throughout the War of Eight Saints, Catherine was, indirectly at least, Salutati's interlocutor, advancing a Christian and prophetic perspective on political affairs in response to the statements of a secular, civic identity on the part of Florence and other Italians. If Salutati's letters represented the voice of Florence, Catherine's were the voice of the church, and her ability to enter into this war of words by letter was the most important effect of Catherine's embrace of the epistolary form.

---

[61] Petrarch explicitly acknowledged this virtue of letters, praising the letter as a literary form of conversation, one that could emulate live speech (Struever, *Theory as Practice*, 8).

[62] Salutati became chancellor of Florence in April 1375. See Ronald G. Witt, *In the Footsteps of the Ancients: The Origins of Humanism from Lovato to Bruni* (2000), 310.

[63] For Salutati's *missive* during the conflict with the papacy, see Ronald G. Witt, *Coluccio Salutati and His Public Letters* (1976), and Daniela de Rosa, *Coluccio Salutati: Il cancelliere e il pensatore politico* (1980). On the War of Eight Saints and Salutati's role more generally, see Witt, *In the Footsteps of the Ancients*, 301–15; and idem, *Hercules at the Crossroads: The Life, Works, and Thought of Coluccio Salutati* (1983), 126–32.

On the other hand, the political meaning in Catherine's letters will not be noticed if the letters are read as spiritual treatises, abstracted from the particular circumstances in which she composed them. Indeed, Catherine's comments on worldly affairs appear to bypass political and other complications to go to the root spiritual issue, and she has accordingly usually been read as either uninterested in politics or naive about worldly affairs. She addressed her main worldly or institutional causes—reform of the church, the return of the papacy to Rome, the Crusade, social peace—in highly traditional terms, calling for a social and political order based on the love of God and neighbor, a true Christian society. But while Catherine's letters emphasized the spiritual conditions of players in the various crises affecting Italy and the church during her public career, they were not therefore apolitical or (for the most part) politically naive. Catherine clearly and consciously marshaled her rhetorical gifts and spiritual renown on behalf of the papacy in its battles against Florence and other Italian city-states during the War of Eight Saints, though she could also be harshly critical of the pope and other church leaders when she perceived that they did not live up to their calling. In this context, spiritual exhortations toward proper self-knowledge addressed to players in Italian civic and ecclesiastical politics contained highly charged political meaning.

## Catherine's Campaign Begins

The political meaning in Catherine's spiritual exhortations can be seen dramatically in several of the earliest letters she wrote following her trip to Florence. Catherine's letters as well as her movements at this time show an immediate sensitivity to the main points of political influence and tension during the run-up to the War of Eight Saints. After helping to nurse victims of an outbreak of plague in late 1374 and early 1375, Catherine entered into one of the most sensitive diplomatic theaters in the intensifying dispute between the papacy and the Tuscan city-states by traveling to Pisa in early 1375 with Raymond of Capua and others of her *famiglia*. The diplomacy of both Florence and the papacy was focused at this time on swaying Pisa and nearby Lucca to their sides. To use the language of the papal bull of 1376 cited above, it is obvious that the "business of the Church" Catherine and Raymond were engaged in at this time had everything to do with the sensitive political position of these crucial port cities.[64] They spent most of 1375 in Pisa, residing at the house of a

[64] On the diplomacy directed at Pisa and Lucca at this time, see Trexler, *The Spiritual Power* (1974), 73–78.

notable citizen, Gherardo Buonconti. As will be seen, Catherine's letters from Pisa reveal an increasingly intense preoccupation with the dispute and its threat to church unity, and develop what was to become a familiar theme in her letters to secular and clerical leaders: a three-pronged program for peace in Italy and the church, consisting of the interdependent goals of Crusade, return of the pope to Rome, and ecclesiastical reform. In addressing these themes Catherine was adhering closely to Gregory XI's main political objectives, as noted above. As in papal policy, the Crusade and the return of the pope to Rome were for Catherine linked inextricably to Italian peace, and it thus represents a misunderstanding to assert, as Gardner does, that Catherine and Raymond went to Pisa not to keep Pisa and Lucca out of the Florentine league but to elicit support for the Crusade. This distinction is practically meaningless: there could be no Crusade—and no return of the pope—without peaceful consolidation of the papacy's political authority in Italy, and support of the Crusade involved an allegiance to the church that would preclude, theoretically at least, support for the growing movement against the church in central Italy. In this sense, Catherine's discussion of the Crusade in her letters was part of her participation in papal diplomacy during the War of Eight Saints, not something separate from it.[65]

A letter Catherine wrote in late 1374 shows an awareness of the political sensitivity of her trip to Pisa, and perhaps an awareness of the sensitivity of the larger ecclesiastical political scene within which her spiritual charism was being mobilized. Shortly after her return to Siena from Florence in autumn 1374, Catherine wrote to the Pisan ruler Piero Gambacorti, declining for the moment an invitation to visit Pisa. Catherine's reply makes it clear that Piero had invited her not only on his own behalf, but also at the bidding of the women of his household (including his daughter Tora, who subsequently entered a reformed Dominican community in conscious imitation of Catherine and was later beatified under the name "Chiara"). Catherine's reply addressed the spiritual motivations of this invitation, but in the context of the mission of Catherine and Raymond on behalf of the church it is very likely that Piero's interests included political goals. Indeed, the political implications surface in Catherine's letter, in which she announced that she was postponing her trip on account of bad

---

[65] On Catherine's involvement in the Crusade movement, see Franco Cardini, "L'idea di Crociata in Santa Caterina da Siena." Cardini gives a very useful chronological summary of Catherine's epistolary efforts on behalf of the Crusade, relating her letters to concrete political developments. See also Paul Rousset, "Sainte Catherine de Sienne et la problème de la croisade," *Revue suisse d'histoire* 25, no. 4 (1975): 499–513, and "L'idée de croisade chez sainte Catherine de Sienne et chez les théoriciens du XIVᵉ siècle," In *Atti del congresso internazionale di studi Cateriniani* (1981), 363–372. See also passing references to Catherine's Crusade letters in Rusconi, *L'attesa della fine*, 27–34.

health and because "right now I would be a source of scandal."[66] While it is possible that Catherine's trip to Florence had already raised eyebrows in Siena—that is, the fact of her traveling at all was scandalous—Catherine's concern about scandal likely also stemmed from the sensitivity of relations between Siena and Pisa at this time, and from Pisa's position in the politics of the church in Italy. Both Siena and Pisa were vying for control of the lands to the west of Siena, and disputes with Pisa over this territory were a regular feature of legislative and diplomatic records in this time. Moreover, the Sienese had reason to be suspicious of Pisan complicity with the agents of the church. Piero Gambacorti had been a conspicuous champion of the papal cause during the wars with the Visconti. And while Florence and Lucca had contributed generously to Sienese defenses against the Salimbeni uprising in October, Pisa had joined Gerard du Puy and Perugia in refusing the Sienese military aid.[67] As with other leaders with whom Catherine communicated during the War of Eight Saints—the Florentine Parte Guelfa elite, for example—Piero's piety cannot be entirely disentangled from the issue of his political identity as a supporter of the papacy. Just as the local political fortunes of the Florentine Guelfs were linked to the state of Florence's relations with the papacy, Piero's signorial control of Pisa also depended to some degree on his support from the Pisan *popolo grasso* and foreign policy ties to the church in Italy.

After traveling to Pisa, and before 25 June 1375, Catherine sent Raymond of Capua to the English soldier of fortune John Hawkwood (known in Italian by various names, including "Giovanni Acuto") to exhort him and his army to volunteer for the Crusade which had recently been proclaimed by Gregory XI.[68] Hawkwood and his men were one of several mercenary troops engaged by both sides in the wars between the papacy and the Visconti; he had most recently fought on the papal side. But in 1375 the pope was forced to settle with Barnabò Visconti, mostly because the Florentines were not willing to contribute the funds the papal army required to continue the war. The peace treaty between the papacy and Barnabò of 6 June

[66] Letter 149/XXII: "Ricevetti una vostra lettara, la quale viddi con affettuoso amore, unde io conosco che non mia virtù nè mia bontà—però che so' piena di peccato e di miseria—ma solo l'amore e la bontà vostra e di coteste sante donne vi mosse umilemente a scrivare a me, pregandomi ch'io debba venire costà. Per la qual cosa io volontariamente verrei adempire el desiderio vostro e loro; ma per ora io mi scuso, ché la impossibilità del corpo mio non mi lassa, e anco vego che per ora io sarei materia di scandalo."

[67] Neri di Donato, 656: "Sanesi richiesero l'abate di Perogia e li Pisani e tutti altri collegati: tutti se ne fe'ro beffe e non mandaro nulla." The league referred to here is the league of Tuscan communes with Urban V and renewed with Gregory XI in 1371 against Barnabò Visconti. For a more general discussion of Piero Gambacorti's relations with Siena and other cities, see Pietro Silva, "Il governo di Piero Gambacorti in Pisa e le sue relazioni col resto della Toscana e coi Visconti," *Bullettino Senese di Storia Patria* 19 (1912): 357–60.

[68] On Hawkwood, see most recently William Caferro, *Mercenary Companies and the Decline of Siena* (1998).

1375 created considerable anxiety in Florence and other Tuscan cities. Not only did this treaty raise the specter of an alliance between the church and Milan against the Tuscan cities, but it let loose Hawkwood's army with no profitable occupation other than ravaging the countryside and threatening the cities themselves. Indeed, news of the peace settlement was taken by the Florentines as confirmation of rumors that the leaders of the Papal States were planning to raise an army to attack Florence and other Tuscan cities, and the peace between the pope and Barnabò Visconti was a mere ruse, with the real object being the subjugation of Tuscany. This anxiety was shared by the Sienese.[69] The air of crisis that the release of the mercenaries engendered was heightened by other difficulties at this time: the cities were just recovering from the plague that had broken out in the second half of 1374, and all of Tuscany was suffering a severe famine that had begun the previous fall, in the midst of which the papal governor of Bologna, Cardinal Guillaume Noellet, refused to authorize the export to Florence of crucial grain stores. At this moment (and after the other nefarious plots of which the papal governors were suspected), the Sienese received a letter from Cardinal Noellet on 13 June, announcing officially the pact between the papacy and the Visconti, and warning the commune that this left the army of Hawkwood unoccupied, "nor do we know in what direction they might go, for they are unbridled by God and evilly disposed."[70] It is, in fact, unlikely that the release of Hawkwood was part of a plot by the pope or by the governors of the Papal States, but it is little wonder that the Sienese, like the Florentines and others, feared the worst.

It is also not surprising that, in this context, Florentine and Sienese officials found Raymond's presence at Hawkwood's camp worthy of notice. On 27 June the Sienese ambassadors to Florence reported, in a letter otherwise devoted to speculation concerning the planned movements of Hawkwood's troops, that a Florentine had encountered Raymond on his way to Hawkwood with two other men, one of whom was "a man of a bad sort and much involved in plots"; when asked their business, Raymond and the others replied that they were traveling "on the orders of Caterina *santa* of Siena, to speak on her behalf to Messer Giovanni about his going on the Crusade." The Florentine informant suspected that this was a trick.[71] In her letter, Catherine urged Hawkwood and his men to sanctify their penchant for warfare by fighting the infidels instead of fomenting discord and violence among Christians:

> It has been the desire of my soul that you change your ways and that you take up the salary and the cross of Christ crucified, you and all your followers and

[69]   Neri di Donato, 658.
[70]   ASS, *Concistoro* 1786, n. 54.
[71]   Ibid., n. 83.

companies. Then you will be one of Christ's companies, going to fight all the infidels who have possession of our holy place, where gentle first truth lived and endured his sufferings and death for us. Thus I beseech you gently in Christ Jesus that which God has decreed, and also the holy father, that you go against the infidels, and you who delight so much in war and fighting, do not make war any longer against Christians, because in this you offend God, but go against them. What a great cruelty it is that we, who are Christians, members bound together in the body of the holy Church, should be persecuting one another.[72]

Leaving aside, for the moment, discussion of Catherine's use of the image of the church as a unified body, it is important to note that Catherine here was representing an explicit policy objective of the pope. Gregory XI, like his predecessors, saw the mercenary companies as a likely source for an army for a general Crusade, and also saw the Crusade as a possible solution for the political and social disruption caused by the mercenary companies in Italy and France.[73] Indeed, at this time Gregory was optimistic that religious disturbances in the Muslim East, as well as a possible ending of the Hundred Years War, would make it possible for a general Crusade to the East to succeed with the participation of the mercenary companies.[74] Thus this letter can be read as evidence of Catherine's enlistment in papal business in Italy at this time. Beyond its representation of papal diplomatic goals, Catherine's letter also expressed a sympathy for the plight of the threatened cities and an understanding of the destabilizing effect of the army on the prospects for peace in Italy—and by extension, the prospects for the return of the pope, the reform of the

[72] Letter 140/XXX: "E già desidera l'anima mia che mutiate e' modi e che pigliate el soldo e la croce di Cristo crocifisso, voi e tutti e' vostri seguaci e compagni; sì che siate una compagnia di Cristo, ad andare contra a' tutti infedeli che posseggono el nostro luogo santo, dove si riposò e sostenne la prima dolce Verità morte e pena per noi. Adunque io vi prego dolcemente in Cristo Gesù che, poi che Dio à ordinato, e anco el santo padre, d'andare sopra gl'infedeli, e voi vi dilettate tanto di far guerra e di combattere, non guerreggiate più i cristiani, però che offendete Iddio, ma andate sopra di loro; ché grande crudeltà è che noi, che siamo cristiani, membri legati nel corpo della santa Chiesa, perseguitiamo l'uno l'altro."

[73] Norman Houseley, "The Mercenary Companies, the Papacy, and the Crusades, 1356–1378," *Traditio* 38 (1982): 253–80, esp. 277–78. Houseley differs with the dominant historiographical line (represented by Denifle, Mollat, and Peter Partner) by asserting that this "papal policy was not based on unrealistic premises," particularly regarding mercenary motivations and the possibility that the companies could be enticed by the spiritual rewards of Crusade. Houseley attributes the failure of this policy to the absence of "a permanent crusading front which would ensure [the companies] paid employment and booty" (279). The idea of using the Crusade as a means to divert internal political strife can be traced to the Peace of God movement and to Urban II's proclamation of the First Crusade at Clermont. See Carl Erdmann, *The Origin of the Idea of Crusade* (1977), 336ff; and H. E. J. Cowdrey, "The Peace and Truce of God in the Eleventh Century," *Past and Present* 46 (1970): 42–67.

[74] Gregory XI, *Lettres secrètes et curiales relatives à la France*, ed. L. Mirot et al. (1935–57), nos. 1852–65, 1896–1907; Houseley, "The Mercenary Companies," 277.

clergy, and the Crusade. The *condottieri* were wildcards in Italian politics, liable to switch sides at any time to fight for the highest bidder. It is possible that Catherine's proposed solution, which would keep Hawkwood's men in the papal service without threatening the safety of the Tuscan cities, and without heightening even further the discontent of the Tuscans with the activities of the papal representatives, was also motivated by a concern that his services might be purchased by the Florentines or by the Visconti and used against the papal forces.

In this last concern, in particular, Catherine's letter to Hawkwood should be read alongside a letter from the same period sent to Barnabò Visconti, in which Catherine similarly appealed to the ideal of a unified church body and employed the Crusade as a means to such unity. Catherine must have sent this letter between 6 June—the date of the pact between the pope and the Visconti—and 24 July, when the Florentines took the dramatic step of entering into an alliance with the Visconti specifically directed against the church.[75] At about the same time, Catherine also wrote to Regina della Scala, Barnabò's wife—a political power in her own right—seeking her help in keeping her husband loyal to the papacy.[76] A reference within the letter to Barnabò to a request from one of his servants suggests that Catherine had had previous contact with representatives of the Milanese despot.[77] This was a crucial diplomatic moment in the intensifying conflict between the papacy and the Florentines, as both sides sought an alliance with Milan, the third point in the triangle of central

[75] Letter 28/XVIII. On the political situation, see Brucker, *Florentine Politics and Society*, 294, and Trexler, *Spiritual Power*, 35. Dupré Theseider dates this letter much earlier, to late 1373 or early 1374, but in fact it can be dated to June–July 1375 with relative certainty. Within the letter, Catherine refers directly to Barnabò's recent reconciliation with the pope. While this would make no sense before the peace treaty between Barnabò and the pope, or after the treaty with the Florentines, it fits in well with Barnabò's status—reconciled officially, but always volatile—between the pact with the pope and the pact with Florence.

[76] Letter 28/XVIII.

[77] Ambassadors from Milan visited Siena in late 1373, residing "nell'albergo dell'Ocha" (Neri di Donato, 653), in the neighborhood of Catherine's family. Perhaps Catherine met them at this time, but there is no other evidence of Catherine's interaction with the larger political world before the crucial events of 1374. A more likely occasion is when Milanese ambassadors visited Siena in January 1375; the Consiglio Generale approved expenses to honor ambassadors from Barnabò and Galeazzo Visconti on 20 January (ASS, *Consiglio Generale* 184, 3–4v). It is interesting to track Barnabò's emissaries alongside Catherine's letters, as evidence of her close attention to the key points of diplomatic interest in 1375. The Florentine priors on 19 September 1374 sent to Siena a letter of safe conduct for a Visconti ambassador to Florence to travel through Sienese territory in order to visit Hawkwood (ASS, *Concistoro* 1784, n. 107). Barnabò wrote to the Sienese government on 2 January 1375, to inform them that he was sending an ambassador to discuss safe passage through Sienese territory for some of his soldiers (ASS, *Concistoro* 1785, n.50). Indeed, the contacts of the Sienese with agents of the Visconti angered the pope, as the Sienese papal physician, Francesco Casini, reported in a letter of 20 December 1374 (ASS, *Concistoro* 1785, n. 42).

and northern Italian political powers. As was discussed in the previous section, the pope and his agents in Italy had noticed with apprehension the diplomatic contacts already begun between Barnabò Visconti and the Sienese while Barnabò was still officially excommunicate and at war with the papacy, and her rhetoric in this letter must be read in the context of fears that the Milanese leader might join the Florentine league.

In the letter, Catherine began by urging Barnabò to turn from concerns for temporal lordship—such lordship is from God, and men can only consider themselves administrators of what God has bestowed—to the lordship of his soul. For the sake of his soul, Barnabò needed recourse to the blood of Christ, and for this he needed the church and union with the pope: "And so only an idiot holds himself back from or acts against this Vicar, who holds the keys to the blood of Christ crucified."[78] Catherine acknowledged the climate of anticlerical rhetoric, and noticeably did not deny the validity of criticism of the clergy. But she warned Barnabò sternly not to make this criticism a pretext for a new war against the pope, the "head" of the body of the church, lest he should be amputated like a "rotten limb" from the body of the church, a metaphor that was to become her usual manner of describing Florence and other cities opposing the papal cause:

> I beg you, for the love of Christ crucified, do not do anything more against your head. And do not marvel if the demon will put it to you and has put it to you under the guise of virtue that it is a just action to wish to go against evil pastors on account of their faults. Do not believe the demon, and do not desire to pass judgment on that which does not touch you. . . . So I say to you, dearest father and brother in Christ gentle Jesus, that God does not wish that you, or anyone, make himself a judge of his ministers. He has reserved this to himself, and he has reserved it to his vicar, and if his vicar does not do it (which he ought to do, and it is bad if he does not do it), humbly we should await the punishment and correction of the highest judge, eternal God. I say to you, and I beg you on behalf of Christ crucified, that you do not meddle in these things any more. Maintain your cities in peace, passing judgment on your subjects when they commit sins, but never on those who are ministers of this glorious and precious blood. Through other hands than theirs you will not be able to receive this blood, and you will not have or receive the fruit of that blood, but you will be, like a rotten member, cut off from the body of the holy Church. No more of this, father. Humbly I want us to lay our head in the lap of Christ in heaven by affection and love, and in the lap of Christ on earth, who stands in his place, through reverence for the blood of Christ, for which blood he holds the keys.[79]

[78] Letter 28/XVII: "Però è stolto colui che si dilunga o fa contra questo vicario, che tiene le chiave del sangue di Cristo crucifisso."

[79] Ibid.: "Pregovi, per l'amore di Cristo crocifisso, che non facciate mai più contra el capo vostro; e non mirate che 'l dimonio vi porrà e v'à posto inanzi il colore della virtù, cioè

Then, as a remedy for his past opposition to the church, and as a means to peace with the pope—"this kind father, Christ on earth"—Catherine invited Barnabò to wage war against the infidels instead of fighting those to whom "we ought to be bound by the bonds of dive and blazing charity." Christians ought to fight against their proper enemy to recover their proper inheritance: "What a shame and disgrace it is for Christians to allow the evil infidels to possess what is rightfully ours." To fight against Christians is to "war only against ourselves."[80]

As in the letter to Hawkwood, the Crusade was a means to unity with the pope, a subjugation of personal, local, and national political identities under the corporate unity of the church. As always, the social issue at stake in the body analogy was the identity of the head, and for Catherine, the head of the social body as well as the spiritual body was unambiguously the pope. Catherine's marshaling of commonplace images of the body—evoking both the mystical body of the church and the Aristotelian body-politic—is a rhetoric in which political identity is bound to spiritual identity, based on membership in an ecclesial body-politic with the pope as its head. This political vision, and the language Catherine used to articulate it in this case, was a regular feature of her interventions as the conflict between the Tuscans and the papacy intensified. At the theoretical level, this blending of the mystical and social images of the body was hardly original to Catherine.[81] What was distinctive, and provocative, about Catherine's use of this imagery was how she attempted through it to influence Barnabò's next move in the Italian political game. Catherine's

---

giustitia di voler fare contra e' mali pastori per lo defetto loro. Non credete al dimonio, e non vogliate far giustitia di quello che non tocca a voi. . . . Così vi dico, carissimo padre e fratello in Cristo dolce Gesù, che Idio non vuole che voi, nè veruno, vi facciate giustizieri de' ministri suoi. Egli l'à commesso a sè medesimo, e esso l'à commesso al vicario suo: e se 'l vicario suo non la facesse (ché la debbe fare, ed è male se non si fa), umilemente doviamo aspettare la punitione e corretione del sommo giudice, Idio eterno. . . . Dicovelo, e pregove da parte di Cristo crocifisso, che non ve ne impacciate mai più. Possedetevi in pace le città vostre, facendo giustizia de' sudditi vostri quando si commette la colpa; ma non per loro, mai, che e' sono ministri di questo glorioso sangue e prezioso. Per altre mani che per le loro voi no 'l potete avere; non avendolo, non ricevete il frutto d'esso sangue: ma sareste, come membro putrido, tagliato dal corpo della santa Chiesa. Or non più, padre! Umilemente voglio che poniamo il capo in grembo di Cristo in cielo per affetto e amore, e di Cristo in terra, la cui vece tiene, per riverentia del sangue di Cristo, del quale sangue ne porta le chiavi."

[80] Ibid.: " . . . ché grande vergogna e vituperio è de' cristiani, di lassare possedere quello che di ragione è nostro a' pessimi infedeli! Ma noi facciamo come stolti e di vil cuore, che non facciamo briga e guerra se non con essonoi medesimi."

[81] On the connections between the idea of Christian society as a *corpus mysticum* and articulations of secular conceptions of the body politic, see Ernst Kantorowicz, *The King's Two Bodies* (1957), esp. 196–97. See also Sarah Beckwith, *Christ's Body*, esp. chap. 2, "Christ's Body and the Imaging of Social Order," 22–44.

argument addressed Barnabò's salvation, but was equally a case against his joining the Florentine league.

The Crusade activity of Catherine and Raymond in Pisa intensified after the apparent settlement of the Visconti conflict and a papal bull announcing a planned Crusade (published on July 1). The pope had enlisted help of the Roman provincial of the Dominicans, the minister general of the Franciscans, and Raymond of Capua in order to canvass Italy for prospective participants and contributors for the Crusade.[82] Shortly after July 1, Catherine wrote to the queen of Naples, Giovanna d'Anjou. Giovanna, whose control of her kingdom depended on papal favor, was a key contributor to military efforts against the Visconti as well as an important source of grain supplies for the Florentines. While her loyalty to the pope could have been considered solid, she also had fostered strong economic and political ties with the Florentines during the years of anti-Visconti wars.[83] Catherine's letter refers to the recently published Crusade decree and to the pope's interest in gauging support for a Crusade among the Italians, urging Giovanna to prepare to contribute to the Crusade effort "so that you might give whatever aid or force is needed to deliver our gentle Savior's holy place from the hands of the infidels, and their souls from the devil's hands."[84] Writing again to Giovanna several months later, Catherine gave this theme added resonance by appealing to Giovanna's status as titular "queen of Jerusalem":[85]

> May I see the fire of holy desire so growing in you at the remembrance of the blood of God's Son that since you are titled queen of Jerusalem, so you will be head and cause of this holy Crusade; so that holy place will not be possessed any longer by those evil infidels, but will be held honorably by Christians, and by you as your own possession.[86]

---

[82] Catherine mentions the papal measures in the letters to Giovanna d'Anjou and Niccolò Soderini described below.

[83] Trexler, *Spiritual Power*, 36–37, 84–5; E. G. Léonard, *Gli Angioini di Napoli* (1967), 564–67.

[84] Letter 133/XXXII: "E però vi prego e constringo, da parte di Cristo crocifisso, che vi disponiate e accendiate el vostro desiderio, ogni ora che questo ponto dolce verrà, di dare ogni aiuto e vigore che bisognarà, acciò che 'l luogo santo del nostro dolce Salvatore sia tratto delle mani dell'infedeli, e l'anime loro sieno tratte delle mani delle demonia, acciò che participino el sangue del Figliuolo di Dio come noi."

[85] Giovanna's ancestor Carlo d'Angiò (Charles Robert d'Anjou, king of Hungary) acquired the royal title to Jerusalem in 1277, but by this time it had been reduced virtually to an empty honorific.

[86] Letter 143/XXXIX: " . . . ch'io vega cresciare tanto in voi el fuoco del santo desiderio, per la memoria del sangue del Figliuolo di Dio, che, come voi sete intitolata reina di Jerusalem, così siate capo e cagione di questo santo passaggio; sì che quello santo luogo non sia posseduto più da quelli pessimi infedeli, ma sia posseduto da' cristiani onorevolmente, e da voi come cosa vostra."

In July and August Catherine wrote letters to other potential support-ers of the Crusade, calling on her correspondents to respond enthusiasti-cally to the papal plan. For example, Catherine wrote in July to the influential Florentine merchant and politician, Niccolò Soderini, one of her contacts among the prominent members of the Parte Guelfa. In the letter, Catherine responded with thanks to a letter Soderini had sent her and some act of charity performed for her—possibly concerning her brother, Benincasa, who had settled in Florence by this time. She also announced the measures the pope had taken to inquire into support for the Crusade among the Tuscans, and called upon Soderini to write in support of the Crusade and encourage others to do so as well.[87]

The beginning of Catherine's letter-writing campaign coincided with the intensification of conflict between Florence and the papacy, and reveals dramatically her connection to the ecclesiastical politics of the moment. It is striking in particular that Catherine moved quickly to visit Pisa, a politically sensitive region governed by a ruler sympathetic to the papal position in the growing conflict, and that at the very beginning of her newly expanded career she wrote letters to Piero Gambacorti, John Hawkwood, and Queen Giovanna of Naples, among others, systematically addressing the key players on the political stage. Catherine's travels and writing campaign were an organized and systematic effort by the support-ers of the papal cause in Italy to enlist her saintly reputation and rhetori-cal skills for that cause. But Catherine was no passive instrument, as is abundantly clear from another letter from this period, the earliest surviv-ing letter to Raymond of Capua, in which Catherine demonstrated to Raymond her authority in the world in terms that reflected larger cul-tural expectations about female holy authority, but also crossed the boundaries of what Raymond, it seems, was willing to accept. This is her famous letter concerning the execution of Niccolò di Toldo, which is the subject of the next chapter.

---

[87] Letter 131/XXXIII.

CHAPTER 3

# Niccolò di Toldo and the Erotics
# of Political Engagement

The mixing of the mystic and the mundane made possible by the epistolary form is illustrated in an especially dramatic way in Catherine's most famous letter, addressed to Raymond of Capua, in which she describes how she converted and accompanied to his execution a young Perugian—Niccolò di Toldo—arrested in Siena in 1374 and executed for a political crime.[1] Catherine's account of her own experiences in this letter, written at a formative moment in her career, scripts her in a public and political drama whose denouement demonstrates boldly her authority in the world. In this letter, Catherine manipulated in a provocative way images central to the current discourse of female religiosity, and central to her own developing reputation, in order to establish for herself an authoritative perspective on political events and affirm for herself a privileged role on the public stage. While Catherine's discourse was inextricably bound up in the terms in which a woman could articulate authority in her culture, a close reading of this letter shows how she took an active

---

[1]    Recent analysis of this letter and its significance includes Daniel Bornstein, "Spiritual Kinship and Domestic Devotions," in Judith C. Brown and Robert C. Davis, eds., *Gender and Society in Renaissance Italy* (1988), esp. 177–79; Joan P. Del Pozzo, "The Apotheosis of Niccolò di Toldo: An Execution 'Love Story,'" *Modern Language Notes* 110 (1995), 164–77; as well my own earlier treatments of this letter in "Catherine of Siena: Rewriting Female Holy Authority," in Lesley Smith and Jane H. M. Taylor, eds., *Women, the Book, and the Godly: Selected Proceedings of the St. Hilda's Conference, 1993*, vol. 1 (1995), 89–104; and "The Evidence of Catherine's Experience: Niccolò di Toldo and the Erotics of Political Engagement," in Mario Ascheri, ed., *Siena e il suo territorio nel Rinascimento* (2001), 53–90.

part in the establishment of her authority, in terms that were not completely consistent with cultural expectations of female visionary sanctity.

To understand what Catherine was doing in this letter, it is necessary to read it with sensitivity to the political setting of Niccolò's execution, as well as the situation of Catherine in the first months of her campaign on behalf of the church in Italy. It is also important to keep in mind that this is the first letter we possess from Catherine to Raymond, and very probably the first she wrote to him. As such it is a striking introduction to her distinctiveness and departure from convention. Catherine's letters to Raymond, unlike her letters to other correspondents, frequently include narrative sections describing crucial experiences; several of these will be discussed in chapter 5.[2] It does not seem misplaced to see Catherine, through a virtuoso manipulation of epistolary convention, as a participant in her own hagiography, recounting her own saintly *geste* to her future biographer. On one level, Catherine here was just telling Raymond what happened to her, using a letter to share experiences with an absent friend. But the meaning of the story was much more far-ranging: an audacious presentation of her identity and authority as well as the nature of her involvement in politics.

## Who Was Niccolò di Toldo, and Why Was He Executed?

As will be seen, in her letter Catherine does not give the name of the condemned man, and Raymond of Capua does not mention the event in the *Legenda maior.* The information we possess about the occasion for the Niccolò di Toldo letter comes largely from hagiographical collections authored by the Sienese Dominican friar and associate of Catherine, Tommaso d'Antonio da Siena, known as "Caffarini," who spearheaded the campaign for her canonization after the death of Raymond of Capua.[3] Caffarini gives his fullest version of the affair in his deposition for the *Processo Castellano,* a collection of testimonies about Catherine's sanctity collected by Caffarini in response to an inquiry by the bishop of Venice in 1414 into Catherine's cult.[4] Here Caffarini discusses the Niccolò di Toldo

---

[2]    For example, in letter 219/LXV, Catherine described her vision of leading the saved into Christ's wounds; in letter 295, she told the dramatic story of her near martyrdom in Florence in 1378; and in letter 272, she described the dialogue with Christ that subsequently formed the basis for her book, and told how Christ—with John the Evangelist and Thomas Aquinas—descended from heaven to give her the ability to write.

[3]    On the hagiographical efforts of Caffarini, see Fernanda Sorelli, "La produzione agiografica del domenicano Tommaso d'Antonio da Siena: esempi di santità ed intenti di propaganda," in Daniel Bornstein and Roberto Rusconi, eds., *Mistiche e devote nell'Italia tardomedievale* (1992), 157–70.

[4]    *Il Processo Castellano,* ed. M.-H. Laurent (1942). This collection was later used by Pius II in his definitive inquiry into Catherine's sanctity, leading to her canonization in 1461.

episode in the context of Catherine's charity toward the sick and imprisoned, noting that she succeeded in converting condemned prisoners
whom priests and learned theologians had not been able to move:

> Indeed once I went to the communal prison with her to visit one condemned
> to death, a young noble from Perugia whose name was Niccolò Toldo. He had
> been employed in some function by the then-senator of Siena, and during
> some unrest had ill-famed the senator of something concerning the city-state.
> For this he found himself thus sentenced without remedy, and chose to throw
> himself into the abyss of desperation. The virgin heard him and, as she was
> entirely jealous for the health of souls, so it happened that he who had at first
> paced his cell like a ferocious and desperate lion, by means of the virgin's
> presence, was so restored that he went devout and willing, just like a gentle
> lamb born to the slaughter, to the place of beheading. And thus he accepted
> death while still at a young age, in the presence of the Virgin and with her
> receiving his head into her hands, with such marvelous devotion that it was
> like the *transitus* of some devout martyr and not the death of one who was con-
> demned for a human crime. And everyone watching, among whom I was one,
> was so moved internally and from the heart that I do not remember any previ-
> ous burial accompanied with as much devotion as that one.[5]

Caffarini gives a shorter, and slightly different version in his *Legenda
minor,* composed between 1416 and 1417 as an adaptation for popular
dissemination of Raymond's lengthy *Legenda maior.* In this version, he
notes that Niccolò's crime was speaking "certain rash words he had spoken against the Sienese state," and refers to the "beautiful letter" in which
Catherine describes the event.[6] Caffarini further identifies Niccolò as the

---

[5]   *Processo Castellano,* 42: "Siquidem cum me invenissem in carceribus communitatis cum
prefato ad capitale supplicium condempnato, qui Nicolaus (de) Toldo nobilis de Perusio
dicebetur, et qui per senatorem tunc Senarum in quodam officio deputatus, cum ex quadam
turbatione ipsum senatorem de quibusdam concernentibus civitatis statum infamasset, ac
per hoc irremediabiliter se sententiatum taliter cerneret, omnino se in baratrum desperatio-
nis iactare volebat. Quod virgo audiens veluti salutis animarum tota zelotipa, cum accessisset
ad ipsum, taliter factum est, ut qui primo tanquam leo ferocissimus et desperatus per
carcerem incedebat, mediante presentia virginis, taliter est reductus quod uti agnus mansue-
tus qui portatur ad victimam, devotus et spontaneus, ad locum decapitationis accessit, et cum
tam admiranda devotione mortem illam cum esset iuvenilis etatis, virgine presente et in suis
manibus caput eius accipiente, suscepit, ut non condempnati ex quovis scelere hominis, sed
per omnes cuiusdam devoti martiris transitus videretur, ac per hoc omnes visceraliter et ex
corde compungerentur, inter quos ego unus fui, in tantum ut non recorder usque tunc alicui
sepulture interfuisse tante devotionis quemadmodum illa fuit."

[6]   Tommaso di Antonio da Siena, *Sanctae Catherinae Senensis Legenda Minor,* ed. E. Frances-
chini(1942), 92: "Quasi similis casus accidit adhuc in ipsa civitate Senarum, personaliter ibi me
presente, de quodam nobili Perusino nomine Nicolaus Tuldi; qui, cum ex quibusdam verbis
statum civitatis concernentibus incaute prolatis ab eo, capitalem sententiam incurrisset, et ex
hoc per carcerem uti deperatus incederet, ex quo virgo visitavit eum atque confortavit, velut
agnus corde letissimo processit ad mortem; cuius anima meritis et orationibus eiusden virginis

young man in the letter in a marginal notation in his copy of Catherine's letters.[7] But Caffarini's interpretation of the event (seemingly colored by his reading of the letter), refers only vaguely to the nature of Niccolò's offense and casts Catherine's intervention in conventional, "saintly" terms: the holy virgin was able by her mere presence to accomplish what priests and theologians, despite their efforts, could not do.

Apart from the hagiography and several references in the Perugian archives (uncovered by Anna Imelde Galletti) to one Niccolò, son of Toldo di Uffreduccio, who served in several civic offices, what is known of Niccolò di Toldo derives from three documents in the Sienese archives.[8] The records of the Concistoro, the Sienese magistracy, show that on 4 June 1375 the magistrates decreed that one Nicolaus de Perusio, "captured by the Lord Senator and his court because of the discord sowed by him in the city of Siena, pernicious and deadly to the state of the present government and against the manifest honor and good reputation and legal authority of the present Lord Senator," be interrogated by the Podestà and Gonfalonieri of the *terzi* of the city and punished according to the full rigor of the law.[9] In addition, Gerard du Puy, abbot of Marmoutier, vicar-general of the Papal States and de facto ruler of Perugia, wrote twice to the Sienese magistracy on behalf of the imprisoned Niccolò. On 8 June, Gerard wrote to inquire into the crime for which Niccolò was being held and to protest Niccolò's innocence.[10] Having received a reply from the Sienese—apparently asserting the truth of the charges against Niccolò—Gerard wrote again on 13 June to ask that he be treated mercifully, "as if he were a subject of the church [*tanquam ipsius ecclesie subditum*]."[11] There is no reference to Niccolò's execution in surviving governmental records, but the necrology of the Sienese Dominican friary includes an entry for one "Nicholaus, *familiarius* of the Lord Senator," who died and was entombed in the cloister of San Domenico on 20 June, the

visibiliter ipso tunc evolavit ad celum. Super qua materia pulcram habemus epistolam."

[7] Siena, Biblioteca Comunale T.II.2, f.119v (Caffarini's marginalia): "Hic fuit mentio de quodam nobili de Perusio, qui fuit decapitatus in Senis, et dictus est Niccolaus Tuldi, de quo habetur in Legenda minori et in contestationibus, et qui in desperatione constitutus, per istam virginem ad Dominum est reductus et miro modo salvatus."

[8] Anna Imelde Galletti, "*Uno capo nelle mani mie:* Niccolò di Toldo, perugino," in *Atti del simposio internazionale Cateriniano-Bernardiniano*, 121–28.

[9] ASS, *Concistoro* 76, f. 16r (printed in Laurent, ed., *Documenti*, 31: " . . . quod Nicolaus de Perusio, captivatus per dominum senatorem et suam curiam propter satam zizaniam per eundem in civitate Senarum letiferam et perniciosam ad statum presentis regiminis et contra manifestum honorem et bonam famam ac legalitatem presentis domini senatoris, ponatur in manibus ac fortia domini potestatis communis ad discutiendum crimen ipsius cum presentia gonfalonieriorum terceriorum civitatis Senarum magistrorum, et deinde puniendum eundem prout debiti iuris rigor precipit observare et delicti qualitas poposceret."

[10] ASS, *Concistoro* 1786, 40; Laurent, ed., *Documenti*, 32.

[11] ASS, *Concistoro* 1786, 52 (13 June 1375); Laurent, ed., *Documenti*, 33.

vigil of the feast of Corpus Christi—not necessarily the same Niccolò, but a very suggestive coincidence.[12]

It is impossible to know for certain the specific nature of the "discord" Niccolò was accused of inciting, and precisely how he threatened the government of Siena and the authority of the senator, but it is not difficult to sketch a likely scenario. As I described in chapter 2, June 1375 was a time of increased tension in the growing dispute between the papacy and Florence, when threats to the Riformatori in Siena on the domestic and foreign fronts combined to make the Sienese especially sensitive to the danger posed by potential alliances between Gerard du Puy and the Salimbeni and their Dodici allies. Gerard du Puy had an established relationship with the Salimbeni, whose lands bordered Perugian territory. Gerard was suspected of complicity in the Salimbeni rebellion of 1374, and his attempt to broker a peace between Siena and the Salimbeni was not friendly to the Riformatori. It is sufficiently clear that the Sienese suspected Niccolò of some kind of political subversion, and Gerard's interventions as Niccolò's patron suggest strongly that Niccolò's subversion was connected to ecclesiastical interests. The senator whom Niccolò served was Pietro Marchese del Monte Santa Maria, who from at least August 1375 was a member of Catherine's network.[13] Pietro's role in the affair is not clear. Was he complicit in Niccolò's activities? Pietro was reconfirmed in office in October for another six-month term, which suggests that he

[12] *I Necrologi di San Domenico in Camporeggio,* n. 1799, 120: "Nicholaus, familarius domini senatoris, mortuus est et sepultus est in angulo claustri in vigilia Corporis Christi [*20 giugno*] et ibi est imago virginis Marie." Laurent in passing dismisses the identification of this man with Niccolò di Toldo. The Catherinian historiography has apparently accepted Laurent's conclusion on its face (see, for example, Galletti, "*Uno capo nelle mani mie,*" 123), but this consensus seems to be ill-founded. Laurent's reasoning (which is never made entirely clear) seems to be based on an alternative identification he finds in the work of the seventeenth-century Sienese antiquarian Ugurgieri, who notes having seen a tombstone with the following inscription "Hic iacet Nicolaus Iannini de Fabriano" in a location that sounds like the spot where "Nicholaus, familarius domini senatoris" was laid in 1375: "Nel muro del claustro dalla parte del refettorio si vede dipinta a fresco o a guazzo una imagine della beatissima Vergine Maria ed un cavaliero genuflesso e sotto vi sono le suddette parole" (Isidoro Ugurgieri Azzolini, *Le pompe sanesi, o vero relazione delli huomini, e donne illustri di Siena, e suo stato* [1649], 2: 449; *Necrologi di S. Domenico,* 269). There are several objections to the assumption that these are references to the same tomb. First, the *necrologio* refers simply to a fresco of the Virgin Mary, as if to an image that predates the tomb, whereas Ugurgieri describes a different image (including a kneeling knight) apparently painted as a memorial to "Nicolaus Iannini." Second, and more basic, Ugurgieri was not describing the fourteenth-century church. Between the fourteenth and seventeenth centuries S. Domenico experienced several destructive earthquakes and a devastating fire. It would be rash to assume that the walls themselves, let alone the disposition of tombs, remained the same.

[13] Catherine wrote Pietro four letters—148/XXXVI, 135/XLII, 180/XLIII, and 170/LXVII—the first of which can be dated to August 1375; see Noffke, *Letters of Catherine of Siena,* 1: 150. As mentioned below in chapter 4, Catherine's close follower Neri di Landoccio Pagliaresi was in Pietro's service in September 1375.

was not suspected of actual conspiracy against the Sienese regime.[14] But there are other reasons to suggest that the senator, who according to Caffarini was "ill-famed" by Niccolò, was compromised by the affair. It is perhaps suggestive that Pietro, who as senator ought to have been specifically responsible for administering justice, did not try Niccolò himself.[15] Perhaps suspicions regarding Niccolò's activities, and Pietro's association with Niccolò, compromised the senator's impartiality in such a way as to force him to give up Niccolò to the magistrates for trial. One possibility is that the discovery of Niccolò's conspiring made Pietro guilty by association for harboring a spy in his household. Another is that Niccolò implicated Pietro in the same subversive activity for which he himself had been arrested. There is evidence that Pietro was, by reputation, considered sympathetic to the church party: in 1376 the Florentine Eight of War wrote to the Bolognese asking them to prorogue to another time the election of Pietro as Bolognese captain, because of his excessive devotion to the church cause.[16] Combining all of the archival and hagiographic evidence, and considering the event in the context of the highly charged political situation in June 1375, it is reasonable to accept Galletti's conclusion that Niccolò was an agent of Gerard du Puy and took a position in the court of Pietro (whose feudal territory included lands in the Perugian *contado*) in order to infiltrate the Sienese political world.[17] In any case, the obvious interpretation of the Niccolò di Toldo affair is that he was arrested and executed for acting in some manner as an agent of the church, and specifically of Gerard du Puy, who was at the time considered the single greatest enemy of the Sienese regime.

Catherine returned to Siena from her work with Raymond in Pisa in June 1375, apparently for the precise purpose of ministering to a Perugian accused of subversion against the Sienese state, and whose chief patron seems to have been the much despised and feared papal governor, Gerard du Puy. Her presence at Niccolò's execution can be seen as consistent with the political trajectory of her career and mission during and after 1374.

---

[14] ASS, *Consiglio Generale* 185, 95v, 14 October 1375.

[15] It is not entirely clear at this stage what the administrative relationship was between the offices of senator and *capitano del popolo*. Elena Brizio ("Reportorio del fondo del Senatore nell'Archivio di stato di Siena," unpublished Laurea thesis, Università degli studi di Siena, 1987) asserts that later than this period the senator became responsible for executing justice, and the *capitano* for leading the Sienese in war. Neri di Donato (pp. 653–54) described an episode in the career of Pietro's predecessor, Ludovico da Mogliano, in which Ludovico judged and had executed some outlaws apprehended by Sienese armies in April 1374. If the senator normally tried prisoners himself, the fact that Pietro turned over Niccolò to the *capitano del popolo* might have signaled that the senator, because he was implicated in the case, was not trusted to be impartial.

[16] They also objected that Pietro was related to the Ubaldini, deadly enemies of the Florentine Eight (Edmund Gardner, *Saint Catherine of Siena*, 190n.

[17] Galletti, "*Uno capo nelle mani mie*," 121–22.

While Catherine in her letter did not address the political details directly, this letter can nevertheless be read in the light of Catherine's intervention into a politically charged situation. Indeed, consideration of the political dimension of the affair is required in order to understand the way in which her ecstatic, mystical rhetoric works in this letter.

## The Niccolò di Toldo Letter

Catherine's letter moves from an exhortation to Raymond to a description of her encounter with Niccolò as a romance culminating in marriage on the scaffold. The letter concludes with Catherine gesturing to an exemplary purpose of her story for Raymond. The letter can thus be divided into three sections, each with distinct rhetorical purposes. The thematic link between the sections is signaled by Catherine's final comments, and by the reappearance of an image that exercises a controlling influence on the letter as a whole: the fragrant and bloody open wound of Christ. In the first section of the letter, Catherine invites Raymond to enter into the open wound in Christ's side; the narrative of Niccolò's death in the central section culminates in Catherine's vision of Niccolò entering after death into Christ's wound; and Catherine concludes the letter by urging Raymond to imitate Niccolò in what she has represented as a kind of martyrdom. As will be made clear below, on the thematic level the exemplarity of Niccolò's death for Raymond depends on the parallels between Catherine's exhortation to Raymond to enter into the open side of Christ and Niccolò's penetration of the wound in Catherine's vision.

In the opening section of the letter, Catherine exhorts Raymond by invoking her own desire to see him "inflamed and drowned in the sweet blood of the Son of God, which blood is blended with the fire of his most burning charity."[18] She goes on to explain that it is to gain humility that Raymond must bathe himself in the blood, since experiencing the love of God engenders humility by inspiring hatred of self. In the course of this explanation, the emotional pitch heightens as Catherine pointedly changes the terms, moving from contemplation of the virtue "charity" to the more affective "love": the "fire of most burning charity" (*fuoco dell'ardentissima carità*) of Christ's blood becomes the "most burning love" (*ardentissimo amore*) with which the lamb was slain. It is *amore*, not *carità*, that teaches the soul hatred of self.

---

[18] Letter 273: "Scrivo a voi e racomandomivi nel prezioso sangue del figliuolo di Dio, con desiderio di vedervi affogato e anegato nel sangue dolce del Figliuolo di Dio, el quale sangue è intriso col fuoco dell'ardentissima carità sua."

Catherine concludes her excursus on the theme of love and humility by extending the sensory imagery of fire and heat, writing that the soul engulfed in blood will emerge purged, "as the iron issues purified from the furnace." She then directs Raymond to the source of the affection necessary for purification:

Enter into the open side (*costato uperto*) of the son of God, which is an open shop, so full of fragrance that sin [itself] becomes fragrant. Therein the sweet bride reclines on a bed of fire and blood, therein is seen and made manifest the secret of the heart of the Son of God.[19]

As in her other letters, Catherine here does not develop images in a logical or linear way, but rather invokes them in patterns or constellations around her theme as her ideas become more complex. Thus the energetic and industrial mood established by the image of the furnace, modified by the commercial tenor of the "open shop" (*bottiga aperta*), is altered radically by the allure of the "sweet bride" (*dolce sposa*). Catherine adds another image to the constellation, proclaiming in an ecstatic apostrophe:

O tapped cask (*O botte spillata*), which gives to every enamored desire drink unto drunkenness, and gives happiness and illuminates every understanding, and fills every memory so that therein one is so exhausted that one cannot hold nor understand nor love anything other than this sweet and good Jesus, blood and fire, ineffable love![20]

Catherine writes that she wants Raymond, fortified by this source of "immeasurable desire," to work to support others in the church:

I want you to do as one who draws water with a pail, the water that is holy desire, and pour the water over the head of your brothers, which are our members, bound in the body of the sweet bride.[21]

Catherine then calls on him to strengthen his resolve and persevere in spite of temptations to waver. As in later letters to Raymond, Catherine suggests that he is too inclined to temporize:

[19] "E così l'anima nesce con perfettissima purità, sì come el ferro esce purificato della fornace. Così voglio che vi serriate nel costato uperto del Figliuolo di Dio, el quale è una bottiga aperta, piena d'odore, in tanto che 'l peccato diventa odorifero. Ine la dolce sposa si riposa nel letto del fuoco e del sangue, ine vede ed è manifestato el segreto del cuore del Figliuolo di Dio."

[20] "O botte spillata, la quale dà bere e inebbrii ogni inamorato desiderio, e dai letitia e illumini ogni intendimento, e riempi ogni memoria che ine s'affadiga, in tanto che altro non può ritenere, né altro intendere, né altro amare se non questo dolce e buono Gesù, sangue e fuoco, ineffabile amore!"

[21] "Poi che l'anima mia sarà beata di vedervi così anegati, io voglio che facciate come colui che attegne l'acqua con la secchia, la quale aqua è 'l santo desidario: versare l'acqua sopra 'l capo de' fratelli vostri, è quali sono membri nostri, legati nel corpo della dolce sposa."

And beware that through the illusions of the demon, which I know have caused you difficulties and will continue, or through the words of creatures, you do not turn to look back, but always persevere when you see things most cold, until we see spilled the blood of sweet and amorous desire.[22]

Thus the themes of love and desire mix with the pervasive influence of blood in this letter, culminating in the sweet fragrance of the open wound of Christ, and anticipating the bloodiness and the amplified eroticism of the narrative of Niccolò's death that follows. Catherine exhorts Raymond to enter into the wound as a motivation to greater commitment in their work in the church, and her story of Niccolò's execution will serve as an example of commitment culminating in amorous shedding of blood.

In the second part of the letter, Catherine introduces the story of Niccolò's execution in a way that provides internal evidence for a political meaning in this affair and in Catherine's relationship with Raymond. Having proposed to Raymond the stimulation of the blood in Christ's wound, Catherine calls him to action:

Up, up my most sweet father, and let us no longer sleep, for I am hearing news which makes me want neither bed nor covers. I have begun already by receiving a head in my hands, which was of such sweetness to me, that the heart cannot conceive, nor tongue speak, nor eyes see, nor ears hear. The desire of God progresses, among the other mysteries done before, and which I do not speak, since it would take too long.[23]

Catherine thus begins her description of Niccolò's execution on a note of expectation, linking the event she is about to describe to other, ongoing projects of God, although her excitement is also reflected in some confusion in this passage: it is not immediately clear what Catherine has "begun already," or how "receiving a head in my hands" begins the action to which Catherine is calling Raymond. The "news" is apparently Niccolò's death and the accompanying visionary experience, which—according to the paradoxical logic of the mystic—makes sense in relation to Catherine's description of the event as beyond sense perception: for having heard what cannot be heard and having seen what cannot be seen, Catherine is about

---

[22] "E guardate che per illusioni di dimonio, le quali so che v'ànno dato impaccio e daranno, o per detto di creatura, non tiriate indietro, ma sempre perseverate, ogni otta che vedeste la cosa più fredda, infine che vediamo spargere el sangue con dolci e amorosi desiderii."

[23] "Su su, padre mio dolcissimo, e non dormiamo più, ché io odo novelle che io non voglio più né letto né testi. O cominciato già a ricevere uno capo nelle mani mie, el quale mi fu di tanta dolcezza, che 'l cuore nol può pensare, né la lingua parlare, né l'occhio vedere, né orecchie udire. Andò el desiderio di Dio, tra gli altri misterii fatti inanzi, e' quali non dico, ché troppo sarebbe longo."

to tell what cannot be told. Catherine's excited language of imminent action here resembles the language she uses elsewhere to introduce news about the Crusade or the return of the pope to Rome. By referring to Niccolò's execution and her own part in it, Catherine is calling to Raymond to join her in a social movement, which she links to the theme of desire ("The desire of God went on"), a movement either of God's desire or desire for God. The sense that Catherine is speaking of a plan to which both she and Raymond are party is strengthened in a subsequent conspiratorial reference to Niccolò as "one whom you know."[24]

Catherine writes that she went to visit Niccolò, comforted him and brought him to confess his sins, and promised to be with him at the time of execution. The next day she visited him and took him to holy communion, which "he had not received in some time." In language redolent of blood and desire—immediately suggesting the terms of the opening section of the letter—Catherine tells Raymond how Niccolò's fear of death is conquered by his love and desire for Catherine:

> But God's measureless and burning goodness tricked him, creating in him such an affection and love in the desire of God, that he did not know how to abide without God, and he said: "Stay with me and do not leave me. Like this I cannot but be alright, and I will die content!" and he had his head resting on my breast. I sensed an intense joy, a fragrance of his blood, and it was not without the fragrance of my own, which I wait to shed for the sweet husband Jesus.[25]

The odor of blood conveys an erotic charge reminiscent of the fragrance of the wound.[26] And Catherine is intimately engaged in the erotic tension of this scene. Niccolò desires Catherine, but is tricked thereby into desiring God.

Just as Catherine acts as God's proxy in this divine trick, her language suggests that Niccolò stands in for Jesus as the husband for whom Catherine waits. With "desire in [her] soul growing," she transfers her own aspiration and longings to Niccolò, extending to him an understanding of his approaching execution as marriage: "Be comforted my sweet brother,

---

[24] "Andai a visitare colui che vi sapete ..."

[25] " ... ma la smisurata e affocata bontà di Dio lo ingannò, creandoli tanto affetto e amore nel desiderio di Dio, che non sapeva stare senza lui, dicendo: 'Sta' meco e non m'abandonare, e così non starò altro che bene, e morrò contento!'; e teneva el capo suo in sul petto mio. Io sentivo uno giubilo, uno odore del sangue suo, e non era senza l'odore del mio, el quale io aspetto di spandere per lo dolce sposo Gesù."

[26] Given medieval medical understanding of semen as blood, the mixing of Catherine's and Niccolò's blood might be read as a description of sexual intercourse; see Danielle Jacquart and Claude Thomasset, *Sexuality and Medicine in the Middle Ages*, trans. Matthew Adamson (1988), 52; and Joan Cadden, *Meanings of Sex Difference in the Middle Age: Medicine, Science, and Culture* (1993).

because soon we shall reach the wedding."[27] Catherine recounts to Raymond Niccolò's transformation from fear to joy, reporting his exultant anticipation of their coming tryst:

"Whence comes such grace, that my soul's sweetness will wait for me at the holy place of justice. . . . I will go all joyous and strong, and when I think that you will be there it will seem to me a thousand years until I arrive."[28]

And Catherine comments: "He spoke such sweet words as to make me burst at the goodness of God."[29]

Before Niccolò arrives, Catherine awaits him "in continual prayer and in the presence of Mary and Catherine, virgin and martyr." Catherine then places her own head on the block, praying for her own martyrdom. Although martyrdom is not granted her, Catherine pleads with Mary that at the moment of death she grant Niccolò peace of heart, and then allow Catherine to "see him attain his goal." Believing that Mary has made her a "sweet promise," and now in ecstasy, Catherine reports that her soul was so full that, despite the multitude of people who had assembled for the execution, she could see no one.[30]

Niccolò arrives, humble "like a gentle lamb" and laughing, and asks Catherine to bless him with the sign of the cross. After blessing him, Catherine instructs him to prepare for the wedding: "Down for the wedding, my sweet brother, for soon you will be in everlasting life!" She then places his neck on the block and reminds him of the blood of the lamb. Niccolò's final words gesture to the role Catherine is playing in this marriage as proxy for Christ: "his mouth said nothing but 'Jesus' and 'Catherine,' and in this way I received his head into my hands, closing my eyes in divine goodness, and saying, 'I want it!' [*Io voglio!*]."[31]

---

[27] "Confortati, fratello mio dolce, ché tosto giognaremo alle nozze."

[28] "'Unde mi viene tanta gratia che la dolcezza dell'anima mia m'aspettarà al luogo santo della giustitia? . . . Io andarò tutto gioioso e forte, a parammi mille anni che io ne venga, pensando che voi m'aspettarete ine."

[29] " . . . e diceva parole tanto dolci che è da scoppiare della bontà di Dio!"

[30] "Aspettà'lo al luogo de la giustita, e aspettai ine con continua orazione e presenzia di Maria e di Caterina vergine e martire. Inanzi che giognesse elli, posimi giù, e distesi el collo in sul ceppo; ma non mi venne fatto che io avessi l'effetto pieno di me ine su. Pregai e constrinsi Maria che io volevo questa gratia, che in su quello punto gli desse uno lume e pace di cuore, e poi el vedesse tornare al fine suo. Empisi tanto l'anima mia che, essendo la moltitudine del popolo, non potevo vedere creatura, per la dolce promessa fatta a me."

[31] "Poi egli gionse, come uno agnello mansueto, e, vedendomi, cominciò a ridere, e volse che io gli facesse el segno della croce; e, ricevuto el segno, dissi: 'Giuso alle nozze, fratello mio dolce, ché testé sarai all vita durabile!' Posesi giù con grande mansuetudine, e io gli distesi el collo, e chinà'mi giù ramentà'li el sangue de l'Agnello: la bocca sua non diceva, se non 'Gesù' e 'Caterina,' e così dicendo recevetti el capo ne le mani mie, fermando l'occhio nella divina bontà, dicendo: 'Io voglio!'"

As if in response to her declaration of desire and assent, Catherine then sees in a vision Niccolò's soul ascend to heaven. Consistent with the fleshly consummation of her encounter with Niccolò, Catherine sees Jesus, "God and Man," receiving first Niccolò's blood into His own blood, "a flame of holy desire . . . into the fire of his own divine charity" and then placing Niccolò's soul in the "open shop of his side," bringing him into union with the crucified Christ:

> O how sweet and inestimable to see the goodness of God, with what sweet-ness and love he awaited that soul departed from the body—turning the eyes of mercy toward him—when he came to enter into the side, bathed in his blood, which availed through the blood of the Son of God. Thus received by God (through the power God was powerful enough to do), the Son, wisdom and incarnate word, gave him and made him share in the crucified love, with which he received the painful and shameful death, through the obedience which he showed to the Father, for the good of the human race.[32]

As in the hortatory section of her letter, Catherine represents union with Christ as entering the wound in his side. By being joined to Christ's cruci-fied and wounded flesh Niccolò's gender is transformed:

> He made a sweet gesture which would charm a thousand hearts. . . . He turned as does a bride when, having reached her husband's threshold, she turns her head and looks back, nods to those who have attended her, and so expresses her thanks.[33]

After seeing Niccolò enter into Christ's side, Catherine concludes by describing her state of happy calm after the ecstasy of her vision, confirm-ing her active role in the consummation of this marriage: "My soul rested

---

[32] "Allora si vedeva Dio e Uomo, come si vedesse la chiarità del sole, e stava aperto e riceveva sangue nel sangue suo: uno fuoco di desiderio santo, dato e nascosto nell'anima sua per gratia, riceveva nel fuoco della divina sua carità. Poi che ebbe ricevuto el sangue e 'l desiderio suo, ed egli ricevette l'anima sua e la misse nella bottiga aperta del costato suo, piena di misericordia, manifestando la prima Verità che per sola grazia e misericordia egli el riceveva, e non per veruna altra operatione. O, quanto era dolce e inestimabile a vedere la bontà di Dio, con quanta dolcezza e amore aspettava quella anima partita dal corpo—vòlto l'occhio de la misericordia verso di lui—quando venne a entrare dentro nel costato, bag-nato nel sangue suo, che valeva per lo sangue del Figliuolo di Dio—Così ricevette da Dio per potenzia: fu potente a poterlo fare—; e 'l Figliuolo, sapienzia verbo incarnato, gli donò e feceli participare el crociato amore, col qualle elli ricevette la penosa e obrobriosa morte, per l'obedientia che elli osservò del Padre in utilità dell'umana natura e generatione."

[33] "Ma elli faceva uno atto dolce, da trare mille cuori—non me ne maraviglio, però che già gustava la divina dolcezza—: volsesi come fa la sposa quando è gionta all'uscio dello sposo, che volle l'occhio e 'l capo adietro, inchinando chi l'à acompagnata, e con l'atto dimostra segni di ringratiamento."

in peace and quiet in such a fragrance of blood that I could not bear to wash away the blood which had splashed on me from him."[34]

In the short final section of the letter, Catherine returns to earth, and comments on the meaning of her vision and its purpose for Raymond. She remarks that "the first stone is already laid," an image that Catherine used in connection with the martyrs—the stones on which the church is built.[35] Catherine concludes the letter by reminding Raymond of her earlier exhortation, and gesturing to the link between the exhortation and Niccolò's execution: "So do not be surprised if I impose on you only my desire to see you drowned in the blood and fire which pours out of the side of Christ."[36] In the exhortational section of the letter Catherine had called on Raymond to enter into the open side of Christ as the source of an emotional engagement that will allow him to persevere in his work for the church, "the bride of Christ." As Catherine's conclusion makes clear, her account of Niccolò's death is meant as a model for Raymond of union with Christ and total commitment to their common cause.

## The Wound in Christ's Side as Female Flesh

The exhortational and narrative sections of this letter are clearly linked by the reappearance of the open wound of Christ and the theme of espousal. Catherine is telling Raymond that he must seek to enter the wound, where he will find the "dolce sposa," just as Niccolò di Toldo was married to Christ in his execution and entered into Christ's side. An echo of Catherine's use of the image of the wound can be found in the *Legenda maior,* but reinterpreted to suit Raymond's rhetorical purposes in that work. Raymond describes how, after Catherine conquers her disgust by

---

[34] "L'anima mia si riposò in pace e in quiete, in tanto odore di sangue che io non potei sostenere di levarmi el sangue, che m'era venuto adosso, di lui."

[35] As Suzanne Noffke points out (*Letters of Catherine of Siena,* 1: 89n), Catherine used the image in this way in two other letters to Raymond of Capua. For example, in letter 295, describing her near death during the civil unrest in Florence in 1378, Catherine made this image explicit: "Sì come facevano i gloriosi martiri, e' quali per la verità si disponevano alla morte, e ad ogni tormento, unde col sangue loro, sparto per amore del sangue, fondavano le mura della santa chiesa." She also used this image in lamenting her own missed opportunity for martyrdom at this time: "Unde io ò da piagnere, pero ché tanta è stata la moltitudine delle mie iniquità che io non meritai che 'l sangue mio desse vita, né alluminasse le menti accecate, né pacificasse il figliuolo col padre, né murasse una pietra col sangue mio nel corpo mistico della santa Chiesa." See also letter 333: "Gattivello padre mio, quanto sarebbe stata beata l'anima vostra e la mia se aveste murata una pietra nella santa Chiesa col sangue vostro, per amore del sangue!"

[36] "Parmi che la prima pietra sia già posta, e però non vi maravigliate se io non v'impongo che 'l desiderio di vedervi altro che anegati nel sangue e nel fuoco che versa el costato del Figliuolo di Dio."

drinking from the cancer of a woman she is nursing, Christ rewards her for this act of self-abnegation by raising Catherine up and letting her nurse at his wound.[37] In the structure of the *Legenda maior,* this experience serves as further authorization for Catherine's ascetic singularity, as well as an intimate union with Christ guaranteeing protection for Catherine in the world. The image as Raymond employs it suggests immediately the topos of Jesus as Mother, which Bynum and others have described, according to which the wound figures as a breast.[38]

But Catherine's use of the image in this letter, although it does convey an idea of feeding (Raymond is to drink the blood from the wound), possesses an eroticism and public sense that distinguishes it both from the *Legenda maior* and from Bynum's emphasis on nutritional meaning. It is an image that appears in one form or another in twenty-nine of Catherine's other letters. Catherine used the image of Christ's wounds sometimes in a provocative way to claim an intimate and privileged space for herself within society, configured as the Body of Christ. For example, in letter 219 she described for Raymond of Capua a mission-defining vision given to her in response to her special request to Christ: she sees herself leading Raymond, her other followers, and all Christians and infidels alike into the wound in Christ's side.[39] Just as in this vision the wound is a threshold beyond which distinctions between Christians and infidels lose meaning, in letter 267, also to Raymond, Catherine described the wounds (*piaghe*) as a place beyond even the highest human authority; reacting to apparent papal disfavor, she instructed Raymond to tell the pope that, should he reject her, she would hide in the wounds of Christ, from which the pope could not drive her, and from which she would continue to fight for the church, *la dolce sposa.*[40] (The two letters to Raymond are discussed in greater length in chapter 5.) In other contexts, she described it as the source of "the secret of the heart," the opposite of self-love;[41] a *caverna* or hiding place;[42] the lance of Christ *cavaliere* (related to the topos of Christ armed with the virtues);[43] and, as in this letter, an open shop.[44]

---

[37] *LM,* pars. 162–63.

[38] Bynum, *Holy Feast and Holy Fast,* 271–72.

[39] Letter 219/LXV.

[40] Letter 267.

[41] For example, in letters 47, 55, 72, 74, and 318.

[42] For example, letters 158, 306, 308, 329.

[43] In letters 97, 256, 260. For example, letter 256, to Messer Niccolò Prior of the Tuscan province of the Templars: "Venne armato questo nostro cavaliere colla corazze della carne di Maria, la quale carne ricevette in sè e' colpi per riparare alle nostre iniquità; l'elmo in testa: la penosa corona delle spine, affondata infine al cerebro; la spada allato: la piaga del costato, che ci mostra el secreto del cuore; la quale è un coltello, a chi à punto di lume, che debba trapassare el cuore e le 'nteriora nostre per affetto d'amore."

[44] In letters 75, 87, and 163.

But unlike other instances of this image in Catherine's letters, the wound in the Niccolò di Toldo letter possesses a particular erotic force and logic. In this, Catherine is following her most likely source for the image of the wound as "an open shop . . . full of fragrance." Although it has not previously been recognized, Catherine's language shows the clear influence of the meditation on the passion in the pseudo-Bonaventuran text, the *Stimulus amoris*.[45] This tour-de-force of affective spiritual literature has recently received attention as scholars have begun to recognize the extent of its influence in late-medieval religious literary culture.[46] Apart from the obvious similarities between Catherine's language and that of this influential text (as will be seen), it is evident that the *Stimulus amoris* was a text familiar to members of Catherine's circle. Also previously unrecognized, Tommaso Caffarini lifted whole passages almost verbatim from this text in a sermon on Catherine's stigmata in his collection of Catherinian hagiography, the *Libellus de supplemento*. Among the passages he appropriated are those that had the most direct influence on Catherine's rhetoric in the Niccolò di Toldo letter.[47] Caffarini's use of the text supports the already strong likelihood that Catherine was also influenced by the *Stimulus amoris,* whether directly or indirectly. It is therefore worth looking at the language of the *Stimulus amoris* in some detail, as an aid to understanding Catherine's parallel rhetoric in her description of the execution of Niccolò di Toldo.

The *Stimulus* author begins by exhorting his readers to be aroused to love of God from love of corporeal things by contemplating Christ on the cross; the flesh of Christ supplants corporal desires through union with Christ's heart in his open side:

> Therefore, soul, if you delight in flesh, love no flesh except the flesh of Christ. For this flesh, whose passion you should meditate in your heart every day, was offered on the altar of the cross for your salvation and the salvation of all mankind. O most desirable passion! O most admirable death! For what is more admirable than that death should give life, wounds heal, blood make white and make clean inward things [*intima*]; that such pain should cause such sweetness; that the opening of his side should join heart to heart?[48]

---

[45] The *Stimulus amoris* is in *S. Bonaventurae Opera omnia,* ed. A. C. Peltier, vol. 12 (1868).

[46] Flora Lewis draws the connection made here between the *Stimulus amoris* and late-medieval affective readings of the Song of Songs, particularly in the Dominican tradition, in "The Wound in Christ's Side and the Instruments of the Passion: Gendered Experience and Response," in Lesley Smith and Jane H. M. Taylor, eds., *Women and the Book: Assessing the Visual Evidence* (1997), 204–29. See also Sarah Beckwith, *Christ's Body;* and Karma Lochrie, *Margery Kempe and Translations of the Flesh* (1991).

[47] See below, notes 49 and 53.

[48] *S. Bonaventurae Opera Omnia,* 12: 633: "Si ergo, anima, carnem diligis, nullam carnem, nisi carnem Christi ames. Haec enim pro tua, et totius humani generis salute, est

Contemplating the wounds, the author shifts to the first person, and regrets that he cannot be joined physically to the crucified Christ. Instead, he resolves mentally to construct three "tabernacles: one in the hands, one in the feet, and one in the side, where I will remain continually—where I will rest, sleep, wake, drink, eat, read, pray, and carry out all my business"; this is an image that Catherine employs in several letters.[49] Evoking vividly the erotic language of the Song of Songs—"My beloved put his hand through the opening, and my insides trembled at his touch" (5:4)—and its association of affection and wounding—"You have wounded my heart, my sister, my spouse" (4:9)—the author describes the entry of the soul into Christ's wound in physical and sexual terms, and clearly shifts the bodily geography of the wound:

> O most loving wounds of our Lord Jesus Christ! For when on a certain time I entered into them with my eyes open, my eyes were so filled with blood that they could see nothing else; and so, attempting to enter further in, I groped the way all along with my hand, until I came unto the most inward bowels of His charity, from which, being encompassed on all sides, I could not go back again. And so I now dwell there, and eat the food He eats, and am made drunk with His drink. There I abound with such delight that I cannot describe it to you.[50]

Having identified his own emotional engagement in the passion with that of the Virgin Mary, "whose soul the sword of her Son's Passion pierced,"

super aram crucis oblata, cujus passionem in corde rumines quotidie. Hujus enim passionis Christi meditatio continua mentem elevabit: quid agendum, quid meditandum, quidque sciendum et sentiendum sit, indicabit: te demum ad ardua inflammabit: te vivificari, et contemni, et affligi faciet: affectus tuos tam in cogitatione, quam in locutione, ac etiam operatione regulabit. O passio desiderabilis! O mors admirabilis! Quid mirabilius, quam quod mors vivificet, vulnura sanent, sanguis album faciat, et mundet intima, nimius dolor nimium dulcorem inducat, apertio lateris cor cordis conjugat."

49 Ibid., 634: "Bonum est enim secum esse, et in ipso volo tria tabernacula facere, unum in manibus, unum in pedibus, sed aliud continuum in latere, ubi volo quiescere, dormire, videre, bibere, comedere, legere, orare, et omnia mea negotia pertractare."

50 Ibid., 634: "O amatissima vulnera Domini nostri Jesu Christi! Nam cum in ea quadam vice oculis subintrarem apertis, ipsi oculi sanguine sunt repleti, sicque nihil aliud videns coepi ingredi manu palpans, donec perveni ad intima viscera charitatis suae, quibus post undique circumplexus reverti nequivi. Ideoque ibi inhabito, et quibus vescitur cibis, vescor, ac inebrior suo potu. Ibi tanta abundo dulcedine, ut tibi non valeam enarrare."

Compare Libellus de supplemento, 237–38: "O amantissima vulnera Domini nostri Iesu Christi, quibus cum aliquem affectum subintrare oculis contingit apertis, statim oportet ut sangine sint repleti, sicque, nichul aliud videns, ingreditur uti manu palpans, donec perveniat usque ad intima sue viscera caritatis, a quibus undique circumplexus retroverti non possit. Ideoque ibi inhabitat et eisdem ibi cibis pascitur quibus vescitur ipse dilector, ac taliter et tam ubertim potatur ut torrente voluptatis divine moro modo inebrietur, tantaque in ibi dulcedine fruitur ut nullis valeat vocabulis explicari."

the author then conflates the wounded Virgin with her wounded Son, and so shifts Christ's gender—a move perhaps suggested by the similarity between *vulnera* and *vulva.*[51]

> He that previously was in the womb of a virgin for sinners now deigns to carry me, his servant, in his bowels. But I greatly fear that the time of being born from him approaches, when I will be deprived of the delights which I am enjoying. But if he has given birth to me, he must then, like a mother, feed me with his breasts, lift me up with his hands, hold me in his arms, kiss me with his lips, and cherish me in his lap, or certainly I know what I will do. Although he gives birth to me, I know that his wounds remain always open, and through them I will again enter into his womb, and entirely repeat this, until I am inseparably gathered up into him.[52]

Addressing the sensuality of his own imagined entry into Christ's flesh, the author asserts that the reader is wrong to think that such bliss need be postponed until after death, and recommends the wounds as a source of physical as well as spiritual delight:

> But believe me, O man, if you wish to enter into him by those straight and narrow holes, not only your soul, but also your body will find marvelous rest and sweetness. And that which is fleshly, and tending to fleshly things, by entering into the wounds will be made so spiritual that you will consider as nothing all delights other than the ones you feel there. Indeed, it may be that sometimes the soul will dictate, for the sake of obedience or some other purpose, that you ought to withdraw; but the flesh, delighted by that sweetness, will say that it must tarry there.[53]

Thus the wounds ought to be the source of all things good; as in Catherine's letter, the wounds are an "open shop." The author of the *Stimulus amoris* endows this image with more obvious meaning by relating

---

[51] Lochrie, *Margery Kempe and Translations of the Flesh,* 70.

[52] *S. Bonaventurae Opera omnia,* 12: 634: "Et qui prius fuerat pro peccatoribus in utero virginali, tunc dignatur me servum suum intra viscera sua comportare. Sed multum timeo, ne veniat partus ejus, et ab illis deliciis excidar, quibus fruor. Sed certe, etsi me peperit, debebit sicut mater me lactare uberibus, levare manibus, portare brachiis, osculari labiis, foveri gremiis, aut certe quid faciam scio. Quantumcumque me pariat, scio, semper sua vulnera sunt aperta, et per ea in ejus uterum iterum introibo, et hoc toties replicabo, quousque ero sibi inseparabiliter conglobatus."

[53] Ibid., 634: "Sed crede mihi, o homo, quia si in ipsum per haec angusta foramina intrare volueris, non solum anima, sed etiam quietum ac dulcedinem mirabilem inveniet corpus tuum: et quod carnale est, et ad carnalia tendit, ex illo vulnerum introitu fiet adeo spirituale, ut caeteras praeter eas, quas sibi sentit, delicias reputes esse nihil. Imo fortasse aliquando anima propter aliquam obedientiam vel utilitatem dictabit esse recedendum, et caro allecta illa dulcedine dicet ibi esse immorandum."

it to the traditional notions of Christ as physician/apothecary, and the wound in Christ's side as the special source of his saving medicine:

> Behold, it is an open shop full of all fragrances, and rich in medicines. Enter therefore through the windows of the wounds, and receive the medicine which heals, restores, preserves, and conserves. Take whatever sort you want; choose what delicate electuaries you desire; and if you would be anointed with most sweet ointments, do not hesitate to enter into those wounds. Behold, the gate of paradise stands open, and by the spear of the soldier the brandished sword is removed away. Behold the tree of life, bored through both in the branches and in the trunk. Unless you set your feet—that is, your affections—in these holes, you cannot obtain its fruit. Behold there is opened the treasury of divine wisdom and eternal charity. Enter, then, at the opening of the wounds, and with knowledge you will obtain great delights.[54]

The author of the *Stimulus amoris* extends to his readers the possibility of immediate and fleshly union with Christ, and associates Christ's fleshliness with His "femininity."

By gendering flesh as female, the author of the *Stimulus amoris* appealed to a medieval topos by now very well known from the work of Bynum and others. By a theological extension of Galenic and Aristotelian theories of conception, which hold that the woman contributes the matter or flesh to the fetus, Christ's incarnation could be understood as an exaltation of feminine *materia*. Christ's fleshliness feminizes Him; a bridegroom in his divinity, Christ became a bride in his humanity. Thus, as Karma Lochrie has argued, encountering Christ's flesh as female provided, for men, a special means to imitate Christ on the cross through abjection and transgression:

---

[54] Ibid., 634: "Ecce aperta est apotheca omnibus aromatibus plena, et medicinalibus opulenta. Per vulnerum ergo fenestras intra, et accipe medicinam sanitivam, restauritivam praeservativam et conservativam. Ibi quascumque volueris species accipe. Ibi quaecumque delicata appetieris electuaria sume. Si etiam suavitatis unguentis volueris deliniri, per illa intrare vulnera non postponas. Ecce aperta est janua paradisi, et per lanceam militis gladius versatilis est amotus. Ecce lignum vitae tam in ramis, quam in stipite perforatum, in quibus foraminibus nisi pedes, id est, affectus posueris, non poteris capere fructus ejus. Ecce apertus est thesaurus divinae sapientiae, et charitatis aeternae. Intra ergo per vulnerum aperturam, et cum cognitione delicias obtinebis."

Compare *Libellus de supplemento*, 239: "Ecce aperta est apotheca omnibus aromatibus et medicinalibus plena: per vulnerum igitur fenestras intretis et accipiatis medicinam sanativam, conservativam, restaurativam et preservativam. Ibi quascumque volueritis species accipite: ibi, quecumque electuaria appetieritis summitate. Si etiam suavitatem unguenti volueritis deliniri, per illa intrare vulnera minime postponatis. Ecce, aperta est ianua Paradisi et Longini lanceam gladius versatilis est amotus. Ecce lignus vite, tam in ramis quam in stipite perforatum, in quibus foraminibus, nisi pedes affectus posueritis, capere fructus eius minime poteritis. O beata lancea et beati clavi qui aperitionem huiusmodi facere meruerunt! Certe quisquis tanto dilectori affectus extitisset, profecto loco illius lancee exire de Christi latere amplius noluisset, sed utique dixisset: 'Hec requies mea in secula seculi; hic habitabo quoniam elegi eam' [Ps. 131: 14]."

In the Crucifixion, the scientific and theological theories of the feminine and the flesh find their most graphic expression. The wounded and bleeding body of Christ, which gives birth to new life for humanity, does so by offering itself as food, as the matter that restores humankind to God. Christ becomes female and mother on the cross when he suffers bodily and when he surrenders his flesh as the *materia* of new life. While the ultimate purpose of the Passion is the redemption of mankind, woman seems to be privileged as the means for this redemption. Such a privileging of the bodily, the physical, and the female allows for the male *imitatio christi* a means by which he calls into question his own transcendent status as spirit, and thereby humbles himself.[55]

Employing a similar association of fleshliness and femininity, the author of the *Stimulus amoris* thus deploys an eroticized image of union with Christ through female flesh as a means to immediate and transforming *imitatio Christi.*

Similarly, Catherine's *dolce sposa* reclining within the wound accentuates the *costato uperto* as an image of female eroticism. Like the author of the *Stimulus amoris*, Catherine appeals to the topos of female fleshly *imitatio Christi* and evokes the erotic spousal language of the *Song of Songs*, particularly according to its dominant late medieval interpretations, in which focus on the poem as a model for the soul's experience of love of Christ supplanted traditional allegorical interpretations.[56] In this tradition, the transfixing of Christ could be understood as an act of love, and his wound seen as the point of entry to the heart: "You have wounded my heart, my sister, my spouse" (*Song of Songs* 4:9). In this way, as for the author of the *Stimulus amoris*, the open wound allows the joining of a human heart with Christ's.[57] Catherine does at times use the phrase *dolce sposa* to represent the church, as she does in this letter when calling on Raymond to spill the blood from the wound on other members of the "body of the sweet bride," and as in the example from letter 267 cited above.[58] But of more pertinence for the Niccolò di Toldo letter, Catherine in some other letters uses *sposa* to denote the human flesh that Christ

[55] Lochrie, "Language of Transgression," 118.

[56] For discussion of the late-medieval history of this topos, see Jeffrey Hamburger, *The Rothschild Canticles: Art and Mysticism in Flanders and the Rhineland circa 1300* (1990), 70–87.

[57] *S. Bonaventurae Opera Omnia*, 12: 633: "Quid mirabilius, quam quod mors vivificet, vulnera sanent, sanguis album faciat, et mundet intima, nimius dolor nimium dulcorem inducat, apertio lateris cor cordi conjungat?"

[58] Other examples include letters 101 and 145. Letter 11, written in 1377 to Pietro, Cardinal of Ostia, contains an extended development of this theme; for example, Catherine opens the letter, "Io Catarina, serva e schiava de' servi di Gesù Cristo, scrivo a voi nel prezioso sangue suo; con desiderio di vedervi uomo virile e non timoroso, acciocché virilmente serviate alla Sposa di Cristo adoperando per onore di Dio spiritualmente e temporalmente, secondo che nel tempo d'oggi questa dolce Sposa ha bisogno."

married in his incarnation, a marriage which she sometimes describes as consummated in his circumcision.[59]

This image of alluring female flesh in the center of Christ's wound thus reinforces the way in which, like the author of the *Stimulus amoris*, Catherine describes union with Christ with an image of sexual union with female flesh. A rounded or arched opening, rather than a horizontal slit, is suggested by the parallel and homonymous images of the *bottiga* and the *botte*. Moreover, the emphasis here is on entering in rather than flowing out. Phallic images prevail: the soul is purified in the blood as an iron is purified in the furnace, and the *botte spillata* (the "tapped cask") is opened with a *spillo* or *spilla*, a metal spike used for puncturing the seal of a cask.[60] The blood that flows from the open wound, as from a punctured cask, is "the blood of sweet and amorous desire," suggesting the blood of the marriage bed, a reading implied as well by the image of the *dolce sposa* reclining on a bed of fire within the open wound. This gendering of Christ's wound is consistent not only with the economy of images in the *Stimulus amoris*, but also with what several scholars have recently identified as a tendency in late medieval visual art to represent the wound in Christ's side as a vulva.[61]

That Catherine uses gendered images of flesh intentionally is clear from how she elsewhere uses spousal images: only female correspondents, and never male ones, are invited to unite themselves to Christ as *sposo*. And when, in letter 267 (discussed above) Catherine speaks of herself as fighting for the *dolce sposa*, she pointedly tells the pope that she will fight *virilmente:* the logic of the image demands that she transform her own gender.[62] Even more striking, Catherine employs the image of the

---

[59] For example, letters 35, 36, 107, 143, 221, 239, 262, and 354.

[60] Niccolò Tommaseo and Bernardo Bellini, *Dizionario della lingua italiana*, vol. 4 (1872), 1109, s.v. "Spillo." Catherine develops this image of Christ as a wine cask in letter 136: "Così vediamo che quella umanità è quella botte che velò la natura divina, e 'l celleraio, fuoco e mani di Spirito santo, la spillò, questa botte, in su legno della santissima croce. Questa sapienza, Parola incarnata, vino dolcissimo, ingannò e vinse la malizia del dimonio, però che elli el prese con l'amo della nostra umanità. Adunque non potiamo dire che non ci abbia dato bere, cioè di tòllare el vino dell'assetato e ineffabile desiderio che elli à de la salute nostra."

[61] For examples, see Flora Lewis, "The Wound in Christ's Side," esp. 205 and 207. See also Richard C. Trexler, "Gendering Christ Crucified," in Brendan Cassidy, ed., *Iconography at the Crossroads* (1993), 107–120, esp. 109; Trexler cites the example of the breviary of Bonne of Luxembourg, reproduced in Jean Wirth, *L'image médiévale* (1989), 329. See also Karma Lochrie, "Mystical Acts, Queer Tendencies," in Karma Lochrie, Peggy McCracken, and James A. Schultz, eds., *Constructing Medieval Sexuality* (1997), 180–200.

[62] Catherine does call on her female correspondents to be "manly," particularly in letters where she exhorts them to prepare for the Crusade. This is a counterexample to Bynum's conclusion that women in the Middle Ages did not employ images of gender transformation as part of their self-expression.

*costato uperto* in such a way as to enforce only heterosexual erotic encounters with Christ.[63] While, in other letters to men, Catherine does not so clearly feminize the *costato uperto,* she nevertheless makes its location at least ambiguous; it is most often disembodied, abstracted from its site on the body of Christ—not to be found on *male* flesh. On the other hand, when Catherine extends to female correspondents the *costato uperto* as the source of union with Christ, she nearly always genders Christ clearly as male, usually by making him *sposo* to her correspondent's *sposa.*[64] Moreover, Catherine addresses several of her female correspondents as if they are praying before the cross, which she never does in letters to males; the *costato uperto* is clearly situated on a real man's body, which becomes a staircase the supplicant climbs with her mind, as in a letter to a group of nuns in Florence:

> To make it possible for us to ascend to this perfection, Christ has made a staircase of his body, and on it has made steps. If you regard the feet, they are fastened and nailed to the cross, placed there for the first stair. This is because we must first rid ourselves of every self-will, because just as the feet carry the body, even so desire carries the soul. Reflect that we can never have any virtue at all if we do not climb this first stair. Once you have climbed it, you arrive at deep and genuine humility. Climb the next stair without delay and you come to the open side of the Son of God. There you find the fiery abyss of divine charity; at this second stair of the open side, you find a shop filled with fragrant spices. There you find God and Man. There the soul is so sated and drunk that it cannot see itself. Just like the drunkard intoxicated with wine, the soul cannot see anything but blood, spilled with such a fire of love. Then it rises up with burning desire and climbs to the next stair, that is the mouth, and there rests itself in peace and quiet, tasting the peace of obedience. And it behaves as does a man who is fully drunk, who, when he is good and full, falls asleep, and when he sleeps he feels neither prosperity nor adversity. Just so the bride of Christ, full of love, falls asleep in the peace of her bridegroom.[65]

[63] The strict heterosexuality of Catherine's image patterns deserves closer attention; it should not be assumed that her images *must* work that way.

[64] As in letters 75, 112, 163, 262, and 288. Letters 97, 182, 300, and 308 do not fit into this pattern, although it is possible to read the image in these letters as serving a merely exemplary function.

[65] Letter 75, to the Florentine monastic communities of San Gaggio and Monte San Savino: "Drittamente, acciò che l'anima possa salire a questa perfezione, el nostro Salvatore à fatto del corpo suo scala, e su v'à fatti gli scaloni. Se raguardate e' piei, essi sono confitti e chiavelati in croce, posti per lo primo scalone; però che in prima die essere l'affetto dell'anima spogliato d'ogni volontà propria, perché, come i piei portano el corpo, così l'effetto porta l'anima. Pensate già mai l'anima à neuna virtù, se non sale questo primo scalone. Salito che tu l'ài, giogni alla vera e profonda umilità; saglie all'altro e non tardare più, e tu giogni al costato aperto del Figliuolo di Dio: ine trovarete el fuoco e l'abisso della divina carità. In questo secondo scalone del costato aperto vi trovarete una bottiga aperta, piena di spezie odorifere. Ine troverete Dio e Uomo: ine si sazia e inebria l'anima, per sì fatto modo

The one time in a letter to a male correspondent that Catherine does refer to the *costato uperto* in the context of this topos of climbing the cross, she does not invite her reader to encounter the body of Christ in this way. Rather, she relates a command from Christ *to her* to ascend up his body, a divine injunction she describes again in the *Dialogue*.[66] The rhetorical precision with which Catherine positions the *costato uperto* with respect to her correspondent's sex shows that she understands the particular erotic potential of the image.

Thus is found the logic of Catherine's imagery in the first part of the Niccolò di Toldo letter, in which she appeals to the topos of female fleshly *imitatio Christi* precisely in order to employ its potential as a site of the kind of affective union with Christ described by Lochrie, and recommended by the author of the *Stimulus amoris*. As Catherine's exhortation to Raymond makes clear, he is to be stirred to an emotional engagement by which he will, through love of Christ, comprehend his own sinfulness and thus achieve humility. Catherine represents the wound as a site of exactly the kind of transgression made possible by the association of femininity with flesh, and the privileging of female *imitatio Christi*.

## Catherine as Sweet Bride in the Body of Christ

It remains to be seen what the implications are of Catherine's manipulation of this image of female flesh for a reading of this letter. Catherine departs from the mystical tenor of the *Stimulus amoris* by evoking the wound in a very public scene. Catherine portrays herself acting in the midst of a social drama and on a public stage; if this is a mystical experience, it is a very public one, and full of social significance. Consistent with the social tenor of this episode, Kathleen Falvey has argued that Catherine's activities are meant to conform to the practices of members of *confortiere* confraternities, who accompanied prisoners to the scaffold in hopes of bringing them to remorse and a good death.[67] But while there is

---

che non vede sè medesima: sì come l'ebbro, che è inebriato di vino, così l'anima allora non può vedere altro che sangue, sparto con tanto fuoco d'amore. Alora si leva con ardentissimo desiderio e giogne all'altro scalone, cioè alla bocca, e ine si riposa in pace e quiete; gustavi la pace dell'obedienzia. E fa come l'uomo che è bene inebriato, che, quando è ben pieno, si dà a dormire; e quando dorme non sente né prosperità né aversità. Così la sposa di Cristo, piena d'amore, s'adormenta nella pace dello Sposo suo."

See also letter 120, to Rabe di Francesco de' Tolomei, and letter 251, to Agnesa di Francesco di Pipino, which employs the image of the cross as tree.

[66] Letter 74, to the Dominican friar Niccolò di Montalcino. Catherine returns to the image in chapters 26, 75, 126, and 166 of the *Dialogue*.

[67] Kathleen Falvey, "Early Italian Dramatic Traditions and Comforting Rituals: Some Initial Considerations," in Konrad Eisenbichler, ed., *Crossing the Boundaries. Christian Piety and*

a possible connection in Catherine's actions to such confraternal practices, in the letter Catherine attributes to herself something much more like the function of a priest. Not only does Catherine represent herself as the sole agent of Niccolò's conversion, but she brings him to confession and communion. And on the scaffold Catherine continues in her priestly role by blessing Niccolò and "officiating" at his wedding. The solitude within which Catherine casts her encounter with Niccolò also emphasizes her lone responsibility for his salvation. Catherine conspicuously excludes onlookers from her story; she makes reference to the crowd only to dismiss them, despite the fact that, in reality, there must have been a great many people there from the start (including, by his account, Caffarini himself). No jailor or other prisoners are mentioned, nor does she acknowledge any companions either in her visit to Niccolò in prison or as she attends him at the place of execution.

This solitude also emphasizes the sudden and surprising appearance of the Virgin Mary and Catherine of Alexandria, who are not shown acting in any way in the drama, but are invoked so that the ensuing action takes place in their presence; the two saintly virgins serve as silent, but conspicuous, witnesses to the execution. The importance of these two figures in the scene is suggested by Catherine's treatment of Niccolò's execution as a marriage, to which she signals her assent by saying, "I want it" (*Io voglio*), and of which she receives his head as a token. Raymond of Capua describes Catherine's mystical marriage to Christ, by which Christ guarantees Catherine continuous communion with him despite her apostolate in the world—thus authorizing her active life—in terms that suggest, as Millard Meiss has argued, that Raymond modeled his description on the pictorial tradition of Catherine of Alexandria's mystical marriage to Christ.[68] Catherine never refers explicitly to her marriage to Christ, although she describes in several places how Christ married humankind by granting the token of the ring of his circumcised flesh (humanity as *sposa*). But by having Catherine of Alexandria and the Virgin Mary as witnesses, she here appears to invoke the same pictorial tradition of the mystical marriage of Catherine of Alexandria, in which the Virgin Mary is often placed between Christ and Catherine as both celebrant and witness. At the same time, she appeals to the popular theme of the marriage of the Virgin Mary. Both are examples of a social scene used to express spiritual realities. The reference

---

*the Arts in Italian Medieval and Renaissance Confraternities* (1991), 33–55. On comforting confraternities in general, see Adriano Prosperi, "Il sangue e l'anima. Ricerche sulle Compagnie di Giustizia in Italia," *Quaderni Storici* 51 (1982): 959–99.

[68] This was a theme that was particularly popular in Sienese art, and in art associated with the Dominicans, who had a special devotion to Catherine of Alexandria as the patron saint of learning.

here operates on several levels at once, necessitating fluctuating identities. Catherine stands in for Christ as Niccolò's prospective husband; scripts herself as Catherine of Alexandria both in her desire for martyrdom and her mystical marriage to Niccolò/Christ; and she acts as the Virgin Mary by standing over Niccolò, whose marriage to Catherine/Christ is consummated in his execution.

The marriage theme in the narrative portion of the letter parallels the reference to the *dolce sposa,* and the vision in which Catherine sees Niccolò enter into the open side of Christ evokes immediately the earlier mention of the wound. Having called on Raymond to seek his bride in the wound of Christ, Catherine describes Niccolò's apotheosis as the consummation of his marriage. By inviting Raymond to seek the *dolce sposa* as the source of union with Christ, Catherine reverses the positions of the bride and bridegroom in the *Song of Songs* by making it the bridegroom who is seeking the bride.[69] Niccolò's consummation of his union with Christ involves his becoming a bride crossing her husband's threshold, beyond which (one imagines) the bridegroom awaits on the marriage bed.[70] Once again, the images show Catherine's care with the sexual logic of spousal and erotic imagery: Raymond as a man goes to meet his bride, while Niccolò—very much a man in his romance with Catherine—must become female in his union with the bridegroom Christ. By portraying Niccolò's union with Christ as a transformation in gender, Catherine represents union with Christ in terms of the abjection and transgression to be found in the female body. The exemplary nature of her story suggests that Raymond too in some sense must be feminized, and thus Catherine appeals to the notion of *imitatio Christi* referred to above. Catherine extends to her male reader the opportunity for conversion by experiencing Christ's fleshliness—Christ's "femininity."

But while Catherine in this letter appeals to a culture of metaphorical language that would have resonated with the members of her spiritual circle, and which is very familiar to historians of late-medieval religion, Catherine's provocative interpretation of her own experience with Niccolò is far from conventional. Having presented Raymond with a feminized and eroticized body of Christ as the source of the reversal necessary for the male to experience the love of Christ on the cross, Catherine then scripts herself in the role of a female *alter Christus* as the agent of Niccolò's conversion, achieved through love of Catherine. In her story of

---

[69] *Song of Songs* 3:1: "In my bed by night I sought him whom my soul loves."

[70] This image suggests the custom in Italian cities of *Menare la donna,* an elaborate procession leading the new bride to her husband's house, and the popular association of the crossing of the husband's threshold with consummation of the marriage. See Christiane Klapisch-Zuber, "Zacharias or the Ousted Father: Nuptial Rites in Tuscany between Giotto and the Council of Trent," in *Women, Family, and Ritual in Renaissance Italy* (1985), 189.

Niccolò's marriage, Catherine represents herself in two roles: she is the bride going to a tryst with her lover, and as Christ's proxy in Niccolò's conversion Catherine is also the bridegroom, a direct parallel to her earlier spousal image; the "sweet bride" awaiting Raymond inside the open wound is a female Christ and Catherine herself. To obey Catherine's command, Raymond must enter into the side of Christ as Niccolò does—through female flesh—and thus Catherine asserts authority by appealing to the privileged position of female flesh as a special access to union with Christ. And so she offers herself to Raymond in the position of the lover, a site of affection through which he can experience the transformation necessary for salvation.

The identification of Catherine with the "dolce sposa" residing within the wound has, thus far, been based mainly on the logic of Catherine's rhetoric, which forces the reader to draw a specific lesson from the story of Catherine and Niccolò. But this reading of the image of the "dolce sposa" as self-referential is borne out in the striking way in which her language in this letter evokes rhetoric used to describe her by others. Catherine's clerical followers, in particular, frequently referred to Catherine as the bride of the Song of Songs, often to explain or comment on her movements in the world and anomalous social position, and sometimes with particular application to the imagery in the Niccolò di Toldo letter.

This is clear, for instance, in a letter Giovanni dalle Celle sent to William Flete in 1376, referring to Catherine's travels:

> You say, most kind father, that the daughter of the King has now arrived in Pisa. Let us run after her not with our fleshly feet but with feet of fire, and affections strong as columns; let us run with branches of palms, beseeching her to come, saying: Come out of Lebanon, O spouse, come. Rise up, my lover, my beautiful one, and come, my dove in the clefts of the rock, that is, nesting in the wounds of Christ.[71]

Giovanni dalle Celle similarly referred to Catherine as the *sposa* of the Song of Songs, residing in the wounds of Christ, in a letter written in 1376 or 1377 to a cleric who had accused Catherine of heresy and warned Giovanni to steer clear of her "exotic" teachings. Giovanni retorted that Catherine's apparent innovations were justified by her special access to Christ's wound, like the Bride of the Song of Songs:

---

[71] Giovanni dalle Celle and Luigi Marsili, *Lettere*, 2: 364: "Dixistis, pater benignissime, quia filia regis iam Pisis advenit. Ocurramus ob viam ei non pedibus carnis sed pedibus ignitarum, affectionum fortium ut colomna; ocurramus cum ramus palmarum provocantes eam ad veniendum atque dicentes: veni de Libano, sponsa veni. Surge amica mea, spetiosa mea, et veni, columba mea in foraminibus petre, id est in vulneribus Christi, nidificans."

You say: "Do not be carried away by exotic and foreign teachings." Truly, her teaching is exotic and foreign. Foreign, I say, because she comes from *far and from the uttermost coasts* and *from the royal thrones*. Whence she can rightly be spoken of as the Bride in the Song of Songs: "The King has brought me into his store-rooms," that is, into the wounds in Christ Jesus, where drunk with the blood of the Savior she effused that gift which you see in her letters. And thus they water the earthly paradise of the Church of Christ, so that this passage in the Song of Songs can refer to her: "Your plants [*emissiones*] are a paradise." And what further moves me is that her teaching is true and ought to be venerated, since the *pen of her tongue* paints with the heart's blood, and what the tongue speaks reveals the conscience within. Nor ought we marvel at this, since her beloved Jesus is as *a bundle of myrrh,* that is Christ Crucified, *abiding between her most pure breasts,* and she is *the beloved dove who tarries in the clefts of a rock,* that is in the wounds of Christ and in the cave of flesh formed by the wound in his side.[72]

William Flete drew the same connection between the dove in the Song of Songs and Catherine's dwelling in the wounds of Christ in his posthumous sermon on Catherine:

At her passing Christ her Spouse could rightly say to her: "Arise from your torments, *my friend,* my spouse, *and come, my dove,* to make your nest *in the clefts of the rock, in the hollows of the wall,* that is, in the wounds of Christ; *show me your face, let your voice sound in my ears, for your voice is sweet*—the voice of your unspeakable endurance—and by your endurance you have won possession of your soul.[73]

In the same sermon, Flete cited Catherine herself to argue that her movements and lack of cloistered stability were compensated for by her residence in Christ's side:

In life she used to sing: "In my virginity I have become the bride of God." I once asked her: "Mother, do you have a house?" She answered thus: "My house is in the side of the crucified Christ who *is the sun of justice*. (Mal 4:2)[74]

---

[72] Ibid. 2: 370–71: "Dixistis: 'Doctrinis variis et peregrinis nolite abduci.' Vere varia et peregrina est doctrina sua. Peregrina dico, quia procul et de ultimis finibus et a regalibus sedibus venit. Unde merito dicere potest cum sponsa in Canticis Canticorum: 'Introduxit me rex in cellaria sua,' hoc est in stimata Iesu Christi, ubi ebria sangione Salvatoris effudit donum illud, quod vos vidistis in epistolis suis; que ita rigant terrestrem paradisum Ecclesie Christi, ut merito dici possit de ea illud Canticorum: 'Emissiones tue paradisus.' Et quod plus me movet, sua vera et veneranda doctrina est, quia calamum lingue tingit in sanguine cordis et quod lingua loquitur, conscientia manifestat. Nec mirum, quia dilectus suus Iesus ut fasciculus mirre, id est Christus crucifixus, inter purissima ubera sua commoratur, et sicut columba dilecta moratur in foraminibus petre, id est in vulneribus Christi et in caverna macerie que est lateris vulnus."

[73] Hackett, *William Flete,* 189.

[74] Ibid., 203.

It is not surprising to find Catherine referred to as the bride of Christ, but the parallel between Catherine's use of the image of the *dolce sposa* and the identification by both Giovanni dalle Celle and William Flete of Catherine as the Bride of Christ living in his wounds, particularly the wound in his side, is striking confirmation that Catherine's readers could easily have understood her marshaling of the images of the wound and the *dolce sposa* in the letter as gesturing to her special role as an agent of her followers' salvation, and explaining her position in the world. Catherine's letter is part of a conversation about her identity, in which she was influenced by her followers (for instance, in her use of the *Stimulus amoris*), and in turn used her letters to shape their understanding of who she was.

## Hagiographic Silence and Assimilation

Yet Catherine's self-presentation in this letter was not completely effective in shaping her posthumous saintly identity. In this letter, Catherine appealed to elements in the hagiographical *vulgata* on her identity and worldly role, and in particular the spousal language whereby her entry into the world and heterogeneous manner of life were justified by her clerical promoters. She also manipulated images of female fleshliness and privileged access to divine gifts. But she employed these images in a way that does not fit precisely into the version of her life that Raymond of Capua constructed in the *Legenda maior;* indeed, Raymond does not mention this letter, despite the fact that the details of the letter seem to have been well known in Catherinian circles in the years immediately after her death. Raymond does recount several occasions on which Catherine intervened for unrepentant prisoners on the way to the gallows in a chapter of the *Legenda maior* devoted to the miracles Catherine performed for the spiritual well-being of others. But he opts to tell a secondhand account of Catherine intervening for prisoners on the scaffold rather than tell the story of Niccolò di Toldo.

Specifically, Raymond's story about prisoners embellishes a story from the *Miracoli,* which describes how two criminals were being transported past Catherine's house in Siena to the place of execution. As was usual, along the way the condemned men were tortured by having their flesh cut with pincers, in response to which they "blasphemed God and the saints as they went along and commended themselves to the devil." This noise drew to the window the people of the house, who called on Catherine to come as well. She, however, hearing their cries of despair, retired to her room and prayed before a picture of the Madonna:

And there with great devotion and love, and fervor of charity and abundance of tears, she begged God for the souls of those men in a way that no tongue can describe, saying to the Crucified: "My Lord Jesus Christ, fountain of mercy and piety, change these hearts which you have created, and which with your martyrdom you have redeemed. You should give them to me." And then she turned to the Madonna: "You have given yourself as advocate for sinners, Virgin and Mother of the Son of God. I demand those men, obtain them for me, and then bestow on me all of the torments you wish for them." Finally, with Catherine praying thus and the cart continuing on its way, when they were near the place of justice, they began to weep and to change their language, saying with very happy expressions: "Ecco la Caterina! Praised be to God and to his mother the Virgin Mary! We are sinners and deserving of this and of all punishments. Lord God, have mercy on our souls." And thus with these words, they were both raised, devout and contrite, on the gallows.[75]

The *Miracoli* story emphasizes several characteristics of Catherine's sanctity, including her ability to intercede with Christ and the Virgin Mary for sinners; her supernatural efficacy in causing remorse for sins, even in hardened criminals, and even without meeting them; and her willingness to suffer for the sins of others. Catherine does not enter the public scene in person, but a key element in this story is the public acknowledgment of Catherine's agency in the prisoners' conversion—"Ecco la Caterina!"— which provides the outward evidence of her otherwise entirely spiritual intervention.

Raymond's version of this story stresses the mystical, apolitical, nature of Catherine's intercession. In the *Legenda maior* Catherine perceives a

[75] *I Miracoli*, 15–16: "Avenne in Siena, non à molto tempo, che passando la giustizia dinanzi all'uscio di Caterina, erano in su uno carro due malfattori che s'andavano attenagliando le loro carni, e per soperchio di dolore o per altro che fosse, essendo male disposti, andavano bestemiando Idio e santi, e raccomandandosi al diavolo ad alte voci, fecionsi alle finestre per vedere le gente di casa, Caterina rimanendosi ella nella camera sola. E veggendo tanta crudeltà, costoro che erano corsi alle finestre chiamarono Caterina che venisse a vedere; di che venendo insino a mezo la sala, e udendo e intendendo le disperate voci di coloro, e insieme sentendo nella camera donde ella era uscita, romore e strida, non giunse a farsi alla finestra per vedergli, ma, subitamente ritornando in camera, gittossi in orazione dinanzi alla tavola della Donna. E quivi con quanta divozione amore e fervore di carità e abundanzia di lacrime ella chiedeva a Dio l'anime di costoro, non è lingua che 'l potesse dire, dicendo al Crocifisso: 'Signore mio Gesù Cristo, fontana di misericordia e di pietà, muta questi cuori che tu creasti, e col tuo martirio gli ricomperasti. Tu gli mi pure darai.' Poi si rivolgeva alla Madonna: 'Tu se' posta avocata per gli peccatori, Vergine e Madre del Figliuolo di Dio. Io richieggo costoro, impetrami costoro, e poi adosso a me ogni tormento che tu vuogli per loro.' Finalmente costei così orando e il carro andando, quando e' furono presso al luogo della giustizia, cominciarono a gridare e a mutare latino, dicendo colle facce molto liete: 'Ecco la Caterina, lodato sia Idio e la sua madre Vergine Maria. Noi siamo peccatori e siamo degni di questo e d'ogni pena. Signore Idio, abbi misericordia dell'anime nostre.' E sì con queste voci, così devoti e contriti furono amendue in su le forche."

host of demons assailing the prisoners, who are converted when a vision of the crucified Christ appears to them. Raymond's version removes the public acknowledgment of Catherine by the prisoners, and has the miracle discovered by Catherine's first confessor, Tommaso dalla Fonte, through the testimony of the priest who accompanied the prisoners to the scaffold.[76] Catherine's account of her active and public participation in Niccolò di Toldo's execution differs strikingly from the mystical and private intercession in the *Miracoli* and *Legenda maior* stories, in which Catherine retires to her room, moving away from the window and the public spectacle. The story Raymond chooses to tell, with Catherine retreating from the public scene deep into her house to accomplish her miracle, fits more happily into his general emphasis on the private sphere of Catherine's activity.

As mentioned already, the letter and the story it tells were included by Caffarini in his Catherinian writings, one of two conspicuous cases where Caffarini recovered a letter addressed to Raymond but omitted in the *Legenda maior*. (The other is the equally provocative letter from 1377 in which she describes to Raymond the revelation that would form the basis for her book, and announces that she has miraculously learned to write, a letter discussed at length in chapter 5.) As has been seen, Caffarini provides details not explicit in the letter, but otherwise shifts attention away from the circumstances of the letter to its evidence of Catherine's saintly intervention for a despairing soul. Further evidence of the way in which this particular event was assimilated into hagiographic categories is in the account of one of Catherine's Dominican followers, fra Simone da Cortona, in his deposition for the *Processo Castellano*. Fra Simone's version elides all particularities of the affair into what he identifies as one of Catherine's common practices:

At that time, many who were to be punished, although desperate because of their misdeeds, proceeded to their deaths without confession. Hearing about this, the kind mother used to keep vigil in prayer over them with pious cries to Christ, and early in the morning would go to visit them in the prison, comforting them and exhorting them to have hope, and in their presence beseeching God that he might punish her, so that she might go freely in their place to die and so arrive at the heavenly banquet. And thus sweetly with words she would soften their hearts, so that they would ask for a confessor and, not without great contrition, confess their sins. And thus the kind mother called lost souls back to Christ, who is the way, the truth, and the life. And this happened many times. And even more, she would accompany them along the way to the place of justice. And when they arrived at the moment of

[76] *LM*, 228–30.

martyrdom, kneeling, she would receive their heads in her hands, and rejoice when she saw her white garment spattered with their blood.[77]

A similar indirect reference to the Niccolò di Toldo affair occurs in a posthumous sermon on Catherine by William Flete:

> In the eternal fatherland she is a woman clothed with the sun, that is, with perpetual splendor, but in this life she was a woman clothed with blood when with abundant love and for the consolation and salvation of her neighbor, she held in her hands the heads of the decapitated in the place of justice: then she was sprinkled with blood.[78]

Whether or not Catherine on more than one occasion visited prisoners in jail, or prayed with them before their execution, it is obvious that the memories of both of these disciples of Catherine were corrupted by her letter on the Niccolò di Toldo execution: it is certainly not credible that the events of Niccolò's death were repeated often. Simone da Cortona and William Flete seem to have combined a reading of Catherine's letter with reference to Catherine's intercessions for prisoners in the *Legenda maior* and elsewhere. In the process, the specific details of the event were lost, and Niccolò himself disappeared.

The manuscript collections in which this letter was copied reflect a similar indifference of Catherine's followers and first readers to the political implications of this and other letters. Copies of the Niccolò di Toldo letter appear in manuscripts from each of the three major families of collections—attributed respectively to Catherine's followers Neri di Landoccio Paglieresi, Stefano di Corrado Maconi, and Caffarini. The earliest extant copy of this letter, in a collection compiled before 1406 (and probably in the 1390s) by Neri di Landoccio Paglieresi, is presented without any information concerning the event described and the identity of the condemned man. This is consistent with the overall presentation, in Neri's collections, of letters in no systematic order and with a minimal apparatus.[79] The other two

---

[77] *Processo Castellano*, 458: "Item tempore illo quamplures plectendi propter eorum demerita tamen desperati sine confessione procedebant ad mortem. Quod sentiens pia mater pernoctabat in oratione super talibus cum piis clamoribus ad Christum et in mane bona hora ibat ad carecerem, confortans tales et exortans ad spem, conquerens coram eis de Deo eo quod faciebat sibi iniuriam quod libenter loco ipsorum voluisset mori ut posset ad celeste convivium pervenire. Et ita dulciter verbis demulcebat eosdem quia petebant confessorem et non sine magna contritione confitebantur peccata sua. Et sic pia mater perditas animas revocabat ad ipsum Christum, qui est via, veritas et vita. Et hoc contigit pluries. Et etiam ulterius usque ad locum iustitie et per viam eos associabat. Et genuflectentes cum ad martirium pervenissent, suis manibus delubra recipiebat gaudebatque quando videbat suam vestem albam illorum stillatum cruore."

[78] Hackett, *William Flete*, 206.

[79] Vienna, Österreichische Nationalbibliotek, Palatino 3514. Neri's other collection

families—descendants of compilations by Stefano di Corrado Maconi and Caffarini—show more active editorial involvement, and represent the importance of Catherine's *epistolario* as evidence for her sanctity; in their writings about her, Caffarini and Catherine's other supporters emphasized the range and prestige of her correspondents to enhance her authority. The Maconian manuscripts group letters *ad statum* and in roughly descending social order, and Caffarini's collection groups the letters in a strict hierarchy with the letters to clerics separated from letters to laypeople. And so in both of these families of manuscripts, the Niccolò di Toldo letter is one among a number sent to Raimondo da Capua. These collections also show an effort to correlate the letters with the hagiographical narrative by adding informational rubrics. For example, copies of the Niccolò di Toldo letter in the Maconian family are accompanied by an especially prolix rubric describing the letter as concerning "a singular grace performed for a young Perugian, who had his head cut off in Siena, and [Catherine] received it into her hands."[80] Thus while the manuscripts help connect the letter to the story in the *Legenda*, they do not help relate what Catherine writes to the details of Niccolò di Toldo affair. Like the hagiography, these manuscripts refer to Niccolò only to identify the object of Catherine's saintly intervention. Catherine acts as a saint should act, and Niccolò becomes, literally, nothing more than an object in the saint's hands.

Raymond's reason for excluding the letter from the *Legenda maior* probably had less to do with the amplified eroticism of Catherine's account— an effect more surprising to modern sensibilities than it would have been to someone steeped in the affective spirituality of the fourteenth century—than with Catherine's provocative self-authorization, and the way in which Catherine scripted herself as exercising her spiritual gifts in public, as a participant in the political scene. For Catherine employed these tropes of female privilege to establish her authority to engage the political and to direct her confessor and superior to a greater level of commitment in the cause within which they were both enlisted. Catherine was not only calling on Raymond to seek salvation through an ecstatic experience. If Niccolò was to be Raymond's model, then Catherine was urging him to

(Florence, Biblioteca Nazionale, Magliabechiano XXXVIII, 130) similarly lacks informational rubrics or introductions. Both of Neri's collections appear to be devotional handbooks, designed for private reading, which might help explain the lack of rubrics. Also, if Neri copied these to be read by him and other intimates of Catherine, it is possible that informational rubrics would have been superfluous.

[80] For example, London, British Library, Harley MS 3480, f. 53r: "Questa lettera mando essa katerina al padre dell'anima sua maestro Raymondo notificandoli una singolare grata inpetrata per uno giovane perugino al quale in siena fu tagliata la testa et ella la ricolse in mano."

make an equal commitment to the cause for which Niccolò was martyred—that is, the cause of the church in Italy. That she represented herself as the agent of Niccolò's and Raymond's salvation through political engagement was a remarkable and provocative statement of Catherine's own role as *dolce sposa*—as representative and the very emblem of the papal cause. If, as suggested above, this letter can be read as Catherine introducing herself to Raymond, one can well imagine that Raymond was as shocked as edified by his new charge!

The political aspects of this letter are established largely by the details of Niccolò's arrest and execution, and by the political context of the rapidly intensifying conflict between the papacy and the Italian city-states in early 1375. But a political meaning is implicit in the image that dominates this letter: the *costato uperto del Figliuolo di Dio*. In this letter, Catherine boldly invoked the body of Christ as a site of personal spiritual engagement, but with all of the social and political resonance that this image carries in her other letters and which, indeed, this image probably always carried in the Middle Ages. In letters to political leaders during the War of Eight Saints, Catherine employed the image of the Body of Christ to represent a hierocratic social and political order, and to argue that political opposition to the pope would also entail estrangement from the spiritual Body.[81] In other instances, Catherine used the wounds of Christ, and especially the wound in his side, to establish her own authoritative perspective on events, her own political space.[82] Writing about the execution of Niccolò di Toldo, at the outset of the War of Eight Saints, Catherine invoked even more dramatically the wound in Christ's side to establish her privileged relationship to the spiritual and political order. Given the political meaning of the Body of the Christ, in medieval writing generally and in Catherine's letters more specifically, the wound here signifies not only a privileged place of intimacy with Christ, but a place at the very center of the political order. Catherine's account of the Niccolò di Toldo affair is not, any more than Raymond's version of her life, an unproblematic representation of her experience or self-understanding, but an example of Catherine manipulating the epistolary genre to construct her own identity, and especially the authority by which she entered into the political scene.

This letter also gives abundant evidence of the qualities of exuberant mysticism and intense affection that drew to her, as she began her worldly career, a group of young elite Sienese men—the core of her *famiglia*—a group that was held together, in large part, through Catherine's letters. The mixing of spiritual and political meaning, seen in the Niccolò di

---

[81] For example, letters 28, 138, 168, and 171.
[82] For example, letters 219 and 267.

Toldo letter and the early letters discussed above, carried over to members of Catherine's *famiglia,* who shared political connections in addition to their attraction to their spiritual *mamma*—a phenomenon that will be explored in chapter 4.

# CHAPTER 4

# *Catherine's Sienese* famiglia:
# *Pious Networks and Political Identities*

The ecstatic and affectionate spirituality of the Niccolò di Toldo letter gives some idea of Catherine's personality. She attracted, at the beginning of her public career, a mixed group of followers—her *famiglia*—including a number of young elite Sienese laymen. For these men, Catherine's identity—bride of the Song of Songs, Christ's spouse, spiritual mother—was no hagiographic commonplace, but an immediate and joyful reality. For her followers, membership in her *famiglia* was based on a highly personal and sentimental attraction to Catherine—their *mamma*. This breathless declaration of filial devotion, in a letter from the Sienese nobleman Stefano di Corrado Maconi to another young Sienese nobleman, Neri di Landoccio Pagliaresi, is typical:

> About what you have written concerning our venerable and sweet Mamma, I am not amazed at this, nor do I doubt it, since I believe of her many greater things than what you have written. For I truly believe and proclaim that our most kind Mamma *is* Mamma, and I have a firm hope that every day I will believe with clearer illumination and proclaim with greater effect that [Catherine] is Mamma![1]

---

[1] Misciattelli, *Lettere di S. Caterina da Siena* 6: 69 (15 January 1379): "Ma di quel che mi scrivi della nostra venerabile e dolce Mamma, di ciò non mi maraviglio, nè anco ne dubito, credendone senza neuna comparazione molto maggiori fatti che non scrivi; però che'io credo veramente e così confesso, che la Mamma nostra benignissima è mamma; e ò ferma speranza che ogni dì con più chiaro lume credarò e confessarò con maggiore efficacia, lei essere mamma."

In his testimony for the *Processo Castellano,* Stefano recounts Catherine's motherly attention in nursing him when he was ill with a fever, with miraculous effect.[2] He describes his conversion as entrance into a family in which the children competed for the attention of their mother; he notes that Catherine's other sons envied him for the motherly affection she showed him, and for giving him such responsibilities as taking dictation of her *Libro.*[3] For Stefano, membership in Catherine's family was explicitly an alternative to mundane family ties and concomitant social and political obligations. After he was accepted into Catherine's circle and began assisting in her correspondence, he began to despise the world and all that belonged to it, considering himself "so blessed by the presence and intimacy of Catherine" that he "thought little of and willingly surrendered ties to parents, brothers, sister, and all other blood-relatives."[4] Indeed, Stefano claimed that the transformation caused by his entrance into Catherine's *famiglia* was so dramatic and decisive that nearly all Siena marveled at it.[5]

In light of this kind of rhetoric, it is not surprising that historians have shown such complete lack of curiosity about the social and political meaning of Catherine's network of followers and supporters. Stefano saw Catherine's *famiglia* as an alternative to his ordinary family and the social and political obligations that families—especially prominent and noble ones like the Maconi—demanded from their male members. This image of Catherine's *famiglia* as an antithesis to worldly families is also an important theme in the *Legenda maior* and echoes Catherine's own language in letters responding to mothers who had expressed concern about their sons' and daughters' affiliations with her. Catherine asserted the prominence of her spiritual motherhood over merely biological mothers, and in 1376 upbraided Monna Lapa—who had apparently complained about Catherine's long absence from Siena—for failing to transcend carnal affection in exchange for the spiritual labor pains of the religious life.[6] The rhetoric of Catherine's *famiglia* thus illustrates the view that feminine imagery and holy women gave late-medieval men access to greater intimacy with Christ precisely because the feminine occupied a marginal space, remote from social and political power, and so allowed men to

---

[2]  *Processo Castellano,* 264.

[3]  Ibid., 262.

[4]  *Processo Castellano,* 260: "et ita, licet indignus, acceptatus fui comes tam sancte societatis, parvipendens atque derelinquens utrumque parentem, germanos, sororem, aliosque consanuineos, me beatum reputans esse pro virginea presentia et familiaritate."

[5]  Ibid.: "et tantam atque talem in me persensi mutationem, ut etiam ab extra temperari non posset, ita ut fere tota civitas miraretur."

[6]  Letter 240. See also letters 112, to Benedetta di Agnolino Salimbeni; 120, to Rabe di Francesco Tolomei; and 247, to Giovanna di Corrado Maconi.

experience a reversal of normal male identity. Accordingly, as this model suggests and Stefano's words confirm, Catherine's motherhood and her *famiglia* was valued precisely because it was at odds with the male sphere of political and social activity.

Yet there is abundant reason to question the categorical distinction between religious identity and political commitment in general, and particularly in the case of Catherine's *famiglia* in Siena. Catherine and her followers maintained ties to their "real" biological families and were thereby implicated in the real politics of Siena at the most mundane level. Even more striking, it is not at all clear that these two families and two identities were really distinct; membership in Catherine's *famiglia* was at times consistent with the political goals of their families and civic political groups. During the War of Eight Saints, the secular authority of the spiritual power was at issue, and in a lesser sense the spiritual authority of secular powers. The distinction between the "spiritual" and the "political" was at least problematic, if not meaningless. Commitment to one side or another in the battles between the papacy and the Italian city-states was both a pious and a political statement, expressing a bond to one or another party in local politics. A clear distinction between the spiritual goals of Catherine and her followers and their political activities is therefore misleading.

As I suggested in Chapter 1, Catherine's public career was in part an extension of her family background. This chapter explores the social and political particularities of some of Catherine's spiritual children, details that have been lost behind the rhetoric of hagiography and spiritual memoir. Reading some of Catherine's letters to her followers with a full knowledge of their political lives makes it possible to understand tension in their commitment to her as not simply the clash between the City of God and the City of Man, but moments in which loyalties to Catherine's *famiglia* brought them into ill-repute with the governing regime or clashed with family obligations. They worked out their devotion to Catherine within specific social, political, and economic situations. This kind of reading demonstrates how the letter was the chief vehicle by which she communicated with her network and mixed in the male political world, so that her letters mixed spiritual encouragement with political exhortation.

In this chapter I will survey the careers of those of her closest Sienese male followers for whom there is most information outside the Catherinian hagiography.[7] They were not a uniform group. Some were members

---

[7] A number of other men are mentioned in one or two episodes in the hagiography. Others are given in a list of Catherine's followers provided by Cristofano di Gano Guidini in his *Libro di memorie* (*Archivio Storico Italiano*, series 1, vol. 4, pt 2: 27–48). He mentions as

of the *popolo,* others nobles; some were in the same sociopolitical group as Catherine's family, but another, Cristofano di Gano Guidini, was a member of the ruling *monte* of the Riformatori. Nevertheless, several generalizations can be made about Catherine's close followers. All were either nobles or of the higher orders in the *popolo.*[8] Further, they acted together in other enterprises. For example, Matteo di Fazio de' Cenni, the rector of the Sienese Misericordia (a hospital that was an important focus of civic piety), was part of Catherine's extended circle in Siena, and she and her followers participated in the charitable activities of the hospital; some of Catherine's followers also used the Misericordia as a meeting place.[9] More dramatically, several of Catherine's *famiglia*—both nobles and elite members of the *popolo*—joined the most prominent civic confraternity, the Compagnia della beata Vergine Maria, a flagellant group that met in the chapel below the Spedale della Scala, the most prominent civic institution in Siena.[10] Membership in confraternities could express political identity as well as pious commitment, which is one of the reasons that

Catherine's followers several men discussed in further detail below: Neri di Landoccio Pagliaresi, Nigi di Doccio degli Arzocchi, Stefano di Corrado Maconi, ser Michele di ser Monaldo, Gabriello di Davino Piccolomini, and Sano di Maco. Those he lists who are not treated below are: Maestro Giovanni di Maestro Senso, Maestro Senso, ser Barduccio Canigiani, Ceracchino di Poncino, ser Francesco Landi, Pietro di Credi, Pietro di Giovanni di Ventura, Sano di Bartolomeo, Cenni di Jacomo, the stationer Pavoluccio d'Andrea, Matteo Forestani, Nanni di Master Meo, and ser Mariano di Bartolomeo.

The notary Barduccio Canigiani was a Florentine who became a close follower of Catherine in the last two years of her life and served in these years as probably her most consistent scribe. Ser Francesco Landi was a Sienese notary and member of the Riformatori, and served on the executive board in 1368 and in the Consiglio Generale in 1373. Pietro di Giovanni di Ventura was a Noveschi who resided in S. Pietro Ovile di sotto in the *terzo* of Camollia. He was with Catherine in the Sienese *contado* in 1377, at which time he carried to Siena her letter defending herself and her *famiglia* to the Sienese magistrates (letter 201); he joined her at some point during her stay in Rome in 1378–80; and later wrote a testimony for the *Processo Castellano.* He served as one of the Defensores in 1368 and 1370, as ambassador to Montalcino in 1373, and on the Consiglio Generale in the first half of 1378. It has not been possible to identify the other men on Cristofano's list with any degree of certainty.

8   In class terms, the distinction between nobles and elite nonnobles was relatively insignificant, especially compared to the gulf between elites and the lower classes, a point stressed by Alessandro Stella in his study of the Ciompi revolt (*La révolte des Ciompi*) and borne out as well in the Sienese Bruco revolt of 1371.

9   For example, in a letter to Neri di Landoccio Pagliaresi in 1379, Stefano di Corrado Maconi notes that he was writing in the company of Matteo, "nella nostra camera alla Misericordia" (Misciattelli, *Lettere di S. Caterina da Siena,* 6: 77).

10   The membership list is in Siena, Biblioteca Comunale, MS. I.V.22 (*Statuti della Compagnia della BVM*), ff. 21v–24r. Catherine's followers who are listed, in the order they appear: Nigi di Doccio, Michele di ser Monaldo, the Franciscan fra Gabriele da Volterra, Sano di Maco, Pavoluccio d'Andrea, Gabriele di Davino Piccolomini, Stefano di Corrado Maconi, Pietro di Credi, Marco Bindi, and Pietro di Giovanni Ventura. A "Stefano di Iachomo" who appears on the list with the marginal notation "morto" could possibly be Catherine's brother.

civic governments were suspicious of them and sometimes sought to outlaw them. The Compagnia della beata Vergine Maria was dominated by magnates and wealthy *popolari,* and so membership was a sign of social achievement in Siena. As Valerie Wainwright has shown, the confraternity had by the 1370s become a stronghold of the Dodici.[11] After the Dodici were proscribed in 1371, the Compagnia became a center of potential subversion, and Catherine looked to them for likely allies in her efforts to bring Siena into peace with Pope Gregory XI and to convince the Sienese regime to recognize the legitimacy of Urban VI after the schism of 1378.[12] And according to one of Stefano di Corrado Maconi's biographers, Stefano at some point used the chapel of the Compagnia to help foment a plot against the Riformatori (more about this below).

All of Catherine's chief lay followers in Siena were active in political life at the same time.[13] To understand their political involvement, some introduction is needed to the structure of political offices in Siena in the 1370s. At the height of executive authority was the Concistoro, which consisted of three separate bodies: the Signoria, the Ordines Civitatis, and the Sapientes de Concistoro. The signorial board was the seat of official executive authority and consisted of fifteen men, the Quindici Defensori. Unlike the Signoria under the Nove and Dodici, the Signoria after 1368 represented the coalition of the "popular" *monti,* although the Riformatori maintained a clear preponderance, which was strengthened by the disenfranchisement of the Dodici in 1371; from 1371 to 1384, the Signoria consisted of twelve representatives of the Riformatori and three Nove. The *popolo minuto* influence was countered to some degree by the Ordines (which consisted of twelve men over the age of twenty-five, four from each *terzo*) and the Sapientes (twenty-four men over the age of twenty-five, eight from each *terzo*), both of which customarily included nobles and Nove in addition to regular membership by Riformatori. Men in the Sapientes and Ordines participated most directly in government. In addition, nobles and prominent members of the *popolo* were often elected to influential ad hoc committees called *balìe,* or chosen for important ambassadorial functions. Nobles, because of their traditional military education and wealth, were the men usually elected as *podestà* (governors) of cities and communities

---

[11] Siena, Biblioteca Comunale I.V.22, f. 23v. Wainwright ("Conflict and Popular Government") shows how the Dodici superceded the Nove as the dominant *monte* in the confraternity, which she takes to be a measure of the social prominence of the Dodici.

[12] Letter 184 (15–27 March 1377), and letter 321 (September–October 1378).

[13] I am grateful to Elena Brizio for sharing with me at a very early stage of my research her unpublished dissertation, "Siena nel secondo Trecento," which includes a prosopography of Sienese office holders during the regime of the Riformatori. This prosopography prompted my initial interest in the political lives of Catherine's followers and proved very useful in directing my own research, which has supplemented and in some cases corrected Brizio's records of the offices held by the Caterinati.

under Sienese rule. All segments of the coalition participated in great numbers in the Consiglio Generale, which was a large communal legislature responsible in this period mainly for ratifying decisions already made in the Concistoro. Also attending the Concistoro was the *capitano del popolo*, the chief military and police officer of the commune. Military and policing functions were also carried out by two officials who were always foreigners, the *podestà* (an increasingly impotent and anachronistic official in this period) and the senator, usually a nobleman (with his own administrative and military retinue) who was responsible in some cases for carrying out wars and passing judgment in political crimes. Directly under the *capitano del popolo* were the leaders of the city's neighborhood military companies, as well as the *capitani dei vicariati*, responsible for the administration of the various military districts in the Sienese *contado*.

Catherine's spiritual sons held a number of these offices at various times. Taken together, the experiences of Catherine's followers bring her *famiglia* much closer to the center of civic politics than the rhetoric of conversion and feminine "liminality" alone would suggest.

## The Wool Master Sano di Maco

Catherine had several close followers from the ranks of the Sienese *popolo grasso* guild aristocracy, men who were politically and socially tied to the *monte dei Dodici*. This was consistent with her own family origins and with the social connections of the Dominicans. These members of Catherine's circle were active officeholders until the expulsion of the Dodici in 1371, after which they occupied minor positions.[14] These men occupied a peculiar and contradictory place within Siena. Like any member of the Dodici who was not specifically identified as an active insurgent against the regime, they were socially and economically substantial but politically proscribed.

Sano di Maco was a Dodici wool master who probably came to know Catherine through business dealings with her family or through shared Dominican friends. He remained a mainstay of Catherine's Sienese circle

---

[14] Examples of these men include Michele di ser Monaldo, mentioned as one of Catherine's followers by Cristofano di Gano, who was notary for the friary of San Domenico, and in this capacity appears in a number of documents connected to Catherine's Dominican and lay followers in the 1370s and later. Mino di Giovanni di ser Mino, a member of one of the most prominent Dodici families (with a history of connections to the Dominicans), contributed a short account of his experience with Catherine for the *Processo Castellano*, in which he gives an eyewitness account of miracles Catherine performed in 1377 at Belcaro, the fortress outside of Siena at which she founded a monastery, and at the Augustinian hermitage of Lecceto.

throughout her public career.[15] Catherine wrote him eight letters from 1375 through 1378, in four of which she addresses all her Sienese *figliuoli* through him.[16] His residence was in San Pellegrino, the neighborhood dominated by the elite members of the wool guild, in the same area where Catherine's father and brothers established workshops. It was adjacent to the *contrada* of Sant'Antonio, where Catherine's family house was. Sano, like Catherine's three brothers, was elected as a Dodici representative to the large executive committee board following the revolution of September 1368 and to the Consiglio Generale on 27 June 1370. Following the banishment of the Dodici from political office in 1371, Sano did not appear again until 1385, after the regime of the Riformatori was overthrown, when he was elected to the Consiglio Generale.[17] He was a long-time member of the elite Compagnia della beata Vergine Maria, and became prior of the Compagnia on at least three occasions—in 1377, 1378, and 1380.[18] Consistent with this impression of Sano as a pious member of the *popolo grasso* is the career of his son, who entered the Benedictine community of Monte Oliveto Maggiore. Catherine sent a letter to him and several other novices in the Olivetan monastery of San Michele in Bosco in Bologna.[19]

Catherine's letters to Sano—and to her other followers through him—strike a consistent theme of perseverance in trials. Catherine alternates between encouragement and criticism as she rallies her *famiglia* around her authority as spiritual *mamma*. These letters present an image of a group of supporters beset by misgivings and local opposition, and of

[15] Sano di Maco is sometimes referred to as "Sanus de Mazacorno" (see, for instance, *Processo Castellano*, 429). While this has led Noffke, for instance, to identify him as "Sano di Maco di Mazzacorno" (*Letters of Catherine of Siena*, 1: 92), this should perhaps be corrected to "da Mazzacorno," Mazzacorno being a variant for "Massa Corno," referring to the farmland on the river Cornia to the south of Siena. In addition, Sano was not a "wool worker" (ibid.), but a wool master (*lanaiuolo*)—an important distinction in socioeconomic status. Sano acted as procurator for Catherine's mother and sister-in-law Lisa after Catherine's death (ASS, *Gabella* 103, f. 50v; ASS, *Diplomatico, Spedale di Siena*, 7 novembre 1384). He also appeared at the chapter of the convent of Santa Caterina (of Alexandria) in 1392 (ASS, *Diplomatico, Patr. dei resti, S. Domenico*, 30 novembre 1392). Sano had at least one child, a daughter named Angela, who is recorded making a donation to San Domenico in 1381 (ASS, *Patrimonio dei Resti* 2190, f. 90v). He is mentioned frequently in correspondence between Catherine's followers (see Misciattelli, *Lettere di S. Caterina da Siena*, 6: 55–85).

[16] Letters to Sano di Maco: 69/XXIV, 147/XXV, 142/XXVI, 232/LXXV. Letters to Sano di Maco "e gli altri figliuoli:" 294, 62, 303, 318. Sano also accompanied Catherine to the founding of her monastery outside of Siena in 1377 and joined her in Rome in 1379 (see *Processo Castellano*, 429, and Misciattelli, *Lettere di S. Caterina da Siena* 6: 68).

[17] ASS, *Concistoro* 1589, f. 18r; ASS, *Concistoro* 55, 101r; ASS, *Consiglio Generale* 474; and Brizio, "Siena nel secondo Trecento," 2: 366, s.v. "Sanus Machi."

[18] See letter from Nigi di Doccio de' Arzocchi to Neri di Landoccio Pagliaresi, 22 May 1380 (Misciattelli, *Lettere di S. Caterina di Siena*, 6: 85).

[19] Letter 36; see Noffke, *Letters of Catherine of Siena*, 2: 125–26.

Sano in particular as a pious layman caught between devotion to Catherine and sensitivity over the scandal of her increasing notoriety, tensions created by the political meaning of Catherine's activities. On a first visit to Pisa in March 1375, Catherine wrote to Sano and emphasized her motherly authority and expectations, promising that she would feed him "like a son" with the food of divine grace, and calling on him to "fight and preach, like a man [*virilmente*]."[20] Writing to Santo from Avignon in July 1376, she encouraged him to remain firm in the face of trials, and willingly to endure with Christ "shame, scorn hunger, thirst, cold, heat, wrongs, and slanders," and rejoice to receive "torture and derision and taunts from the world." She warned Sano to ignore the "words sown by the devil" whether spoken by evildoers or by the "Servants of God," a likely reference to criticism she received from all sides, including some clerics, for her travels and intervention in the dispute between the pope and the Florentines.[21]

The pressures of public criticism evidently grew more intense for Sano and Catherine's other followers in Siena during her stay with the Salimbeni in the summer and fall of 1377. The Salimbeni were not only a powerful family which had been in almost constant revolt against the Riformatori, but they were also suspected of alliances with ecclesiastical forces in the war between the church and the Florentine league, of which Siena was a member. It is not surprising, therefore, that this trip marked Catherine and her followers as a subversive group in Siena. Catherine wrote to Sano at this time, acknowledged that her followers' confidence in her was being weakened by the pressure of worldly scandal, and urged her followers not to be swayed by murmurings and complaints from neighbors who presumed to judge the "servants of God." She called on Sano to reject worldly delights and status, and resist the tricks of the devil, who places murmuring and complaining words in the mouths of one's neighbors. Implicitly comparing herself and her followers to Christ and his disciples, she warned her followers not to exhibit the imperfect love of Christ's disciples before the Passion, who fled as soon as he was removed from them.[22] From this audacious parallel, she shifted to a more personal and domestic appeal, reassuring her children and calling on them to be good sons who would please their mother:

---

[20] Letter 69/XXIV.

[21] Letter 232/LXXV.

[22] Letter 294: " . . . anco è fatto come l'amore imperfetto de' discepoli di Cristo che essi avevano inanzi la passione: dilettandosi molto della presenzia sua, l'amavano, ma perché l'amore non era fondato in verità,—eravi del piacimento e diletto loro—però mancò quando fu tolta la presenzia sua; e non seppero portare la pena con Cristo, ma per timore fuggirono. Guardate, guardate che questo non tocchi a voi. Voi vi dilettate molto della presenzia, e in absenzia fate fuoco di paglia, ché, tolta la presenzia, ogni piccolo vento e piova lo spegne, e non ne rimane altro che fumo nero di tenebra di conscienzia."

Do not wonder because I am not with you. Good sons do more when the mother is not with them, because they wish to demonstrate to her the love that they have for the mother, and by this enter more into her graces when she returns. . . . I beg you, Sano, read this letter to all the children. And all pray to God for us, that it might be given to us to accomplish the honor of God—which has already begun—and the salvation of souls. We have no other desire, nor do we wish to adopt any other, in spite of anyone who has wanted or wants to impede us.[23]

In other letters, Catherine similarly emphasized for Sano the theme of perseverance in the spiritual battle, and juxtaposed the judgment of the human will, voiced by the murmurings of neighbors, and the judgment of the divine will.[24]

It is clear that the Sienese *signori* and others highly placed within Sienese government thought Catherine was up to something other than the "salvation of souls," and that others were complaining about her, even clerics and perhaps members of her own circle. Catherine's repeated use of the image of spiritual battle and her exhortations to defeat the enemies of the soul in the letters to Sano should be read in light of these complaints and the overt concern of the Sienese regime about her "plotting" with the church and Sienese subversives.[25] Catherine's images in these letters slide easily between spiritual and human affairs: the enemies of the soul are also enemies of Catherine, speaking against her public activities. What for Catherine was a conflict between human judgment and divine will was, for the Sienese regime, a conflict between Siena and the city's enemies. Sano and Catherine's other followers, who unlike Catherine remained within Siena and subject to Sienese jurisdiction, were caught in between these two modes of interpretation. Catherine wrote letters to other followers at this time in which she similarly upbraided them for pusillanimity and lack of commitment to her; for example, she addressed her "flock" in Siena through Matteo de' Cenni, rector of the Hospital of the Misericordia, urging them to "be true sheep; do not be afraid of your

---

[23] Ibid.: " . . . siate figliuoli fedeli, forti e perseveranti in Cristo dolce Gesù: così sconfiggerete le tentazioni del demonio e le parole sue, che egli dice ponendosi per le lingue delle creature. . . . e non mirate perché io non vi sia, ché i buoni figliuoli fanno più quando la madre non è presente che essendo presente, volendo mostrar l'amore che essi ànno a la madre, e per più venirle in grazia. . . . Voi prego, Sano, che a tutti e' figliuoli leggiate questa lettera; tutti pregate Dio per noi, che ci dia a compire l'onore suo, il quale è cominciato, e la salute dell'anime, che altro desiderio non voliamo né altro adoperare, a malgrado di chi el voleva e vuole impedire."

[24] For example, letter 62.

[25] For example, letter 69/XXIV, and letter 62, in which Catherine moves from discussing the spiritual battle to reproaching Sano and her *figliuoli* in Siena for complaining about others under the guise of good intentions, a charge that can be related to letter 294 and its criticism of her followers' lack of confidence in Catherine and her mission.

own shadows."[26] Sano was a member of a prominent but politically disenfranchised social group, beset by enemies within the city and compromised further by the scandal of being one of Catherine's *figliuoli,* and so experienced in a particularly direct way the tensions of that commitment, and had particular reason for misgivings over Catherine's increasingly public notoriety. Catherine's rhetoric throughout her public career sought a universal perspective beyond city walls and civic responsibilities, and it is this perspective that she communicated in her letters to Sano. For Sano and others within Siena, the detachment from local ties necessitated by complete commitment to Catherine was much more complicated than what Catherine or her hagiographers conveyed.

### Nanni di ser Vanni Savini, Dodici Rebel

While Sano di Maco's sociopolitical background combined with his relations with Catherine might have made him suspect in Siena, another Dodici member of Catherine's *famiglia*—the wealthy banker Nanni di ser Vanni Savini—would have been considered especially obnoxious by the regime. Nanni's continuous connection with Catherine and her *famiglia* can be deduced from references to him in several of Catherine's letters from 1375 through 1378. Nanni donated his fortress of Belcaro, a short distance from Siena, to Catherine to found a new monastery, some time before September 1376.[27] Within Catherine's *famiglia* he served as a messenger and bearer of letters and money.[28] For example, in a letter of 1378 to Neri di Landoccio Pagliaresi, with Catherine in Florence, Stefano di Corrado Maconi noted that he had sent to Neri by way of Nanni di ser Vanni a "very fine letter" ("capitolo molto bello") written by William Flete against the Florentines.[29] Raymond of Capua describes in the *Legenda*

---

[26] Letter 124: "Adunque siate pecorelle vere, e non temete dell'ombre vostre." See also letter 128, to Gabriele di Davino Piccolomini, and letter 216, to Nigi di Doccio Arzocchi.

[27] Catherine received a papal license for the monastery during her stay in Avignon, to which she departed in September 1376, so Nanni must have offered her the fortress before that date. Catherine petitioned the Sienese government for permission to take possession of the fortress on 25 January 1377 (ASS, *Consiglio Generale* 187, f. 9r–v; printed in Laurent, ed., *Documenti,* 41–43.

[28] Catherine refers to "Nanni," without further identification, in five letters: 228, 273/XXXI, 198/IV, 80, and 365. Since there does not seem to have been anyone else of this name active in Catherine's *famiglia,* it is very likely that these references are to Nanni di ser Vanni.

[29] Misciattelli, *Lettere di S. Caterina da Siena* 6: 64 (Stefano di Corrado Maconi to Neri di Landoccio Pagliaresi, dated Siena, 22 May 1378): "Mandoti per Nanni di ser Vanni uno Capitolo molto bello che 'l Baccelliere à fatto per gli fiorentini." (William Flete is almost always referred to in the Catherinian literature as "the Bachelor," in reference to his university degree.)

*maior* how Catherine converted Nanni, an expert in the art of vendetta "notorious among all the worldly minded men of Siena," who was fomenting a series of private feuds under the pretext of seeking peace. Raymond tells how Nanni was sent to Catherine by William Flete, and how in Raymond's presence Catherine brought Nanni to contrition and conversion through her interior prayer. Nanni confessed to Raymond and made peace with his enemies. A few days later he was arrested and imprisoned by civic authorities and seemed likely to have awaited execution, but in the end he was released after suffering only the loss of "a great deal of property," and thereupon donated Belcaro to Catherine. Raymond notes that he became Nanni's confessor for several years subsequently, and that Nanni experienced a "thorough and long-lasting" change in his life—although Raymond, cautiously, only vouches for the time he was Nanni's confessor.[30]

Other evidence of Nanni's career conflicts with Raymond's account, or at least colors the story differently. Nanni's imprisonment, his loss of property, and even his donation of the castle of Belcaro to Catherine can all be related to his role as a conspicuous participant in Dodici- and Salimbeni-led activity against the ruling government in the early 1370s. By the time of the revolutions that brought the Riformatori to power in 1368–71, Nanni had established himself as one of the most prominent and wealthy citizens of Siena. As Valerie Wainwright has noted, Nanni was one of several very wealthy Dodici who were able to gain political and social ascendancy during the regime of the Nove, and thus achieved even more exalted status once the Dodici came to power in 1355.[31] He served in a number of offices between the 1368 revolution and the Revolt of the Bruco in 1371—for instance, acting as an ambassador to one of the mercenary companies (in March 1371)[32] and to Florence (in May 1371), and serving on select committees concerned with the governing of Lucignano, monetary affairs, and the city grain supply.[33]

---

[30] *LM*, pars. 235–39.

[31] As a measure of his wealth, Nanni was taxed at the tenth highest rate in the *terzo* of Città (the section of the city in which much of Siena's "old money" was concentrated) in the Lira of 1371. His sister, Margarita, married Nicolò di Pietro Malavolti, a member of one of the five most prestigious noble families, and brought a handsome dowry of 1,200 gold florins (Wainwright, "Conflict and Popular Government," 75 and 78n).

[32] Neri di Donato, 637.

[33] Nanni was elected to the Sapientes per Lucignano five times in 1371, on 18 January, 5 April, 17 April, 2 May, and 22 May (ASS, *Concistoro* 59, f. 35r and 30v; 60, 4v and 22r). He was elected one of the *sapientes per denari* on 4 May 1370; one of the *ufficiales per biado* on 9 May 1370; and one of the *sapientes per la Lira* on 3 April 1371 (ASS, *Concistoro* 55, f. 3v and f. 9v; and 59, f. 24r). He was chosen as ambassador to the *compagnie di venture* on 22 March 1371 (ASS, *Concistoro* 59, f. 13v) and as ambassador to Florence on 31 May 1371 (ASS, *Concistoro* 60, 30r; and Neri di Donato, 637). See also Brizio, "Siena nel secondo Trecento," 2: 290, s.v. "Nannes ser Vannis."

Elected as one of the grain officials in May 1370, he was one of a number of officials replaced after grain riots that summer, in which many of the same *popolo minuto* wool workers who would participate in the Revolt of the Bruco the following year demonstrated against supposed hoarding of grain by members of the Dodici and Nove.[34] In the reprisals that followed the Revolt of the Bruco and the Salimbeni-led coup the following year, Nanni was—like Catherine's brothers—identified as one of the enemies of the regime and fined; according to Neri di Donato, he was one of the two most heavily penalized men.[35] A year later, Nanni was identified as a co-conspirator with Gonuzo Salimbeni and several Dodici in a plot against the regime, for which he was imprisoned and fined.[36] And Nanni is listed as one of the *ribelli* reconciled with the commune in August 1375 in the settlement of the Salimbeni revolt of 1374–75, and thereby identified as one of the Salimbeni allies punished for aiding in the rebellion.[37] Nanni was one of a number of members of the Salimbeni/Dodici cohort who traveled to Florence in June 1375 for discussions of the settlement of the treaty between the Salimbeni and the Sienese regime.[38] Neri di Donato notes that on 11 June Agnolino di Giovanni Salimbeni and several others traveled to Florence "with all the banished rebels and opponents of the commune of Siena, without a good man among them."[39] Nanni donated the fortress of Belcaro to Catherine as an act of piety, but only after it had been razed, along with the Sienese property of the Salimbeni and others, by the *popolo* in the early stages of the 1374 Salimbeni revolt.[40] It is very hard to imagine that Nanni would have been permitted to take possession again of a fortress so close to the walls of Siena. Whether because of his conversion or because of the change in his worldly fortunes resulting from civic punishments, Nanni—such a conspicuous and volatile participant in civic affairs before 1375—does not surface again in the documents as a political player after the settlement of the Salimbeni revolt August 1375.[41]

[34] Neri di Donato, 636, and Valerie Wainwright, "The Testing of a Sienese Popular Regime," 150–51.

[35] Neri di Donato, 642.

[36] Ibid.

[37] Nanni is listed in the account of the settlement in ASS, *Consiglio Generale* 185, 69v.

[38] Sienese ambassadors to Florence wrote to the Sienese governors on June 5 about Nanni's arrival and his reasons for his visit (ASS, *Concistoro* 1786, 34).

[39] Neri di Donato, 658: "Agnolino di Joanni Salimbeni e 'l priore de' Salimbeni andoro a Fiorenza a dì XI di giugno, per cagione de la detta pace, con Marco Bindi e Biagio da Montemassi e Bartolomeo di Masso e Nicolò d'Antonio Barnini e Mone e quello di Lorenzo Ughetti e Pavolo di Veltro e Battacone, con tutti le sbanditi ribelli e contrari al communo di Siena, senza uno omo buono."

[40] Neri di Donato, 656.

[41] There is one reference to Nanni in the records of the Concistoro for 14 May 1376 (ASS, *Concistoro* 80, f. 7r), on which day he was given leave to travel outside Siena.

Raymond's account of his crimes is misleading, perhaps intentionally so. Nanni did lose property and could certainly have been arrested, but his notoriety in Siena was due to his activities against the regime, not his engagement in *vendette*.

Nanni is an intriguing nexus in the developing network around Catherine of Siena at the outset of the War of Eight Saints. It was Nanni, enemy of the Riformatori, who engaged the spiritual direction of William Flete. Again, Flete may have been the conduit for the first contacts between Catherine and her circle and the Salimbeni family, with whom Nanni was so notoriously identified. Nanni's movements in June 1375 are also intriguing. In Florence, he presumably met with the Florentines charged with negotiating the peace between the Salimbeni and the Sienese commune, among whom were Buonaccorso di Lapo and Carlo and Leonardo Strozzi–leaders of the propapal Albizzi faction of the Parte Guelfa, men with close connections to Raymond and to Catherine herself as well as to their mission. Some time shortly after June 20, Catherine apparently sent Raymond to the English *condottiere* John Hawkwood to invite him to enlist in a planned Crusade; a Florentine informant spotted him there along with two companions, one of whom was "a man of a bad sort and much involved in plots." In her letter to Raymond recounting the execution of Niccolò di Toldo, a letter that was probably written during his embassy to Hawkwood, Catherine greets "Nanni and Jacomo." There's no way to know for certain, but given his presence in Florence at the time and his intimacy with Raymond and Catherine, this very likely means that Nanni di ser Vanni was one of Raymond's companions. He moved between the Salimbeni, the Florentine Parte Guelfa and propapal elites, and Catherine and Raymond in their mission on behalf of the church.[42]

Speculation aside, what can be known of Nanni's career reveals the political trajectory of the mission of Catherine and Raymond in the spring of 1375. Nanni links the religious reformer and sometime opponent of the Riformatori, William Flete; the regime of the Dodici, which had maintained strong ties to papal interests in Italy; the rebellious Salimbeni cohort, themselves suspected by the Sienese of receiving encouragement and support from the papal governor Gerard du Puy; and the ecclesiastical diplomacy on which Catherine and Raymond embarked in early 1375. Catherine's *famiglia* was simultaneously a spiritual association and a political movement.

---

[42] The "Nanni" of the Niccolò di Toldo letter has not previously been identified with Nanni di ser Vanni, but there is no other "Nanni" mentioned anywhere in connection with Catherine. Burlamacchi, among others, assumed that "Nanni" was a diminutive of "Giovanni," but this assumption is mistaken. Nanni di ser Vanni is referred to in Latin records of the communal government as "Nannes ser Vannis."

## The Notary Cristofano di Gano Guidini

Far more information concerning the life of Cristofano di Gano Guidini survives independent of Catherinian hagiography: ten volumes of notarial cartularies covering his entire career from 1362–1409 in addition to his own autobiographical *Memorie*. It depicts his family life, public career, and spiritual aspirations, including an engaging description of his relations with Catherine.[43] Cristofano joined Catherine's circle sometime before 1375, through the agency of two of her noble followers, Neri di Landoccio Pagliaresi and Nigi di Doccio Arzocchi, and became one of her core followers.[44] In 1378, during Catherine's stay in Florence, he acted as an envoy between Catherine and her followers in Siena, and was with Catherine at the time of her near martyrdom during the Ciompi revolt (described in chapter 5).[45] He helped promulgate Catherine's writings by translating her *Libro* into Latin.[46] Caffarini, in his deposition for the *Processo Castellano*, noted that Cristofano was one of Catherine's scribes and responsible for one of the collections of her letters after her death, and described communications between himself and Cristofano regarding Catherine's prospects for canonization. Bartolomeo Dominici also described Cristofano as one of Catherine's most devoted followers.[47]

Cristofano's *Libro di memorie* gives particularly colorful evidence of his investment in Sienese civic life, and the way in which he negotiated his relationship with Catherine within other commitments. Cristofano describes how he sought Catherine's advice in choosing a wife. Under her influence, Cristofano had been considering embracing the religious life.

[43] The autograph manuscript of Cristofano's *Libro di memorie* is ASS, *Ospedale di S. Maria della Scala*, 1188. The narrative portions of this book are published in *Archivio Storico Italiano*, series 1, vol. 4, pt. 2, 27–48. All references here are to the printed edition. Some financial notations included in the original are not reproduced in the edition. On the financial activity represented in the MS, see Giovanni Cherubini, "Dal libro di ricordi di un notaio senese del Trecento," in *Signori, contadini, borghesi: Ricerche sulla società italiana del basso medioevo* (1974), 393–425.

[44] Cristofano di Gano Guidini, *Libro di memorie*, 31. Both Neri and Nigi served on the Ordines at the same time that Cristofano became notary to the *capitano del popolo* in January and February 1375 (see ASS, *Concistoro* 75, ff. 1–2), at which time they could easily have met.

[45] In her letter to Raymond of Capua describing these events (letter 295), Catherine refers Raymond to "Cristofano" for a complete account. In Letter 298, Catherine writes from Florence to Stefano di Corrado Maconi in Siena, instructing Stefano, if he cannot come to Florence himself, to respond to her letter by way of "Cristofano," the bearer of Catherine's letter.

[46] Cristofano also wrote a life of Giovanni Colombini, the Sienese founder of the Gesuati, a work that is now lost, but which was used by Feo Belcari in his fifteenth-century life of Colombini (Cherubini, "Dal libro di ricordi di un notaio senese del Trecento," 394).

[47] *Processo Castellano*, 41, 54–5, 57, 69–70, 73, 89, and 445. On his role in the collections of Catherine's letters, see E. Dupré Theseider, "Il problema critico delle lettere di Santa Caterina da Siena." *Giornale storico della letteratura italiana* 69 (1933): 117–278.

But conscience-stricken after his mother pleaded that he not abandon her, he decided to marry, and asked Catherine (who was in Pisa) for advice in choosing between three marriage prospects.[48] Cristofano quotes Catherine's reply in full, although she reproached him for a lack of commitment and for insincerity. Christ commanded his followers to abandon their parents, so what he claimed as conscience was in fact the devil's temptation.[49] Catherine, as elsewhere, asserted the absolute priority of spiritual affiliation over worldly families and obligations, though it is clear that she did not expect Cristofano to be swayed by her argument. Her tone, rather than reproachful, could be read as affectionate mocking of a follower whom she knew to be committed only so far, unlike several others who went on to become religious of one sort or another, like Neri di Landoccio Pagliaresi, Francesco Malavolti, and Stefano di Corrado Maconi. Further, despite her comments and reluctance to involve herself in matters that "concern worldly people, not me," Catherine, seeing that he was determined "to embroil himself in the perverse and wicked world," gave in to Cristofano's request, and made a specific recommendation; apparently Catherine was familiar with the girls in question, or at least with their families.[50] Having taken care to ask Catherine's opinion, Cristofano did not in fact take her advice, and on 28 October 1375 contracted marriage with a different choice: Mattia, daughter of one of Catherine's fellow *mantellate*, Caterina di Ghetto. They had seven children, one of whom he named "Caterina," out of veneration for St. Catherine as well in honor of his mother-in-law. Mattia died, along with six of their seven children, in an outbreak of plague in 1390.[51]

A modern reader is immediately struck by the fact that Catherine's letter, and Cristofano's explanation, portray his piety as less-than-dauntless. But his presentation of the letter without apparent embarrassment is evidence, perhaps, of how unrealistic a religious commitment had been for him. Further, Cristofano expected his readers to understand the nature of his choice and to sympathize with his reasons. As he points out, his mother had made considerable sacrifices in his interest. Cristofano's mother was born into one of the provincial branches of the Piccolomini, one of the most prominent Sienese noble families. His father Gano died in the Black Death of 1348, leaving behind such big debts that his mother

---

[48] Cristofano di Gano Guidini, *Libro di memorie*, 31–32.

[49] Letter 43/XLIV.

[50] Ibid.: "Del fatto della sposa io vi rispondo che mal volontieri di questo io mi impaccio, però che s'apartiene a' secolari più che a me; non di meno non posso contradire al vostro desiderio, considerato la condizione di tutte e tre, ch'ognuna è buona. Se vi sentite di non curarvi perch'abbi auto altro sposo, potetel fare, poi che volete impacciarvi in el malvagio e perverso secolo. Se lasaste però, prendete quella di Francesco Ventura da Camporeggi."

[51] Ibid.

could not even recover her dowry. She thus had good reason to remarry, a choice that likely would have meant leaving Cristofano to be raised by her dead husband's family.[52] Instead, she returned with her son to her natal family. With the help of his maternal grandfather, Manno di Minuccio Piccolomini, Cristofano was educated and obtained positions tutoring the sons of two *novesche* families in Siena and also apprenticed in the notarial arts. From 1362, throughout the last years of Dodici rule and first years of the Riformatori, presumably through his mother's family connections and his new contacts in Siena, he obtained positions of authority in his native region of the Sienese *contado,* acting on five different occasions as Sienese vicar in Armaiolo.[53] By 1375, Cristofano began regularly obtaining notarial offices in the Palazzo Pubblico, acting for instance as notary to the *capitano del popolo* in 1375 and as notary to the Concistoro twice during the Riformatori (in 1376 and 1378) and at least once during the regime of the Dieci Priori, which followed the fall of the Riformatori in 1385.[54] His volumes of minutes to the Concistoro deliberations are idiosyncratic and apparently unique in this period, in that the first entry always begins with the invocation "Ave Maria." By choosing to marry he recognized his mother's sacrifice and the beneficial results for his career and also became a property-holder and entered into political office. With Mattia's dowry of 350 florins, he bought a house in the Ovile section of Siena as well as a piece of land in his native region of Armaiolo.[55] Cristofano served on the Consiglio Generale in 1377, 1382, and 1384;[56] and became one of the fifteen-member signorial board of

52 Klapisch-Zuber, "The 'Cruel Mother,'" 117–31.

53 Cristofano di Gano Guidini, *Libro di memorie,* 30.

54 Cristofano's appointment as notary to the *capitano del popolo* is noted in ASS, *Concistoro* 75, f. 2. He was notary to the Concistoro in January to February 1376 (ASS, *Concistoro* 79) and March to April 1378 (*Concistoro* 90). He is identified reading to the assembled Consiglio Generale a letter sent to the *concistoro* on 25 April 1378 (ASS, *Consiglio Generale* 187, f. 165v). Concerning his notariate after the 1385 revolution, see Cristofano di Gano Guidini, *Libro di memorie,* 30. For Cristofano's other notarial assignments in the Palazzo, including stints as election official and tutor to notarial apprentices, see ASS, *Concistoro* 78, 21v (3 December 1375); *Concistoro* 88, f. 40v (7 December 1377); *Concistoro* 94 (6 December 1378) and 24 (24 December 1378); *Concistoro* 96, f. 18 (13 April 1379); *Concistoro* 100, f. 12 (16 January 1380). His increasing status is signaled by the increases in salary he reports in the *Libro di memorie:* paid 300 lire and 1/3 for service his first time as notary to the concistoro, he received 800 lire the second time, and 1,000 lire from the new regime after 1385 (*Libro di memorie,* 30).

55 Cristofano di Gano Guidini, *Libro di memorie,* 40. In the Lira of 1385, Cristofano was taxed 8 denarii for his house in San Pietro d'Ovile (ASS, *Lira* 21, f. 104v). The size of Mattia's dowry is high for the bride of a notary in this period. (I am grateful to Edward English for this observation.) This confirms the importance of Cristofano's family background in his success.

56 ASS, *Concistoro* 84, f. 36v (6 June 1377); 114, f. 37r (28 December 1382); 122, f. 67v (23 June 1384); and see Brizio, "Siena nel secondo Trecento," 2: 111, s.v. "ser Cristofanus Gani."

Defensores in 1383 and 1384.[57] From 1388 to his death in 1409, Cristofano was notary for the largest and most venerable Sienese charitable institution, the Spedale di Santa Maria della Scala.

While clearly pious, Cristofano was (as Catherine suggested) deeply invested in Sienese affairs, exhibiting a particularly civic piety in the invocations of his Concistoro volumes, and in his attachment to the Spedale della Scala. Indeed, while Catherine's other nonnoble close followers were associated with political entities that were disenfranchised or outlawed under the Riformatori, Cristofano was actually a member of the governing *monte*, and identified with the "new men" who mostly constituted that *monte*.[58] Cristofano's rapid advancement might well have owed much to the expulsion of the Dodici and their families from public life. Since notaries were typically *dodicini*, there was need for new men to fill notarial offices in Siena after 1371. Cristofano's identification is not itself a clear register of his political commitments; as a "new man" in Sienese politics in the 1370s, Cristofano was by definition a member of the Riformatori. As a member of Catherine's *famiglia*, he undoubtedly leaned toward the papal party and objected to the Sienese alliance with Florence against the pope, just as later he clearly did support Sienese reconciliation with the papacy and loyalty to Urban VI.[59] Also, the fact that he was rehired as notary to the Concistoro under the Dieci Priori also suggests that he was not identified as an opponent of the higher orders in Sienese society, nor as an especially active proponent of the Riformatori. More important than what might be inferred about his political views is his proximity throughout his career to Sienese government. In this respect his notarial positions are more significant than his elective offices (which during Catherine's lifetime were not especially prestigious), since his activities in the Palazzo placed him in close familiarity with both the protagonists and the policies of Sienese government throughout the War of Eight Saints and Catherine's public career. Thus he could have served for Catherine and her circle as a source of information and influence within the Palazzo Pubblico, a link to the very center of political life. In sum, Cristofano was a man of pronounced civic piety, devoted to Catherine both during her life and after her death, but in the context of a variety of his other more ordinary obligations and commitments.

[57] Cristofano di Gano Guidini, *Libro di memorie*, 31.

[58] This is implicit in his probably overstated emphasis, at the beginning of the *Libro di memorie*, of his humble origins: "In prima sia manifesto a chi vedrà questa scrittura, come io ser Christofano di Gano predetto so' di vile nazione" (*Libro di memorie*, 28). Also, insofar as it is possible to identify them in Brizio's prosopographical study, it appears that all of the godparents Cristofano names for his children (*Libro di memorie*, 43–47) were Riformatori.

[59] See his letter from Siena to Neri di Landoccio Pagliaresi in Rome, 14 January 1379, in which he reports on the likelihood of Sienese support for Urban VI (Misciattelli, *Lettere di S. Caterina da Siena*, 6: 68).

## The Nobles

The true core of Catherine's *famiglia*, her "bella brigata," was young members of the Sienese noble families. Neri di Landoccio Pagliaresi, Nigi di Doccio Arzocchi, Gabriele di Davino Piccolomini, Francesco di Vanni Malavolti, and Stefano di Corrado Maconi were all members of Catherine's circle beginning in at least 1374. These young men shared social backgrounds and education, and came from families (with the exception of the Malavolti) that all resided within neighboring sections of the *terzo* of San Martino. They grew up together and must have known each other well before entrance into Catherine's circle, and several of them (particularly Stefano di Corrado and Neri di Landoccio) maintained intimate friendships after her death. Like Sano di Maco, Nigi di Doccio, Stefano di Corrado, and Gabriele di Davino became members of the Compagnia della beata Vergine Maria prior to 1378.[60]

Since the advent of the Nove in 1287, Sienese governmental authority had been officially in the hands of the *popolo*, with the nobles excluded from the Signoria. While family honor and habitual *vendette* between the various clans made it difficult for them to unify under one banner, on the occasions when the nobles did achieve at least partial and temporary solidarity the consequences for a popular regime could be grave.[61] Both the Nove and the Dodici fell at least in part as a result of actions of the noble families, and the nobles could not have enjoyed any more than did the Nove and Dodici the emergence into political authority during the Riformatori of the lower elements of the *popolo*. Indeed, the revolution that toppled the Riformatori in 1385 was engineered by the nobles. With the exception of the Tolomei, the nobles were at least latent dissidents throughout the 1370s and early 1380s. Nevertheless, it was practically impossible to do without them, since they were usually among the only Sienese with enough money to administer the key financial offices of the Gabella and Biccherna, as well as having the resources in personnel and fortified property in the *contado* to man important military and territorial governing posts. Elena Brizio has shown that, despite the theoretical exclusion of the nobles from the regime itself, the noble families were

---

[60] Siena, Biblioteca Comunale, MS I.V.22. While Nigi appears to have joined long before the other noble Caterinati on the membership list, Stefano and Gabriele appear to have joined at the same time: Stefano's name follows immediately after Gabriele's, and both names are written in the same hand, which is different from the hand that wrote the names before and after theirs.

[61] In both the revolutions of 1355 and 1368, the revolt of the nobles was occasioned by the visit of the emperor, or of an imperial vicar, to the Siena. Whereas one noble family could not easily agree to follow the leadership of another family, since this would imply a loss of status, they could make common cause under the imperial banner without compromising honor or their standing amongst Sienese families.

present in force throughout Sienese government during the Riformatori.[62] Among these families, the Tolomei and Salimbeni exercised special
influence on Sienese politics, and must be set aside as being exceptional
cases. The Tolomei were fully represented in government during the
Riformatori, as noble protectors of the regime. The Salimbeni engineered
the revolt in 1368 that put power in the hands of a popular government,
and were soon after barred from governmental offices because of their
naked ambitions for signorial control. The other noble families, on the
other hand, were constant but ambivalent participants in the governing
coalition.

Like other members of their natal families, Catherine's noble *figliuoli*
were elected to political offices in Siena during the Riformatori. Participation in political offices was part of familial strategies for individual and
group aggrandizement. As Elena Brizio has suggested, it is possible at
times to discern a division of responsibilities within larger families, with
some members concentrating on select executive offices and leaving to
others representation in the Consiglio Generale.[63] The political offices
Catherine's spiritual sons held in Siena represent their continued implication in mundane family alliances and family obligations. Not only did
they regularly seek and obtain seats on the large and heterogeneous legislative body of the Consiglio Generale, but they also attained election to
the Ordines and the Sapientes, the two advisory bodies that, with the
Defensores, constituted the Sienese Concistoro—the very center of
Sienese political authority. In the records of these years, one can often
find two or more of these men serving on the Consiglio Generale at the
same time. Given Catherine's family background, her public activities,
and her clerical network, the suspicions of the Sienese regime in 1377
about the activities of Catherine's *famiglia* were not unreasonable. The
regime, observing groups of her noble *figliuoli* in political offices, might
easily have looked on Catherine's followers as a faction within the government, and a potential source of political opposition.

Gabriele di Davino Piccolomini, a member of one of the largest and most
prominent Sienese noble clans, entered Catherine's circle by around 1375,
joined her at the Rocca d'Orcia for part of her trip there in late summer
1377, traveled with her to Rome in November 1378, and after her death
devoted himself to service with one of the Sienese hospitals.[64] Like several
other Caterinati, by 1378 he had become a member of the Compagnia della

---

[62]  Brizio "Siena nel secondo Trecento."

[63]  Brizio, "L'elezione degli uffici politici," 16–62.

[64]  On Gabriele's participation in Catherine's circle, see the testimony of Tommaso Caffarini in *Processo Castellano*, 40. On his travels with Catherine, see Gardner, *Saint Catherine of
Siena*, 89, 213, and 288. Gabriele is referred to a number of times in the records of the hospital of Santa Caterina (named after Catherine of Alexandria), which was founded by the

beata Vergine Maria.[65] Gabriele joined a long list of members of his clan in the Consiglio Generale for semestral terms in 1370 through 1376, and then again in 1378–79.[66] The break in Gabriele's attendance in the Consiglio Generale in 1377 might, in part, be explained by his accompanying Catherine in her travels in the Sienese *contado* in that year. Nigi di Doccio Arzocchi, from one of the smaller noble clans, had apparently become one of Catherine's circle by 1374, at which time Cristofano di Gano Guidini reports that he was introduced to Catherine by Nigi and Neri di Landoccio Pagliaresi. Nigi also joined the Compagnia della beata Vergine Maria and maintained contacts with others of Catherine's circle after her death.[67] Nigi served in the Consiglio Generale for seven semesters from 1370 through 1379; in 1372 he was twice a failed candidate for the commune's chief economic councils, the Gabella and the Biccherna; in November 1373 he was chosen as *podestà* of the Sienese subject community of the Abbadia di San Salvatore (near Montalcino); and was elected to the Concistoro as one of the Ordines in 1372, 1375, and 1379.[68] Gabriele and Nigi were among the followers left behind in Siena whom Catherine sought to reassure when she and her group came under deepening suspicion during her stay with the Salimbeni in autumn and winter 1377 and as the hostilities between the papacy and Florence reached their most intense moment. Not surprisingly, considering their continued ties to Sienese political life, Catherine wrote them letters resembling those sent to Sano di Maco.[69]

Also typical of the dual allegiances maintained by Catherine's followers is the career of Francesco di Vanni Malavolti, a member of one of the oldest and most powerful Sienese clans and one of Catherine's most intimate followers from around 1375. In his testimony for the *Processo Castellano*, Francesco describes his conversion after being introduced to Catherine by Neri di Landoccio Pagliaresi, a period of sinful relapse while Catherine was away in Avignon, a second conversion and reintegration into the *famiglia*, and an eyewitness account of miracles Catherine performed in

---

Nove family of the Petroni and attached to one of the major Sienese charitable/medical institutions, the Misericordia, whose rector Matteo di Fazio de' Cenni was also one of Catherine's circle.

[65] Siena, Biblioteca Comunale, MS. I.V.22, f. 23v.

[66] ASS, *Concistoro* 55, f. 108r; 67, f. 39r; 71, 59v; 74, f. 22v; 76, f. 49v; 80, f. 64r; 94, f. 52r. A letter home from a Sienese ambassador to Avignon in January 1375 refers to a letter from the *signori* carried to him by "Gabriele de' Piccolomini" (ASS, *Concistoro* 1785, 56). It is possible that Gabriele di Davino was the emissary referred to here, but there were two other Piccolomini named Gabriele also active in Sienese politics at this time.

[67] Siena, Biblioteca Comunale, MS. I.V.22, f. 21v.

[68] ASS, *Concistoro* 55, f. 106v; 63, f. 2r; 65, ff. 26r–v; 67, f. 27r; 67, ff. 39r–41r; 72, ff. 42v–55r; 73, f. 54r; 74, f. 22v; 75, f. 2r; 76, f. 49v; 80, f. 65r; 82, f. 49r; 94, f. 52v; 96, f. 2r; 97, 50v.

[69] Letters 128 and 216.

summer 1377 at the Salimbeni stronghold in the Val d'Orcia and in Montepulciano.[70] After Catherine's death, against his family's opposition (and with the help of an encouraging vision from Catherine), Francesco entered the monastery of Monte Oliveto Maggiore in 1388, served for several years in various offices within the Olivetan order, and in 1411 was made abbot of the Benedictine monastery of Sant'Emiliano (near Sassoferrato) by Pope Gregory XII.[71]

Until he embarked on the monastic life, Francesco took regular part in Sienese political life, following in the footsteps of his father, Vanni di Francesco Malavolti, an influential noble who had been a prominent participant in the noble coup d'état in September 1368. Francesco was elected to the Ordines in September 1377, and to the Consiglio Generale in July and December 1374, June 1375, December 1376, December 1377, December 1382, and March 1385, immediately after the noble coup d'état that ended the government of the Riformatori.[72] Unlike Catherine's other followers, Francesco remained involved in Sienese secular politics long after her death, a fact that might be linked to the relative vigor with which his family, among the noble clans, exercised political authority. For instance, his election to the first Consiglio Generale under the Priori, the regime that followed Riformatori, should be seen in the context of the central role played by members of his family, with the Salimbeni and Piccolomini, in the coup. Francesco's activity in 1377, before Catherine's death, demonstrates most dramatically his movement between her circle and the Palazzo Pubblico. He was with Catherine in the Sienese *contado* in the summer of that year, during the beginning of her mission in the lands of the Salimbeni.[73] He was then elected to the Ordines in September, serving in the Concistoro in September and October 1377, while Catherine was under great suspicion in Siena for her connections to the papacy, the Salimbeni, and the affair of the abbot of Sant' Antimo (described in chapter 5). In other words, Francesco provided Catherine with a connection in government at a particularly sensitive moment in her career, an affiliation that could have strengthened the

---

[70] Francesco's account, in which his conversion is followed briefly by his return to former ways during Catherine's trip to Avignon, suggests that he had not joined Catherine's circle long before 1376 (*Processo Castellano*, 376–79).

[71] *Processo Castellano*, xxv.

[72] ASS, *Concistoro* 72, f. 47v (election to Consiglio Generale, 1 July 1374); *Concistoro* 74 (Consiglio Generale, 19 December 1374); *Concistoro* 76, f. 49v (Consiglio Generale, 19 June 1375); Concistoro 82, f. 57v (Consiglio Generale, 30 December 1376); *Concistoro* 86, f. 2r (Ordines, 1 September 1377); *Concistoro* 88, ff. 50r–51r (Consiglio Generale, 28 December 1377); *Concistoro* 114, f. 34r (Consiglio Generale, 28 December 1382); Concistoro 129, f. 26v (Consiglio Generale, 27 March 1385).

[73] Brizio has Francesco elected to the Consiglio Generale on 29 June 1377, but there is no reference to this election in the relevant volume of *Concistoro* records (vol. 84).

apprehensions of the Riformatori over Catherine's activities and caused them to treat Catherine and her *famiglia* not as a politically marginal group, but as a potentially subversive party within government.[74]

Two further nobles, whose stories warrant special attention, negotiated the conflicts between familial and civic obligations and membership in Catherine's *famiglia* differently.

## Neri di Landoccio Pagliaresi

Neri di Landoccio Pagliaresi, a member of one of the lesser Sienese noble families, was one of Catherine's closest followers during her public career, serving regularly as her scribe and compiling some of the first collections of her letters after her death.[75] He was also a poet, whose surviving works include long verse adaptations of the stories of Barlaam and Josephat and of Santa Eufrosina as well as a number of *laudi*.[76] Neri's *laudi*, as well as his original contributions to the hagiographical accounts he used for his longer works, express a characteristic penitential élan and intense spiritual longing, emphasizing the theme of the restless soul, longing for the peace of union with God—a sentiment that resonates also in Catherine's writings. Neri's choice of Eufrosina as a poetic subject was perhaps related to the fact that, as Raymond of Capua notes in the *Legenda maior*, Catherine as a young girl was nicknamed "Eufrosina" and took as an early model the story of Santa Eufrosina, who disguised herself as a man in order to enter a monastery and so evade marriage. Neri's "Leggenda di santo Giosofà" is a poetic reworking of the popular medieval hagiographical story of Barlaam and Josephat, itself a Christianization of the life of Buddha. Both of his longer poems are stories of noble youths who turn away from worldly power and wealth to embrace a life of asceticism and prayer, a popular hagiographic theme that had special application to Neri's career.

---

[74] In her letter of September 1377 to the Capitano del Popolo, Salvi di ser Pietro (letter 122), after defending herself against charges of political scheming, Catherine sends greetings to Francesco: "Conforta Francesco in Gesù Cristo."

[75] A letter in Pagliaresi's hand is one of Catherine's eight surviving original letters (Siena, Biblioteca Comunale, MS. T.III.3). And he is cited in the Caterinian sources, along with Stefano Maconi and the Florentine notary Barduccio Canigiani, as one of the scribes who took dictation of Catherine's *Libro della divina dottrina* in late 1377 and 1378. Two manuscripts of the letters that are all or in part in Neri's hand are Vienna, Österreichische Nationalbibliotek, Palatino 3514, and Florence, Biblioteca Nazionale, Magliabechiano XXXVIII, 130.

[76] Giorgio Varanini, ed., *Cantari religiosi senesi del Trecento: Neri Pagliaresi, fra Felice Tancredi da Massa, Niccolò Cicerchia* (1965); and Neri Pagliaresi, *Rime sacre di certa o probabile attribuzione*, ed. Giorgio Varanini (1970). On Neri's career and writings, see Varanini's biographical sketch in *Cantari religiosi*, and F. Thomas Luongo, "Neri Pagliaresi," *Dictionary of Italian Literary Biography*.

In the early 1370s Neri was a young noble increasingly prominent in public office and known as well as a poet—possibly of secular verse (though none of these survive).[77] A rising political figure, he was elected to the Consiglio Generale on 1 September 1370; named as a candidate (but not elected) to the position of *podestà* of Montalcino in January 1371; elected to the Ordines on 1 November 1372; elected again to the Consiglio Generale in November 1372 and December 1373; and finally elected to the Ordines again on 1 January 1375.[78] This series of offices, particularly his two terms on the Ordines, shows that by 1375 Neri had become an undoubtedly well-known participant in communal politics, joining other family members in running the commune.[79]

But Neri turned away from civic politics during his time with Catherine. His entry into Catherine's circle is marked by a letter he received from her while he was in Asciano with the Dominican friar Bartolomeo Dominici, probably in Lent 1372.[80] Catherine acceded to Neri's request to receive him as her son, and exhorted him to raise himself above worldly affairs. Neri must have been a regular part of Catherine's circle before 1374, when Cristofano di Gano Guidini in his *Libro di memorie* recalled that Neri introduced him to Catherine. Neri was therefore one of the first laymen to enter Catherine's *famiglia*, and from the beginning of her public career was one of the most committed and passionate of her followers; references to Neri can be found in all the Catherinian hagiography, including the testimonies given by several of her followers for the *Processo Castellano*. In addition to Cristofano, Neri was responsible for introducing to Catherine several young noblemen who became her close followers, including Stefano di Corrado Maconi and Francesco di Vanni Malavolti. While Neri continued to hold political office in the first few years of his connection to Catherine, after his term on the Ordines in 1375, he never again held public office.[81] In this

---

[77] In his account of Neri in the *Processo Castellano* (quoted below), Francesco di Vanni Malavolti recalled reading with pleasure a number of Pagliaresi's poems. Varanini in 1965 speculated that this might be a reference to secular verse, perhaps destroyed by Pagliaresi after his conversion.

[78] ASS, *Concistoro* 57, f. 1v; 60, f. 55r; 58, f. 11v; 67, f. 3v; 67, f. 39v; 70, f. 60v; 75, c. 2r. See also Brizio, "Siena nel secondo Trecento," 2: 294, s.v. "Nerius dni Landoccius de Pagliarensibus."

[79] For example, his father, Landoccio di Neri de' Pagliaresi, held a number of offices during the Riformatori, including serving on the Ordines with Neri in 1375 (ASS, *Concistoro* 77, f. 1v).

[80] Letter 99/VII; see Noffke, *Letters of Catherine of Siena*, 1: 11–13.

[81] On Neri's conversion see the comments of Francesco di Vanni Malavolti in the *Processo Castellano* (p. 377): "[Neri], cum quo pro maiori parte temporis conversabar tum quia erat multum virtuosus et morigeratus, tum quia erat valens et pulcher rithmorum compositor, in quibus plurimum illo tempore delectabar. Iste Nerius, post multum temporis ex quo fueramus ad invicem, me nesciente qum pluries audierat de fama istius gloriose virginis Catherine ac etiam fuerat sibi locutus, propter quod immutatus et homo alter effectus."

respect Neri was unique among Catherine's lay followers. But Neri did not thereby cease his public and political activity. As Catherine's career moved from Siena to the broader terrain of ecclesiastical politics in Tuscany and beyond, the theater of Neri's political activity shifted from the Palazzo Pubblico to Catherine's *famiglia*. Neri can be found in early September 1375 in the service of the Sienese senator Pietro Marchese del Monte Santa Maria, himself one of Catherine's contacts.[82] As such he was following in the footsteps of Niccolò di Toldo, who as a member of Pietro's staff was arrested and executed for subversion in June 1375. From 1376, Neri figures continuously in the records of the activities of Catherine and her *famiglia*. Neri was present with Catherine in Avignon. He probably traveled to the papal Curia in spring 1376 as part of a diplomatic advance party with Raymond of Capua before Catherine's own trip in late May.[83] After Catherine and her *famiglia* left Avignon, Neri was found with Catherine in Pisa in November and December 1376, where letters from Stefano di Corrado Maconi reached him at the Dominican monastery of Santa Caterina.[84] He traveled with her to celebrate the founding of her monastery at Belcaro in spring 1377, and then was one of her company during her stay with the Salimbeni in the Val d'Orcia in the following summer and autumn.[85] In 1378 Neri was with Catherine in Florence, and again in Rome in 1378–79.[86] Sometime before 22 June 1379 Catherine sent Neri to Perugia, probably as bearer of a letter exhorting the Perugian governors to give

[82]   This can be deduced from Catherine's letter 135/XLII, to Pietro on 2 September 1375, in which she asks the senator to allow Neri to visit her in Pisa: "Se Neri vuole venire qua, pregovi che voi el lassiate venire."

[83]   See letter 226, sent to Raymond of Capua in Avignon probably in February or March 1376: "Credo che Neri verrà costà, perché mi pare che sia bene di mandarlo a corte. Informatelo di quello che fa bisogno d'adoperare per la pace di questi membri putridi che sono ribelli alla santa Chiesa, però che non si vede più dolce remedio a pacificare l'anima e 'l corpo che questo." While in Avignon, Neri served on at least one occasion as an emissary between Catherine and the pope. See Letter 218/LXXIV: "Pregovi, reverendo padre, che di quello che Neri, portatore di questa lettara, vi dirà, che, se elli è possibile a voi ed è vostra volontà, voi glili diate e concediate."

[84]   For these two letters, sent from Siena on 29 November 1376 and 8 December 1376, see Misciattelli, *Lettere di S. Caterina da Siena*, 6: 54–59.

[85]   For Neri's presence at Belcaro, see *Processo Castellano*, 428 (testimony of Mino di Giovanni di ser Mino). That Neri was with Catherine is also clear from the postscript to letter 56, sent to fra Simone da Cortona from the Rocca d'Orcia in Autumn 1377: "Neri gattivo, mio negligente figliuolo, vi si racomanda, e io ve ne strengo che preghiate Dio che gli tolga tanta negligenzia." In addition, there survive two letters from a despairing disciple of Catherine (identified only as "F. S.") addressed to Neri at the Rocca (Misciattelli, *Lettere di S. Caterina da Siena*, 6: 60–62).

[86]   See for instance a letter to Neri in Florence from Stefano di Corrado Maconi dated 22 May 1378 (Misciattelli, *Lettere di S. Caterina da Siena*, 6: 62–65), and letters to Neri in Rome from Stefano and Cristofano di Gano Guidini on 14 January, 15 January, 22 June, and 2 July 1379 (Ibid., 67–80).

their allegiance to Urban VI.[87] She sent him on a similar mission to Queen Giovanna of Naples, who had thrown her support to Clement VII, in the second half of 1379; Neri was still in Naples when Catherine died 29 April 1380. A letter addressed to him there on 22 May from Nigi di Doccio Arzocchi describes Catherine's death and the circumstances of the "orphans," her followers.[88]

After Catherine's death, Pagliaresi settled in a hermitage outside the Porta Nuova in Siena; Stefano Maconi and other Cateriniani wrote to him there throughout the 1390s.[89] During his last years he remained in contact with Catherine's followers, and worked to collect, transcribe, and disseminate Catherine's letters; one of the most important manuscripts in the formation of the Catherinian *epistolario* is in his hand.[90] Two long poems from these years take as their point of departure the death of Catherine: the *laude* "Su, al cielo è ritornata," and the *capitolo* "Spento è el lume che per certo accese."[91] The *laude* celebrates Catherine's life and her arrival in Paradise. The *capitolo* begins with the rejoicing of the blessed over Catherine's arrival in heaven, but turns quickly to the poet's own sorrow, bereft of his spiritual guide and support, and pleads for her intercession and protection. The poem goes on to consider Catherine's relationship with the world, castigating worldly leaders for refusing to recognize her authority and her advocacy, and closes with a warning of divine retribution for those who disparage God's servants.

## Stefano di Corrado Maconi

The ambiguities of the relationship for Catherine's noble followers between their worldly obligations and their ties to Catherine's *famiglia* are perhaps best illustrated in the career of Stefano di Corrado Maconi, whose declarations of filial devotion and conversion to Catherine's *famiglia* are featured in this chapter's introduction. Information about Stefano's career exists in his testimony for the *Processo Castellano* and many other references in the accounts of other Caterinati.[92] Stefano

[87] See letter 339, to the Priory of Perugia, and Fawtier, *Sainte Catherine de Sienne* 2: 250–1.
[88] See letter 192, which Catherine sent to Neri in Naples on 4 December 1379. See also letters to Neri in Naples from fra Bartolomeo Dominici 1 September 1379, and from Nigi di Doccio Arzocchi on 22 May 1380, describing Catherine's death and the circumstances of the *famiglia* after her death (Misciattelli, *Lettere di S. Caterina da Siena*, 6: 82–6).
[89] Misciattelli, 6: 87–133.
[90] Vienna, Oesterreichische Nationalbibliotek, Palatino 3514. See Dupré Theseider, "Un codice inedito dell'epistolario di S. Caterina da Siena," *Bullettino dell'Istituto storico italiano e Archivio muratoriano* 48 (1932): 17–56.
[91] Neri Pagliaresi, *Rime Sacre*, 187–90, 199–215.
[92] Stefano's testimony is *Processo Castellano*, 257–73.

became a Carthusian after Catherine's death, and eventually became prior general of the order's Roman observance during the schism. He is commemorated as "*beato* Stefano Maconi" in Carthusian literature, including a biography by the Sienese Carthusian Bartolomeo Scala published in 1626.[93] While Bartolomeo does not cite documentary sources, he includes many details that he was probably able to cull from documents that were destroyed in the period of the dissolution of the order–especially the archives of the Certosa di Pontignano, outside of Siena, of which Bartolomeo was prior.[94]

In 1376, on the advice of a companion, Stefano sought Catherine's help in settling a vendetta that placed the Maconi—one of the smaller of the Sienese noble families—at the mercy of more powerful rivals. According to Bartolomeo Scala, the other families involved were the Tolomei and Rinaldini. Catherine miraculously brought the Tolomei and Rinaldini to make peace.[95] As described in his testimony for the *Processo Castellano,* on meeting Catherine in 1376 Stefano quickly became one of her closest followers, traveling with her to Avignon in 1376 and Florence in 1378, and eventually joining her in Rome just before her death in 1380. He formed close friendships with other men in Catherine's circle, especially Neri di Landoccio Pagliaresi, with whom Stefano maintained an active correspondence during Catherine's life and after her death. In fulfillment of Catherine's final wish for him, Stefano became a Carthusian in 1381, entering the Sienese Certosa di Pontignano, in which he served as prior from 1382 to 1389.[96] In 1389, Stefano was made prior of the Certosa of Milan at the request of Gian Galeazzo Visconti, with whom Siena had formed an alliance against Florence that year. He held this position until 1398, during which time he oversaw the beginnings of the construction of the new Carthusian foundation in the ducal city of Pavia. In 1398, he was elected prior general of the Urbanist faction of the Carthusians, a position he held until 1410, after which he again served as prior of Pontignano and then as prior of Santa Maria delle Grazie in Pavia, where he died in 1424.[97]

Indeed, Stefano fulfilled the promise of the sudden and irrevocable conversion experienced on meeting Catherine in 1376. At the same time, other evidence of his activities during the years he was one of Catherine's

---

[93] Bartolomeo da Siena, *De vita et moribus beati Stephani Maconi senensis cartusiani ticinensis cartusiae olim coenobiarchae libri quinque* (1626).

[94] Giovanni Leoncini, "Un certosino del tardo medioevo: don Stefano Maconi," *Die Ausbreitung kartäusischen Lebens und Geistes im Mittelalter,* vol. 2, *Analecta Cartusiana* 63.2: 54–107.

[95] Stefano describes the situation in his testimony for the *Processo Castellano* (259), but does not give the names of the other families.

[96] Stefano renounced his inheritance rights on the occasion of his embracing the religious life in a document of 19 March 1381 (ASS, *Diplomatico, Patrimonio dei Resti, Certosa di Pontignano,* 19 March 1380 [old style]).

[97] *Processo Castellano,* xvi–xix.

*famiglia* adds considerable nuance to the apparently straightforward change of loyalties in his conversion from his worldly family to Catherine. First is Stefano's regular election, alongside other members of his family and clan, to Sienese political offices during these years. He was elected to terms on the Consiglio Generale in December 1373, July 1374, December 1374, June 1375, December 1376, December 1377, December 1378, June 1379, and May 1380—some nine months before he entered Pontignano.[98] In addition, Stefano was elected to the Ordines on one occasion, late in his political career, in July 1379.[99] Second, and perhaps related to his political offices, Stefano spent a surprisingly large amount of time apart from Catherine and the *famiglia* during the period when, by his and other accounts, he had become one of her most devoted and intimate followers, as well one of her primary scribes. For instance, on the return trip from Avignon in 1376, Stefano left the *famiglia* in Pisa in November to return early to Siena;[100] he stayed behind in Siena when Catherine and company journeyed to her new monastery in the Sienese *contado* in April 1377 and does not appear to have traveled with her to the Val d'Orcia that December;[101] while he went with Catherine to Florence in March 1378, he returned to Siena in March or April and thus was not present for Catherine's near martyrdom during the Ciompi revolts;[102] he stayed behind in Siena when Catherine made her final trip, to Rome in November 1378, only to join her in March of 1380 just before her death.[103]

It is clear from comments Catherine made in several of her letters to Stefano in 1378 and 1379 that his absence from her *famiglia* was due in large part to his obligations to his own family. But it is likely that Stefano's political activity and family obligations were related, and jointly responsible for keeping him in Siena. For example, Stefano's early return to Siena in November 1376 can be connected to his election to the Consiglio Generale a month

[98] ASS, *Concistoro* 71, f. 6or; 72, ff. 47v–55r; 74, f. 22v; 82, f. 49r; 88, f. 44rv; 94, f. 51r; 97, f. 50v; 102, 29v.

[99] ASS, *Concistoro*, 98, 3r.

[100] There exist two letters from Stefano in Siena to Neri di Landoccio in Pisa, dated 29 November and 8 December 1376 (Misciattelli, *Lettere di S. Caterina da Siena*, 6:54–59).

[101] Stefano does not mention that trip in his testimony for the *Processo Castellano*, and the testimony of Francesco di Vanni Malavolti, the most thorough account of the trip, does not mention Stefano among the witnesses to various miracles Catherine performed in the Val d'Orcia. It is unlikely that Francesco would have omitted mentioning his presence, especially given Stefano's ecclesiastical prominence by the time of the *Processo Castellano*.

[102] That Stefano had returned to Siena from Florence is clear from his letter to Neri di Landoccio Pagliaresi in Florence, dated 22 May 1378 (Misciattelli, *Lettere di S. Caterina da Siena* 6: 62–65), and from Catherine's letters to him at this time (letters 298 and 365).

[103] See two letters from Stefano in Siena to Neri di Landoccio Pagliaresi in Rome, dated 15 January and 14 July 1379 (Misciattelli, *Lettere di S. Caterina da Siena*, 6: 72–80). Ten of Catherine's twelve letters to Stefano were sent to him from Rome after November 1378; these are letters 319, 205, 332, 222, 329, 324, 320, 195, 368, and 369.

later, and his remaining in Siena in 1378 through 1379 related to an intensification of his political participation expressed in his election to the
Ordines in July 1379. Stefano may have felt a family obligation to participate
in political life more, for instance, than Gabriele di Davino Piccolomini or
Francesco di Vanni Malavolti because of his relatively greater prestige within
his clan, which was considerably smaller and less potent than the Piccolomini and Malavolti. According to his biographer, Stefano was trained for
family leadership, which is borne out by the lead he took in seeking out
Catherine's assistance in settling the Maconi feud with the Tolomei and
Rinaldini in 1376 and by his quick promotion within the Carthusian order.
In other words, whatever tensions Catherine's other followers experienced
in negotiating their dual loyalties to Catherine and to secular affairs and
family business, it may be that Stefano found it even more difficult than the
others to shift completely from his worldly family to Catherine's *famiglia*.

It is tempting to see in this evidence of his continued immersion in
worldly affairs a simple contradiction of Stefano's account of the complete change of life brought about by meeting Catherine. Catherine complained repeatedly in letters to him—sometimes harshly—about Stefano's
refusal to give up the worldly business preventing him from complete
devotion to Christ and, it is implicit, keeping him from embracing a religious vocation.[104] Moreover, in several of these letters she identified Stefano's family ties as the source of his worldly encumbrances and the
secular business that kept him from joining her and her *famiglia,* and
called on him to sever such bonds. For example, in a letter to Stefano
from Rome in early 1379, after exclaiming "Oh how blessed will be my
soul when I see that you have cut yourself off from the world actually and
mentally," Catherine exhorted him, "Hide yourself in the wounds of
Christ crucified, flee from the world, depart from the house of your parents."[105] And after Stefano's return from Florence to Siena in 1378, when
Catherine wrote him in congratulation for having escaped from some
bandits who had taken him prisoner in the *contado* on his way home, she
quickly adapted this event to her rhetorical purpose:

---

[104] For example, her final letter to him (letter 369), from late 1379 or early 1380, contains a stinging criticism of his lack of will in failing to follow through on his stated desire to
reject his worldly state, reflected in his remaining in Siena while Catherine and others of
her *familiari* were in Rome.

[105] Letter 329: "Oh quanto sarà beata l'anima mia, quando io ti vedrò avere tagliato da
te il mondo—attualmente e mentalmente . . . Niscondeti nelle piaghe di Cristo crocifisso;
fuggi dinanzi al mondo, esce dalla casa de' parenti tuoi; fuggi nella caverna del costato di
Cristo crocifisso, acciò che possi venire a terra di promissione." As Antonio Volpato points
out in his edition of her letters, by urging Stefano to depart from the house of his family,
Catherine here evokes familiar scriptural language, from Genesis 12:1 and Psalm 44:11. In
a similar vein, see also letter 205 (December 1378).

So my soul desires that, since the sweet eternal bridegroom has saved you miraculously and delivered you from their hands, I beg him now to deliver you from the others, who are even greater and more cruel enemies than these. These were enemies of the body, but the others are enemies of the soul. And this is the truth: those of the worldly household are our enemies, and especially those who are most closely related to us, who it does not appear are concerned with anything but their own interests. When you have been liberated from them, you will be out of prison; the sun will rise. Now you are at the dawn, which does not permit you fully to savor or discern virtue, because it is not yet the time of the sun, when you will be released from these domestic enemies. But I want, dearest son, that you comfort yourself in this time of the dawn, because soon the sun will rise, and we will hear those sweet words: "Leave the dead to bury the dead, and follow me."[106]

What might seem to be merely a conventional evocation of a familiar scriptural passage (from Matthew 8:22), is in fact a dramatic disparagement of Stefano's family obligations, given the circumstances of Stefano's "miraculous" release from the bandits. In his renunciation of inheritance rights on entering the Certosa di Pontignano, Stefano acknowledged having received four hundred gold florins from his father, Corrado di Leoncino Maconi, to pay ransom when he was captured by bandits in the *contado*.[107] As Catherine probably knew, Stefano in fact owed his safe release to his father's intervention, which makes her warning against the self-interest of domestic relations even more insistent and almost shocking. From Catherine's perspective, at least in these letters, Stefano's political activity and other worldly responsibilities impeded his spiritual progress.

But the obligations of Stefano's political and family life and his spiritual aspirations were not necessarily in the stark opposition that Catherine's strongest language would imply. For all Catherine's criticism and warnings concerning family obligations, in her letters she also repeatedly cautioned Stefano neither to offend his parents, nor to cause them scandal. For example, even as she complained about Stefano's absence while

---

[106] Letter 365: "Ora desidera l'anima mia che, puoi che 'l dolce sposo eterno vi campò miracolosamente e trassevi delle mani loro, così prego lui che tosto ti tragga degli altri, e' quali ci so maggio nemici e più crudeli che non erano eglino: questi erano nimici del corpo, ma gli altri sono nemici dell'anima. E così è la verità: che e' dimestici dell'uomo sicondo el mondo sono nostri nimici; e spezialmente quegli che ci so' più congiunti, che non pare che attendano altro che alla loro utilità. Quando tu sarai diliberato da loro, escito fuore di prigione, sarà levato el sole. Ora se' nell'aurora, che anco ben bene non ti lassa gustare nè discernere la virtù, perché non se' ancora nel tempo del sole che tu sia sciolto da questi nemici dimestici. Ma io voglio, carissimo figliuolo, che tu ti conforti ora in questo tempo dell'aurora, però che tosto ne verrà el sole. Udiremo quelle dolci parole: 'Lassa i morti seppellire a' morti, e tu mi seguita.'"

[107] ASS, *Diplomatico, Patrimonio dei Resti*, Certosa di Pontignano, 19 March 1380.

she was in Florence, she advised him to rejoin her only if he could do so without "scandal and upset" to his parents.[108] While he was in Siena and apart from Catherine, Stefano was still an active part of Catherine's network and could serve as a nexus of communication for Catherine and her Sienese followers, distributing letters from her and spreading news.[109] He could also be of service to her and her *famiglia* both practically and politically. For example, in a letter from Florence in May 1378, Catherine asked Stefano to attempt to procure some money that had been promised to Raymond, if he could do so "without scandal."[110] In a letter from Rome in late 1379, Catherine informed Stefano that she had written letters in support of Urban VI to the Sienese *signori* and to the Compagnia della beata Vergina Maria, and called on Stefano to exhort his fellow members of the Compagnia actively to promote the Urbanist cause as part of a large campaign that would "light a fire in all of Italy."[111] Another example of Catherine employing Stefano, probably in connection with the antischismatic campaign, is letter 324, in which she commanded him from Rome in 1379 "in the name of Christ crucified" to comply with any request for assistance from "the prior" (perhaps Raymond of Capua, at that time prior of Santa Maria della Minerva in Rome) or any ambassador from him, as if the request had come from Catherine herself.[112] Whether or not Stefano's picture of a complete transformation of life in joining Catherine's circle was a sentimental idealization, the situation he found himself in from 1376 to 1381 was clearly not so simple as a choice between worldly and spiritual family ties.

It is also reasonable to suppose that Stefano brought to communal politics the perspective of a member of Catherine's *famiglia*. As with Catherine's other followers, this is difficult to prove, but a sense of Stefano's position in Siena and attitude toward the governing regime can be gathered from two letters he wrote to Neri di Landoccio in 1379, while the latter was in Rome with Catherine. In the first, he described with some bravado how he and another one of Catherine's followers, Pietro di Giovanni Venture, lobbied

[108] Letter 365 (May or June 1378): ". . . ma con scandalo e turbazione del padre e della madre, no, infino che lo scandalo fosse necessario."

[109] See, for example, Catherine's letter 332 (1 January 1379), in which she asks Stefano to deliver a letter to William Flete, and letter 320 (10 April 1379), in which she asks that he pass on a letter to "Matteo" (perhaps the Dominican fra Matteo de' Tolomei). Stefano's letters from Siena to Neri di Landoccio while the latter was in Pisa, Florence, and Rome in 1376–1379, show the extant of Stefano's contact with the Caterinati, both in and outside Siena.

[110] Letter 298 (May 1378).

[111] Letter 368 (December 1379): "Fa' che tu sia fervente, e non tiepido, in questa operazione, e in stimolare e' frategli e maggiori tuoi della Compagnia, che faccino la loro possibilità in quello ch'io scrivo. Se sarete quello che dovete essere, metterete fuoco in tutta Italia, non tanto costì."

[112] Letter 324.

successfully to oppose a proposed visit to Siena by an ambassador of the antipope, and even offered to help seize the ambassador; he assures Neri about "the good disposition that exists today in our wicked city, as opposed to the pain you felt previously in seeing it hold against obedience to the holy Church."[113] In the second letter, sent in June 1379, Stefano responded to Neri's skepticism concerning the good intentions of the Sienese regime toward Urban VI. The papacy had required money and troops in order to raise the interdict and the city had not complied. After explaining that resources in the city were scarce at that time, on account of the extortionate demands of some military companies in the *contado*, he reported that he had nevertheless been a vocal advocate of compliance with the papal terms and even was reprimanded for speaking more on the subject than was proper.[114]

Perhaps Stefano exaggerated his own efforts, but his comments can be taken as a good indication of his political position in Siena. Beyond this, there is also Stefano's relationship with the bishop of Narni, the Sienese Jacomo di Sozzo Tolomei, who was papal nunzio in Siena to negotiate the lifting of the interdict during the War of Eight Saints. Stefano's contact with the bishop, and his desire to enter into the bishop's service, dated at least from May or June 1378, at which time Catherine referred in a letter to Stefano's plans to become part of the bishop's *famiglia* in order to receive an exemption from the interdict.[115] Whether or not Stefano ever formally attached himself to the bishop of Narni, he did associate with him informally. In effect, in addition to representing his clan, by 1379 Stefano was acting in Sienese politics as a visible adherent of the church and papal diplomacy. This was entirely consistent with his position as a member of Catherine's *famiglia*. Indeed, Stefano's reputation as someone sympathetic to the church, both on account of his pro-Urbanist statements and his connection to Catherine, might have contributed to his election to the Ordines in July 1379, shortly after the second of the two letters to Neri cited above. As the city moved toward a peace treaty with Urban VI, perhaps his affiliation with Catherine and the church party, suspect on other occasions, at this moment served the interests of the regime as it sought to placate the pope.

Much more dramatic, if unverifiable, evidence of Stefano's political stance in Siena can be found in an episode recounted by Bartolomeo da

---

[113] Misciattelli, *Lettere di S. Caterina da Siena*, 6: 70–71 (15 January 1379): "Questo ti scrivo acciò che abbi qualche poca d'allegrezza della buona disposizione che oggi è in nostra città tapinella, in cambio della pena che ad altro tempo ài avuta, vedendola tenere contra l'obbedienza della santa Chiesa."

[114] Misciattelli, *Lettere di S. Caterina da Siena*, 6: 73–74.

[115] Letter 298, in which Catherine advised to await a peace treaty and the lifting of the interdict.

Siena. Bartolomeo tells how Stefano, a member of the Compagnia della beata Vergine, was drawn into a conspiracy of nobles who, using the chapel of the confraternity as their meeting place, plotted a coup against the magistrates of the city and the leaders of the *popolo,* who were oppressing the nobles. Without having been told of this affair, Catherine nevertheless perceived Stefano's thoughts and commanded him to perform penance—one drop of blood for every conspiratorial word—in the same chapel where the plot had been hatched. Interestingly, Bartolomeo has Catherine upbraid Stefano as much for the impracticality of the plot—it will end merely in slaughter—as for the sacrilege of using a chapel for such a purpose:

> Come now, Stefano my son, is it thus that you rush headlong to the destruction of both soul and body? What mad plots are you considering? Return to your heart, son, return. I desire that you immediately set aside these civil conspiracies. Do you really think that the house of God will ever offer for conspirators an inviolable refuge in the heart of the Republic? You will fail utterly.[116]

It would be rash to accept as completely accurate the details of a hagiographic work written more than two hundred years after the facts; it would also be unwise to dismiss this story too quickly. Like other episodes in which Bartolomeo fills in details not known from Stefano's own account—for example, his identification of the Maconi family enemies in 1376—the details in this story are specific and at least ring true. Probably, Bartolomeo depended on some earlier documents or tradition rather than invented the stories and details. The story of Stefano's plotting illustrates Catherine's prophetic gift, but does not reflect well on the sanctity of Stefano, Bartolomeo's subject. And at the risk of arguing in a circle, it is entirely plausible that a conspiracy against the Riformatori might have been based among the membership of the Compagnia, a group of pious social elites with political and economic reasons for opposing the "popular" regime of the Riformatori who also could justify toppling the government because the regime's alliance with Florence against the pope had resulted in the papal interdict. Stefano's letters, in which he disparaged the Sienese regime for its past opposition to the papacy, as well as his ties to Catherine and her circle, suggest that he would have been sympathetic with such a plot.

---

[116] Bartolomeo da Siena, *De vita et moribus beati Stephani Maconi,* 255–56: "Hem Stephane fili, ecquem praeceps in interitum animae simul et corporis ruis? Ecque insana versas animo consilia? Redi ad cor fili redi; et quas civiles coniurationes pertexere animum subiit, deponas prorsus volo. An putas Domum Dei tanquam inviolabile asylum conspirantibus in viscera rei publicae effugia olim futura? falleris omnino."

Finally, Stefano's religious career was a continuation of, not a break with, his family connections and his public life in Siena. The bare details of Stefano's career from 1381 until his death in 1424 suggest some obvious conclusions. When Stefano finally did give in to Catherine's ambition for him and became a monk, he entered a Carthusian foundation—the Certosa di Pontignano—that, according to Bartolomeo da Siena, was built in large part out of the generosity of the Maconi.[117] After his 1381 profession, Stefano was made prior of that monastery before the end the following year, a speedy preferment that must have been at least partly due to his family connections and experience in public life.[118] Bartolomeo describes how, after his entry into the religious life at Pontignano, Stefano possessed great authority in Siena, and acted as an arbiter in feuds and took on the civic roles expected of a well-respected civic religious leader.[119] It is unlikely that he ceased to play a civic role or exert influence even after he moved to Milan in 1389. His appointment there came at the direct request of Gian Galeazzo Visconti, the "Count of Virtue" and duke of Milan, in the year Siena became a client city of Milan by way of a mutual defense treaty against the Florentines; in 1399 this relationship was formalized when the Sienese accepted Gian Galeazzo as their lord. Stefano was brought to Milan in order to direct the construction of the new Certosa in the new ducal city of Pavia, but his appointment was also undoubtedly part of Gian Galeazzo's strategy to forge links to his new client state. Possibly, Stefano's appointment was made at the request of the Sienese. In any case, it would be very surprising if Stefano did not serve at the ducal court as an unofficial ambassador for his home city, as would have been expected of any Sienese with access to a foreign political or ecclesiastical leader.[120]

This chapter has sought to restore some of the social and political particularities of Catherine and her followers that have been elided by

[117] Ibid., 56.

[118] The exact date of Stefano's profession is not known for certain. Stefano's renunciation of his inheritance rights, on 19 March 1381 (as cited above), probably took place not long before his entrance into the monastery. According to Bartolomeo da Siena (*De vita et moribus beati Stephani Maconi*, 60), his profession was on 25 March 1381. Laurent (*Processo Castellano*, xvii) points to a letter from Stefano to Neri di Landoccio on 30 May 1381, in which Stefano refers to his profession as a recent event, as evidence that the profession probably took place in May. Another letter from Stefano to Neri, dated 14 December 1382, makes it clear that he had been elected Prior by that date.

[119] Bartolomeo da Siena, *De vita et moribus beati Stephani Maconi*, 87.

[120] The best example in Siena in this period of the way in which an official of a royal or ecclesiastical court could function in this way is the Sienese Francesco Casini, physician to popes Gregory XI and Urban VI, who sent the Sienese accounts of papal pronouncements or sentiments, as for example he did in communicating to the Sienese papal displeasure over Siena's receiving a Visconti embassy in 1374. On unofficial ambassadors in this period, see Andrea Giorgi, "Il carteggio del Concistoro della Repubblica di Siena," 204–15.

hagiographical emphasis on her spiritual goals and the spiritual aspirations of her *famiglia*. It should be clear why the Riformatori viewed Catherine's group with such suspicion. While it would be both reductionist and an overstatement of the political coherence of Catherine's followers to see them as a party, it is certainly true that her close followers in Siena, like her more general network, were disposed by their social backgrounds to be enemies of the ascendant *popolo minuto* in Siena and in Florence. Like the members of the Parte Guelfa in Florence, the pious motivations of Catherine and her followers for supporting the papal cause against the Tuscan league were of a piece with their social and political identities. The line between political and pious authority, even between political and sacred spaces, was obviously blurred. For the nobles and other elite men who were Catherine's lay followers in Siena, association in an ostensibly religious and apolitical fraternity like Catherine's *famiglia* or the Compagnia della beata Vergine Maria was a way to claim a degree of political authority not available in a political scene dominated by *gente nuova*. Similarly, despite Catherine's statements of detachment and distance from worldly affairs, her network of followers gave her influence and a status within the political world that she, as a woman—even a saintly woman—would not otherwise have been able to claim.

# CHAPTER 5

# Prophetic Politics: Catherine in the War of Eight Saints

This chapter presents the heart of this book's argument for placing Catherine on the Italian political and cultural map, Catherine's movements and letters during the War of Eight Saints. The letters show the complex relationship between political realities and her prophetic reputation as she plunged, with her *famiglia*, into the political crisis engendered by the hostilities between Florence and the papacy. Catherine's letters are the clearest evidence of the way in which Catherine, even as she sometimes appealed to expectations regarding her female prophetic authority, transgressed boundaries to address a broad and influential audience. However much politics were written out of her life in later times, her saintly identity took shape within the circumstances of Tuscan and ecclesiastical politics in the 1370s.

As Catherine entered into Italian affairs in early 1375, with her *famiglia* already well established, the conflict between Florence and the papacy was intensifying. Hostility toward the papacy was already high in Florence.[1] An escalation in tensions, and a movement from a cold to a hot war, came in June when the papacy released John Hawkwood's army from papal service, unleashing an immediate threat to the Tuscan cities.[2] Catherine's letter to the mercenary leader shortly before this event anticipated its destabilizing effect, even if her solution—the enlistment of Hawkwood and his army in the Crusade—in retrospect

---

[1]  Peterson, "The War of Eight Saints," 185.
[2]  On Hawkwood and his effect on the economic and political fortunes of cities like Siena, see Caferro, *Mercenary Companies.*

Figure 2. The Rocca d'Orcia

appears unrealistic.[3] Florence negotiated a settlement with Hawkwood on June 21, paying the mercenary 130,000 florins not to attack the city, and recommended that other cities do the same. Shortly after the settlement, and the "discovery" of the plot to hand over the neighboring town of Prato to Berenger, abbot of Lézat and papal nuncio in Italy, the Florentines resolved to raise the funds necessary to pay Hawkwood by levying an oppressive tax on the clergy of the city and sequestering the estates of leading prelates. According to one account, the imposition on the bishop of Florence, the bishop of Fiesole, the abbot of Vallombrosa, and others amounted to thirty thousand florins. The regime sought to impose a forced loan on other clerics: for every denarius imposed by the pope (by way of the payment to Hawkwood), a florin to the camera of the commune.[4] This action was enthusiastically supported in Florence, where fear of the machinations of the papal governors fostered extreme anti-ecclesiastical sentiment. This was already a characteristic feature of Florentine religious culture.[5] The Fraticelli, who preached that the pope was anti-Christ and that all clergy ordained since John XXII were illegitimate, had long found a receptive audience in Florence, particularly among the lower classes.[6] The regime's measures were supported by prestigious orthodox religious figures like the Vallombrosian Giovanni dalle Celle, a staunch opponent of the Fraticelli, who wrote that "no innocent person can be excommunicated," assuring one of his Florentine lay correspondents that he need only be sure not to vote for measures to kill or capture the pope or any other clergy and or religious.[7] Giovanni, one of Catherine's loyal supporters outside of Siena, had a strong following among pious, socially prominent Florentines. Another reform-minded religious leader, the Augustinian humanist Luigi Marsili, also supported the commune's seizure of clerical wealth, referring to it as a "blessed enterprise." Appealing both to Florentine/Italian cultural identity and to a reformist spirit, Marsili argued that the commune's actions were directed against the *French* clergy attempting unjustly to impose their political will in Italy, and that the measures should be considered a war against corruption in the church, and as such would receive God's sanction; any excommunication resulting from these actions would be unjust and therefore

[3] Catherine was far from the only person actively promoting a general Crusade in 1375, and while her enthusiasm and her attempt to recruit a mercenary like Hawkwood might now seem naive, it was much less obviously so at the time.
[4] Trexler, *Spiritual Power,* 113–114.
[5] Ibid., 115.
[6] Brucker, *Florentine Politics and Society,* 303. On the Fraticelli in Florence, see also Marvin B. Becker, "Florentine Politics and the Diffusion of Heresy in the Trecento: A Socio-Economic Inquiry," *Speculum* 34 (1959): 60–75.
[7] Giovanni dalle Celle, Luigi Marsili, *Lettere* 2: 265–6.

invalid.[8] This was precisely the justification for antipapal actions that Catherine anticipated in her letter to Barnabò Visconti discussed in chapter 2. The enthusiasm for these measures was such that the committee of eight men elected on 7 July to collect these funds became known popularly as the "Eight Saints." Siena and Pisa were also forced to pay off Hawkwood in subsequent months, and Siena followed Florence's lead in trying to raise the necessary funds with a tax on the clergy.[9]

Another early intervention in Catherine's letter-writing campaign also failed to achieve its end, as Barnabò Visconti formed an alliance with Florence on 24 July. For Florence, this definitive step toward war with the papacy represented a decided shift of power from the leadership of the Parte Guelfa to the *gente nuova*. Indeed, in face of the vehemence of Florentine public opinion, there was little that the Parte leaders could do to stem the overtly antipapal policy taken by the commune at this time.[10] In August the commune created a special eight-man *balìa* to prepare for war. This committee, the Eight of War, all of whom were determined opponents of the Parte Guelfa, served as de facto governors of Florence in the subsequent months. Throughout the autumn and winter, the regime sought to create a league of Tuscan cities in anticipation of armed conflict with the papal forces and to sow discord among the Papal States, a diplomatic barrage articulated by Coluccio Salutati, the new chancellor of Florence. Salutati complained that the ecclesiastical hierarchy was menacing Florence and cited several specific complaints: the refusal to provide grain for the city during the famine, the plot to take Prato, and the unleashing of Hawkwood against the city.[11] Some cities, Arezzo for example, joined the league immediately. Siena initially resisted repeated appeals from the Florentines to preserve its liberty by enlisting in the league, but on 6 November decided to join. While the Sienese regime was determined to ally the commune with Florence and the league, there were also concerns within the city about any resulting threats to Sienese sovereignty or even independence.[12] It is likely that these stated concerns masked anxieties (pious or political) about

[8]   Brucker, *Florentine Politics and Society*, 301–2; Trexler, *Spiritual Power*, 115.

[9]   The Sienese accord with Hawkwood was announced in the Consiglio Generale on 30 June (ASS, *Consiglio Generale* 185, 52v). On 3 July Piero Gambacorti wrote to the Sienese, reporting a Pisan pact with Hawkwood (ASS, *Concistoro* 1786, 89r). On 17 July, the Sienese Concistoro deliberated taxing clerics in order to raise the money to pay Hawkwood, in explicit imitation of the Florentines (ASS, *Concistoro* 77, 12r–v).

[10]   After the discovery of the Prato plot in late June, the commune renewed a ban on citizens holding neighboring episcopal sees. This action was directed at the patrician families—the Ricasoli, Corsini, Strozzi, Albizzi, Baroncelli, Tedaldi, Tornaquinci, Cavalcanti—who formed the backbone of the Parte and who received the lion's share of papal preferments in Florence. See Trexler, *Spiritual Power*, 112; Peterson, "War of Eight Saints," 185.

[11]   Brucker, *Florentine Politics and Society*, 300; Peterson, "War of Eight Saints," 187–88.

[12]   The Sienese Concistoro deliberated about the invitation to join the league with the Florentines and Barnabò Visconti beginning on 27 July, deciding to send ambassadors to

entering into a military league explicitly understood to be "against evil clerics."[13] Meanwhile, the crucial cities of Pisa and Lucca remained uncommitted, but it was clear that they could not long withstand the pressure from Florence. (Salutati wrote to the Pisans, exhorting them to "Wake up!")[14] Florentine agitation succeeded in causing rebellions against the papal governors throughout the winter. Early December saw a revolt in Città di Castello, which was followed in close succession by rebellions in Gubbio, Sassoferrato, Urbino, Todi, and Forlì. On 1 January, Gerard du Puy surrendered the city of Perugia.[15] By the beginning of 1376, nearly the entire Papal State had revolted.

Catherine and Raymond continued their efforts on behalf of the pope. A papal privilege of 17 August 1376 confirmed Raymond as Catherine's director, recognizing their mission to work for the Crusade and "other business of the Holy Roman Church."[16] Catherine and Raymond remained in Pisa through September, when she returned briefly to Siena, leaving Raymond in Pisa busy with affairs for the Crusade. She left Siena almost immediately for Lucca, and then returned again to Pisa. Evidently, Catherine was being employed by the church party to help maintain Pisan and Luccan neutrality, a conclusion suggested by one of her letters to some female followers in Siena, in which she explains that she has delayed her return to Siena "on account of some service to the Church

---

Florence but agreed to nothing for the time being (ASS, *Concistoro* 77, 17r–v). The Florentine Priors wrote to the Sienese magistrates on 8 August, chiding them for their hesitation in taking measures to protect their own liberty and wrote again with a similar message on 10 August (ASS, *Concistoro* 1787, 11 and 13). On 16 August, the Concistoro deliberated further about the league, deciding to refer the decision to the Consiglio Generale (ASS, *Concistoro* 77, 22v). Since in this period communal policy was usually set by the Concistoro, with the Consiglio Generale acting often merely as a rubber stamp for the decisions taken by the magistrates, it is very likely that the governing regime had already decided to join the league. The concerns subsequently voiced in the Consiglio Generale suggest that the members of the Concistoro were more uniformly enthusiastic about entering the league than the Sienese population at large. The Consiglio Generale deliberated about this matter on 6 September, deciding that the Sienese Captain of War—and no foreign official—ought to lead any forces of the league that would enter into Sienese territory (ASS, *Consiglio Generale* 185, 82r). On 6 November, the Consiglio Generale yielded to the arguments of Pietro di Giacomo Tolomei (one of the Sapientes in the Concistoro in July and in November 1375) and voted to enter the league, under the condition that the Florentines and other participants of the league would not give help to the Aretini in the dispute between Siena and Arezzo over Lucignano (ASS, *Consiglio Generale* 185, 105v).

[13]  Neri di Donato, 658.

[14]  Peterson, "War of Eight Saints," 187.

[15]  Neri di Donato (659) records these developments with evident amazement: "In tutto e per tutto ogni città, castella e rocche e cassari, che la Chiesa tenea di qua, signori e sottoposti de la Chiesa in pochi dì di ribellaro, e cacciaro li uffitiali loro e abattero loro forteze, e féro cose inistimabili e incredibili: fu quasi un sogno." On the revolt of the Perugini, with the help of agents of the league, see Neri di Donato, 659–70.

[16]  Laurent, ed., *Documenti*, n. 38.

and the wishes of the holy father."[17] A letter to her first confessor, fra Tomasso dalla Fonte, from Pisa in December suggests that her movements were causing murmurings against her in Siena, now formally allied with the Florentines. Catherine exulted that "the whole world is against us," and responded to fra Tomasso's apparent request that she return by saying that the archbishop of Pisa had asked the master general of the Dominicans to allow her to remain for several more days.[18] Several letters also attest to her continued activities on behalf of the Crusade.[19]

Catherine expressed increased consternation over the growing conflict, particularly the rebelliousness of Florence and its allies. In late summer or early autumn, Catherine wrote to Elizabeth, the queen mother in Hungary, seeking her help in gaining the cooperation of her son, the Angevin king Louis I, in the plans of the pope, particularly concerning the Crusade. As a member of the house of Anjou, Louis was one of the traditional Guelf allies of the pope, but at this moment he was in a particularly sensitive position, being courted both by the pope and by the Florentines, who had been seeking an alliance with him since at least 1374. Louis had already received embassies from the Sienese government seeking his support for the league, and from the bishop of Siena seeking support for the papacy.[20] Catherine begged Louis to come to the aid of the church, "this bride bathed in the blood of the lamb, which you see that everyone is harassing, Christians as well as infidels," and struck a familiar theme by reminding Louis that he needed the church's gift of the Holy Spirit just as the church needed his help.[21] As in earlier letters to Hawkwood and Barnabò Visconti, Catherine cast the political issue in spiritual terms, offering Elizabeth and Louis a

---

[17] Letter 108/XLIX, to the *mantellate* Monna Giovanna di Capo and Francesca: "Non vi maravigliate se non ne siamo venute, ma tosto ne verremo, se piacerà alla divina bontà. Per alcuna utilità della Chiesa e volontà del padre santo ò sostentato un poco el mio venire. Priegovi e comandovi a voi, figliuole e figliuoli, che tutti preghiate, e offeriate orazioni sante e dolci desideri dinanzi a Dio per la santa Chiesa, però che molto è perseguitata."

[18] Letter 139/XLVI.

[19] In a letter to Monna Giovanna and other *mantellate* in Siena (letter 132/XLVIII), Catherine referred to a meeting with ambassadors from the queen of Cyprus regarding the Crusade. In a letter, probably from either Siena or Lucca (letter 157), Catherine encouraged Vanni and Francesco, sons of Niccolò de' Buonconti (her host in Pisa), to join the Crusade.

[20] On 6 April 1374, the Florentine priors sent to Siena an account of one of their embassies to Louis, in which he reportedly expressed his fervent desire to preserve the liberty of the Tuscan communes, but declined to enter into a league until the communes had themselves entered (ASS, *Concistoro* 1784, n.20). The bishop of Siena, the Franciscan Guglielmo dei Guasconi, was sent to Hungary by the pope in autumn 1375; see Paolo Nardi, "I vescovi di Siena e la curia pontificia dall'ascesa della parte Guelfa allo scoppio dello scisma d'occidente (1267–1378)," in Achille Mirizio and Paolo Nardi, eds., *Chiesa e vita religiosa a Siena dalle origini al grande giubileo* (2002), 175.

[21] Letter 145/XL: "Pregovi, per l'amore di Cristo crucifisso, che voi soveniate a questa sposa, bagnata del sangue dell'Agnello, ché vedete che ogni uno le fa noia, e cristiani e infedeli."

spiritual *quid* for a political *quo*, salvation for support of the pope in the Italian conflict.

At around the same time Catherine wrote a letter to the queen of Naples, another traditional Angevin ally of the pope, and similarly transformed the terms of the political argument by urging Giovanna to come to the aid of the church, "a mother who feeds her children at her breast with the sweetest life-giving milk," adding, "it is a foolish and mad child that does not help such a mother when the rotten member rebels and opposes her."[22] Catherine here played on a rhetorical commonplace by appealing to the queen's duty to come to the aid of mother church, but in a way that resonated with Giovanna's political position: she was a feudal subject of the pope, and thus in a special way a "daughter" of the church. Indeed, Catherine used this metaphor repeatedly in her letters to Giovanna, an obvious rhetorical device to portray Giovanna's political position in spiritual terms.

Catherine frequently identified the rebellious cities as "rotten members" in the body of the church in her letters throughout the conflict between the pope and the Florentine league. In a letter she wrote from Pisa to her Sienese follower Matteo di Fazio de' Cenni, rector of the hospital of the Misericordia, Catherine disclosed that the persecution of the church would accomplish a divine plan that would find its fulfillment in the Crusade:

> Now is the time to lament, to weep, to grieve: the time is ours, son, because the bride of Christ is persecuted by Christians, false and rotten members. But be comforted, because God will not scorn the tears and sweat and sighs that are poured out in his presence. My soul in grief rejoices and exults, because among the thorns it smells the scent of the rose that is about to open. Sweet first truth says that with this persecution he fulfills his will and our desires. Again, I rejoice and exult in the sweet fruit that is being made in Christ on earth, over the business of the Crusade [*santo passaggio*], and again in what has been done and is being done here and is to be done though divine grace.[23]

---

[22] Letter 138/XLI: "Ché voi sapete che ella è quella madre che notrica e' figliuoli al petto suo, dando lo' latte dolcissimo che lo' dà vita. Bene è stolto e matto quello figliuolo che none aita la madre, quando el membro putrido le ribella ed è contra a lei. Voglio che siate quella figliuola vera che sempre soveniate alla madre vostra."

[23] Letter 137/XLV: "Ora è il tempo di gridare, di piangere, e di dolersi: el tempo è nostro, figliuolo, però che è perseguitata la Sposa di Cristo da' cristiani, falsi membri e putridi. Ma confortatevi, ché Dio non dispregerà le lagrime, sudori e sospiri che sono gittati nel cospetto suo. L'anima mia nel dolore gode e essulta, perché tra la spina sente l'odore della rosa ch'è per aprire. Dice la prima dolce Verità che con questa persecutione adempie la volontà sua e' desiderii nostri. Ancora, godo del dolce frutto che s'è fatto in Cristo in terra sopra a' fatti del santo passaggio, e ancora di quello che è fatto e fa qui ed è per fare, per la divina grazia."

It is impossible to do justice here to the rich pattern of images that Catherine employed in this brief letter, but it is important to pause to note the prophetic perspective Catherine claimed on the political situation and on her activities and the activities of her followers. In a tone of lamentation that invoked implicit scriptural precedent, Catherine identified the situation of Italy and the church in the 1370s in Old Testament terms ("the time is ours"), and then linked to the resolution of the political crisis the success of her own projects in Pisa ("what has been done and is being done here"), the Crusade in particular. The image of the rose, in part at least an evocation of martyrdom, appears in several of Catherine's other letters in connection with the Crusade.[24]

Letters from late 1375 also show Catherine advising ecclesiastical leaders and lobbying them for support for church reform, the return of the pope, and the Crusade. Probably in November or December 1375, Catherine wrote to the papal nuncio Berenger of Lézat (chief suspect in the Prato affair), whom she may have met in Pisa when he was sent to Italy by the pope to mediate between Siena and the Salimbeni in spring 1375. Referring to a letter she had received from Berenger, in which he had asked her several questions, Catherine responded by urging the pope to resist pressure from his relatives and to be less lenient in correcting the sins of the prelacy; she assured Berenger that she had assumed his sins for him, and that God had pardoned him; and she recommended that he exert himself not so much in temporal affairs, but work to see that the pope appoint good pastors rather than the "wolves and devils incarnate" of the existing prelacy: "They care about nothing but food and beautiful palaces and pretty youths and big horses. Ah me, that what Christ acquired on the wood of the cross is being thus spent on prostitutes." She pleaded with him to encourage the pope to appoint new cardinals and other pastors not through flattery or simony, but to find holy men of good reputation: "Let him not favor a noble more than a merchant, because virtue is what makes a person noble and pleasing to God."[25] That Berenger had requested Catherine's insight into the policy of the pope in the reform of the church and had asked for her prayers or intercessions

---

[24] For example, letter 270, sent to Gregory XI in April 1377: " . . . ché tra le spine nasce la rosa: e tra le molte persecuzioni ne viene la reformazione della santa Chiesa, la luce che fa levare la tenebre de' cristiani, e la vita degl'infedeli, e la levazione della santissima croce."

[25] Letter 109/LI: " . . . farne ciò che voi potete, trare e' lupi e' dimoni incarnati de' pastori: a veruna cosa attendono se nonne in mangiare e belli palagi e belli giovini e grossi cavalli. Oimé ché quello che Cristo acquistò in su el legno della croce, sì si spenderà con le meretrici. Pregovi che, se ne doveste morire, che voi diciate al padre santo che ponga rimedio a tante iniquità, e, quando venrà el tempo di fare e' pastori e cardenali, che non si faccino per lusinghe né per denari né simonia: ma pregatelo, quanto potete, che'egli attendi e miri se truova la virtù, e buona e santa fama nell'uomo. Non miri più a gentile che a mercennaio, ché la virtù è quella cosa che fa l'uomo gentile e piacevole a Dio."

for him, shows that by this time her prominence within the papal party was acknowledged. And Catherine took advantage of the opportunity to try to influence the pope. This exchange between Catherine and this high clerical official reveals her making active use of the role as court prophetess (a second Birgitta), part of the role for which she had been enlisted in the cause of the church in 1374. While letters to John Hawkwood, Barnabò Visconti, and Giovanna d'Anjou show Catherine attempting to convince important political figures to cooperate in papal plans, the letter to Berenger shows Catherine attempting to influence the policy of the papal party by holding the pope and his representatives in Italy to a high reformist standard.

## 1376: Escalating Conflict and the Trip to Avignon

Two letters Catherine wrote in January 1376 to highly placed ecclesiastical officials show her once again attempting to influence the pope. There had been many rumors concerning the pope's return to Rome throughout the autumn and winter, and so to Nicola da Osimo, notary and secretary to Gregory XI, Catherine pleaded that he diligently encourage the pope to set out for Rome and launch the Crusade.[26] Having heard that the pope was planning to promote Elias of Toulouse, the master general of the Dominicans, to another office, she asked Nicola to recommend for his vicar Stefano della Cumba, who had been procurator of the order from 1367 to 1374, and who had apparently met Raymond of Capua when Raymond was in Rome as prior of the Minerva.[27] Catherine further suggested that if Nicola needed help with this or any other matter, he should send for Raymond. She wrote a similar letter around the same time to Iacopo da Itri, archbishop of Otranto, whom Catherine had probably met when in 1375 he passed through Pisa as apostolic nuncio. Both letters reflect Catherine's careful efforts in this period to influence the pope. In both letters she mentioned that she had written to the pope on this matter, but had made no specific recommendation, only asking that he seek the advice of Nicola and the archbishop of Otranto.[28]

In the mentioned letter to the pope—the earliest extant letter from Catherine to Gregory XI, presumably also sent in January 1376—Catherine sought to shape the pope's approach to the crisis in Italy with themes to which she would return in later letters to him as the war intensified.

---

[26] Letter 181/LV.

[27] Noffke, *Letters of Catherine of Siena*, 1: 256–57n. The papal court had resided in Rome from October 1367 to September 1370 at the end of the pontificate of Urban V.

[28] Letter 183/LVI, to the archbishop of Otranto; and letter 181/LV, to Nicola da Osimo.

Indeed, this letter should be read in possible reaction to—or anticipation of—the papal response in early 1376 to the rebellions in Italy, which was to attack Florentine commerce in retaliation for the Florentine role in the uprisings.[29] Catherine pointed away from temporal measures as a solution, exhorting Gregory to seek peace through reform and a unifying Crusade, and by returning to Rome, even against the pressures of the French prelacy. To appreciate the full force of Catherine's admonitory exhortations, it is important to note that, while she repeatedly attacked the Florentines and their allies in her letters during the war, her advice to the pope and prelates showed sympathy for the rebellious Tuscans. She laid ultimate responsibility for the crisis on the prelates governing the church, and on the pope for not correcting them. Echoing the concerns in the letters to Nicola da Osimo and Iacopo da Itri, Catherine exhorted the pope—whom she addressed by the affectionate *babbo* (daddy)—not to give in to self-centeredness and fear of incurring displeasure of others by avoiding reform of the those under his authority. Clearly referring to the rebellious cities, Catherine blamed the rotten state of these members of the body of the church, which was corrupted by "vermin," on the lack of correction by their pastors, who in turn had not been corrected by Gregory. She urged him to act bravely (strongly implying that he had not been brave up to now): "If until now you haven't been very firm in truth, I want you, I beg you, for the little time that is left, to be so—manfully and like a virile man—following Christ, whose vicar you are." And she urged him to achieve peace through reform, devoting himself only to spiritual matters, and to appoint good pastors and governors of his cities. The rebellion of the "rotten members" was caused by bad pastors and governors. Above all, he must return to Rome, make peace with the rebellious cities, and launch the Crusade:

> Up, father no more negligence. Raise the standard of the most holy cross, for with the fragrance of the cross that you will acquire peace. I beg you to invite those who have rebelled against you to a holy peace, so that all the war might be turned onto the infidels. Take comfort, take comfort, and come, come, to console the poor little servants of God, your children. They are waiting for you with affectionate and loving desire.[30]

29 Trexler, *Spiritual Power*, 44–108.
30 Letter 185: "Se per infino a qui non ci fusse stato bene fermo in verità, voglio e prego che si facci, questo punto del tempo che c'è rimaso, virilmente e come uomo virile, seguitando Cristo di cui vicario sete. E non temete, padre, per veruna cosa che avenga, di questi venti tempestosi che ora vi sono venuti, cioè di questi putridi membri che ànno ribellato a voi: non temete, ché l'aiuto divino è presso. Procurate pure alle cose spirituali, a buoni pastori e buoni rettori delle città vostre, però che per li mali pastori e rettori avete trovata ribellione: poneteci remedio e confortatevi in Cristo Gesù, e non temete. Mandate inanzi e compite, con vera e santa sollicitudine, quello che per santo proponimento avete cominciato, dell'avvenimento vostro e del santo e dolce passaggio, e non tardate più, ché per lo tardare sono avenuti molti inconvenienti e 'l demonio s'è levato e leva per impedire che

Catherine closed the letter by reference to the appointment of a vicar for the Dominicans, and by alerting Gregory to the fact that Pisa and Lucca were in a precarious state "because they have received no comfort from you, and by the contrary party are being goaded and threatened" into joining the league. She reminded the pope that she was pleading with them to stay out of the league and urged Gregory to write to them, especially to Piero Gambacorti, with encouragement.[31]

In the first half of 1376, as the rebellion against the papal governors continued and the pope began to take punitive measures against Florence, Catherine continued lobbying high prelates for a change in the church's strategy in Italy. Writing, for example, to Cardinal Giacomo degli Orsini, the protector of the Sienese commune at the papal Curia, Catherine called for a shift from temporal to spiritual methods: "Do not pay so much attention to transitory things, but pay attention to the saving of souls." She asked him to exhort the pope to appoint good pastors and administrators, and to launch the Crusade: "This will be the way to arrive at peace."[32]

In Florence, the successes of the winter were received as a vindication of the policy of the Eight and the proponents of war against the papal governors, and as a divine approval of Florence's opposition to evil clerics. In this climate of overwhelming public approval for the actions of the Eight, all opposition to war was silenced in favor of unity around the banner of Florentine liberty.[33] This is the context for a letter of general encouragement Catherine wrote in early 1376 to Angelo da Ricasoli, bishop of Florence and member of a notable Guelf patrician family.[34] The Florentine message was carried beyond Florence through the letters of Coluccio Salutati to other Italian cities, in which he invoked the ideal of

---

questo non si faccia, perché s'avede del danno suo. Su, padre, non più negligenzia; rizzate el gonfalone de la santissima croce, ché con l'odore de la croce acquistarete la pace. Pregovi che coloro che vi sono ribelli voi gl'invitiate a una santa pace, sì che tutta la guerra caggia sopra gl'infedeli. Spero, per la infinita bontà di Dio, che tosto mandarà l'aiutorio suo. Confortatevi confortatevi, e venite venite a consolare i povarelli servi di Dio e figliuoli vostri. Aspettianvi con affettuoso e amoroso desiderio."

[31] Ibid.: "So' stata a Pisa e a Lucca infino a qui, invitandoli, quanto posso, che lega non faccino co' membri putridi che sono ribelli a voi: stanno in grande pensiero, perché da voi non ànno conforto e da la contraria parte sempre sono stimolati e minacciati che la faccino: per infino a qui al tutto non ànno consentito. Pregovi che ne scriviate anco strettamente a missere Piero, e fatelo sollicitamente e non v'indugiate."

[32] Letter 223. Not unusually, Catherine's argument here was circular. She called for a Crusade as a means to peace, but also called for reconciliation in order to launch the Crusade. See also Letter 177/LXI, to Pietro Cardinale Portuense (from whom the Florentines had sought help as a mediator).

[33] Peterson, "War of Eight Saints," 186.

[34] Letter 88/XXVIII.

Republican Rome in urging the Italian cities to unite as Italians in opposition to foreign prelates:

> How sad to see noble Italy, whose right it is to rule other nations, itself suffer slavery! What a sight to see this abject barbarism seize upon Latium with ferocious cruelty, creating havoc and preying upon the Latins! Therefore arise . . . and expel this abomination from Italian territory, and protect those who desire liberty. Do not allow these Gallic devourers to oppress your Italy with such cruelty![35]

Against this rhetoric of Italian identity, Catherine's letters at this time to the Florentines and other Italian cities urged the alternative of the church, the source of salvation.

Catherine's awareness of the rhetorical terms of the dispute can be seen, for instance, in a letter from this period to one of her prominent Guelf friends, Niccolò Soderini, who at this time (January or February) was serving as one of the Florentine priors. Like other members of the Guelf elite, he was forced at this time to give up any attempt at shifting the Florentine policy and reasserting the interests of the Parte. Catherine upbraided Niccolò for not working for peace and attacked one of the avowed rationales (in the apologetics of Luigi Marsili, for example) for the Florentine actions: that the Florentines were not stepping outside the church, but only attacking its unjust administrators. As in her earlier letter to Barnabò Visconti, Catherine dismissed any attempt to separate opposition to the institution from sacramental membership in the church. The church is one body, and the blood is part of the body: "And if I should say, "I do not act against [Christ]," I say that you do act against him when you act against his vicar, who takes his place. . . . If you are against the holy Church, how can you share in the blood of the Son of God, since the Church is none other than that same Christ?"[36] By rebelling against the pope, the Florentines were removing themselves from the body of the church, as well as showing themselves to be ungrateful and disobedient sons of their papal father. More pointedly, Catherine argued that their *lega* (league) against the pope was counterproductive, since it would deprive them of their *legame* (bond) to God:

> What worse can happen to us than to be deprived of God? Well might we have many bonds (*legame*) and, having made a league (*lega*), be bound

---

[35] Letter to the Romans, January 1376, quoted in Brucker, *Florentine Politics and Society*, 300.

[36] Letter 171/LX: "E se io dicessi: 'Io non fo contra lui'; dico che tu fai contra lui, quando fai contra el vicario suo, la cui vece tiene. . . . Se tu se' contra la santa Chiesa, come potrai participare el sangue del Figliuolo di Dio, ché la Chiesa non è altro che esso Cristo?"

(*legati*) to many cities and creatures, which if there is not the bonding
(*legame*) and the assistance of God, will be worth nothing.[37]

Catherine used similar rhetoric in a letter to the magistracy of Lucca, the
Anziani, from the first part of 1376, when it was becoming clear that the
Lucchesi would join the Florentine league.[38] Writing apparently from
Lucca, probably between 14 January (when the Anziani had resolved to
join the league) and 14 March (when Lucca along with Pisa formally
joined the league) Catherine urged the Anziani not to be swayed by "fear
of losing your peace or your state, or by the threats of these demons" who
had been encouraging them to oppose the pope: "You have not [yet]
been cut off from the head, from the one who is strong, and you are not
bound (*legati*) to the weak and rotten limb, cut off from his strength.
Take care, take care, that you do not make such a bonding (*legame*)!"[39]

In the meantime, the economic measures taken by the pope were dam-
aging enough to convince the Florentines tentatively to look for a settlement; this was also an opportunity for the Guelfs to attempt a shift in
communal policy. But the prospects for rapprochement were dashed on
19 March, while ambassadors from Florence were on their way to Avignon, when the city of Bologna revolted against the papal government.
There was no doubt that the Florentines and the other members of the
league were largely responsible for the revolt, and this nullified for the
moment any possibility of a truce between Florence and the pope.[40] Cit-
ing the Florentine responsibility for the uprisings in the various cities of
the Papal States, on 31 March the pope placed Florence under interdict,

[37] Ibid: "O che peggio potiamo avere che essere privati di Dio? Bene potremmo avere
assai legame e, fatta lega, legati con molte città e creature: che, se non c'è el legame e l'aiutorio di Dio, ci vaglia nulla."
[38] Lucca had determined to side with the league on January 14, and formally entered it
on March 12 (Noffke, *Letters of Catherine of Siena*, 1: 239). The intention of the Luccans and
Pisans to join the league was known before March; for example, on 29 February, the Sienese
sent ambassadors to Florence for discussions with the representatives of the league, that is,
Pisa, Lucca, Florence, and Barnabò Visconti (ASS, *Consiglio Generale* 186, 18v).
[39] Letter 168/LIII: "Non vi movete per veruno timore di perdere la pace e lo stato
vostro, né per minacce che questi dimoni facessero a voi, però che non vi bisogna; ma confortatevi, con uno santo e dolce ringratiamento, ché Dio v'à fatta grazia e misericordia, però
che non sete sciolti dal capo, da colui che è forte, e non sete legati nel membro debile e
putrido, tagliato dalla sua fortezza. Guardate guardate che questo legame voi non faceste."
[40] See, for example, the comments of Neri di Donato (p. 660) on the resulting disman-
tling of papal authority in Italy and the Florentine role: "In poco di tempo non rimase in
Toscana e nella Marca e nel Ducato e nel Patrimonio terra alcuna a la Chiesa, quasi si può
dire che non ubidissero a la Chiesa o loro uffitiali; tutte si volsero, chi a comuno, chi a signore e chi a magiore, e quasi poco o nulla rimase a la Chiesa, e ciò tutto per operatione e
justitia di Dio per li normi pecati de' malvagi e iniqui pastori, prelati e cherici de la Chiesa
santa di Dio. E anco per operatione, sollecitudine e procaccio de' Fiorentini, Dio promise
tutto questo: *Cum manibus inimicis meis vindicabo vindictam meam*."

and excommunicated thirty-six Florentines considered most responsible for communal policy.[41]

At some point before the revolt of Bologna and the declaration of interdict, it seems that Catherine's friends within the Parte Guelfa sought her help in pleading their cause before the pope. It is also likely that they, along with Catherine and Raymond, had begun to contemplate Catherine's going to Avignon herself to address the pope on this matter.[42] Catherine did write to the Florentine *signori*, probably in April, offering her intervention with the pope. At the same time, she also issued a strongly worded criticism of the prevailing justification of the Florentine position as a reaction to evil clerics rather than an assault on the church itself, and a warning to the Florentine leaders not to delay: "Do not wait for the wrath of God to descend on you; for I tell you, this injury he considers to have been done to him, and so it was."[43] Urging the Florentines to end their rebellion, she invoked the Crusade and the concomitant vision of Christian unity based on recovery of the Holy Land:

> Open, open the eyes of your understanding, and do not walk in such blindness, for we are not Jews nor Saracens, but we are Christians baptized and ransomed in the blood of Christ. So we ought not go against our head [the pope] for any injury we have received, nor should one Christian go against another, but we ought to do this against the infidels, since they have done us an injury, for they possess what is not theirs, but ours.[44]

Catherine's rhetoric of Christian identity in this letter is similar to that used in her letters to John Hawkwood and Barnabò Visconti, but stronger and more insistent. The increased intensity of Catherine's language was perhaps in direct response to the letters of Coluccio Salutati in this period and their rhetoric of Italian identity.

Meanwhile Raymond traveled to Avignon on 24 March 1376 with an urgent message for the pope from Catherine, and possibly at the behest of Catherine's Florentine friends. In the letter Raymond carried with him, Catherine reiterated her call for the pope to reform the pastors of the church, return to Rome, and launch the Crusade, and pleaded with

---

41   Brucker, *Florentine Politics and Society*, 310.

42   Cardini, "Caterina da Siena, la Republica di Firenze," 317.

43   Letter 207/LXVIII: "Oimè oimè, figliuoli miei, piangendo ve 'l dico, e ve ne prego e constringo da parte di Cristo crucifisso, che vi riconciliate e facciate pace con lui, e none state più in guerra: none aspettate che l'ira di Dio venga sopra di voi, ché io vi dico che questa ingiuria elli la riputa fatta a sé, e così è."

44   Letter 207/LXVIII: "Aprite aprite gli occhi del cognoscimento e none andate in tanta cechità, però che noi non siamo giuderi né saracini, ma siamo cristiani batteggiati e ricomprati del sangue di Cristo. Non doviamo dunque andare contra al capo nostro per neuna ingiuria ricevuta, né l'uno cristiano contra all'altro, ma doviamo fare questo contra li infedeli, che ci fanno ingiuria, però che possegono quello che none è loro, anco è nostro."

him not to stop seeking peace because of what had happened in Bologna.[45] Shortly after this, Catherine wrote again to the pope, urging him to be merciful in his dealings with the rebellious cities, and as a sign of the role she increasingly saw for herself in the spiritual struggle represented by the rebellions, offered herself in their place for punishment ("If you want to make a vendetta and render justice, take it out on me"), and blamed the discord on the "stench of my sins."[46] In April, after the pope had sought her insight into the prospects for his return to Rome, now scheduled for the end of the year, Catherine advised the pope not to provoke the rebellious cities, referring specifically to Gregory's plan to send an army of Breton mercenaries to Italy.[47] Instead of sending armies, the pope should come himself "as a meek lamb," and she warned him that any other approach would be a violation of God's will.[48]

Catherine articulated her vocation and her role as a peacemaker most clearly in a letter she sent to Raymond in Avignon in April 1376. Like the Niccolò di Toldo letter, this was one of a number of dramatic statements of self-identity Catherine addressed to Raymond at various points in her career. In the letter, Catherine reported to Raymond a series of revelations, in which Christ had confirmed to her that the current persecution of and corruption within the church was part of the divine plan of reform. She then described to him a powerful vision:

---

[45] Letter 206/LXIII: "Non vi dilongate però dalla pace, per questo caso, che è avenuto, di Bologna, ma venite: ch'io vi dico ch'e' lupi feroci vi mettaranno el capo in grembo come agnelli mansueti, e domandaranovi misericordia."

[46] Letter 196/LXIV: "Ma se volete fare vendetta e giustitia, pigliatela sopra di me, misera miserabile, e datemi ogni pena e tormento che piace a voi, infine alla morte. Credo che per la puzza delle mie iniquità sieno venuti molti defetti e grandi inconvenienti e discordie. Dunque sopra me, misera vostra figliuola, prendete ogni vendetta che volete." Noffke, following Dupré Theseider (*Epistolario*, 268), dates this letter between the previous letter to the pope and the publishing of the interdict against Florence in Siena on April 15, reasoning that either the interdict had not been proclaimed yet or Catherine had not yet heard of it. On the other hand, Catherine would have heard about the pope's action, as all of Europe did, shortly after March 31, though the date on which the interdict was published in various cities depended on local political circumstances. The interdict itself did not go into effect until May, and the precise consequences for the Florentines of the interdict depended largely on how far the pope was willing or able to take the ban in order to harm Florentine merchant activity throughout Europe (see Trexler, *Spiritual Power*, 44–108). Thus Catherine in this letter could have been urging the pope to mitigate the effects of a decision already made.

[47] The Bretons were sent, with the army of John Hawkwood, against Bologna; letters from the Eight to the Sienese on June 11 and 28 inform the commune about the movements of the mercenary armies (ASS, *Concistoro* 1788, nos. 48, 55). Florence and Siena sent troops to support the Bolognese. Neri di Donato (p. 662) reports that the army of the league was routed by an army of more than 10,000 Bretons.

[48] Letter 229/LXIX: "E guardate che, per quanto voi avete cara la vita, voi non veniate con sforzo di gente, ma con la croce in mano come agnello mansueto: facendo così, adempirete la volontà di Dio, ma venendo per altro modo la trapassereste e non l'adempireste."

As the fire of holy desire grew in me, marveling, I saw the Christian people and the infidels enter into the side of the crucified Christ, and I passed into their midst, through the desire and effect of love, entering with them in Christ sweet Jesus accompanied by my father St. Dominic and *Iohanni singulare*,[49] with all my children. Then he placed the cross on my shoulder and the olive branch in my hand, as if he wanted—and so he said—that I should carry it to the one people and to the other: "Say to them: I bring you word of a great joy!"[50]

This vision is a stunning declaration of Catherine's sense of her own authority and her special mission in the church, a prophetic perspective that transcended normal ecclesiastical authority. Catherine frequently used the image of the body of Christ to represent social and political unity—found, for example, in the letters to Barnabò Visconti and to the Florentines—and to express her intimacy with Christ and thus her authority, as in the Niccolò di Toldo letter. But this letter represents an even bolder understanding by Catherine of her mission and her authority, in connection to her increasingly significant role in the conflicts affecting the state of the church. And her vision of herself leading the infidels into the wound represents her fullest ambitions for the Crusade, the hope that the Crusade would result in the conversion of the infidels. While this might seem an extremely naive expectation, Catherine was far from alone in connecting war against the infidels to the infidels' conversion.[51]

Catherine herself departed for Avignon in late May 1376 with a small group of her followers and arrived at the Curia on 18 June, where (according to her hagiographers) she was received by the pope on several occasions. The interdict had taken effect in Florence on 11 May, and

[49] Undoubtedly a reference to the evangelist John, "the beloved disciple." The prominence of John in this vision can be explained by the way in which this vision evokes the Book of Revelation, but also by appeal to the visual register of Catherine's references to the body of Christ. As discussed in chapter 3, when Catherine in her letters evokes the wounded body of Christ, she sometimes does so in a way that suggests visual contemplation of a crucifix or crucifixion scene. And the beloved disciple is a standard character in late-medieval Italian representations of the crucifixion.

[50] Letter 219/LXV: "E crescendo in me el fuoco del santo desiderio, mirando, vedevo nel costato di Cristo crucifisso intrare el popolo cristiano e lo infedele; e io passavo, per desiderio e affetto d'amore, per lo mezzo di loro, e intravo con loro in Cristo dolce Gesù accompagnata col padre mio santo Domenico e Iohanni singulare, con tutti quanti i figliuoli miei. Allora mi dava la croce in collo e l'ulivo in mano, quasi come volesse, e così diceva, che io la portasse all'uno popolo e all'altro; e diceva a me: 'Di' a loro: "Io vi annunzio gaudio magno."'"

[51] The idea of fighting the Crusade to convert the infidels was current at least from the early thirteenth century, persisting in the fourteenth century in the writings of such Crusade theorists as Ramon Lull and Marino Sanudo, and could be understood in terms of the Crusade preparing the way for missionaries, or as compelling conversion in itself. See Benjamin Z. Kedar, *Crusade and Mission: European Approaches to the Muslims* (1984), 108ff.

almost immediately the corresponding prohibitions throughout Europe against Florentine businesses began to take their toll on the commune's finances.[52] Negotiations in July and September failed when the pope initially refused to meet with the Florentine ambassadors, and then made exorbitant demands in exchange for peace. These failures in negotiations had the effect of hardening Florentine political opinion against the pope, and the commune intensified its efforts to mobilize support in Italy for the war. Moreover, in autumn additional steps were taken to confiscate and liquidate clerical property in order to pay for the war; this appealed to the desires of many of the Florentine public to see the clergy stripped of some of their wealth, but also damaged negotiations with the pope.[53]

Catherine remained in Avignon until November while the pope departed for Italy with his court in September. During her stay she evidently sought to influence the French royal family to support the papal program. Louis, the duke of Anjou, apparently promised her that, if the pope would launch a Crusade, he would raise and lead an army himself.[54] She wrote a letter to the French king, Charles V, urging him to stop his wars with England, because that conflict was diverting resources and energies from the Crusade: he should be fighting infidels, not Christians.[55] It is not clear what, if any, influence she had on these men, or what other agenda the duke of Anjou might have been furthering by contacting her.[56] Her more pressing business concerned papal relations with the Florentines and the prospects for the return of the Curia to Rome. From Avignon she wrote the Florentines two letters that reflected her increasing impatience with their refusal to submit to the pope, as well as a sense that the Florentines had not dealt honestly in employing her mediation. While her friends in Florence might have engaged her help in honest miscalculation of the political situation in Florence, it is also possible that her mission was used by the Florentines as a delaying tactic.

Catherine had traveled to Florence prior to leaving for Avignon, and stayed with several of her followers in the house of Niccolò Soderini. Raymond of Capua tells how Catherine was asked by the priors to intercede for them with the pope, which might be true, but the Eight—not the

[52] Trexler (*Spiritual Power*, 44–108) details the varying effectiveness of the interdict in various crucial centers of Florentine trade. There is no doubt, however, that it cut Florence off from several of its key markets for cloth and alimentary supplies. The interdict was published in Pisa on June 29, and in Naples on July 15. On August 19, news reached Florence that all the Florentines had been expelled from Naples.
[53] Brucker, *Florentine Politics and Society*, 317–18; Trexler, *Spiritual Power*, 122–23.
[54] After a wall collapsed at a banquet Louis was giving, killing several guests, Catherine wrote to him (letter 237) in order to encourage him to use the occasion to turn from temporal affairs and devote his efforts to the Crusade.
[55] Letter 235.
[56] See Fawtier, *Sainte Catherine de Sienne*, 2: 229–231.

priors—drove the Florentine government at this time. As Franco Cardini notes, this might have given Catherine the impression that she had received an official office without actually committing the Florentines to anything.[57] If Catherine perceived that the Florentines were sending mixed messages, this confusion (intentional or not) might have resulted from the political conflicts within Florence: while an unfavorable peace settlement would have helped the cause of the Parte Guelfa (members of which dominated the Priorate at this time) by casting doubt on the wisdom of the war policy of the regime, the Eight needed a good peace to vindicate their actions in the previous year and maintain their political support.[58] In any case, on 28 June she wrote to the Eight of War complaining that their ambassadors had not yet arrived, and that the new taxes on the clergy adopted in Florence at that time were giving fuel to the many papal advisors who sought to continue the war (and forestall the pope's departure from Avignon). The delay and the taxes also threatened to compromise Catherine, who had been telling the pope of the good intentions of the Florentines.[59] In August or September, she complained by letter to one of her friends, the Guelf leader Buonaccorso di Lapo, that the Florentine ambassadors sent to Avignon were not exhibiting the repentance that the Florentine *signori* had shown in their communications with her; moreover, the ambassadors would have nothing to do with her, contrary to a promise made by the *signori* that they would confer with her in their approach to the pope.[60]

Meanwhile, in addition to her meetings with Gregory, Catherine sent him six letters while she stayed in Avignon, and another three in the few months following the pope's return to Italy.[61] Given the French resistance to the pope's plan to return to Rome, Catherine was in a politically sensitive position. According to the accounts of companions like Stefano di Corrado Maconi, Catherine was subjected to severe tests while in Avignon. A group of learned prelates interrogated her, apparently seeking to expose her as a heretic, but they found her doctrinally sound. The pope's physician, the Sienese Francesco Casini, later commented to Stefano di Corrado Maconi that "had they not found that this virgin had a solid foundation, she would never have made a more unfortunate voyage."[62] And the Sienese Dominican Bartolomeo Dominici reported that the wife

---

57 Cardini, "Caterina da Siena, la Republica di Firenze," 321.
58 Brucker, *Florentine Politics and Society,* 329.
59 Letter 230/LXXII.
60 Letter 234/LXXXII.
61 The following letters to the pope can be dated between June 1376 and January 1377: letters 218/LXXIV, 255/LXXI, 233/LXXVI, 231/LXXVII, 238/LXXX, 239/LXXXI, 252/LXXXVIII, 209, and 285.
62 *Processo Castellano,* 269–70.

of the pope's nephew sought to test Catherine by driving a hairpin into her foot while Catherine was in ecstatic prayer. Catherine remained rapt from her senses, though the pain in her foot was later severe.[63] It is possible that the pope was keeping Catherine at a distance, but the fact that she wrote him letters when she was theoretically capable of meeting with him face to face does not in itself mean that she was out of favor with Gregory. Once again, Catherine could say more in her letters than she could have said in a papal audience.

Indeed, her letters to Gregory XI grew increasingly urgent and critical of his inaction and wavering under the pressure of his French advisors and rumors of plots against his life in Italy. For example, in a short note Catherine sent Gregory at this time she responded to French cardinals who were delaying the pope's departure by urging him to follow the model of pope Clement VI, who payed close attention to the advice of his cardinals. Catherine retorted that Gregory should instead model himself on Urban V, Gregory's immediate predecessor, who acted against the advice of his Curia in returning to Rome.[64] Catherine exhorted Gregory in surprisingly lusty terms, playing on the traditional image of Rome as bride of the pope (and more generally, on the see as bride of the bishop): "Go quickly to your bride, who awaits you all pale, so that you can put the color back into her."[65] In another letter, Catherine complained of Gregory's cowardice in remaining in Avignon and avoiding reform:

Ah me, ah me, my most sweet father, forgive my presumption in saying what I have said and what I am compelled by gentle First Truth to say. His will, father, is this, and this is what he is asking of you. He demands that you take justice against the abundance of sins that are committed by those who feed and graze in the garden of the holy Church, saying that animals should not be eating the food of men. Since he has given you the authority and you have accepted it, you ought to use your strength and power, and if you are not willing to use it, it would be better to refuse it, and more to the honor of God and the salvation of your soul.[66]

[63] Ibid., 303–304.
[64] Letter 231.
[65] Ibid.: "Andate tosto a la Sposa vostra, che v'aspetta tutta impalidita, perché le poniate el colore." On the scriptural and apocalyptic implications of this image, see Amanda Collins, *Greater than Emperor*, 62–63. Collins notes that Clement VI, in expressing a desire to return to Rome, had wished "to gaze upon her ample bosom" (quoted from Diana Wood, *Clement VI: The Pontificate and Ideas of an Avignon Pope* [1989], 77n).
[66] Letter 255/LXXI: "Oimè oimè, padre mio dolcissimo, perdonate alla mia presunzione, di quello ch'io v'ò detto, e a dire costretta so' dalla prima dolce Verità di dirlo. La volontà sua, padre, è questa e così vi dimanda: egli vi dimanda che facciate giustizia dell'abondanzie delle molte iniquità, che si commettono per coloro che si notricano e pasciono nel giardino della santa Chiesa, dicendo che l'animale non si debba notricare del cibo degli uomini. Poi che esso v'à dato l'autorità, e voi l'avete presa, dovete usare la virtù e potenzia

From this startling suggestion—Gregory should reform the church or resign the papacy—Catherine proceeded to accuse him of irresponsibility in not seeking peace with the Tuscan cities. And then, consistent with Catherine's sense of her own authority as annunciated in her vision of 1 April, she threatened to go over Gregory's head: "Act in this way, so that I do not complain to Christ Crucified about you, for there is no one else to whom I can appeal, since there is no one higher on earth."[67]

Gregory did eventually leave Avignon for Italy, arriving in Corneto by the end of the year, where he negotiated with the Romans concerning the return of the papal court to Rome. Catherine returned to Siena by mid-December and continued, to some extent, to involve herself in the negotiations of the Tuscan cities with the pope.[68] The Sienese ambassadors to the pope were seeking, as part of the terms of peace, the return of the port of Talamone, which had been seized by the Pisan prior of the Hospitallers with aid from the armies of the church. Catherine wrote to the pope regarding this embassy, calling on him to make peace and accept the Sienese apologies for joining the league.[69] In the meantime, the war continued. In mid-December, the papal city of Ascoli surrendered to the league, and an attempt on the part of the church to take back Città di Castello failed, as did an attack on Bolsena.[70] Nevertheless, on 21 December, Rome submitted to the pope, clearing the way for his return. In Florence, the winter and spring saw division and growing opposition to war, which the Parte Guelfa sought to manipulate for political gain. But tensions between the papacy and the Florentine league were heightened again in February, when the Breton soldiers in the service of the bishop of Geneva stationed in Cesena, the last city in Romagna loyal to the pope, responded to an armed revolt by committing wholesale slaughter of the inhabitants of the city, including women

vostra; e non volendola usare, meglio sarebbe a rifiutare, e più onore di Dio e salute dell'anima vostra sarebbe."

[67] Ibid: "Fate sì ch'io non mi richiami a Cristo crocifisso di voi, ché ad altro non mi posso richiamare, che non c'è maggiore in terra."

[68] Catherine wrote at least one letter to a Florentine follower at this time (letter 130, to Ippolito degli Ubertini). Her other activities with respect to Florence are less certain. According to the biographer of Catherine's follower, Stefano di Corrado Maconi, the Florentine Guelfs at this time wanted Catherine to visit Florence, but she refused on the grounds that such a trip would be scandalous. She sent Stefano instead with a message to the Eight, urging them to make peace, but a rumor spread through the city that a "Catherinated Sienese" was inducing the Eight to subject the city to the pope, and Stefano was attacked by a mob. (Bartolomeo da Siena, *De vita et moribus beati Stephani Senensis Carthusiani* [1626] book 1, chap. 8; Gardner, *Saint Catherine of Siena,* 202.)

[69] Letter 285.

[70] Neri di Donato (664–65) concludes his descriptions of these two battles and the deaths they caused with the ironic comments, "E queste sono le indulgentie che dànno ogi li pastori de la Chiesa," and "Queste sono ogi l'opere de' pastori."

and children.[71] While Catherine never mentioned the Cesena affair explicitly, a letter to Gregory XI written on 16 April concludes in a tone of apocalyptic despair that might have been a response to the massacre and the moral disrepute it cast on the papal cause: "Ah me! We have fallen under the sentence of death, we have made war upon God."[72]

## 1377: Mission to the Salimbeni

Catherine's activities in 1377, more than in 1375 and 1376, brought her directly into the ambit of Sienese politics, but in a way that emphasizes the interconnectedness of many local Sienese concerns with Italian issues. For example, in January she wrote to Pietro di Giacomo Tolomei, a leader of his clan and one of the most dominant political personalities during the regime of Riformatori, to ask for his help in obtaining the release of the brother of Raymond of Capua, a soldier in the papal army who had been taken prisoner by the Prefect of Rome in one of the battles between the armies of the church and the Tuscan league.[73] Catherine might have assumed that Pietro was well placed to give this help, not only because of his high position within Siena and Siena's participation in the league, but also because the Tolomei dominance of the Riformatori made them close allies of the Florentine regime.[74]

[71] The shock and outrage with which Italians reacted to the massacre can be seen in contemporary accounts like that of Neri di Donato (p. 665), who emphasizes the bloodthirsty role of the cardinal of Geneva in leading the massacre against the desires even of John Hawkwood. As is clear from a letter from the Florentines Priors (written by Coluccio Salutati) to the Sienese Concistoro, the Florentines made the most of the massacre as an example of clerical perfidy (ASS, *Concistoro* 1790, 53, 9 February 1376/7).

[72] Letter 270: "Oimè, caduti siamo nel bando della morte e aviamo fatta guerra con Dio."

[73] Letter 254. See Gardner, *Saint Catherine of Siena*, 199. Luigi delle Vigne, Raymond's brother, was in the service of the queen of Naples, and was captured during the battle of Bolsena, during which Giovanna's army, which had been sent to fight against Viterbo, was completely defeated by the combined forces of Francesco di Vico, prefect of Rome, and the Florentines. Neri di Donato (p. 665) comments on the outcome of the battle with evident satisfaction, and notes that many of those fighting for the papal side were relatives of the pope or otherwise of families with connections to the prelacy: "Quelli de la Chiesa furo rotti e fune presi e morti molti, e fu preso el detto nipote del papa con XX cavalieri, tutti parenti del papa e de' cardenali; sichè tutti gli ebero a man salve."

[74] While Catherine did have close relations with one branch of the Tolomei (the family of Francesco di Giacomo Tolomei), Pietro was of another branch. He held more elective offices than any other noble during the years of the Riformatori, frequently holding positions on the magisterial board, the Concistoro (see Brizio, "Siena nel secondo Trecento," 344). As mentioned above, it was Pietro who, as a member of the Concistoro, urged the Consiglio Generale to agree to membership in the Florentine league in November 1375 (ASS, *Consiglio Generale* 185, f. 105v). Not surprisingly, in addition to asking for Pietro's intercession in the matter of Luigi delle Vigne, in her letter to Pietro, Catherine also argues against those who say that they are fighting unjust pastors and not the church itself, her

Several other letters written in the early part of the year also illustrate how Catherine's interest in issues of ecclesiastical and Tuscan politics merged with local concerns of the Sienese at this time, especially concerning the security of Sienese territory to the south and west of the city, which provided crucial sources of food and salt as well as Siena's only access to the sea. Of particular concern was the area to the south of the city dominated by the towns of Montalcino and Montepulciano, and further south into the Val d'Orcia. It was in this region that the most volatile of the Sienese noble families—the Salimbeni, the Aldobrandeschi counts, and the Tolomei—fought among themselves and against the commune for control of castles and land. This area was also of great strategic importance during the War of Eight Saints, lying at the southernmost end of Tuscany at the border of the Papal States.[75] The area to the southwest of the city, between Siena and its sometime port at Talamone, was subject to occasional incursions by the Pisans (the cause of cold relations between Siena and Piero Gambacorti in late 1374) as well as by the mercenary armies. In spring 1376, men of Piero Gambacorti, the Salimbeni, and the Aldobrandeschi conti di Santa Fiora joined together to seize some Sienese lands in this area.[76] And in July 1376, the Sienese port town of Talamone and the surrounding region were invaded and taken for the church by an army led by the Tuscan province of the Knights of St. John of Jerusalem (the Hospitallers), who were based in Pisa. Sienese armies were able to retake some of the territory surrounding Talamone during the rest of 1376, but the port itself was still held by the *frieri* (as the Hospitallers were known in Tuscany).[77] The recovery of Talamone was at the forefront of issues facing the Sienese government from the end of 1376 and through 1377; the Sienese ambassadors sent to greet the pope in November on his return to Italy were charged in particular with negotiating to reacquire the port.[78]

In March or April, Catherine wrote to Niccolò Strozzi, prior of the Tuscan province of the Hospitallers—that is, the leader of the army that had occupied Talamone—encouraging him to arm himself spiritually for battle against the infidels, a likely reference to a papal plan to send

usual tack in letters to supporters of the league during the War of Eight Saints.

[75] Both the Sienese and Florentines feared that Gerard du Puy had ambitions to extend his dominion west from Perugia into the Sienese *contado*.

[76] Neri di Donato, 661. The Concistoro discussed the Pisan actions against Sienese lands on 16 May (ASS, *Concistoro* 80, f. 9v) and the Consiglio Generale considered this affront to "the honor of the commune" on 18 May (ASS, *Consiglio Generale* 186, ff. 59r–v).

[77] An account of the military actions in and around Talamone are in Neri di Donato, 661–62. The Consiglio Generale discussed the situation on 15 July (ASS, *Consiglio Generale* 186, f. 79).

[78] Gardner, *Saint Catherine of Siena*, 203–4.

the Hospitallers to Rhodes in the spring of 1377.[79] Probably around the same time, she wrote to a group of young Florentine men in the circle of Giovanni dalle Celle, exhorting them to join the *frieri* in the anticipated Crusade.[80] And on Holy Thursday (March 26) 1377, Catherine sent a letter to a group of prisoners in Siena, encouraging them to derive spiritual benefit from their sufferings and offering them the model of Christ *cavaliero*, fighting the devil on the spiritual battlefield.[81] Catherine frequently employed this image in letters to soldiers, as well as to men whom she was encouraging to enlist in the Crusade. Given recent events and Catherine's other letters regarding the *frieri* around this time, the prisoners to whom she wrote on Holy Thursday were most likely *frieri* captured in the battles against Siena in July 1376.[82]

While these letters show Catherine engaged, at least indirectly, in an issue of concern to the Sienese government, she entered into an area of central anxiety for the regime when, in late July or August, she traveled with a complement of her lay and clerical associates into the Sienese *contado* to stay at the Rocca d'Orcia, the stronghold of Agnolino di Giovanni Salimbeni, the *capo* of the Salimbeni family. The truce of 1375 between the Sienese and the Salimbeni had not kept the members of that family at peace for very long. In 1376 Cione di Sandro Salimbeni acted to extend his domain by claiming the ownership of Monte Antico (near Montalcino), conquering and naming himself *signore* of the city of Chiusi, and seizing the Castello di Celle from Orvieto.[83] Cione was also said to be

[79] Letter 256. Gregory announced in a letter of 8 December 1375 that the Hospitallers would send an expedition of 500 cavalry and 500 shields in spring 1377 for purpose of defending Rhodes against Turkish advances (Theseider, *Epistolario*, 192n). Catherine possibly assumed that this *passagium particolare* would be the beginning of a *passagium generale*—a full-scale Crusade. On Niccolò Strozzi, see Anthony Luttrell, "Gregory XI and the Turks: 1370–1378," *Orientalia Christiana Periodica* 46 (1980): 416.

[80] Letter 257/L, to Conte di Monna Agnola and companions.

[81] Letter 260: "Dico ch'egl'è cavaliere: venuto in questo campo della bataglia à combatuto e vénto le dimonia."

[82] Luttrell (p. 416n), following Burlamacchi (in Tommaseo, ed., *Le lettere di S. Caterina da Siena* 2: 13) takes Neri di Donato to be saying that a single *friere* seized Talamone and was subsequently imprisoned—in other words, that only one man was imprisoned. But from context it seems clear that "el friere" must be a way of referring to a group or company of Hospitallers; obviously it was a group of knights and not an individual who was able to seize the lands. This reading is confirmed by Neri's subsequent references to "el friere" and "i frieri" (661–69).

[83] On Cione di Sandro's attempt to claim Monte Antico in August 1376, see Neri di Donato, 662. The Florentine Eight of War attempted to intervene in Cione's dispute with Siena over Monte Antico (ASS, *Concistoro* 1376, ff. 54 and 55, both dated 31 October 1376). On 6 January 1377, the Concistoro discussed Cione di Sandro's claims (ASS, *Concistoro* 83, ff. 9v–10; see also ff. 14–15v, and 18r–v). The Consiglio Generale took up the issue of Monte Antico on 8 February, discussing Cione's offer to sell Monte Antico to the commune, which the Consiglio Generale considered in light of the fact that the commune already considered that land to be Sienese property (ASS, *Consiglio Generale* 187, f. 11v). On Cione's seizure of Chiusi, see Neri di Donato, 666.

responsible for invasions of armies of the church into the Sienese *contado* in 1377.[84] Niccolò Salimbeni was implicated in June 1376 in a plot to take lordship of Casole and other lands of Siena and Florence.[85] Agnolino di Giovanni was not as volatile as other members of his family, but his movements were nonetheless viewed with suspicion, for instance when he was encountered by a Sienese agent on his way from visiting the papal stronghold of Foligno in January 1377.[86] In mid-1377, the Salimbeni occupied Bibbiano and exacted general devastation in that part of the Sienese *contado*.[87] And added to these sources of disorder, members of the Salimbeni family were at odds with Spinello di Giacomo Tolomei, whose power was centered near Montepulciano; this culminated in Spinello attacking the Salimbeni lands in spring 1378.[88]

Even before the trip, Catherine had been in contact with several female members of the Salimbeni family. In April, she had written to one of Agnolino's sisters, Isa di Giovanni, inviting her to join the Dominican *mantellate*, and to another sister of Agnolino, Benedetta di Giovanni, recruiting her for a monastery Catherine was founding outside Siena;[89] she also wrote to

[84] Neri di Donato (667) comments on the invasion of soldiers of the church in the Maremma, and notes that this was said to be the doing of Cione di Sandro. Also, the Sienese ambassadors to Perugia met up with Agnolino di Giovanni Salimbeni north of Siena in January 1377 and were informed by one of Agnolino di Giovanni's companions that the soldiers who had ridden into the *contado* were troops cashiered from the papal armies after the battles over Bologna, and that Cione di Sandro was responsible for the invasion (ASS, *Concistoro* 1790, n.25, 9 January 1376/7).

[85] Neri di Donato (662–63) reports that Niccolò del Mozo of Siena, who had previously rebelled against the Riformatori, was amnestied and returned to Siena from Rome and reported a plot wherein Niccolò Salimbeni was going to take Casole and other lands of the Sienese and Florentines. In reaction to this news, three men were arrested, interrogated, and beheaded, and Niccolò (Neri di Donato does not specify whether this is Niccolò del Mozo or Niccolò Salimbeni) was banished.

[86] The letter cited above, from the Sienese ambassadors to Perugia (ASS, *Concistoro* 1790, n.25, 23 January 1376/7). The ambassadors remark that Agnolino had traveled to Foligno "incontanente." The lord of Foligno, Trincio dei Trinci, a strong supporter of the papal cause, was Agnolino's uncle (the brother of Agnolino's mother, Biancina di Giovanni Salimbeni). As mentioned below, Catherine wrote to Trincio and his brother Corrado in late summer 1377 (letter 253) and to Trincio's wife in November (letter 224) after Trincio was killed in a civic uprising.

[87] See Franco Salimei, *I Salimbeni di Siena* (1986), 151; and Alessandra Carniani, *I Salimbeni, quasi una signoria: tentativi di affermazione politica nella Siena del Trecento* (1995).

[88] See Neri di Donato, 671, and Sienese executive and legislative reaction throughout April and May 1378 (ASS, *Concistoro* 91, ff. 9, 21, 29, 42, and 48v; *Consiglio Generale* 187, f. 156).

[89] This is the monastery, Santa Maria degli Angeli, converted from a fortress donated to Catherine by Nanni di ser Vanni, as mentioned in chapter 4. Catherine petitioned the Sienese government for permission to take possession of this fortress on 25 January 1377 (ASS, *Consiglio Generale* 187, f. 9r–v; printed in Laurent, ed., *Documenti*, 41–43.) This foundation, which did not survive Catherine's death by more than a few years, remains something of a mystery. It is not known, for example, what sort of rule the monastery was intended to follow or under whose jurisdiction it operated.

Agnolino to seek his help in this matter.[90] According to Francesco di Vanni Malavolti (one of Catherine's companions on this trip), the purpose of the trip was to settle a dispute between Cione di Sandro and Agnolino di Giovanni Salimbeni over a castle claimed by both men, an argument that threatened to erupt into a wholesale war between the armies of these two powerful lords. She traveled first to Montepulciano because it was between the strongholds of the two cousins, and then to Cione's castle of Castiglioncello, and finally to Agnolino at the Rocca d'Orcia.[91] This dispute, and the precise nature of Catherine's involvement in it, remains obscure. Indeed, the tangle of feuds and plots at this time among the Salimbeni, Tolomei, and Aldobrandeschi—not to mention the agents of the papacy, Sienese, and Florentines—is probably impossible to unravel entirely.[92] Contact with the Salimbeni likely prompted two letters Catherine wrote during her stay in the *contado* to Salimbeni relatives who were directly engaged on the papal side of the conflict with the Florentines: the Trinci in Foligno and the Belforti in Volterra.[93]

Whatever her exact involvement in the family relations of the Salimbeni, there is no question that Catherine saw her activities during this time as continued involvement in the dispute between the pope and the Florentines. For example, in a letter to the archbishop of Pisa late in 1377, Catherine called on the prelacy to use her and other "servants of God" as "spies," in order to gauge popular sentiments in the conflict.[94]

[90] Letters 112 and 113, to Benedetta di Giovanni d'Agnolino; letter 114, to Agnolino di Giovanni d'Agnolino; letter 115, to Isa di Giovanni d'Agnolino. In the letter to Benedetta, Catherine suggests that she come to the Rocca during Catherine's upcoming visit there; from this one can infer that Catherine was not visiting the *contado* simply to confer with Benedetta, but that her invitation to the Rocca had other purposes, and maybe predated, the discussions of Benedetta's religious vocation.

[91] *Processo Castellano,* 391–92.

[92] This is one of the areas concerning which the diplomatic and legislative records are often maddeningly laconic, referring without explanation to the "novità" of Agnolino, or the "novità" of Cione. A full understanding of the relations of these lords to each other and to Siena and other cities would require a study of its own.

[93] Letter 253, to Trincio dei Trinci, Signor of Foligno, and his brother Corrado; these were the brothers of Biancina di Giovanni d'Agnolino Salimbeni, mother of Agnolino di Giovanni and Catherine's hostess at Rocca d'Orcia. In this letter, Catherine consoled the brothers for the opposition they were facing from their subjects, who were seeking the moment of the War of Eight Saints to attempt to oust the Trinci and erect a popular government. She congratulated them for their service to the church, and assured them that while those who served the church would be thanked, those who opposed the church will be punished. A short time after this letter, Trincio was killed by a popular uprising in Foligno; Catherine wrote a letter of consolation to his wife, Jacoma (letter 264). Catherine also wrote to Benuccio di Piero and Bernardo di Uberto de' Belforti (Letter 103). The Belforti were an especially powerful Guelf family. According to Fawtier (*Sainte Catherine de Sienne* 2: 240–41), Benuccio was the son of Pietro di Ottaviano de' Belforti and Angiola di Benuccio di Sozzo di Francesco de' Salimbeni.

[94] Letter 243: "E so bene che tutto voi non potete vedere, ma mettete le spie de' servi di Dio, che v'aitino a vedere, però che fino a la morte si die fare ciò che si può per amore del

Catherine's intervention was not welcomed by the Sienese, who would have had reason to fear her influence—and the influence of Raymond of Capua and her other *famigliari*—in this sensitive area of local concern. Sienese anxiety about Catherine's activities can be inferred from several letters Catherine wrote to the Sienese magistracy and others during her stay in the *contado*. In August or September, Catherine wrote to the Sienese *signori* in reply to a letter from the governors demanding that she return to Siena to help settle some dispute within the city. Catherine prefaced her response to the request with a striking attack on the moral standing of the government in a lengthy disquisition on "self-love" and "servile fear," vices that cause a kind of "blindness," and which Catherine therefore regularly identified as the root causes of bad political decisions.[95] Among the effects of these vices on civic governments, Catherine wrote, was that evil people were heeded and left unpunished while the just servants of God were condemned, despite the fact that they sought only "the honor of God and the salvation of souls, and the peace and quiet of the cities," spiritual and temporal goals that Catherine presented as interconnected.[96] In response to the request that she return and accomplish a truce within the city, Catherine first denied her ability to help in such affairs, and then asserted that she had been commanded by God to remain in the *contado* on account of some needs of the Dominican monastery of Sant'Agnese of Montepulciano and in order to accomplish peace among the Tolomei. In contrast to her earlier note of humility, Catherine reminded the *signori* that the Tolomei affair was one "you know you have been trying to settle for some time, and have not brought to an end."[97] Catherine wrote in a similar vein in September to the Sienese goldsmith Salvi di ser Pietro, an influential member of the Riformatori who was serving as *capitano del popolo*.[98] Salvi had apparently informed her

---

Salvatore nostro."

[95] Letter 123.

[96] Letter 123: "Oh cechità d'amore proprio e timore disordinato, tu giugni a tanta cechità che non tanto che tu condanni la comune gente e gli iniqui uomini—e' quali giustamente si potrebbero condennare, e temere de le falsitadi loro—, ma tu lassi el timore de lo iniquo e condanni il giusto, recandosi a di petto i poverelli servi di Dio, e' quali cercano l'onore di Dio e la salute dell'anime e la pace e la quiete de le cittadi; non restando mai i dolci desiderii, e la continua orazione, lagrime e sudori, d'offerire dinanzi a la divina bontà. Come dunque ti può patire, amor proprio e timore servile, di temere e giudicare coloro che si dispongono a la morte per la tua salute, e per conservare e crescere in pace e in quiete lo stato tuo?"

[97] Ibid.: "Unde io non veggo che testé a questi dì io possa venire, per alcuna cosa di bisogno che io ò a fare per lo monasterio di santa Agnesa; e per essere co' nipoti di missere Spinello per la pace de' figliuoli di Lorenzo, la quale sapete che, già è buono tempo, voi lo cominciaste a trattare, e non si trasse mai a fine."

[98] Letter 122. See Brizio, "Siena nel secondo Trecento," 2: 364, s.v. "Salvi ser Petri." At the end of this letter, Catherine greets "Francesco," probably a reference to Francesco di

of rumors in Siena about her activities in the *contado*. Catherine responded that God had commanded her to continue in her work despite "such murmurings and suspicions concerning me and my father fra Raimondo."[99] It was in this letter that Catherine issued the self-justificatory statement quoted at the beginning of this book's introduction, in which she addressed specifically the accusation that she and her companions were plotting with the Salimbeni: "The citizens of Siena do a very shameful thing in believing or imagining that we are here for making plots in the lands of the Salimbeni, or in any other place in the world." The specificity of the accusation, as well as the fact that Catherine felt obliged to respond to it, shows how deeply she and her *famiglia* were implicated in Sienese politics as well as the broader politics of the War of Eight Saints. Once again, whether Catherine was merely saving souls or plotting with the Salimbeni was a matter of perspective. In fact, she was doing both.

Catherine wrote again to the *signori* in November or December, this time from the monastery of Sant'Antimo, near Montalcino, where she was visiting her friend Abbot Giovanni di Gano.[100] The abbot was involved at this time in a jurisdictional dispute with the archpriest of the nearby city of Montalcino. Apparently a local nobleman had claimed possession of a parish in Montalcino and, with the approval of the archpriest, gave his young son the prebend. Abbot Giovanni objected—the boy was not even in clerical orders—and this led to a battle with the archpriest concerning the jurisdiction over the parish. During the dispute, the archpriest laid some charge against Abbot Giovanni with the Sienese government, very possibly related to his association with Catherine.[101] A letter Catherine wrote to the abbot in September makes it clear that Giovanni di Gano had

---

Vanni Malavolti, who was one of the Ordines of Siena in September and October 1377 (ASS, *Concistoro* 86, 2r).

[99] Letter 122: "Ora vi dichiaro se volontà è di Dio che io stia: e dico che avendo io grandissimo desiderio di tornare per timore di non offendere Dio nel mio stare, per tante mormorazioni e sospetti quanti di me è preso e del padre mio frate Ramondo, fu dichiarato da quella Verità che non può mentire a quella medesima serva sua, dicendo: 'Persevera di mangiare a la mensa a la quale io v'ò posti.'"

[100] Giovanni had attended the opening of Santa Maria degli Angeli in April.

[101] The basis of the dispute is clear from two letters to the Sienese Concistoro in November from Fillipo da Montalcino, a Franciscan friar who was a vicar for Abbot Giovanni di Gano. In his letters, fra Fillipo defended the abbot eloquently and charged the archpriest with pride and ambition (ASS, *Concistoro* 1792, 64 [5 November 1377], and 70 [13 November 1377]). There does not appear to be any record of the charge that the archpriest laid against Abbot Giovanni. Catherine's comments in her letter to the Concistoro (letter 122) suggest that the archpriest's accusation concerned Giovanni's connection to Catherine. In that letter, Catherine defended the abbot and then immediately answered accusations against her own activities. The sense that Giovanni was brought under suspicion because of his connection to Catherine is also implicit in Catherine's letter to Giovanni (letter 250).

complained to Catherine about her trip to the Salimbeni; in the letter, Catherine encouraged the abbot to endure patiently scandals and murmuring.[102] From Sant'Antimo, Catherine sent her *famigliare* Pietro di Giovanni di Ventura to the Sienese to account for her actions by word of mouth, and with a letter warning the *signori* that attacks on the servants of God offend Him, and would result in great ruin for Siena: "You do not want to set the servants of God against you, for all other things make it clear that God feels more deeply injured when scandals and infamy are lodged against his servants."[103] She blamed the charges against the abbot— "the greatest servant of God in these parts in a long time"—on the malice of the archpriest. In an ironic reference to the standard rhetoric employed by the members of the Florentine league, Catherine pointed out that the Sienese had complained often about the corruption of the clergy, and here they had a cleric actually fighting corruption and they were trying to thwart him! She had heard about complaints against her made to the *signori* on account of her travels to the Salimbeni lands, to which she responded indignantly that she and her followers were doing nothing but "offering sweet and loving desires to God, with copious tears and sighs, to give cover so that divine judgments do not fall on us." And Catherine insisted that "no ingratitude or thoughtlessness [*ignoranzie*] of my fellow citizens" would deter her from working unto death for their salvation. All she and her followers were doing was saving souls, the "trade" to which God had set them.[104]

Catherine's references to her *famiglia* in these letters shows that it was not just Catherine alone that the Sienese mistrusted, but also the men with whom she was associated. The Sienese would have been concerned about the involvement of a cleric like Raymond of Capua, with such close ties to the papacy; indeed, Raymond's movements had already attracted attention. Evidently the Sienese regime also viewed Catherine's *famiglia* as a dissident group. Again, the letters Catherine wrote to Sano di Maco and

[102] Letter 250.
[103] Letter 121: "Non vogliate ponere i servi di Dio contra di voi, ché tutte l'altre cose pare che Dio sostenga più che la ingiuria gli scandali e le infamie che sono poste a' suoi servi."
[104] Letter 121: "Del mio venire con la mia famiglia, anco v'è fatto richiamo e messo sospetto, secondo che m'è detto; non so però se egli è vero. Ma se voi costate tanto a voi, quanto voi costate a me e a loro, in voi e in tutti gli altri cittadini non caderebbero le cogitazioni e le passioni tanto di leggiero; e turrestevi l'orecchie per non udire. Cercato ò io e gli altri, e cerco continuamente, la salute vostra dell'anima e del corpo, non mirando a veruna fadiga, offerendo a Dio dolci e amorosi desiderii con abondanzia di lagrime e di sospiri, per riparare che i divini giudicii non vengano sopra di noi e' quali meritiamo per le nostre iniquitadi. Io non so' di tanta virtù che io sappia fare altro che imperfezione; ma gli altri che sono perfetti e che attendono solo all'onore di Dio e a la salute dell'anime, sono coloro che 'l fanno. Ma non si lassarà però, per la ingratitudine e per l'ignoranzie de' miei cittadini, che non s'adoperi infino a la morte per la salute vostra."

other followers in Siena at this time, taking them to task for their pusillanimity and lack of commitment to their cause, show that, like the abbot
of Sant'Antimo, her supporters were worried about the suspicions her
activities raised, and perhaps feared for their own positions.

The sensitivity of the terrain on which Catherine moved is also clear
from a letter she wrote during her stay with the Salimbeni to Rabe di
Francesco Tolomei, the mother of a group of Tolomei with whom Catherine was on good terms: Rabe's son, the Dominican friar Matteo, was a
close follower of Catherine and accompanied her on the trip into the *contado*, and two of her daughters were Dominican *mantellate*. Rabe's eldest
son, Giacomo di Francesco Tolomei, according to Raymond of Capua,
had been converted by Catherine. Rabe had apparently written to Catherine or to one of the Dominican friars in her entourage requesting
urgently that Matteo return to Siena on account of the illness of one of
his sisters. Catherine responded by inquiring about the health of Rabe's
daughter, but followed with warnings about the dangers of self-love that
suggest that Catherine thought the illness a ruse to entice Matteo away
from Catherine.[105] In August, Giacomo di Francesco Tolomei had written
to the Sienese magistrates from the Dominican friary of Santa Caterina in
Pisa, denying a report that he had been in the lands of the Salimbeni.[106]
Rabe's attempt to remove Matteo from Catherine's company at the Rocca
d'Orcia was probably a response to Sienese suspicions of her sons as conspirators with the Salimbeni.[107]

During her stay with the Salimbeni, Catherine did not lose touch with
the main theater of the ongoing conflict between Florence and the
papacy. While Florentine sentiment was divided in the later part of 1377
between supporters of continued war and proponents of peace with the
papacy, the pope still insisted on an exorbitant indemnity—1 million
gold florins—as a condition of peace, which gave the upper hand to the
Eight and their supporters. In reaction, the Florentines on 2 October
announced a new forced loan on the clergy in the same amount
demanded by the pope. And on 6 October, amid renewed calls for war,
the Signoria called for the violating of the interdict. Mass was celebrated
by order of the Signoria on the morning of 8 October. While some
clergy refused to cooperate and were forced to flee the city, many friars

[105] Letter 120. Rabe's motivation has been thus interpreted by most of the students of
Catherine's letters.
[106] ASS, *Concistoro* 1791, 65 (4 August 1377).
[107] There were clearly divisions within these large family groups. Neri di Donato gives
several examples of Tolomei and Salimbeni fighting together, just as members of one clan
occasionally fought against each other (as with the dispute between Agnolino di Giovanni
and Cione di Sandro that Catherine reportedly settled). Rabe might have been concerned
about retaliation from the regime, but also perhaps from the more powerful branches of
the Tolomei, especially that headed by Pietro di Giacomo.

in particular supported the governmental action, and exhorted the people to attend mass.[108]

Catherine's ardent supporter, the Vallombrosian abbot Giovanni dalle Celle, was one of the religious who was outspoken in his defense of the Florentine violation of the interdict. Catherine criticized Giovanni dalle Celle's position in harsh terms in a letter written in October 1377, a letter which culminates in a dire pronouncement on the indifference of the hierarchy and Curia to the state of the church: "I see the Christian Religion lying dead, and I neither lament nor weep over him."[109] From Catherine's perspective, Giovanni and other Florentine clerics who supported their regime's defiance of the interdict were guilty of violating the blood of Christ. Giovanni should have urged pious officials (perhaps a reference to the Guelf elites) to surrender their positions and, if necessary, their lives, rather than cooperate in the sinful policy of the government:

> For you know that in no manner, not for fear of punishment or of death . . . is it licit for us to commit a small sin. . . . I tell you that, if we and the other servants of God, if we do not argue with many prayers, in order to correct such an evil in the others, the divine judgment will come, and Divine Justice will bear abroad her rod.[110]

If only one person was willing to sacrifice his life, Catherine urged, it would be enough to avert a deserved divine punishment for the city's sin and enough to convert the secular authorities—to "break the heart of Pharaoh." Despite a use of the first person plural that suggests identification with Giovanni's situation, Catherine in this letter unambiguously distinguished her position from his: Catherine, unlike Giovanni, was boldly opposing the sinful actions of the church's opponents and was willing to offer her life to bring an end to the conflict. Given Catherine's strong criticism, it is not perhaps surprising that when Giovanni dalle Celle sent some young men under his tutelage to visit Catherine during her stay in the Rocca d'Orcia, some members of Catherine's circle refused to associate with them.[111]

---

[108] Brucker, *Florentine Politics and Society*, 329–32; Trexler, *Spiritual Power*, 146–52.

[109] Letter 296: "Oimè, oimè, oimè, disaventurata l'anima mia! Veggo giacere il morto della religione cristiana, e non mi doglio né piango sopra di lui."

[110] Ibid. "però che voi sapete che in neuno modo, non di pena o di morte, ma per adoperare una grande virtù, non c'è licito di commettere una picciola colpa. . . . Dicovi che, se noi e gli altri servi di Dio non ci argomentiamo con molte orazioni, e gli altri con correggiarsi di tanti mali, el divino giudicio verrà, e la divina giustizia trarrà fuore la verga sua."

[111] Giovanni dalle Celle, Luigi Marsili, *Lettere* 2: 372. Giovanni dalle Celle complained in particular that "Maestro Giovanni," presumably the abbot of Sant'Antimo, Giovanni di Gano da Orvieto, had refused to speak to them, but noted that Catherine had received them warmly.

Catherine did not restrict her harsh words to the Florentines. In October or November, Catherine wrote to Pietro cardinal of Ostia and Nicolà da Osimo in apparent criticism of the pope's intransigency. She instructed these prelates to urge the pope to worry less about the cities lost in the conflict and more about the lost souls; God would hold him accountable for souls lost during his pontificate.[112] She also wrote a very similar letter around this time to the bishop of Florence, Angelo da Ricasoli, who had fled his city to a monastery near Siena to avoid being compelled to violate the interdict.[113] A very powerful letter Catherine sent to Raymond of Capua in Rome around this time shows that she had incurred the displeasure of the pope. Gregory had perhaps heard some of Catherine's criticism. In addition, while Catherine had assured the pope that his return to Rome was God's will and would lead to peace, his trip had been full of hardships and danger, and he still faced opposition throughout the Papal States and Tuscany. It is likely that Gregory blamed her now for his decision to leave Avignon, just as previously he had sought her support for this plan. If Catherine was wrong, then she was a false prophet—and if this was the pope's complaint against her, then Catherine and her supporters could have been in very serious trouble indeed.[114] In any case, it is clear enough from Catherine's response that she felt her authority was at stake, and she responded to the pope through Raymond.

She wrote that the pope was responsible for the "disaster and loss and irreverence toward Holy Church and her ministers," because he did not act on Catherine's urgent advice to return to Rome, reform the clergy, make peace with the rebellious cities, and launch the Crusade. Indeed, if he would only follow Catherine's advice, he would "reacquire both temporal and spiritual things." At the same time, as if to outdo her critics, Catherine offered an extravagant self-accusation: "I, wretched, am the cause of all these evils and your pains because of the smallness of my virtue, and especially because of my disobedience."[115] Catherine's

---

[112] Letter 11, to Pietro, cardinal of Ostia, and letter 282, to Nicolà da Osimo, both from late autumn or early winter.

[113] Letter 242.

[114] Raymond of Capua in the *Legenda maior* shows great sensitivity to the issue of Catherine's reputation as a false prophet by asserting that, contrary to her reputation, she never predicted the launching of a Crusade (which never happened). It is worth noting as well that Catherine's reputation as the saint who brought the papacy back to Rome was in the decades following her death a source of great embarrassment for her followers, since the return of Gregory XI precipitated the schism, a much worse catastrophe than the Avignon papacy. Jean Gerson accordingly used Catherine and Birgitta as examples of the danger of prophetesses; see Dyan Elliot, "Dominae or Dominatae?"

[115] Letter 267: "Di tutti questi mali e pene vostre io miserabile ne so' cagione per la poca mia virtù, e per molta mia disobedienzia."

emphasis on her own responsibility was more than a little ironic, in light of the fact that the pope was blaming her for his mistakes (made against her advice), and also served to emphasize the contrast between her efforts and the pope's lack of commitment. Catherine's self-accusation was thus a radical appraisal of her own role in worldly affairs: if her inadequacies were the cause of the crises, it would be her intercession that would preserve the church. But in fact Catherine was not the cause of the crises, and she continued with a bold defense of her actions and a defiant statement of her authority:

> And to whom will I go, if you abandon me? Who will protect me? To whom will I flee, if you hunt me down, and the persecutors are persecuting me, and I seek refuge from you and from the other servants of God? And if you abandon me, taking out your displeasure and indignation on me, I will hide in the wounds of Christ crucified, of whom you are the vicar. And I know that He will receive me, because He does not desire the death of the sinner. And having been received by him, you will not be able to hunt me. Moreover, we will stand in your place and fight manfully with the arms of virtue for the sweet spouse of Christ. In Him I wish to end my life, with tears, with sweat, and with sighs, and to offer blood and the marrow of my bones. And if all the world hunts me down, I will pay this no mind, resting myself in the breast of the sweet spouse. Pardon me, most holy Father, all my ignorance and the offence I have given to God and to your Sanctity. The truth is what will excuse me and set me free—truth eternal.[116]

Once again, Catherine marshaled the image of the wounds as a site of her own intimacy with Christ. Indeed, the realm within which she was fighting was beyond papal jurisdiction, and her authority, which depended on intimacy with Christ, was far beyond that of the pope, who was merely Christ's vicar. Given the nature of this message, it is no wonder that Catherine closed the letter with encouragement for Raymond to approach the pope "with a manly heart, and without any discomfort or servile fear."[117]

[116] Ibid.: "E a cui ricorro, se voi m'abbandonaste? chi mi soverrebbe? a cui rifuggo, se voi mi cacciaste? E' persecutori mi perseguitano, e io refuggo a voi e agli altri figliuoli e servi di Dio. E se voi m'abbandonaste pigliando dispiacere e indignazione, e io mi nasconderò nelle piaghe di Cristo crucifisso, di cui voi sete vicario: so che mi riceverà, perché non vuole la morte del peccatore. Essendo ricevuta da lui, voi non mi cacciarete; anco staremo nel luogo vostro a combattere virilmente con l'arme de la virtù per la dolce Sposa di Cristo. In lui voglio terminare la vita mia, con lagrime, con sudori, e con sospiri, e dare el sangue e le mirolla dell'ossa. E se tutto el mondo mi cacciasse, io non me ne curarò, riposandomi, con pianto e con molto sostenere, al petto de la dolce sposa. Perdonatemi, santissimo padre, ogni mia ignoranzia e offesa che io ò fatta a Dio e a la vostra Santità. La verità sia quella che mi scusi, e me deliberi: Verità etterna."

[117] Ibid: "A voi dico, padre carissimo, che, quanto è possibile a voi, siate dinanzi alla Santità sua con virile cuore, e senza alcuna pena o timore servile."

## Catherine's Revelation and Writing Miracle

In this climate of tension during her stay with the Salimbeni, during which Catherine and her supporters were being attacked from both sides in the dispute between the pope and the Italian cities, she wrote to Raymond of Capua (now engaged in some ecclesiastical diplomacy in Pisa) one of her most extraordinary and important letters. Catherine first encouraged Raymond to endure the bitterness of persecution: "One should not turn back because of the thorns of many persecutions, for he is very foolish who passes up a rose out of fear of the thorns."[118] She then described her own response to the situation, shifting to the third person (referring to herself as a "servant of God") to tell Raymond about a remarkable experience of dialogue with God:

> Whence, having read the letters and understanding everything, I implored a servant of God to offer tears and sweat before God for the Bride and for the infirmity of Babbo. Whence suddenly through divine grace there swelled a desire and a happiness beyond all measure. And waiting for morning to come in order to have Mass, which was on Mary's day; and the hour of Mass having arrived, she took her place with true knowledge of self, ashamed before God on account of her imperfections. And raising herself above herself with restless desire, and peering with the eye of her intellect into eternal Truth, she asked of him four petitions, holding herself and her father [i.e., Raymond] in the presence of the Bride of Truth.[119]

The four petitions, which with God's responses provide the structure for the body of the letter, were for reform of the church; for the whole world; for Raymond's salvation; and for someone "I cannot name in writing." Anyone who is familiar with Catherine's writings will recognize these petitions as the framework for her book, the *Libro di divina dottrina* or *Dialogo*, which she evidently began to compose at this time.[120] God's responses to the petitions lay out the perspective of divine providence on the trials and

[118] Letter 272: "E non si debbe lassare né vollere el capo indietro per le spine de le molte persecuzioni, perocché troppo sarebbe matto colui che lassasse la rosa per timore de la spina."

[119] Ibid.: " . . . unde, lette le lettare e inteso tutto, pregai una serva di Dio, che offerisse lagrime e sudori dinanzi da Dio per la sposa e per la infermità del babbo. Unde subbito per divina grazia le crebbe uno desiderio e una allegrezza sopra a ogni modo. E aspettando che venisse la mattina per avere la Messa—che era il dì di Maria—e venuta l'ora della messa, si pose nel luogo suo con vero cognoscimento di sé, vergognandosi dinanzi da Dio de la sua imperfezione. E levando sé sopra di sé con ansietato desiderio, e speculando con l'occhio dell'intelletto nella verità eterna, dimandava ine quattro petizioni, tenendo sé e 'l padre suo dinanzi a la sposa de la verità."

[120] On the production and textual history of the *Dialogo*, see Cavallini's introduction to S. Caterina da Siena, *Il Dialogo della divina provvidenza ovvero Libro della divina dottrina*, ed. Giuliana Cavallini (1968).

corruption of the church, including the scandal of unfit pastors. On this issue, Catherine once again turned from her ostensible correspondent Raymond to address the pope. At this point in the letter, it begins to become difficult to differentiate God's voice from Catherine's:

> And thus it pleased the kindness and mercy of God to reveal to me his secrets, confronted with which, most sweet Father, the tongue fails us, and the intellect seems to be darkened, so much is it narrowed in its vision. Desire persists restlessly, so much so that all the powers of the soul shout out as one their will to leave the earth, since it is full of such imperfection, to rise up and obtain their goal, and enjoy with the true citizens the supreme eternal Trinity, where one see them giving glory and praise to God, and where shine the virtues, the fame, and the desire of the true ministers of God and the perfect religious, which shine in this life like a burning lamp placed in the candelabra of the Holy Church, and give light to the whole world. Ah me, Babbo, what a difference there was between them and these of today! About these he lamented with the fervor of a great justice, saying: "Those have taken the form of the fly, which is such an ugly animal, that it lands on something sweet and fragrant, and does not mind, after it has departed, to then land on disgusting and filthy things. In the same way these wicked people are in position to taste the sweetness of my blood, and they do not care, so that they rise from the table of the altar—from guarding and ministering my body and the other sacraments of the Holy Church (which are fragrant and full of sweetness and softness, so much so that they give life to the soul that tastes them in truth, and without this the soul cannot love). These, I say, do not think of then landing themselves in as much filth as their minds and bodies can wallow in, so that not only does such iniquity stink to me, but even the demons are disgusted by such miserable sin."[121]

---

[121] Ibid.: "E poi che a la benignità e pietà di Dio piacque di manifestare sé medesimo e le cose segrete sue—a le quali cose, padre dolcissimo, la lingua ci viene meno, e l'intelletto pare che ci s'offuschi, tanto è assottigliato el suo vedere—el desiderio vive spasimato, in tanto che tutte le potenzie dell'anima gridano a una di volere lassare la terra, poiché c'è tanta imperfezione, e dirizzarsi e giognere al fine suo a gustare co' veri cittadini la somma eterna Trinità, ove si vede rendere gloria e loda a Dio; ove rilucono le virtù, la fame e 'l desiderio de' veri ministri e perfetti religiosi, e' quali stettero in questa vita come lucerna ardente posta in sul candelabro de la santa Chiesa, a rendere lume a tutto quanto il mondo.Oimè, babbo, quanta differenzia era da loro a quelli che sono al dì d'oggi, de' quali si lamentava con zelo di grande giustizia, dicendo: 'Costoro ànno preso la condizione della mosca, che è tanto brutto animale, la quale, ponendosi in su la cosa dolce e odorifera, non si cura, poiché ella è partita, di ponersi in su le cose fastidiose e immonde. Così questi iniqui sono posti a gustare la dolcezza del sangue mio; e non si curano, poi che sono levati dalla mensa dell'altare, da consecrare e ministrare el corpo e 'l sangue mio e gli altri sacramenti de la santa Chiesa (e' quali sono odoriferi pieni di dolcezza e di grande soavità, in tanto che dà vita all'anima, che el gusta in verità, e senza esso non può vivere), essi non si curano di ponersi in tanta immondizia, quanto e' pongono la mente e 'l corpo loro: che, non tanto che ella puta a me tanta iniquità, ma le dìmonia ànno a schifo questo peccato tanto miserabile.'"

Having described for Catherine the condition of sinners in various degrees of self-love, God distinguished between false devotion and the devotion of the true "servants of God," who approach God through an interior affection and not only through their words. The terms of this discussion slide easily between the subject of God's forbearance and Catherine's own need to endure the offenses of sinners, in imitation of the mercy God holds out continuously to sinners. Catherine's voice becomes one with God's as the theme of sinners rejecting God's mercy evokes Catherine's experience as a servant of God unjustly attacked by sinners scandalized by her intercessions on their behalf:

> And so opening the eye of the intellect in obedience to his command, in the depths of his charity, she saw for herself how he was the supreme eternal goodness, and how for love alone he had created and redeemed with the blood of his son all creatures who possess reason, and with this same love had given what he had given. Tribulation and consolation, everything given for love and to provide for the salvation of man, and not for any other end. And he said, "The blood spilled for you demonstrates to you that this is the truth. But these ones, blinded by the self love which they possess for themselves, are scandalized with much intolerance, judging as evil and to their damage and ruin and hateful that which I do for love and for their good, to spare them from eternal punishments, and to gain for them eternal life. Why then do they complain about me, and hate what they ought to hold in reverence? And why do they judge my hidden judgments, which are all just?"[122]

God then revealed to Catherine the secret of his mercy toward the subject of her fourth petition, a man who had been condemned to death (perhaps a reference to Niccolò di Toldo). God explained that what the world might view as cruelty had been allowed in order to obtain this man's salvation, on account of his love for the Virgin Mary, "so that with his blood in my blood he might have life." God's final words exhorted Catherine to continue "to ask me for mercy for these and for the entire world. Conceive, my children, and give birth to this child, the human

[122] Ibid.: "Unde aprendo l'occhio dell'intelletto, per obedire al comandamento suo, nell'abisso dalla sua carità, allora si vedeva come elli era somma ed eterna bontà, e come per solo amore elli aveva creati e ricomprati del sangue del Figliuolo suo tutte le creature che ànno in sé ragione; e con questo amore medesimo dava ciò che elli dava: tribolazione e consolazione, ogni cosa era dato per amore e per provedere alla salute dell'uomo, e non per alcuno altro fine. E diceva: 'El sangue sparto per voi vi manifesta che questo è la verità. Ma essi, come acecati per lo proprio amore che ànno di loro, si scandalizzano con molta impazienzia, giudicando in male, e in loro danno e ruina e in odio, quello che io fo per amore e per loro bene, per privarli de le pene eternali, e per guadagno dar lo' vita eterna. Perché dunque si lagnano di me, e odiano quello che debbono avere in reverenzia, e vogliono giudicare gli occulti miei giudicii, e' quali sono tutti dritti?'"

race, with hatred and sorrow for sin and with blazing and yearning love."[123]

The body of the letter concludes with Catherine in the afterglow of ecstasy, full of the pain and longing of returning to herself from the heights of divine union, from which she said she was able to unburden herself through the consolation of writing. She then returned to her initial theme, for which the long dialogue with God had been an illustration, closing the body of the letter by exhorting Raymond, "That is why I said I long to see you a follower and lover of truth." Remarkable as the letter is up to this point, it contains an even more stunning postscript. At the end of the letter, Catherine (with syntax that is even more than usually scattered) announced to Raymond that in her visionary experience she had learned to write:

> This letter, and another that I have sent you, I wrote with my own hand in the Isola della Rocca, with many sighs and an abundance of tears, so much so that the eye, seeing, did not see. But I was full of wonder at myself and at the goodness of God, considering his mercy toward creatures who have reason in them, and [considering] his Providence, of which he has been so generous toward me, that, deprived of this consolation [comfort, relief], which through my ignorance I never knew, he has provided by giving me the ability to write, so that when descending from the heights I might have a little something with which to vent my heart, so that it not burst. Not wishing me to be taken yet from this shadowy life, in a marvelous way he fixed this in my mind, just as a master does to a pupil to whom he gives an exemplar. Whence, as soon as he had departed from me with the glorious evangelist and Thomas Aquinas, thus sleeping I began to learn. Pardon me for writing too much, for the hands and the tongue are in accordance with the heart.[124]

[123] Ibid.: "E mirando con ansieto desiderio, dimostrava la danazione di colui per cui era adivenuto el caso e di cui era pregato, dicendo: 'Io voglio che tu sappi che per camparlo dall'eterna dannazione, ne la quale tu vedi ch'egli era, io gli permissi questo caso, a ciò col sangue suo nel sangue mio avesse vita; perché non avevo dimenticato la reverenzia e amore che aveva alla mia dolcissima madre Maria, si che per misericordia l'ò fatto quello che gl'ignoranti tengono in crudeltà. . . . io t'invito a chiedere misericordia a me per loro e per tutto quanto il mondo. Concepete, figliuoli, e partorite el figliuolo dell'umana generazione, con odio e dispiacimento del peccato, e con affocato e spasimato amore.'"

[124] Ibid.: "Questa lettera, e un'altra ch'io vi mandai, ò scritte di mia mano in su l'Isola della Rocca, con molti sospiri e abondanzia di lagrime, in tanto che l'occhio, vedendo, non vedeva; ma piena d'amirazione ero di me medesima, e dela bontà di Dio—considerando la sua misericordia verso le sue creature che ànno in loro ragione—, e de la sua providenzia, la quale abondava verso di me, che per refrigerio, essendo privata de la consolazione—la quale per mia ignoranzia io non cognobbi—m'aveva dato e proveduto col darmi l'attitudine dello scrivere, a ciò che, discendendo de l'altezza, avessi un poco con chi sfogare el cuore, perché non scoppiasse. Non volendomi trare ancora di questa tenebrosa vita, per amirabile modo me la formò nella mente mia, sì come fa el maestro al fanciullo, che gli dà l'essemplo. Unde, subito che fuste partito da me, col glorioso evangelista e Tommaso d'Aquino così dormendo cominciai ad imparare. Perdonatemi del troppo scrivere, però che le mani e la lingua s'accordano col cuore."

What is one to make of such an amazing letter, full of startling announcements and so audaciously self-authorizing? It seems clear that Raymond of Capua, the letter's putative addressee, did not know what to make of it: as with Catherine's description of the death of Niccolò di Toldo, Raymond neither cited this letter nor mentioned the writing miracle in the *Legenda maior*. (The miracle was included in later hagiographical works, most notably the *Legenda minor* of Tommaso Caffarini.) Twentieth-century Catherinian scholars, too, have not known what to do with it. Fawtier initially took Raymond's silence as sufficient cause to dismiss the letter as a fraud perpetrated by Caffarini. But this position eventually became obviously untenable, for among other reasons that the letter exists in several early manuscripts connected to Catherine's close followers; any fraud would have had to involve her entire *famiglia*.[125] Other than Raymond's silence, the only reason to doubt this letter is discomfort with its contents, particularly the writing miracle. And indeed Catherinian scholars like Fawtier, Hurtaud, and Grion eventually equivocated on the matter of the letter's authenticity, but held categorically that, whatever else was true, Catherine had never learned to write.[126] It is worth noting that Volpato and Noffke do not question the letter's authenticity in their work on the edition and translation of Catherine's letters. And readers from outside the narrow world of Catherinian studies have had no problem with the letter; for example, Marina Zancan, Claudia Papka, and Jane Tylus have all centered interpretations of Catherine's letters on this text. Indeed, Zancan has cut through the "problem" of the miracle neatly (though in a way that creates interesting other problems for Catherine's readers) by rejecting out of hand the possibility that Catherine did not know how to write, even before the events she describes in this letter.[127] But evidence that the letter continues to cause problems for students of Catherine can be found in Karen Scott's failure to acknowledge the existence of this letter, let alone discuss its significance, in an essay addressed specifically to the subject of Catherine as a writer of letters.[128]

Discomfort with this letter, on the part of Raymond and later scholars, can be traced to the ways in which it complicates Catherine's reputation as a mystic saint and spiritual author. To begin with the dramatic postscript,

[125] Most significantly, letter 272 is included in Vienna, Österreichische Nationalbibliotek, Palatino 3514, written in the hand of Catherine's close follower Neri di Landoccio Pagliaresi.

[126] Robert Fawtier, *Sainte Catherine de Sienne* II: 198; Alvaro Grion, *Santa Caterina da Siena*, 165f. On the other hand, Dupré Theseider argued for the authenticity of the letter: "Sono autentiche le lettere di S. Caterina?" *Vita cristiana* 12 (1940): 244. In his final statement on this question, Dupré Theseider allowed for the possibility that Catherine had indeed learned to write: "Caterina da Siena," in *Dizionario biografico degli Italiani*, vol. 22, 361–79.

[127] Zancan, "Lettere di Caterina da Siena," 594.

[128] Karen Scott, "*Io Caterina*," 87–121.

Catherine's account of her own movement from inspiration to writing in the postscript to this letter invokes an important trope in late-medieval spirituality when she excuses her prolixity by writing to Raymond that "my hands and tongue are in accordance with my heart." In other words, her external words reflect internal experience of divine love; indeed, the authority of her words is guaranteed by the spiritual experience she has just described in the body of the letter. But Catherine is doing more here than appealing to a general principle of late-medieval spiritual culture; she is quoting a well-known *dictum* on this theme, one that appears prominently in a letter from around the same time written by her supporter Giovanni dalle Celle. In this letter, the Vallombrosian abbot responded to an Augustinian friar who had read one of Giovanni's letters in praise of Catherine and had in response written to Giovanni charging Catherine with novelty in her teaching and cautioning Giovanni against placing excessive trust in her. Giovanni responded to this criticism by arguing that authentic teaching derives from interior experience of divine love, and so Catherine's intimacy with God conferred authority and confirmed that her teaching was true: "what further convinces me that her teaching is true and venerable, is that the brush of her tongue paints with the blood of her heart, and that which the tongue speaks makes manifest the conscience within."[129] Although not noted by the editor, this line is in fact a slightly adapted quotation from the *Letter to Severinus on Charity* by "Frater Ivo," a twelfth-century monk apparently in the orbit of Bernard of Clairvaux.[130] Catherine's "my hands and tongue are in accordance with my heart" echoes the argument of the *Letter to Severinus* about the connection between interior love and external teaching, and indeed reads as a vernacular paraphrase of the line quoted by Giovanni dalle Celle.

It is impossible to know for certain whether Catherine had received a copy of the letter of Giovanni dalle Celle—she could have known the *Letter to Severinus* from some other source, or easily have absorbed the substance of its argument from her followers and from other texts—but it is in fact very likely she did receive it. Giovanni dalle Celle, William Flete, and others seem to have forwarded to each other copies of whatever they

[129] *Lettere di Giovanni dalle Celle*, 370–71: "Et quod plus me movet, sua vera et veneranda doctrina est, quia calamum lingue tingit in sanguine cordis et quod lingua loquitur, conscientia manifestat."

[130] Gervais Dumeige, ed., *Épître à Séverin sur la charité* (1955): "Illum, inquam, audire vellem, *qui calumum lingue tingeret in sanguine cordis, quia tunc vera et veneranda doctrina est, cum quod lingua loquitur conscientia dictat*, caritas suggerit et spiritus ingerit." This influential treatise, circulating sometimes under the authority of St. Bernard's name and sometimes attributed to Richard of St. Victor, provided an extended argument for the model of experiential and affective authority so influential in the fourteenth century and was so well-known (at least among religious of a spiritual bent) that Giovanni could be certain that he was appealing to an authority familiar to his correspondent.

had written concerning Catherine, so it is very unlikely that Catherine's immediate circle—and Catherine herself—did not at some point obtain Giovanni's letter quoting the *Letter to Severinus*. Indeed, as has already been mentioned, a group of Giovanni dalle Celle's followers visited Catherine at the Rocca d'Orcia in 1377, during the period in which she experienced her revelation and wrote Letter 272, and it is likely that the Vallombrosian's letter came into Catherine's circle at that time. The relationship—whether direct or indirect—between the postscript to Letter 272, the letter of Giovanni dalle Celle, and Frate Ivo's *Letter to Severinus on Charity* suggests strongly that Catherine learned about herself, and developed the language she used to explain herself, in the context of a regular exchange among her supporters of texts and letters. Contrary to any hagiographical emphasis on the exclusively divine nature of Catherine's inspiration, Catherine's authority and even her self-understanding depended on the ways in which her clerical and other associates glossed her experience and explained her identity. In other words, Catherine's sanctity itself was a product of an epistolary conversation.

In addition, while the letter does in some ways fit Catherine's reputation as a mystic author, it also dramatically breaches the bounds of that saintly identity. On the plus side, in addition to the fact that the letter describes Catherine receiving a series of divine revelations, her ability to write emerged from the experience of ecstatic union with God. The writing miracle emphasizes the supernatural source of her new ability and her own passivity as a vessel of divine wisdom, fixed in her mind by well-placed masters, "the glorious evangelist"—probably John the Evangelist—and Thomas Aquinas, while she slept.[131] But however much Catherine here appealed to aspects of the received image of her authority, she also claimed it for herself in a way that put this letter radically at odds with accepted norms of female sanctity, and especially with Raymond's portrait of her. Catherine in this letter gestured dramatically to the pen in her hand in such a way as to violate the conventional image of a female mystic, and indeed the very terms by which her public was prepared to read her.[132] And while the body of the letter communicated

---

[131] "The glorious evangelist" is almost certainly John. Not only does Catherine elsewhere show particular regard for John the Evangelist (see, for instance, note 49 above), but he was a model in the Middle Ages for prophetic insight—a particularly apt master for Catherine in this instance. Early readers connected to Catherine's circle made this assumption. In the manuscript Antonio Volpato uses for his edition of this letter (Vienna, Österreichische Nationalbibliotek, Palatino 3514), while the original scribe, Neri di Landoccio Pagliaresi, has written only "glorioso evangelista," a second contemporary hand has added "Iohanne" above the line. Earlier editions, including that of Dupré Theseider (*Epistolario di Santa Caterina*), included "Iohanne" as part of the text of the letter.

[132] The humility and lack of self-promotion expected of female mystics in the later Middle Ages typically demanded that they commit their revelations to writing only with exaggerated

divine revelations and a significant visionary experience, the obvious relationship between this letter and her *Libro* points to the process of Catherine's composition of the book, emphasizing her active role in the generation of her own texts in such a way as to unsettle expectations attached to "mystic" or "prophetic" literature. Catherine here was simultaneously the source of divine revelation and an author engaged in the very mundane process of literary experimentation, expansion, and revision that leads to a book.

Moreover, in this revelation Catherine the woman never receded from the stage in favor of the divine voice; rather, it is all too obvious that God was speaking Catherine's language, and that Catherine was putting words in God's mouth. Less obvious, but maybe even more important, is the fact that the letter (as a letter and unlike the book) links Catherine's visionary experience and her writing miracle to the historical moment, the particular tensions and challenges in the church and the world that prompted her exchange with God as well as her communication of this exchange to Raymond. The divine dialogue was a radical and bold assertion of her authority as a true servant of God, speaking with God's voice and called to endure with patience those who unjustly attacked her out of the ignorance of their sinful self-love.

This is an effect lost when the revelation described in this letter is read only in Catherine's book, and when Catherine is read exclusively as a spiritual author. What appears in her *Libro* as spiritual teaching with eternal application, transcending any particulars of Catherine's experience in the world, in letter form was bound up much more obviously in the historical moment. This letter disrupted, and continues to disrupt, the image of Catherine as a "spiritual" author by connecting Catherine's most important and transcendent revelation to the exigencies of the War of Eight Saints, a public and political significance in her prophetic intervention that is intelligible as soon as the revelation is read in context, as a letter addressed to a particular correspondent at a particular moment in history. That the potential of this letter for complicating the reception of Catherine's "revelations" was appreciated by Raymond is suggested by an interesting chronological "mistake" he made concerning the dating of Catherine's dictation of her *Libro*. While he acknowledged that Catherine had begun dictating her book earlier, Raymond located the major part of her dictation in a short period of time following the election of Pope Urban VI and peace settlement between the new pope and Florence, which was announced in August 1378—thus almost a full year

---

reluctance, often having been compelled to do so by their confessors or other male superiors. On the mystical aversion to the pen, see Elliot, "*Dominae* or *Dominatae?*"

from the date of the letter in which Catherine announced to Raymond her revelation and miracle.[133] Raymond thus further distanced Catherine's *Libro* from Catherine's letter and abstracted Catherine's revelation from its historical circumstances.

## 1378: Florence and the Ciompi Revolt

It is perhaps unlikely that Raymond delivered to the pope Catherine's messages from this period, at least verbatim, because by early 1378 Catherine was sufficiently returned to Gregory XI's good graces that he decided to send her on another mission to Florence. Behind this trip lay the designs of Catherine's friends among the Parte Guelfa, who sought to use her visit as part of their campaign to move public sentiment toward peace with the papacy, and against the Eight.[134] Public opinion within Florence had been divided over the war ever since the string of military victories for the league ended in early 1377, and the regime had heightened public anxieties by defying the interdict, thereby forcing the general populace either to violate the papal edict or oppose the governing regime. The Parte, at this point in the hands of its extremist wing, saw this climate of hesitation as an opportunity to regain political ascendancy. Thus starting in winter 1377–78 members of the Parte aggressively reintroduced the controversial practice of *ammonizione*, by which individuals were denounced and thereby disqualified from holding public office, a mechanism the Parte had frequently used in the past to eliminate opponents of Guelf hegemony.[135]

Catherine arrived in Florence with some of her followers in March, residing initially in the house of Niccolò Soderini, and later with Piero Canigiani, who built a house for her. Catherine's presence in Florence was immediately noted by Florentine citizens sensitive to connections to prominent Guelfs, as was indicated by a Florentine chronicler:

> In that year there arrived in Florence a woman by the name of Caterina . . . and being reputed very holy, and unsullied and of good life and honest, she began to censure the camp opposed to the Church. These who adhered to the Parte went to see her enthusiastically, and among others these were the

---

[133] LM, chap. 332.

[134] According to Raymond of Capua, the pope had been advised that "si Catherina de Senis ibit Florentiam, ego habebam pacem" (LM, par. 423, 965). Raymond records this immediately after recounting (in par. 422) a conversation with Piero Soderini concerning the potential for gaining peace by putting the Florentine government in the hands of the Guelfs, and notes that he informed the pope of this conversation.

[135] Brucker (*Florentine Politics and Society,* 336–51) describes at length the atmosphere of political "terror" created by the Guelf attacks.

masters Niccolò Soderini . . . and another was Stoldo di Bindo Altoviti and another Piero Canigiani, and these were the ones who praised her most greatly.[136]

On the other hand, some Florentines perceived her visit as part of a Guelf plot, a not unreasonable assumption considering her connections to powerful Guelfs:

> She was led, either by her own will, or by the malicious influence of those who were great supporters of the Parte, to say that the *ammonizione* were good, in order that the Parte might be able to end the war. For this she was esteemed like a prophet by those of the Parte, but by the others held to be a hypocrite and wicked woman.[137]

That Catherine might very well have approved of the *ammonizione* as a means to ending the war is confirmed by a conversation Raymond of Capua recalled having had in Siena with Niccolò Soderini, in which Soderini suggested that it would be necessary to proscribe merely a few key supporters of the war in order to allow leaders of the Parte Guelfa to arrange peace with the pope. Raymond's account of Soderini's comment gives a clear sense of the Guelf perspective on the connection between Florentine relations with the papacy and internal political struggles: "You may be certain that the Florentine people as a whole, particularly every sound man of that city, desire peace; but a certain few malicious men, who for our sins today govern our city, are the ones who are impeding the peace."[138] Raymond noted as well that, after becoming prior of Santa Maria sopra Minerva in Rome, he mentioned this conversation to the

---

[136] Marchionne di Coppo Stefani, *Cronaca fiorentina di Marchionne di Coppo Stefani*, Niccolò Rodolico, ed., *Rerum Italicarum Scriptores*, vol. 30 (1903), 306: "Nel detto anno addivenne che in Firenze avea una femmina, la quale avea nome Caterina. . . . [*lacuna*], ed essendo stata tenuta di santissima, netta e buona vita ed onesta, cominciò a biasimare la brigata contro alla Chiesa. Questi, che mestavano alla Parte, molto la vedeano volentieri, ed infra gli altri erano li maestri uno Niccolò de' Soderini, lo quale gli avea fatto a casa sua una camera, e in questa alcuna volta era stata; l'altro era Stoldo di messer Bindo Altoviti e l'altro Piero Canigiani; questi erano quelli che sommamente la lodavano. Ed è vero ch'ella sapea sì con buono naturale e sì con molto accidentale le cose ecclesiastiche, e sì dettava, e scrivea molto bene. E Piero Canigiani lassò a piè di S. Giorgio perava pietre e legni, e conducea lassù; tale che quando fu poi arsa la casa sua, egli non ebbe rispetto a beata Caterina, ma per sè adoprò lo predetto lavorio."

[137] Ibid: "Fu costui condotta, o per sua voglia, o con malizia introdotta per stimolo di costoro molte volte all Parte a dire ch'era buono l'ammonire, acciochè all Parte si provedesse di levare la guerra; di che era costei quasi una profetessa tenua da quelli della Parte e dagli altri ipocrita e mala femmina."

[138] *LM*, par. 421, 965: "'Habeatis pro certo, quod populus Florentinus universaliter et omnes probi viri civitatis ejusdem vellent pacem: sed quidam maligni et pauci, qui peccatis nostris exigentibus hodie civitatem nostram gubernant, sunt qui pacem impediunt.'"

pope. This suggests that Raymond, at least, was well informed of the political strategies of the Parte leaders and was cooperating with them. Catherine's unpopularity among opponents of the Guelfs and others in Florence might also have been fostered by her outspoken opposition to the violation of the interdict, as in the letter to Giovanni dalle Celle mentioned above. Catherine addressed this issue directly in a letter she wrote from Florence to Pietro Cardinale di Luna, in which she attacked the clergy—and particularly the mendicants—of Florence for supporting the defiance of the interdict.[139]

Catherine's appearance in Florence as a public ally of the Parte Guelfa placed her at risk when opposition to the Parte erupted in a series of uprisings known collectively as the Revolt of the Ciompi. While this civic unrest was fostered and to some extent directed, in its early stages, by elements of the Florentine middle classes who opposed the Parte Guelfa, the revolt was driven by the poor and unenfranchised workers of the wool industry against their masters of the wool guild and other *popolo grasso* elites.[140] As a class struggle, the Ciompi revolt can very usefully be compared to the earlier Sienese Bruco revolt, and just as Catherine's brothers were targeted in that unrest, Catherine as an ally of the Parte Guelfa was apparently attacked during the Ciompi revolt. On June 22, the Eight of War retaliated against the *ammonizione* by passing legislation disenfranchising leaders of the Parte while a crowd mostly consisting of wool workers attacked and burned the houses of prominent Guelfs. The houses of the Castiglionchio, Canigiani, Albizzi, Corsini, and Soderini—all allies of Catherine—were destroyed, and the crowd attacked the lodging that Piero Canigiani had built for Catherine near the church of San Giorgio.[141] Catherine described in a dramatic letter she sent to Raymond of Capua shortly after the uprising how she was sought out by the crowd, threatened, but not killed. For Catherine this was a lost opportunity for martyrdom, and to accomplish through her death, among other things, peace between the Florentines and the pope:

My desire to give my life for the Truth and the sweet Bride of Christ was not fulfilled. But the Eternal Bridegroom played a great joke on me, as Cristofano

---

[139] Letter 284.

[140] Stella, *La révolte des Ciompi*, interprets the revolt as reflecting in Florence sharp divisions of the population along class lines. On the Ciompi revolt and conditions of the wool industry in this period, see Franco Franceschi, *Oltre il "Tumulto." I lavoratori fiorentini dell'arte della lana fra Tre e Quattrocento* (1993). See also Brucker, *Florentine Politics and Society*, 363–73; Trexler, *The Spiritual Power*, 106–7; and essays by Victor Rutenburg, Charles de la Roncière, and John M. Najemy in *Il Tumulto dei Ciompi. Un momento di storia fiorentina ed europea, Convegno Internazionale di Studi, Firenze, 16–19 settembre 1979* (1981).

[141] Cardini, "Caterina da Siena, le repubbliche di Firenze," 324; Stefani (317–20) lists the individuals whose property was attacked, including most of Catherine's supporters in Florence.

[di Gano Guidini] will tell you fully by word of mouth. So I have reason to weep, because the multitude of my iniquities was so great that I did not deserve that my blood should give life, nor illumine darkened minds, nor bring the son to peace with the father, nor cement with my blood a stone in the mystical body of the holy Church. It seemed that the hands of the one who wanted to do this [i.e., kill her] were bound. And the words I said, "I am she. Take me, and let this family be," were a sword which passed straight to his heart.[142]

Raymond's more sensational version in the *Legenda maior* tells how the crowd were awed by her words and left her and her followers unharmed. Raymond included this episode in the final section of his work, devoted to Catherine's patience, in order to emphasize Catherine's imitation of Christ and willingness to be martyred—the traditional sine qua non of the confessor saint.[143] But here what is interesting in this story is the way in which Catherine was seen by Florentines as involved in the political disputes of the War of Eight Saints, and by implication, suspect in local politics because of the propapal views of the Parte Guelfa elite and Catherine's relationship with prominent Guelfs.

After the uprising, Catherine and her companions moved for a time outside the city walls, then returned to live in hiding within the city, where she presumably stayed when unrest built into full-scale revolution in July. The unrest in Florence had the indirect effect of speeding the settlement of ongoing negotiations with the pope. The peace treaty was finally arranged on 28 July, and proclaimed in Florence on 1 August, an event celebrated in several of Catherine's letters to her followers around this time.[144] Catherine and her companions probably departed the city shortly after the peace announcement. Her Florentine supporters in the Parte Guelfa had mostly flown from the city after the June uprisings, after which some of them were banished from the city and others were disqualified from political office by being declared *grandi*. These events prompted Catherine to write letters to Niccolò Soderini, Ristoro Canigiani, and Pietro Canigiani, encouraging them in their trials and urging them to take solace in being banished from the worldly cares of political offices.[145] A more radical revolt in August

[142] Letter 295: " . . . ma non fu adempito il desiderio mio di dare la vita per la verità e per la dolce Sposa di Cristo. Anco mi fece lo sposo eterno una grande beffa, sì come Cristofano a bocca pienamente vi dirà. Unde io ò da piagnere, però che tanta è stata la moltitudine delle mie iniquitadi che io non meritai che 'l sangue mio desse vita, né alluminasse le menti accecate, né pacificasse il figliuolo col padre, né murasse una pietra col sangue mio nel corpo mistico della santa Chiesa. Anco, parve che fussero legate le mani di colui che voleva fare; e dicendo io: 'Io sono essa. Tolle me e lassa stare questa famiglia,' erano coltella che drittamente gli passavano il cuore."
[143] *LM*, par. 427, 966.
[144] For example, letter 303, to Sano di Maco and other "figliuoli."
[145] Letter 297, to Niccolò Soderini; letters 299, 258, 266, and 279, to Ristoro Canigiani;

resulted in a regime more directly tied to the wool workers, and opposed by the middle classes who had originally made common cause with the wool workers in the regimes that resulted from the June and July revolts.

In August, shortly after her return to Siena, Catherine wrote to the new *signori* of Florence, congratulating them on their peace with the pope in a manner that suggests that she took some of the credit herself: "My intention had been to visit you, and to celebrate with you the holy peace, for which I have labored for so long, insofar as I have been able according to my abilities and my slight virtue; if I had had more virtue, I might have accomplished more of value [*più virtù avrei adoperato*]." She acknowledged her unpopularity with the ascendant parties in Florence, noting that she was forced to leave the city because "the devil has unjustly set people's hearts very much against me."[146] Catherine exhorted the leaders of the new government to accomplish unity in the city, and urged them to place the government of the city only "in the hands of virtuous, wise, and discrete men . . . older and experienced men, not children." She warned against the practice of banishing political opponents: "exiles never make a good city."[147] These commonplaces were in fact politically loaded, given Catherine's association with the Parte Guelfa, who were now the ones being exiled. Her call for the appointment to political office not of *fanciulli*, but of "uomini virtuosi, savi e discreti . . . maturi, esperti" was a standard trope in the medieval defense of oligarchical rule against political newcomers, similar, for example, to William Flete's defense of the Dodici in his letter to the Sienese government cited above.[148]

---

and letter 96 to Pietro Canigiani.

[146] Letter 377: "Non credetti scrivarvi, ma a bocca con voce viva vi credetti dire queste simili parole, per onore di Dio e vostra utilità, ché mia intenzione era di visitarvi e fare festa con voi della santa pace, per la quale pace io tanto tempo mi so' afadigata in ciò che io ò potuto secondo la mia possibilità e la mia poca virtù; se più virtù avessi avuta, più virtù avrei adoperato. Fatta festa e ringraziato la divina bontà e voi, mi volevo partire, e andarmene a Siena. Ora pare che 'l dimonio abbia tanto seminato ingiustamente ne' cuori loro verso di me, che io non ò voluto ch'essi agiunghino più offesa sopra offesa, però che quanto più se n'agiugnesse, più cresciarebbe ruina."

[147] Ibid.: "Unde io vi priego per l'amore di Cristo crocifisso che per l'utilità vostra voi non miriate a mettere governatori nella città più uno che un altro, ma uomini virtuosi, savi e discreti, e' quali col lume della ragione diano quello ordine che è di necessità, per la pace dentro e per confermazione di quella di fuori, la quale Idio ci à conceduta per la infinita sua misericordia, d'avere pacificati i figliuoli col padre, e rimesse noi pecorelle nell'ovile della santa Chiesa. . . . Vogliono essere uomini maturi, esperti, e non fanciulli, così vi priego che facciate; e ingegnatevi di tenere i cittadini vostri dentro e non di fuore, però che usciti non fece mai buona città, la quale reputo mia."

[148] The argument that government ought to be restricted to the experienced, the best, and the wise was a mainstay of oligarchic conservativism in *duecento* and *trecento* Italian political theory, employed by, among others, Brunetto Latini, Tolomeo da Lucca, Remigio de' Girolami, and Marsiglio da Padua; see Lauro Martines, *Power and Imagination: City-States in Renaissance Italy* (1979), 149–75.

## 1378–80: The Issues Change

By August 1378 two of Catherine's objectives of the prior several years had been achieved: the return of the pope to Rome and peace between the pope and the Tuscan cities. Negotiations with the Florentines had been completed by Pope Urban VI, the successor of Gregory XI, who died on 27 March. Catherine wrote Pope Urban several letters after his election, informing him about the situation in Florence, urging him to complete the peace, and to take up the cause of ecclesiastical reform in his appointments to clerical offices.[149] The history of Urban VI's disputed election, and the schism that was precipitated by the election of Clement VII on September 20, are too well known to require lengthy description here. Like Raymond of Capua, who was employed in important diplomatic roles by the new pope, Catherine also entered into the dispute as a vehement proponent of the Urbanist party.

At this final stage in her career, Catherine's concerns took her away from any particular attention to Sienese or Tuscan politics. Her letters on public affairs from this time until her death were concerned, almost exclusively, with the schism, as she attempted to dissuade prominent supporters of Clement like Queen Giovanna of Naples, the king of France, and Pietro Cardinale di Luna. Catherine herself went to Rome in late November, apparently by papal invitation; Raymond of Capua records that Catherine asked the pope to command her to make the trip, in order to quell murmurings about her travels. Urban appears to have conceived of a gathering in Rome of prominent holy people in support of his pontificate. Catherine was invited, along with William Flete and Giovanni dalle Celle, to each of whom Catherine wrote about the pope's plan. It is not known whether Giovanni made the trip, but William Flete refused to leave the solitude of his hermitage, prompting a strong remonstrance from Catherine. She spent the final year of her life in Rome, surrounded by a group of her followers, writing in support of Urban.[150] An excruciating illness of several months' duration finally ended her life on 30 April 1380.

---

[149] Catherine's first letter to Urban (letter 291) can be dated to late June 1378; she wrote him again in July (letter 302), August (letter 346), September (305), October (306).

[150] On the pro-Urbanist group that gathered around Catherine in Rome, see G. G. Meersseman, "Gli amici spirituali di S. Caterina a Roma alla luce del primo manifesto urbanista," *Bullettino Senese di Storia Patria* 69 (1962): 83–123.

# Conclusion

The narrative of Catherine's movements and epistolary activity during the War of Eight Saints detailed in chapter 5 should make it clear that Catherine's statements of political marginality—as expressed, for instance, in the letter quoted at the beginning of this book's introduction—cannot be taken on face value. Catherine's perspective was her own, not that of church leaders or the pope or even Raymond of Capua and her Dominican superiors. But she nevertheless emerges from this narrative of her travels and letters in the role of an agent of the church in Italy during the War of Eight Saints. The circumstances and demands of that conflict provided conditions that made possible her movement into the public eye and occasioned the letters for which she is famous. And read within their political settings, many of Catherine's letters take on clear political meaning, as well as a dominant ideological identification with the papal side in the dispute with the Italian cities, a dispute in which statements of spiritual goals could easily double as political rhetoric. What was at stake in the War of Eight Saints was the political authority of the spiritual power, the very distinction between the spiritual and the political. Thus the pope and supporters like Catherine saw the Florentines and their allies as rebelling against the church and committing sacrilege by violating the interdict. And the Florentines and their defenders (including clerics like Giovanni dalle Celle and Luigi Marsili) argued that they were opposing the unjust extension of the political jurisdiction of corrupt prelates, and so were not in rebellion and thus not liable to spiritual punishment.

In this context, an apparently apolitical ideal like peace, for example, invoked frequently in the letters surveyed here, took on a specific political meaning. It is true that Catherine's strongest calls for peace in its most limited sense—the absence of violence—occur in letters to the ecclesiastical leaders, as when Catherine wrote to the pope urging him to avoid violence in his response to the rebellions in Italy (206/LXIII and 196/LXIV). But peace in its fullest meaning entails a conception of good order, and it is in this sense that Catherine's appeals to peace could be strikingly political. When, for example, Catherine exhorted the Florentine government after the Ciompi revolution to establish peace by not taking reprisals against her allies in Florence, the Parte Guelfa leaders, "peace" was part of a rhetoric defending social elites and their continued participation in government (377). In this case, Catherine's rhetoric paralleled and was no less political than that employed by William Flete in 1371 and Gerard du Puy in 1375 to argue for the reintroduction of the Dodici to participation in the Sienese government. Even more significant in the context of the issues involved in the War of Eight Saints is the fact that Catherine appealed in her letters to an ideal of social and political peace, a society united in the Body of Christ, which assumes the social and political as well as spiritual leadership of the pope. This hierocratic social vision—a conflation of the spiritual and institutional church—placed Catherine clearly on the side of the church in the dispute with Florence. This can be seen, for example, in her letter to Barnabò Visconti (140/XXX), in which she argued that further rebellion against the pope, the head of the body, would cut Barnabò off from access to the blood of the body and thus salvation. This can be seen also in the way that Catherine repeatedly dismissed Florentine rhetoric during the dispute, refusing to admit that opposition to the pastors of the church could be reconciled with full membership in the Christian body. So, for example, she warned Niccolò Soderini (171/LX) and the Anziani of Lucca (168/LIII) that membership in the Florentine league would cut them off from the body of Christ; the Florentine *lega* violated the Christian's *legame* with God. Similarly, she insisted to Giovanni dalle Celle (296) that violation of the interdict was an offense against the blood of Christ. The same argument was implicit every time Catherine referred to the rebellious cities as "rotten members" of the ecclesial body.

And this argument lies behind Catherine's evocation, as in the letter to Hawkwood, of the traditional purpose and justification of Crusade: the establishment of peace among Christians by turning violence outward, against the non-Christians. While the Crusade, in Catherine's vision and as the object of perennial cultural preoccupation, was an ideal that transcended the political situation of the 1370s, it is nevertheless true that Catherine's Crusade appeals had a specific meaning in the context of the War of Eight Saints. The Crusade for Catherine was alternately a prerequisite for and a product of a Christendom unified around papal leadership. Thus an invitation to join the Crusade effort—directed, for example, to volatile political figures like John Hawkwood, Barnabò Visconti, and Giovanna d'Anjou—was also an overture to alliance with the papacy at a moment when its power was threatened politically in Italy. Catherine's Crusade letters engaged a kind of identity politics by evoking Christendom as a source of identity to override "local" allegiances. This is clear, for example, when she called on John Hawkwood (letter 140/XXX) and Barnabò Visconti (letter 28/XVIII) to cease involvement in wars between Christian polities and instead fight the infidels. Catherine's use of the Crusade as a vehicle for language of identity was even more dramatic when (in letter 207/LXVIII) she upbraided the Florentines for violating what should have been their primary loyalty: for "we are not Jews or Saracens." This attempt to shift the grounds of political identity from local and national loyalty to universal, Christian allegiance took on a geographical character in her evocation of the outrage of the infidels unjustly possessing "what is ours": the Holy Land served as an alternative homeland intended to supplant identification with city or nation. Catherine's Crusade rhetoric can thus be understood as a direct response to the sort of rhetoric employed by the Florentines in justifying their opposition to the leaders of the church's political state: for example, Coluccio Salutati's appeal to an idea of Italian unity against the French or Limousin clerics. To whatever extent Catherine's rhetoric appealed to her prophetic distance from the world, she was at the same time deeply invested in worldly politics.

To return to the episode with which this book began, it should be clear now that Catherine's rhetoric of political marginality in response to Sienese concerns about her activities in 1377 obscured the political meaning and objectives of her career as well as the continued ties of her followers to civic political life in Siena and Florence. Catherine's sanctity and the devotion of her followers were inflected with political meaning; and a political crisis, the War of Eight Saints, was the occasion that gave her sanctity meaning on a large stage. This is not to diminish Catherine's sanctity, downplay the devotion of her followers, or reduce religion to politics, but rather to understand religion, as a category of historical analysis, as invested inextricably in particular circumstances. And it is not to lessen the importance of understanding the dominant discourses of female sanctity in the late Middle Ages, to which Raymond of Capua and Catherine's other followers appealed in arguing for her sanctity, which Catherine herself sometimes employed in her letters, and which have figured so prominently in recent studies of medieval female saints and feminine religiosity. But these discourses cannot be taken simply as representative of Catherine's experience. To understand Catherine's career, one must appreciate not only the discourses of sanctity she and her followers employed, but also the circumstances within and the ends for which they employed them. Catherine's involvement in the politics of the 1370s was not a secondary part of her career, an ancillary relation to some essential core of saintly or spiritual identity. Catherine's sanctity and her involvement in worldly affairs were fully interrelated.

One implication of this linking of Catherine's sanctity to the political developments of the 1370s is that the politics of that period cannot be understood fully apart from their religious component. To treat sanctity as set apart from politics and other social pressures and identities makes as little sense as to view the War of Eight Saints apart from the pious commitments that informed the political identities of citizens in Florence, Siena, and other cities. Indeed, what this book has revealed about Catherine's place in the propaganda wars is a reminder of the role that religious commitment played in the articulation of Florentine civic ideology, a role that David Peterson has shown was written out of Florentine history beginning in the fifteenth century.[1] Decades before Coluccio Salutati argued for Florentine republicanism as an alternative to Milanese despotism, he urged a republican vision of Italy against the political ambitions of the church and political identity based on loyalty to the pope. In this way the Florentine commitment to republicanism, as worked out during the War of Eight Saints and tested in such episodes as the defiance of the interdict imposed by Gregory XI, was a religious problem, not merely a secular ideology.

As for Catherine herself, her sanctity was not something separate from her engagement in worldly affairs. Catherine was a young woman shaped by the particularities of Sienese and Tuscan social life and deeply implicated in the political contests that dominated Tuscany in the 1370s, and this social and political setting shaped her emergence as a saint. In contrast to the more stable religious category later constructed for Catherine by Raymond of Capua and Tommaso Caffarini, Catherine's early religious and social identity, while in many ways peculiar to herself, owed much to the model of experimentation and female independence of the Sienese *mantellate*, and independent and forceful women like her mother. Catherine's public career developed not out of proverbial obscurity, or in contrast to her family background, but in a way that was consistent with the social and political situation of her family within Siena. As a political figure in the 1370s, Catherine was effectively in league with the Sienese political groups to which her family had been tied, particularly the disenfranchised guild elites of the Dodici and their Salimbeni allies. While Catherine's lay followers expressed their relations with Catherine as spiritual commitments in contrast to their worldly obligations, the evidence of their continued activities in civic life represents a more complicated mixing of pious aspirations

---

[1] Peterson, "The War of Eight Saints."

and civic commitments, and also brings Catherine much closer to the center of real politics than she appears in the hagiography and in her own writings when they are read ahistorically. Catherine's appearance on the larger stage of Italian and ecclesiastical politics in 1374 was made possible by the needs of the papacy as Gregory XI and the governors of the Papal States sought to consolidate church possessions in Italy in face of opposition from Florence and other cities. The trajectory of her career after 1374 ties her clearly to the papacy and papal allies like the Florentine Parte Guelfa elites, however much Catherine did not accept passively her role as a papal agent. There was no Catherine of Siena without the War of Eight Saints.

This reinterpretation of Catherine's career also calls for a reevaluation of her writings, particularly her letters, and of Catherine's status as an author. Raymond of Capua introduced Catherine's writings in the *Legenda maior* by emphasizing Catherine's mystic authorship, an image of her as a passive vehicle for divine communication. For Raymond as well as for subsequent readers, Catherine's status as an author, like her saintly authority in general, rested on her essential distance from the world she addressed in her writings, and on the estrangement of her texts from the political and other contexts within which they were composed. To be accepted as authoritative, Catherine's writings had to be abstracted from their history and Catherine's own agency in the production of her texts reduced. The effect of the hagiographical construction of Catherine's authorship lingers in the history of modern critical disdain for Catherine's literary ability, and also in the unease with which Catherinian scholars have approached the "problem" of Catherine's literacy, especially her announcement in 1377 that she had learned to write. It has proven difficult to appreciate Catherine's highly original use of spiritual rhetoric and prophetic language in letters, as well as to reconcile Catherine's saintly persona and evidence of her agency in the production of her texts.

Catherine's epistolarity, her use of this relatively flexible genre of writing to mix mysticism in mundane affairs, should be appreciated as an apt expression of her investment in the political scene and of the entire enterprise of her career. Read in the context of the political discourse of the 1370s, Catherine's letters become part of the process whereby she created a community within which her saintly authority would be recognized, vehicles for her to interject her sanctity and prophetic authority into worldly affairs. In Catherine's description of the execution of Niccolò di Toldo, her writing-miracle letter in 1377, and in other less dramatic cases, the meaning of her letters is transformed by understanding the circumstances in which she wrote. Her letters sometimes employed the rhetoric of affective, feminine spirituality and sanctity, but this was not an expression of some static category or identity she embodied. On the contrary, this rhetoric was part of a constellation of images and tropes

Catherine deployed in order to create her own authority and communicate a prophetic perspective on worldly politics. It is my hope that one result of this attempt to explore the political meaning of Catherine's career is that Catherine appears more fully an author, in charge of the marshaling of the terms in which her saintly authority could be recognized. In restoring Catherine to her own history, I hope I have begun to return the pen to her hand.

# Bibliography

ARCHIVES AND MANUSCRIPTS

Siena
   Archivio di Stato (ASS)
      Arti
      Casa della Misericordia
      Concistoro
      Consiglio Generale
      Diplomatico
      Legato Bichi-Borghesi
      Spedale di Siena
      Diplomatico, Patrimonio Resti
      Certosa di Pontignano
      San Domenico
      Gabella
      Lira
      Notarile
      Ospedale di S. Maria della Scala
      Patrimonio Resti, San Domenico
   Biblioteca Comunale
      A.IV.1
      B.VI.12
      B.IX.18
      H.X.47
      I.V.22
      T.II.2

# BIBLIOGRAPHY

Florence
  Archivio di Stato
    Provvisioni
  Biblioteca Laurenziana
    Strozziano XXXI
  Biblioteca Nazionale
    Magliabechiano XXXVIII, 130
  Biblioteca Riccardiana
    1267
London
  British Library
    Harley 3480
Vienna
  Österreichische Nationalbibliotek
    Palatino 3514

PRINTED SOURCES

Bartolomeo da Siena. *De vita et moribus beati Stephani Senensis Carthusiani.* Siena: Ercole Gori, 1626.

*Cantari religiosi senesi del Trecento: Neri Pagliaresi, Fra Felice Tancredi da Massa, Niccolò Cicerchia.* Edited by Giorgio Varanini. Bari: Laterza, 1965.

*Canzoni d'amore e madrigali di Dante Alighieri, di M. Cino da Pistoia, di M. Girardo Novello, di M. Girardo da Castel Fiorentino, di M. Betrico da Reggio, di M. Ruccio Piacente da Siena, riproduzione della rarissima edizione del 1518.* Edited by Giulio Piccini. Florence: Landi, 1899.

Catherine of Siena. *Opere della Serafica Santa Caterina da Siena.* Edited by Girolamo Gigli. 4 vols. Siena-Lucca: Bonetti, 1707–1721.

———. "Le lettere di Santa Caterina da Siena." Edited by Antonio Volpato. In *Santa Caterina da Siena: Opera Omnia.* Edited by Fausto Sbaffoni. Pistoia: Provincia Romana dei Frati Predicatori, 2002.

———. *Le lettere di S. Caterina da Siena, ridotte a miglior lezione.* Edited by Niccolò Tommaseo. 4 vols. Florence: G. Bargera, 1860.

———. *Le lettere di S. Caterina da Siena, ridotte a miglior lezione, e in ordine nuovo disposte con note di Niccolò Tommaseo.* Edited by Piero Misciattelli. 6 vols. Siena: Giuntini Bentivoglio, 1913–22.

———. *Epistolario di Santa Caterina.* Edited by Eugenio Dupré Theseider. Vol. 1. Rome: R. Istituto storico italiano per il Medio Evo, 1940.

———. *Il Dialogo della divina provvidenza ovvero Libro della divina dottrina.* Edited by Giuliana Cavallini. Testi Cateriniani, 1. Rome: Edizioni Cateriniane, 1968.

———. *The Letters of Catherine of Siena.* Translated by Suzanne Noffke. Vol. 1. Binghamton: Medieval and Renaissance Texts and Studies, 1988.

———. *The Letters of Catherine of Siena.* Translated and edited by Suzanne Noffke. Vols. 1–2. Medieval and Renaissance Texts and Studies, 202–203. Tempe, AZ: Arizona Center for Medieval and Renaissance Studies, 2000–2001.

*Dominican Penitent Women.* Edited and translated by Maiju Lehmijoki-Gardner, with contributions by Daniel E. Bornstein and E. Ann Matter. Classics of Western Spirituality. New York: Paulist Press, 2005.

Dominici, Giovanni. *Lettere spirituali.* Edited by M.-T. Casella and G. Pozzi. Spicilegium Friburgense, 13. Fribourg: Edizioni Universitarie Friburgo Svizzera, 1969.

Doni, Anton Francesco. *La Libreria.* Edited by Vanni Bramanti. Milan: Longanesi, 1972.

Flete, William. *Lettera a Raimondo da Capua in lode di Caterina da Siena.* Translated by Giacinto D'Urso. Florence: Baccini and Chiappi, 1974.

Frater Ivo. *Épître à Séverin sur la charité.* Edited by Gervais Dumeige. Paris: J. Vrin, 1955.

Gigli, Girolamo. *Vocabolario Cateriniano del dialetto sanese.* Siena-Lucca: Bonetti, 1717.

Giovanni dalle Celle and Luigi Marsili. *Lettere.* Edited by Francesco Giambonini. Istituto Nazionale di Studi sul Rinascimento, Studi e Testi, 22. 2 vols. Florence: Olschki, 1991.

Gregory XI. *Lettres secrètes et curiales relatives à la France.* Edited by L. Mirot et al. Paris: 1935–57.

Guidini, Cristofano di Gano. *Libro di Memorie.* In *Archivio Storico Italiano,* series 1, vol. 4, pt. 2, 27–48.

Jean de Roquetaillade. *Liber secretum eventum.* Edited by Robert E. Lerner and translated by Christine Morerod-Fattebert. Fribourg: Éditions Universitaires Fribourg Suisse, 1994.

Laurent, M.-H., ed. *Documenti. Fontes Vitae S. Catharinae Senensis Historici.* Vol. 1. Florence: Sansoni, 1936.

Luchaire, Julien. *Documenti per la storia dei rivolgimenti politici del Comune di Siena dal 1354 al 1369.* Lyon: A. Rey; Paris: A. Picard et fils, 1906.

*I Miracoli di Caterina da Iacopo da Siena di Anonimo Fiorentino.* Edited by M.-H. Laurent and Francesco Valli. *Fontes Vitae S. Catherinae Senensis Historici,* vol. 4. Florence: Sansoni, 1936.

*I Necrologi di San Domenico in Camporeggio.* Edited by M.-H. Laurent. *Fontes Vitae S. Catherinae Senensis Historici,* vol. 20. Siena: Università di Siena, 1937.

Neri di Donato. *Cronaca Senese di Donato di Neri e di suo figlio Neri.* In *Cronache Senesi.* Edited by Alessandro Lisini and Fabio Iacometti. *Rerum Italicarum Scriptores,* vol. 15, Pt. 6, 569–685. Bologna: Nicola Zanichelli, 1936.

Neri Pagliaresi. *Rime Sacre di certa o probabile attribuzione.* Edited by Giorgio Varanini. Florence: Le Monnier, 1970.

*Il Processo Castellano.* Edited by M.-H. Laurent. *Fontes Vitae S. Catherinae Senensis Historici,* vol. 9. Milan: Fratelli Bocca, 1942.

Pseudo-Bonaventure. *Stimulus amoris.* In *S. Bonaventurae Opera Omnia,* vol. 12, edited by A. C. Peltier. Paris: Ludovicus Vives, 1868.

Raymond of Capua. *Legenda Sancti Catherine Senensis.* In *Acta Sanctorum,* 3 (April), 862–967. Paris: Victor Palme, 1866.

———. *B. Raymundi Capuani XXIII Mag. Gen. O.P. Opuscula et Litterae.* Edited by H. M. Cormier. Rome: 1899.

——. *The Life of Saint Catherine of Siena by Raymond of Capua*. Translated by Conleth Kearns. Wilmington, DE: Michael Glazier, 1980.

Singleton, Charles S., ed. *Canti carnascialeschi del Rinascimento*. Scrittori d'Italia, 159. Bari: Laterza, 1936.

"Statuto dell'università ed arte della lana di Siena, diviso in otto distinzioni, 1298–1309." In *Statuti Senesi scritti in volgare ne' secoli XIII e XIV e pubblicati secondo i testi del R. Archivio di Stato in Siena*, vol. 1. Edited by Filippo-Luigi Polidori, 128–384. Bologna: Gaetano Romagnoli, 1863.

Stefani, Marchionne di Coppo. *Cronaca fiorentina di Marchionne di Coppo Stefani*. Edited by Niccolò Rodolico. *Rerum Italicarum Scriptores*, vol. 30, pt. 1. Città di Castello: S. Lapi, 1903.

Taurisano, Innocenzo M., ed. *I Fioretti di santa Caterina da Siena*. Rome: Ferrari, 1950.

Tommaso di Antonio da Siena "Caffarini." *Tractatus de Ordine FF. de Paenitentia S. Dominici di F. Tommaso da Siena*. Edited by M.-H. Laurent. *Fontes Vitae S. Catharinae Senensis Historici*, vol. 21. Florence: Sansoni, 1938.

——. *Sanctae Catherinae Senensis Legenda Minor*. Edited by E. Franceschini. *Fontes Vitae S. Catherinae Senensis Historici*, vol. 10. Milan: Fratelli Bocca, 1942.

——. *Libellus de Supplemento: Legende prolixe Virginis Beate Catherine de Senis*. Edited by Giuliana Cavallini and Imelda Foralosso. Rome: Edizioni Caterininane, 1974.

Ugurgieri Azzolini, Isidoro. *Le pompe sanesi, o vero relazione delli huomini, e donne illustri di Siena, e suo stato*. Pistoia: Pier'Antonio Fortunati, 1649.


SECONDARY WORKS

Aers, David. "The Humanity of Christ: Reflections on Orthodox Late Medieval Representations." In *The Powers of the Holy: Religion, Politics, and Gender in Late Medieval English Culture*, edited by Aers and Lynn Staley, 15–42. University Park: Penn State Press, 1996.

Antonelli, Roberto. "L'Ordine domenicano e la letteratura nell'Italia pretridentina." In *Letteratura italiana*, vol. 1, *Il letterato e le istituzioni*, edited by Albert Asor Rosa, 681–728. Turin: Einaudi, 1982.

Antoni, Claudio G. *Sistemi stilistici ed espressione mistica. Saggi sulla tradizione cateriniana*. Pisa: ETS, 1984.

*Atti del Congresso internazionale di studi cateriniani, Siena-Roma, 24–29 aprile 1980*. Rome: Curia Generalizia O.P., 1981.

Balestracci, Duccio, and Gabriella Piccinni. *Siena nel trecento. Assetto urbano e strutture edilizie*. Florence: Edizioni CLUSF, 1977.

Barbero, Alessandro. *Un santo in famiglia: Vocazione religiosa e resistenze sociali nell'agiografia latina medievale*. Turin: Rosenberg and Sellier, 1991.

Becker, Marvin B. "Florentine Politics and the Diffusion of Heresy in the Trecento: A Socio-Economic Inquiry." *Speculum* 34 (1959): 60–75.

——. "Church and State in Florence on the Eve of the Renaissance (1343–1382)." *Speculum* 37 (1962): 509–27

——. *Florence in Transition*. Baltimore: Johns Hopkins University Press, 1967.

——. *Medieval Italy: Constraints and Creativity*. Bloomington: Indiana University Press, 1981.

Beckwith, Sarah. *Christ's Body: Identity, Culture, and Society in Late Medieval Writings*. London: Routledge, 1993.

Bell, Rudolf. *Holy Anorexia*. Chicago: University of Chicago Press, 1985.

Bellomo, Manlio. *Ricerche sui rapporti patrimoniali tra coniugi*. Ius nostrum, 7. Milan: Giuffrè, 1961.

Bennett, Judith M. *Ale, Beer, and Brewsters in England: Women's Work in a Changing World, 1300–1600*. New York: Oxford University Press, 1996.

Benvenuti-Papi, Anna. "Frati mendicanti e pinzochere in Toscana, dalla marginalità sociale al modelli di santità." In *Temi e problemi nella mistica femminile trecentesca*, 109–35. Todi: Accademia Tudertina, 1983.

——. *"In Castro Poenitentiae": Santità e società femminile nell'Italia medievale*. Italia Sacra, 45. Rome: Herder, 1990.

Biddick, Kathleen. "Genders, Bodies, Borders: Technologies of the Visible." *Speculum* 68 (1993): 389–418.

——. *The Shock of Medievalism*. Durham, NC: Duke University Press, 1998.

Bornstein, Daniel. "Spiritual Kinship and Domestic Devotions." In *Gender and Society in Renaissance Italy*, edited by Judith C. Brown and Robert C. Davis, 173–92. London: Longman, 1988.

——. *The Bianchi of 1399: Popular Devotion in Late Medieval Italy*. Ithaca, NY: Cornell University Press, 1994.

Bornstein, Daniel, and Roberto Rusconi, eds. *Mistiche e devote nell'Italia tardomedievale*. Nuovo Medioevo, 40. Naples: Liguori, 1992.

——. *Women and Religion in Medieval and Renaissance Italy*. Chicago: University of Chicago Press, 1996.

Boureau, Alain. "The Letter-Writing Norm, a Mediaeval Invention." In *Correspondence: Models of Letter-Writing from the Middle Ages to the Nineteenth Century*, edited by Roger Chartier and translated by Christopher Woodall, 24–58. Princeton: Princeton University Press, 1997.

Bowsky, William M. *A Medieval Italian Commune: Siena Under the Nine, 1287–1355*. Berkeley: University of California Press, 1981.

Branca, Vittore. *I mistici: Fioretti di San Francesco, Lettere di Santa Caterina*. Milan: Dante Alighieri, 1964.

Brizio, Elena. "L'elezione degli uffici politici nella Siena del Trecento." *Bullettino Senese di Storia Patria* 98 (1991): 16–62.

——. "Siena nel secondo Trecento: Organismi istituzionali e personale politico dalla caduta dei *Dodici* alla dominazione viscontea (1368–1399)." Ph.D. diss., Università degli Studi di Firenze, 1992.

Brucker, Gene A. *Florentine Politics and Society, 1343–1378*. Princeton, NJ: Princeton University Press, 1962.

Butler, Judith. *Gender Trouble: Feminism and the Subversion of Identity*. New York: Routledge, 1990.

——. *Bodies That Matter: On the Discursive Limits of "Sex."* New York: Routledge, 1993.

Bynum, Caroline Walker. *Jesus as Mother: Studies in the Spirituality of the High Middle Ages*. Berkeley: University of California Press, 1982.

——. *Holy Feast and Holy Fast: The Religious Significance of Food to Medieval Women.* Berkeley: University of California Press, 1987.

——. *Fragmentation and Redemption: Essays on Gender and the Human Body in Medieval Religion.* New York: Zone Books, 1991.

Cadden, Joan. *Meanings of Sex Difference in the Middle Age: Medicine, Science, and Culture.* Cambridge: Cambridge University Press, 1993.

Caferro, William. *Mercenary Companies and the Decline of Siena.* Baltimore: Johns Hopkins University Press, 1998.

Camargo, Martin. "Where's the Brief? The *Ars Dictaminis* and Reading/Writing between the Lines." *Disputatio* 1 (1996): 1–17.

Camporeale, Salvatore. *Lorenzo Valla: Umanesimo e teologia.* Florence: Istituto nazionale di studi sul Rinascimento, 1972.

Cardini, Franco. "Caterina da Siena, la repubblica di Firenze e la lega antipontificia. Schede per una riconsiderazione." *Bullettino Senese di Storia Patria* 89 (1982): 300–325.

——. "L'idea di crociata in S. Caterina da Siena." In *Atti del simposio internazionale Cateriniano-Bernardiniano, Siena, 17–20 aprile 1980,* edited by Domenico Maffei and Paolo Nardi, 57–87. Siena: Accademia Senese degli Intronati, 1982.

Carniani, Alessandra. *I Salimbeni, quasi una signoria: tentativi di affermazione politica nella Siena del Trecento.* Siena: Protagon, 1995.

Cecchini, Giovanni. "I Benincasa di Cellole." *Bullettino Senese di Storia Patria* 56 (1949): 114–20.

Centi, Timoteo. "Il memoriale delle mantellate Senesi contemporanee di S. Caterina." *Rivista di storia della chiesa in Italia* 1 (1947): 409–18.

Chabot, Isabelle. "'Sola, donna, non gir mai.' La solitudini femminili nel Trecento." *Memoria. Rivista di storia delle donne* 3 (1986): 7–24.

——. "Diritti e risorse patrimoniali." In *Storia delle donne italiane,* vol. 2, *Il lavoro delle donne, Parte I: L'età medievale,* edited by A. Groppi, 47–70. Rome-Bari: Laterza, 1996.

——. "La loi du lignage: Notes sur le système successoral florentin (XIV$^e$–XV$^e$ siècles)." *Clio: Femmes, Histoire et Sociétés* 7 (1998): 51–72.

——. "Lineage Strategies and the Control of Widows in Renaissance Florence." In *Widowhood in Medieval and Early Modern Europe,* edited by Sandra Cavallo and Lyndan Warner, 127–44. London: Longman, 1999.

Chartier, Roger, ed. *Correspondence: Models of Letter-Writing from the Middle Ages to the Nineteenth Century.* Translated by Christopher Woodall. Princeton: Princeton University Press, 1997.

Cherubini, Giovanni. "Dal libro di ricordi di un notaio senese del Trecento." In *Signori, contadini, borghesi: Ricerche sulla società italiana del basso medioevo,* 393–425. Biblioteca di Storia, 17. Florence: La Nuova Italia, 1974.

*Christianity and the Renaissance: Image and Religious Imagination in the Quattrocento.* Edited by Timothy Verdon and John Henderson. Syracuse, NY: Syracuse University Press, 1990.

Collins, Amanda. *Greater than Emperor: Cola di Rienzo (ca. 1313–54) and the World of Fourteenth-Century Rome.* Ann Arbor: University of Michigan Press, 2002.

Constable, Giles. *Letters and Letter-Collections.* Typologie des sources du moyen âge occidental, 17. Turnhout: Brepols, 1976.

Cowdrey, H. E. J. "The Peace and Truce of God in the Eleventh Century." *Past and Present* 46 (1970): 42–67.

*The Crannied Wall: Women, Religion, and the Arts in Early Modern Europe.* Edited by Craig A. Monson. Ann Arbor: University of Michigan Press, 1992.

*Creative Women in Medieval and Early Modern Italy: A Religious and Artistic Renaissance.* Edited by E. Ann Matter and John Coakley. Philadelphia: University of Pennsylvania Press, 1994.

Crescimbeni, Giovanni. *L'istoria della volgar poesia.* Rome: Per il Chracas, 1698.

Croce, Benedetto. "Letteratura del Trecento. Letteratura di devozione." *La Critica* 3rd ser. 29 (1931): 321–40.

De Certeau, Michel. The *Mystic Fable: The Sixteenth and Seventeenth Centuries.* Translated by Michael B. Smith. Chicago: University of Chicago Press, 1992.

——. "Mystic Speech." In *Heterologies: Discourse on the Other,* translated by Brian Massumi, 80–100. Minneapolis: University of Minnesota Press, 1986.

Del Pozzo, Joan P. "The Apotheosis of Niccolò di Toldo: An Execution 'Love Story.'" *Modern Language Notes* 110 (1995): 164–77.

De Rosa, Daniela. *Coluccio Salutati: Il cancelliere e il pensatore politico.* Florence: 1980.

De Sanctis, Francesco. *Storia della letteratura italiana.* Edited by Niccolò Gallo. Turin: Einaudi, 1958.

Dionisotti, Carlo. *Gli umanisti e il volgare tra Quattro e Cinquecento.* Florence: F. Le Monnier, 1968.

Dondaine, A. "Sainte Catherine de Sienne et Niccolò Toldo." *Archivum Fratrum Praedicatorum* 19 (1949): 168–207.

Drane, Augusta. *The History of St. Catherine of Siena and Her Companions.* 2 vols. London: Burns and Oates, 1880.

Dupré Theseider, Eugenio. "Un codice inedito dell'Epistolario di S. Caterina da Siena." *Bullettino dell'Istituto storico italiano* 48 (1932): 17–56.

——. "Il problema critico delle lettere di Santa Caterina da Siena." *Giornale storico della letteratura italiana* 69 (1933): 117–278.

——. "Il supplizio di Niccolò di Toldo." *Bulletino Senese di Storia Patria* 12 (1935): 162–64.

——. "La rivolta di Perugia nel 1375 contra l'abate di Monmaggiore e i suoi precedenti politici." *Bollettino della R. Deputazione di storia patria per l'Umbria* 35 (1938): 69–166.

——. "La duplice esperienza di S. Caterina da Siena." *Rivista Storica Italiana* 62 (1950): 533–74.

——. "L'attesa escatologica durante il periodo avignonese." In *L'attesa dell'età nuova nella spiritualità della fine del Medioevo, 16–19 ottobre 1960.* Convegni del Centro di studi sulla spiritualità medievale, 3. Todi: Accademia tudertina, 1962.

——. "Caterina da Siena, santa." In *Dizionario biografico degli Italiani,* vol. 22, 361–79. Rome: Istituto della Enciclopedia italiana, 1979.

D'Urso, Giacinto. *Il genio di S. Caterina: Studi sulla sua dottrina e personalità.* Rome: Edizioni Cateriniane, 1971.

Elliot, Dyan. "*Dominae* or *Dominatae?* Female Mysticism and the Trauma of Textuality." In *Women, Marriage, and Family in Medieval Christendom: Essays in Memory of Michael M. Sheehan, C.S.B.,* edited by Constance M. Rousseau and Joel T. Rosenthal, 47–77. Kalamazoo, MI: Medieval Institute Publications, 1998.

Erdmann, Carl. *The Origin of the Idea of Crusade.* Princeton: Princeton University Press, 1977.

Falvey, Kathleen. "Early Italian Dramatic Traditions and Comforting Rituals: Some Initial Considerations." In *Crossing the Boundaries. Christian Piety and the Arts in Italian Medieval and Renaissance Confraternities,* edited by Konrad Eisenbichler, 33–55. Kalamazoo, MI: 1991.

Farmer, Sharon. "The Beggar's Body: Intersections of Gender and Social Status in High Medieval Paris." In *Monks and Nuns, Saints, and Outcasts: Religion in Medieval Society,* edited by Sharon Farmer and Barbara H. Rosenwein, 153–71. Ithaca, NY: Cornell University Press, 2000.

Fawtier, Robert. *Sainte Catherine de Sienne: Essai de critique des sources.* 2 vols. Paris: E. de Boccard: 1921–1930.

Fawtier, Robert, and Louis Canet. *La double expérience de Catherine Benincasa.* Paris: 1948.

Ferroni, Giulio. "L'Io e gli altri nelle *Lettere* di Caterina da Siena." In *Les femmes écrivaines en Italie au moyen âge et à la renaissance. Actes du colloque international, Aix-en-Provence, 12, 13, 14 novembre 1992,* 139–156. Aix-en-Provence: Publications de l'Université de Provence, 1994.

Franceschini, Franco. *Oltre il "Tumulto": I lavoratori fiorentini dell'arte della lana fra Tre e Quattrocento.* Biblioteca di Storia Toscana Moderna e Contemporanea, Studi e Documenti, 38; Florence: Leo S. Olschki, 1993.

Gajano, Sofia Boesch, and Odile Redon. "La *Legenda maior* di Raimondo da Capua, costruzione di una santa." In *Atti del simposio internazionale Cateriniano-Bernardiniano, Siena, 17–20 aprile 1980,* edited by Domenico Maffei and Paolo Nardi, 15–36. Siena: Accademia Senese degli Intronati, 1982.

Galletti, Anna Imelde. "*Uno capo nelle mani mie:* Niccolò di Toldo, perugino." In *Atti del simposio internazionale Cateriniano-Bernardiniano, Siena, 17–20 aprile 1980,* edited by Domenico Maffei and Paolo Nardi, 15–36. Siena: Accademia Senese degli Intronati, 1982.

Gardner, Edmund. *Saint Catherine of Siena: A Study in the Religion, Literature, and History of the Fourteenth Century in Italy.* London: Dent, 1907.

*Gender and Society in Renaissance Italy.* Edited by Judith C. Brown and Robert C. Davis. London: Longman, 1998.

Getto, Giovanni. *Letteratura religiosa del Trecento.* Florence: Sansoni, 1967.

Gill, Katherine. "Open Monasteries for Women in Late Medieval and Early Modern Italy: Two Roman Examples." In *The Crannied Wall: Women, Religion, and the Arts in Early Modern Europe,* edited by Craig A. Monson, 15–48. Ann Arbor: University of Michigan Press, 1992.

——. "*Scandala:* Controversies Concerning *Clausura* and Women's Religious Communities in Late Medieval Italy." In *Christendom and Its Discontents: Exclusion, Persecution, and Rebellion, 1000–1500,* edited by Scott L. Waugh and Peter D. Diehl, 177–206. Cambridge: Cambridge University Press, 1996.

Giorgi, Andrea. "Il carteggio del Concistoro della Repubblica di Siena (Spoglio delle lettere: 1251–1374)." *Bullettino Senese di Storia Patria* 97 (1991): 193–573.

Grion, Alvaro. *Santa Caterina da Siena: dottrina e fonti.* Cremona: Morcelliana, 1953.

Guarnieri, R. "Pinzochere." In *Dizionario degli istituti di perfezione*, vol. 7, 1721–49. Rome: Edizioni Paoline, 1983.

Hackett, Benedict. *William Flete, O.S.A., and Catherine of Siena: Masters of Fourteenth-Century Spirituality*. The Augustinian Series, 15. Villanova, PA: Augustinian Press, 1992.

Hamburger, Jeffrey. *The Rothschild Canticles: Art and Mysticism in Flanders and the Rhineland circa 1300*. New Haven: Yale University Press, 1990.

Hay, Denys. *The Church in Italy in the Fifteenth Century*. Cambridge: Cambridge University Press, 1977.

Henderson, John. *Piety and Charity in Late Medieval Florence*. Chicago: University of Chicago Press, 1994.

Herlihy, David, and Christiane Klapisch-Zuber. *Tuscans and Their Families*. New Haven: Yale University Press, 1985.

Houseley, Norman. "The Mercenary Companies, the Papacy, and the Crusades, 1356–1378." *Traditio* 38 (1982): 253–80.

Howell, Martha C. *The Marriage Exchange: Property, Social Place, and Gender in Cities of the Low Countries, 1300–1550*. Chicago: University of Chicago Press, 1998.

Hughes, Diane Owen. "From Bridepiece to Dowry in Mediterranean Europe." *Journal of Family History* 3 (1978): 262–96.

Hyde, J. K. *Padua in the Age of Dante*. Manchester: University of Manchester Press, 1966.

Isaacs, A. K. "Magnati, Comune e Stato a Siena nel Trecento e all'inizio del Quattrocento." In *I ceti dirigenti nella Toscana tardo comunale, Atti del III convegno, Firenze, 5–7 dicembre 1980*, 81–96. Florence: Papafava, 1983.

Jacquart, Danielle, and Claude Thomasset. *Sexuality and Medicine in the Middle Ages*. Translated by Matthew Adamson. Princeton: Princeton University Press, 1988.

Jourdan, Édouard. "La date de naissance de Sainte Catherine de Sienne." *Analecta Bollandiana* 40 (1922): 365–411.

Kantorowicz, Ernst. *The King's Two Bodies*. Princeton: Princeton University Press, 1957.

Karras, Ruth Mazo. *Common Women: Prostitution and Sexuality in Medieval England*. New York: Oxford University Press, 1996.

Kedar, Benjamin Z. *Crusade and Mission: European Approaches to the Muslims*. Princeton: Princeton University Press, 1984.

Kent, D. *The Rise of the Medici*. Oxford: Oxford University Press, 1978.

Kiekhefer, Richard. *Unquiet Souls: Fourteenth-Century Saints and Their Religious Milieu*. Chicago: University of Chicago Press, 1984.

Kirshner, Julius. "Wive's Claims against Insolvent Husbands in Late Medieval Italy." In *Women of the Medieval World: Essays in Honor of John H. Mundy*, edited by Julius Kirshner and Suzanne F. Wemple, 256–303. Oxford: Basil Blackwell, 1985.

Klapisch-Zuber, Christiane. *Women, Family, and Ritual in Renaissance Italy*. Translated by Lydia Cochrane. Chicago: University of Chicago Press, 1985.

Kleinberg, Aviad M. *Prophets in Their Own Country: Living Saints and the Making of Sainthood in the Later Middle Ages*. Chicago: University of Chicago Press, 1992.

Kristeller, Paul Oskar. *Medieval Aspects of Renaissance Learning*. Durham, NC: Duke University Press, 1974.

Kuehn, Thomas. *Law, Family, and Women: Toward a Legal Anthropology of Renaissance Italy*. Chicago: University of Chicago Press, 1991.

Lansing, Carol. *The Lament for the Dead*. Ithaca, NY: Cornell University Press, forthcoming.

Laurent, M.-H. "Alcune notizie sulla famiglia di S. Caterina." *Bullettino Senese di Storia Patria* 44 (1937): 365–74.

——. "De litteris ineditis Fr. Willelmi de Fleete (cc. 1368–1380)." *Analecta Augustiniana* 18 (1942): 303–27.

Lehmijoki-Gardner, Maiju. "Writing Religious Rules as an Interactive Process–Dominican Penitent Women and the Making of Their Regula." *Speculum* 79 (2004): 660–87.

Léonard, E. G. *Gli Angioini di Napoli*. Milan: Varese dall'Oglio, 1967.

Leoncini, Giovanni. "Un certosino del tardo medioevo: don Stefano Maconi." *Die Ausbreitung kartäusischen Lebens und Geistes im Mittelalter*, vol. 2, *Analecta Cartusiana* 63.2: 54–107.

Lesnick, Daniel R. *Preaching in Medieval Florence: The Social World of Franciscan and Dominican Spirituality*. Athens, GA: University of Georgia Press, 1989.

Lewis, Flora. "The Wound in Christ's Side and the Instruments of the Passion: Gendered Experience and Response." In *Women and the Book: Assessing the Visual Evidence*, edited by Lesley Smith and Jane H. M. Taylor, 204–29. British Library Studies in Medieval Culture. Toronto: University of Toronto Press, 1997.

Lisini, A., and A. Liberati. *Geneologia dei Piccolomini di Siena*. Siena: Enrico Torrini, 1900.

Lochrie, Karma. "The Language of Transgression: Body, Flesh, and Word in Mystical Discourse." In *Speaking in Two Languages: Traditional Disciplines and Contemporary Theory in Medieval Studies*, edited by Allen J. Frantzen, 115–140. Albany: State University of New York Press, 1991.

——. *Margery Kempe and Translations of the Flesh*. Philadelphia: University of Pennsylvania Press, 1991.

——. "Mystical Acts, Queer Tendencies." In *Constructing Medieval Sexuality*, edited by Karma Lochrie, Peggy McCracken, and James A. Schultz, 180–200. Minneapolis: University of Minnesota Press, 1997.

Lumia, Gianna. "Morire a Siena. Devoluzione testamentaria, legami parentali e vincoli afettivi in età moderna." *Bulletino Senese di Storia Patria* 103 (1996): 103–285.

Luongo, F. Thomas. "Catherine of Siena: Rewriting Female Holy Authority." In *Women, the Book and the Godly: Selected Proceedings of the St. Hilda's Conference, 1993*, vol. 1, edited by Lesley Smith and Jane H. M. Taylor, 89–104. Oxford: D. S. Brewer, 1995.

——. "The Evidence of Catherine's Experience: Niccolò di Toldo and the Erotics of Political Engagement." In *Siena e il suo territorio nel Rinascimento*, edited by Mario Ascheri, 53–90. Siena: Il Leccio, 2001.

——. "Cloistering Catherine: Religious Identity in Raymond of Capua's *Legenda maior* of Catherine of Siena." *Studies in Medieval and Renaissance History*, n.s. 3 (2005).

———. "Catherine of Siena." In *Dictionary of Literary Biography: Italian Literature of the Fourteenth Century,* edited by T. J. Cachey, Jr. and Z. B. Baranski. Columbia, SC: Bruccoli Clark Layman, forthcoming.

———. "Neri Pagliaresi." In *Dictionary of Literary Biography: Italian Literature of the Fourteenth Century,* edited by T. J. Cachey, Jr. and Z. B. Baranski. Columbia, SC: Bruccoli Clark Layman, forthcoming.

Luttrell, Anthony. "Gregory XI and the Turks: 1370–1378." *Orientalia Christiana Periodica* 46 (1980): 391–417.

Maffei, Domenico, and Paolo Nardi, eds. *Atti del simposio internazionale Cateriniano-Bernardiniano, Siena, 17–20 aprile 1980.* Siena: Accademia Senese degli Intronati, 1982.

Makowski, Elizabeth. *Canon Law and Cloistered Women: Periculoso and its Commentators, 1298–1545.* Washington, DC: Catholic University Press, 1997.

Mandonnet, P. "Sainte Catherine de Sienne et la critique historique." *Année dominicaine* 59 (1923): 6–17, 43–52.

Marrara, D. "I magnati e il governo del Comune di Siena dallo statuto del 1274 alla fine del XIV secolo." In *Studi per Enrico Fiumi,* 239–76. Pisa: Pacini, 1979.

Martines, Lauro. *Power and Imagination: City-States in Renaissance Italy.* London: Allen Lane, 1979.

Mazzei, A. "Breve storia della nobile e celebre famiglia senese dei Sozzini dalle sue origini alla sua estinzione (sec. XIV–XIX)." *Bullettino Senese di Storia Patria* 73–75 (1966–1968): 131–45.

Meersseman, Gilles Gerard. *Dossier de l'ordre de la pénitence au XIII<sup>e</sup> siècle.* Spicilegium Friburgense, 7. Fribourg: Editions Universitaires Fribourg Suisse, 1961.

———. "Gli amici spirituali di S. Caterina a Roma alla luce del primo manifesto urbanista." *Bullettino Senese di Storia Patria* 69 (1962): 83–123.

Miccoli, Giovanni. "La storia religiosa." In *Storia d'Italia,* vol. 2, *Dalla Caduta dell'impero romano al secolo XVIII,* 431–1079. Turin: Einaudi, 1974.

Molho, Anthony. *Marriage Alliance in Late Medieval Florence.* Cambridge: Harvard University Press, 1994.

Mollat, G. "Relations politiques de Grégoire XI avec les Siennois et les Florentins." *Mélanges d'Archéologie et d'Histoire* 68 (1956): 335–76.

———. *The Popes at Avignon, 1305–1378.* Translated by Janet Love. London: Thomas Nelson, 1963.

*Il movimento religioso femminile in Umbria nei secoli XIII–XIV: Atti del convegno internazionale di studio nell'ambito delle celebrazioni per l'VIII centenario della nascita di S. Francesco d'Assisi, Città di Castello, 27–29 ottobre 1982.* Edited by Roberto Rusconi. Florence: Nuova Italia, 1984.

Muir, Edward. *Civic Ritual in Renaissance Venice.* Princeton, NJ: Princeton University Press, 1981.

———. "The Virgin on the Street Corner: The Place of the Sacred in Italian Cities." In *Religion and Culture in the Renaissance and Reformation,* edited by Steven Ozment, 25–40. Kirksville, MO: Sixteenth Century Journal Publishers, 1989.

Nardi, Paolo. "I vescovi di Siena e la curia pontificia dall'ascesa della parte Guelfa allo scoppio dello scisma d'occidente (1267–1378)." In *Chiesa e vita religiosa a*

*Siena dalle origini al grande giubileo,* edited by Achille Mirizio and Paolo Nardi, 153–77. Siena: Cantagalli, 2002.

Papka, Claudia Rattazzi. "The Written Woman Writes: Caterina da Siena Between History and Hagiography, Body and Text." *Annali d'Italianistica* 13 (1995): 131–47.

Paton, Bernadette. *Preaching Friars and the Civic Ethos: Siena, 1380–1480.* Westfield Publications in Medieval Studies, 7. London: Centre for Medieval Studies, Queen Mary and Westfield College, University of London, 1992.

Peterson, David S. "Out of the Margins: Religion and the Church in Renaissance Italy." *Renaissance Quarterly* 53 (2000): 835–79.

——. "State-Building, Church Reform, and the Politics of Legitimacy in Florence, 1375–1460." In *Florentine Tuscany: Structures and Practices of Power,* edited by William J. Connell and Andrea Zorzi, 122–43. Cambridge: Cambridge University Press, 2000.

——. "The War of Eight Saints in Florentine Memory and Oblivion." In *Society and Individual in Renaissance Florence,* edited by William J. Connell, 173–214. Berkeley: University of California Press, 2002.

Petrocchi, Giorgio. "S. Caterina da Siena." In *La prosa del Trecento,* 105–18. Messina: Editrice universitaria, 1961.

——. "La letteratura religiosa del Trecento." In *Storia della letteratura italiana,* vol. 2, *Il Trecento,* edited by Emilio Cecchi and Natalino Sapegno, 637–82. Milan: Garzanti, 1965.

——. "La *pace* in S. Caterina da Siena." In *La pace nel pensiero, nella politica, negli ideali del Trecento,* 11–26. Todi: Presso L'Accademia Tudertina, 1975.

Prosperi, Adriano. "Il sangue e l'anima. Ricerche sulle Compagnie di giustizia in Italia." *Quaderni Storici* 51 (1982): 959–99.

Reeves, Marjorie. *The Influence of Prophecy in the Later Middle Ages: A Study of Joachimism.* Oxford: Oxford University Press, 1969.

Riley, Denise. *"Am I That Name?" Feminism and the Category of "Women" in History.* Minneapolis: University of Minnesota Press, 1988.

*La rivolta dei Ciompi di Siena: 1371.* Edited by Giovanni Cherubini. Florence: Università degli Studi di Firenze, Fac. Lettere e Filosofia, 1970–71.

Rosa, C. "Il personale politico-amministrativo dello Stato senese (1385–1399)." Tesi di laurea, Università di Siena, 1985.

Rousset, Paul. "Sainte Catherine de Sienne et la problème de la croisade." *Revue suisse d'histoire* 25, no. 4 (1975): 499–513.

——. "L'idée de croisade chez sainte Catherine de Sienne et chez les théoriciens du XIVᵉ siècle." In *Atti del congresso internazionale di studi Cateriniani,* 363–72. Rome: Curia Generalizia O.P., 1981.

Rusconi, Roberto. *L'Attesa della fine: Crisi della società, profezia ed Apocalisse in Italia al tempo del grande scisma d'Occidente, 1378–1417.* Rome: Istituto Storico Italiano per il Medio Evo, 1979.

Rutenburg, Victor. "La vie et la lutte des Ciompi de Sienne." *Annales E. S. C.* 20 (1965): 95–109.

*S. Chiara da Montefalco e il suo tempo: Atti del quarto convegno di studi storici ecclesiastici organizzato dall'Arcidiocesi di Spoleto, Spoleto 28–30 dicembre 1981.* Edited by Claudio Leonardi and Enrico Manesti. Perugia and Florence: La Nuova Italia, 1985.

Salimei, Franco. *Salimbeni di Siena*. Rome: Editalia, 1986.

Sapegno, Natalino. *Scrittori d'Italia: Antologia per lo studio della letteratura italiana nelle scuole medie superiori*. Florence: La nuova Italia, 1963.

Scott, Joan. "The Evidence of Experience." *Critical Inquiry* 17 (1991): 773–97.

Scott, Karen. "'This is Why I Have Put You among Your Neighbors': St. Bernard's and St. Catherine's Understanding of the Love of God and Neighbor." In *Atti del simposio internazionale Cateriniano-Bernardiniano, Siena, 17–20 aprile 1980*, edited by Domenico Maffei and Paolo Nardi, 279–94. Siena: Accademia Senese degli Intronati, 1982.

——. "St. Catherine of Siena, 'Apostola.'" *Church History* 61, no. 1 (March 1992): 34–46.

——. "*Io Caterina*: Ecclesiastical Politics and Oral Culture in the Letters of Catherine of Siena." In *Dear Sister: Medieval Women and the Epistolary Genre*, edited by Karen Cherewatuk and Ulrike Wiethaus, 87–121. Philadelphia: University of Pennsylvania Press, 1993.

——. "Urban Spaces, Women's Networks, and the Lay Apostolate in the Siena of Catherine Benincasa." In *Creative Women in Medieval and Early Modern Italy*, edited by E. Ann Matter and John Coakley, 105–19. Philadelphia: University of Pennsylvania Press, 1994.

Silva, Pietro. "Il governo di Piero Gambacorti in Pisa e le sue relazioni col resto della Toscana e coi Visconti." *Bullettino Senese di Storia Patria* 19 (1912): 357–60.

Sorelli, Fernanda. "La produzione agiografica del domenicano Tommaso d'Antonio da Siena: Esempi di santità ed intenti di propaganda." In *Mistiche e devote nell'Italia tardomedievale*, edited by Daniel Bornstein and Roberto Rusconi, 157–70. Nuovo Medioevo, 40. Naples: Liguori, 1992.

Starn, Randolph. *Contrary Commonwealth: The Theme of Exile in Medieval and Renaissance Italy*. Berkeley: University of California Press, 1982.

Stella, Alessandro. *La révolte des Ciompi: Les hommes, les lieux, le travail*. Recherches d'Histoire et de Science Sociales / Studies in History and the Social Sciences, 57. Paris: École des Hautes Études en Sciences Sociales, 1993.

Sticco, Maria. "Santa Caterina da Siena." In *Letteratura italiana*, vol. 1, *I minori*. Milan: Marzorati, 1961.

Struever, Nancy. *Theory as Practice: Ethical Inquiry in the Renaissance*. Chicago: University of Chicago Press, 1990.

Taurisano, Innocenzo M. "Le fonti agiografiche cateriniane e la critica di R. Fawtier." *Letture cateriniane* 1 (1928): 311–82.

——. "S. Caterina ed il ritorno del Papato a Roma." *Memorie Domenicane* 46 (1929): 89–111.

——. "Il supplizio di Niccolò di Toldo e S. Caterina (nota)." *Memorie Domenicane* 54 (1937): 3–9.

*Temi e problemi della mistica femminile trecentesca, Centro di studi sulla spiritualità, Todi 14–17 ottobre 1979*. Todi: Accademia Tudertina, 1983.

Thibault, Paul. *Pope Gregory XI: The Failure of Tradition*. Lanham, MD: University Press of America, 1986.

Tommaseo, Niccolò, and Bernardo Bellini. *Dizionario della Lingua Italiana*. 4 vols. Turin: Unione Tipografica, 1861–79.

Trexler, Richard C. *The Spiritual Power: Republican Florence under Interdict*. Studies in Medieval and Reformation Thought, 9. Leiden: E. J. Brill, 1974.

———. *Public Life in Renaissance Florence*. New York: Academic Press, 1980.

———. "Gendering Christ Crucified." In *Iconography at the Crossroads*, edited by Brendan Cassidy, 107–20. Princeton, NJ: Princeton University Press, 1993.

Trinkaus, Charles. *In Our Image and Likeness: Humanity and Divinity in Italian Humanist Thought*. 2 vols. London: Constable, 1970.

*Il Tumulto dei Ciompi. Un momento di storia fiorentina ed europea*. Convegno Internazionale di Studi, Firenze, 16–19 settembre 1979. Florence: Olschki, 1981.

Tylus, Jane. "Caterina da Siena and the Legacy of Humanism." In *Perspectives on Early Modern and Modern Intellectual History: Essays in Honor of Nancy S. Struever*, edited by Joseph Marino and Melinda W. Schlitt, 116–141. Rochester, NY: University of Rochester Press, 2001.

Van Ree, A. W. "Raymond de Capoue: Éléments biographiques." *Archivum Fratrum Praedicatorum* 33 (1963): 159–241.

Vauchez, André. *La spiritualité du moyen âge occidental*. Vendôme: Presses universitaires de France, 1975.

———. *La sainteté en occident aux derniers siècles du moyen âge. D'apres les procès de canonisation et les documents hagiographiques*. Rome: École Française de Rome, 1981.

———. *Les laïcs au moyen âge: Pratiques et expériences religieuses*. Paris: Cerf, 1987.

———. *The Laity in the Middle Ages: Religious Beliefs and Devotional Practices*. Translated by Margery J. Schneider. Notre Dame: University of Notre Dame Press, 1993.

———. *Sainthood in the Later Middle Ages*. Translated by Jean Birrell. Cambridge: Cambridge University Press, 1997.

Wainwright, Valerie. "Conflict and Popular Government in Fourteenth-Century Siena: Il Monte dei Dodici, 1355–1368." In *I ceti dirigenti nella Toscana tardo comunale*, 57–80. Florence: Papafava, 1983.

———. "The Testing of a Popular Sienese Regime. The *Riformatori* and the Insurrections of 1371." *I Tatti Studies: Essays in the Renaissance* 2 (1987): 107–70.

Weinstein, Donald. *Savonarola and Florence: Prophecy and Patriotism in the Renaissance*. Princeton: Princeton University Press, 1970.

Weinstein, Donald, and Rudolph M. Bell. *Saints and Society: The Two Worlds of Western Christendom, 1000–1700*. Chicago: University of Chicago Press, 1982.

Weissman, Ronald F. E. *Ritual Brotherhood in Renaissance Florence*. New York: Academic Press, 1982.

Wirth, Jean. *L'image médiévale*. Paris: Méridiens Klincksieck, 1989.

Witt, Ronald G. *Coluccio Salutati and His Public Letters*. Geneva: Librarie Droz, 1976.

———. *Hercules at the Crossroads: The Life, Works, and Thought of Coluccio Salutati*. Durham, NC: Duke University Press, 1983.

———. *In the Footsteps of the Ancients: The Origins of Humanism from Lovato to Bruni*. Leiden: Brill, 2000.

*Women and Faith: Catholic Religious Life in Italy from Late Antiquity to the Present*. Edited by Lucetta Scaraffia and Gabriella Zarri. Translated by Keith Botsford. Cambridge: Harvard University Press, 1999.

*Women and Religion in Medieval and Renaissance Italy*. Edited by Daniel Bornstein and Roberto Rusconi. Chicago: University of Chicago Press, 1996.

Wood, Diana. *Clement VI: The Pontificate and Ideas of an Avignon Pope.* Cambridge: Cambridge University Press, 1989.

Zancan, Marina. "Lettere di Caterina da Siena." In *Letteratura italiana. Le opere,* vol. 1, *Dalle origini al cinquecento,* edited by Alberto Asor Rosa, 593–633. Turin: Einaudi, 1992.

——. "Lettere di Caterina da Siena. Il testo, la tradizione, l'interpretazione." *Annali d'Italianistica, Women Mystic Writers* 13 (1995): 151–61.

Zarri, Gabriella. "Le sante vive. Per una tipologia della santità femminile nel primo Cinquecento." *Annali dell'Istituto storico italo-germanico in Trento* 6 (1980): 371–445.

——. *Le sante vive: Profezie di corte e devozione femminile tra '400 e '500.* Turin: Rosenberg and Sellier, 1990.

# Index

The letter C is an abbreviation for Saint Catherine of Siena. Boldface numbers refer to letters of Saint Catherine.

Aers, David, 17
Albizzi faction, 60, 66, 135, 160n10, 199; papal support of, 59
Alfonzo da Vadaterra, visit from, 56–58, 71
Angela da Foligno, 73
Angelo da Ricasoli, letters to, 167, 187
Anziani of Lucca, letter to, 169, 204
Arzocchi, Nigi di Doccio, 140, 142, 147; letter to, 132n26
Avignon: C's letters to pope and trials during stay, 174–75; C's trip to, 172–75; papacy in, 57; pope's departure from, 176; Raymond's travels to, 170

Bartolomeo Dominici, 145; letter to, 56; testimony about C, 64, 136, 174–75
Bartolomeo Scala, 148
Bartolomeo da Siena, 153–54, 155
Belcaro, monastery at, 132, 133, 146, 180. See also Santa Maria degli Angeli
Belforti family, and letter to, 181n93
Bellanti, Andrea di Naddino, 64n24
Benincasa family. See Iacopo di Benincasa, family of
Benvenuti, Anna, 26
Berenger, abbot of Lézat, 61, 159; letter to, 164–65
Bianco da Siena, 23
Birgitta of Sweden: as model, 73; prophetic role, 56–58; *Revelations*, 73
Boccaccio, Giovanni, 9, 59
Bornstein, Daniel, 13, 16
Boureau, Alain, 75

Brizio, Elena, 140, 141
Bruco, 5, 47, 65, 66; Revolt of the, 44–46, 63, 66, 133, 134
Buonaccorso di Lapo, 66, 135; letter to, 174
Buonconti, Gherardo, 81
Butler, Judith, 16n34
Bynum, Caroline Walker, 14–15; interpretation of gendered identities, and C, 17–18, 19, 25

Caffarini. See Tommaso di Antonio da Siena, called Caffarini
Canigiani, Barduccio, 66, 77, 126nn7, 10
Canigiani, Piero, 197, 199; letter to, 200, 201n145
Canigiani, Ristoro, 66; letters to, 200, 200n145
Casini, Francesco, 155n120, 174
Catherine of Alexandria, Saint: invoked in letter as witness, 100, 112–13; monastery named for, 55n83, 146
Catherine of Siena, Saint (C)
    character and personality: affection and familiarity, 72, 76, 121; constant engagement in writing, 73–75; as independent religious woman, 8, 16, 51, 54–55, 73; main worldly or institutional causes, 80, 81; as self-authorizing, 121, 193, 196; as transgressor of boundaries, 3, 19, 75, 157
    family: brothers, 30–31, 35, 41–42, 44, 48; clash with, over vocation, 28–29,

Catherine of Siena, Saint *(continued)*
—works, letters, in general *(continued)*
  images and metaphors: blood and
    shedding of blood, 98, 99, 101–2;
    body of Christ, 15, 103, 105, 107,
    121, 168, 172, 204; building stones,
    102; C as Bride of Christ, 112, 114;
    Christ *cavaliero*, 179; church as Bride
    of Christ, 102, 163; church as
    human body, 86, 87, 163, 166, 168,
    204; church as mother, 163; *dolce
    sposa*, 97, 102, 103, 108–10, 116,
    121; gender transformation,
    106–10, 113, 114, 116; open wound
    of Christ, 96, 101, 102, 103, 106,
    108–11, 121, 188; the rose, 164, 189
  images and metaphors, examples of,
    listings, 103nn41, 42, 43, 108n58,
    109n59, 110n64, 111nn65, 66,
    121nn81, 82
  recipients: *famiglia*, 1–2, 77, 129–32,
    142, 200; Florentine leaders,
    170–71, 201, 204; key political and
    church leaders, 64–65, 75, 76, 89,
    165, 187, 202, 205; leaders in
    Lucca, 169, 204; leaders in Perugia,
    146–47; monastic communities,
    110n75; Sienese *signori*, 127, 152,
    182
  subjects and views: assertion of mission
    and self-authority, 116, 121, 193,
    196; church reform, 164, 167,
    189–90; criticism of Pope Gregory,
    176, 187, 197; ideal of unified
    church body, 81, 85; ideal of social
    and political peace, 81, 84–85, 166,
    167, 173, 199, 204; mixing of politi-
    cal and spiritual, 80, 121–22, 131,
    162–63, 207–8; priority of spiritual
    affiliation over worldly/family obli-
    gations, 137, 150–51; return of
    papacy to Rome, 21, 166, 187, 200;
    social and political order, 121, 168,
    174, 204; support of papacy, 82–89,
    164, 186; vice in government, 182;
    vice of self-love, 72–73. *See also* Cru-
    sade to Holy Land; War of Eight
    Saints
  themes: C as servant of God, 1–2,
    182–83, 184, 191–92, 196; Holy
    Land, 205; intimacy and union with
    God, 183, 189, 191, 193, 194, 195;
    love, 72–73; marriage, 96, 99–100,
    102, 112–13; motherhood, 15, 103,
    124–25; perseverance, 129, 130,
    131, 189; union with Christ, 101,
    102, 188

Catherine of Siena, Saint *(continued)*
—works, letters, in general *(continued)*
  letters, individual, by number
    **11,** 187
    **18/XIII,** 50–51
    **28/XVIII,** 85–88, 160, 205
    **31/XII,** 64–65
    **36,** 129n19
    **43/XLIV,** 137
    **62,** 131n25
    **69/XXIV,** 130, 131n25
    **74,** 111n66
    **75,** 110
    **88/XXVIII,** 167
    **99/VII,** 145
    **103,** 181n93
    **108/XLIX,** 161–62
    **109/LI,** 164
    **112,** 124n6, 181n90
    **113, 114, 115,** 181n90
    **120,** 111n65, 124n6, 185
    **121,** 184
    **122,** 1–2, 144n74, 182–83
    **123,** 182
    **124,** 131–32
    **127/XX,** 56
    **128,** 132n26, 142
    **130,** 176n68
    **131/XXXIII,** 89
    **132/XLIII,** 162n19
    **133/XXXII,** 88
    **135/XLII,** 146n82
    **137/XLV,** 163
    **138/XLI,** 76, 183
    **139/XLVI,** 162
    **140/XXX,** 76, 83–84, 157, 204, 205
    **143/XXXIX,** 88
    **145/XL,** 162
    **149/XXII,** 81–82
    **157,** 162n19
    **168/LIII,** 169, 204
    **171/LX,** 168–69, 204
    **177/LXI,** 167n32
    **181/LV, 183/LVI,** 165
    **185,** 165–67
    **192,** 147n88
    **196/LXIV, 206/LXIII,** 171, 204
    **207/LXVIII,** 170, 205
    **216,** 132n26, 142
    **218/LXXIV,** 146n83, 174n61
    **219/LXV.** *See* Raymond of Capua,
      important letters to
    **223,** 167
    **226,** 146n83
    **229/LXIX,** 171–72
    **230/LXXII,** 174
    **231/LXXVII,** 174n61, 175

Salimbeni family: as allies of Dodici, 63,
94, 133, 134; C's contacts with and letters to, 180, 181, 181nn90, 93; conflicts
within, 181, 185n107; coup attempt by,
45–47; and Gerard du Puy, 62, 94, 135;
political activities, 1, 5, 43, 61, 135; powerful position of, 6–7, 130, 179–80;
revolt by, 62, 69, 134, 141
Salimbeni territory, trip to: background
and context, 1, 6–7, 179–80; C's reasoning about, 181, 182; companions on,
141, 143, 146, 179; miracles performed
during, 142–43; Sienese concern about,
1–2, 6, 130, 182–84. See also Rocco
d'Orcia
Salutati, Coluccio, 9, 20; C as interlocutor,
79; letters of, and their importance, 74,
79, 167–68, 170, 206; political activity,
4–5, 160, 161
Salvi di ser Pietro, letter to, 182–83
San Domenico, Church of, 24, 34, 47
Sano di Maco: background and political
involvement, 126n10; letters to, 129–30,
184–85, 200n144; and pressures of public criticism, 130–32
Santa Maria degli Angeli, 180n89,
183n100. See also Belcaro, monastery at
Sant'Antimo, C's mission to, 183–84, 185
Savini, Nanni di ser Vanni, 69; as Dodici,
133–34; donation to C., 132, 133, 134,
180n89; function in famiglia, 132, 135;
political activity, 135
Scott, Karen, 12, 64, 193
Siena in late trecento: political unrest, 42–47,
61–63; society, 29–30; strategic area to
south, 6–7, 178–80. See also noble families, Sienese; popolo, in Siena; Sienese government and politics; Sienese
governmental structure
Sienese government and politics, 56; C's
interest in, 176, 177; decision to join
league with Florence, 160–61, 161n12;
relations with Florence, 5–6, 60–63; relations with Pisa, 82, 176, 178; suspicion
about C's activities, and her answers, 1–3,
6, 130, 182–84; suspicion of papacy, 62;
ties to Tuscan and Italian politics, 6, 63,
160–61, 177–80. See also Dodici; Nove;
Riformatori; War of Eight Saints
Sienese governmental structure
Concistoro: deliberations, minutes to,
138, 139; makeup, 127–28
Consiglio Generale, 128; decisions by,
161n12
Ordines Civitatis and Sapientes, 127

Sienese governmental structure (continued)
Signoria, 31, 127, 140, 185; appeals to,
68, 152
Simone da Cortona, 118, 119
Soderini, Niccolò, 66; letters to, 89,
168–69, 200, 204; visits to, 173, 197
Stefano della Cumba, 165
Stimulus amoris, 34, 104, 109; influential
passage in, 104–8, 111
Strozzi, Carlo, 66, 135
Strozzi, Leonardo, 135
Strozzi, Niccolò, letter to, 178–79

Talamone, struggle over, 176, 178
Tolomei, Francesco di Giocomo, 177n74
Tolomei, Giacomo di Francesco, 185
Tolomei, Jacomo di Sozzo, 153
Tolomei, Matteo di Francesco, 185
Tolomei, Pietro di Giacomo, 161n12,
177–78n74; letter to, 177
Tolomei, Rabe di Francesco, 185; letter to,
111n65, 124n6, 185
Tolomei, Spinello di Giacomo, 180
Tolomei family, 148, 177n74; allies of Flo-
rentines, 63; conflicts within, 181, 182,
185n107; political activities, 45, 46n60,
63n20, 140, 185; role in government,
141, 177
Tommaso di Antonio da Siena, called Caffarini, 66, 112; accounts by, 104, 118, 136;
biographical adaptations by, 40–41, 54;
and C's public activities, 64; collection of
C's letters, 120, 121; and execution of Niccolò di Toldo, 91–92; letter to, 56
—works
Legenda minor, 92, 193
Libellus de supplemento, 104
Tommaso dalla Fonte, 118; advice and
instruction from, 31, 33, 34, 35; as confessor and relative, 32, 47, 66; letter to,
162; lost account by, 27
Trexler, Richard C., 173n52
Trincio dei Trinci, 62, 180n86, 181; letter
to, and death, 181n93
Tuscan city-states, league against papacy,
3–5, 79, 160–61, 166–68; Bologna,
Lucca, Pisa joining, 169; reasons for, 59,
60; Siena joining, 160–61. See also War of
Eight Saints
Tylus, Jane, 9, 193

Urban VI, pope; C's gathering of support
for, 78, 202; C's letters to, 72, 76, 202,
listed, 202n149; election of, 196, 202;
political support for, 139, 152, 153